# The Great Violinists

## Margaret Campbell

D1494333

ROBSON BOOKS

This edition published in 2004 by Robson Books,
The Chrysalis Building, Bramley Road, London W10 6SP.

An imprint of Chrysalis Books Group plc

First published in Great Britain in 1980 by Paul Elek Ltd, Granada Publishing.

Copyright © 1980, 2004 Margaret Campbell

The author has made every reasonable effort to contact all copyright holders.
Any errors that may have occurred are inadvertent and anyone who for any
reason has not been contacted is invited to write to the publishers so that a
full acknowledgement may be made in subsequent editions of this work.

British Library Cataloguing in Publication Data
A catalogue record for this title is available from the British Library.

ISBN 1 86105 623 0

Typeset by SX Composing DTP, Rayleigh, Essex
Printed by Bell & Bain Ltd, Glasgow

# Foreword
## *By Ruggiero Ricci*

The violin is probably the most hellish invention ever conceived by man, a beautiful and treacherous work of art that demands our constant attention but can never be completely dominated. We must adapt to her individual characteristics and hope that she will respond with a gracious nod to our own uniqueness. 'Treat her right, and she'll treat you right,' Jascha Heifetz once told me.

The problems, even for the high priests, are considerable: 'I used to sleep on the chin rest,' confided David Oistrakh as we recalled the slavish hours of practice required. 'How do you keep the violin from going out from under your chin when you downshift?' asked Szigeti. We all have some nightmare gremlin waiting to pounce during that elusive perfect performance. 'You mustn't pay attention to my fingerings,' Kreisler warned me, 'I never could play in first position.' Why do we go on? The gratification that comes if one can melt a heart or draw tears is worth the countless hours spent trying to play double harmonics and blistering our fingers with pizzicato.

The hallmarks of some of today's performers are over-sweetness and excessive feelings, as compared to the dry sound, bad shifting, and eccentricities that characterised many of our forebears. Every violin player thinks he's the greatest. If he doesn't, then forget him. Paganini, Wieniawski, Ysaÿe, Kreisler, Heifetz, Oistrakh – all were great and all were different. None was conformist. And yet, as we see in this book, every great violinist embodies in his playing the influence of his predecessors; this shared inheritance, added to and subtly transformed by his own unique stamp, becomes in turn a legacy to future generations.

The gipsy, the jazzman, and the Hochschule professor are all branches of the fiddler's family tree; Margaret Campbell's remarkable work now shows us the fascinating pattern of its growth.

# Contents

# Acknowledgements

Many people have helped me in my researches and I regret that space does not permit me to mention them all by name. In the 1980 edition there is a comprehensive list of those who assisted with the original publication, many of whom, sadly, are no longer with us. Nonetheless I remain indebted to them for their help and I must mention three of those who also provided assistance with this second edition; they were Josef Gingold, Yehudi Menuhin and Yfrah Neaman.

I would like to say how very grateful I am to Maxim Panfilo whom I met in Helsinki six years ago and who offered to help me in documenting the Russian school of violin playing of which he has made a study. He generously provided me with copies of his own researches and gave me permission to quote from them as I wished, and throughout the time I was working on the new edition, he seemed never to tire of my numerous questions, to all of which he miraculously found answers. The chapter on the Russian school would never have materialised, but for his help.

Julie Anne Sadie was my very sympathetic and knowledgeable editor with whom it was a pleasure to work, and I would also like to thank Jennifer Lansbury who has helped in the final publication of this book.

Acknowledgement is made to publishers and copyright-holders for their kind permission to quote from the following:

Leopold Auer, *Violin Playing As I Teach It*, Duckworth & Co. Ltd, 1960; Dr Herbert R. Axelrod, *Heifetz*, Paganiniana Publications, 1976 (by permission of Herbert R. Axelrod); Hector Berlioz, *The Memoirs of Berlioz*, translated and edited by David Cairns (translation and original material copyright © David Cairns 1969), Alfred A. Knopf, Inc., 1969; Sir Adrian Boult, *My Own Trumpet*, Hamish Hamilton Ltd, 1973; Donald Brook, *Violinists of Today*, Barrie & Rockliff Ltd, 1948; Carl Flesch, *The Art of Violin Playing*, Carl Fischer, 1924 (by permission of Carl F. Flesch); Carl Flesch, *Memoirs of Carl Flesch*, translated by Hans Keller, Bois de Boulogne: W. Reeve/Rockliff, 1957 (by permission of Mrs Joan H. Hartfield and Carl F. Flesch); Ivan Galamian, *Principles of Violin Playing and Teaching*, Prentice-Hall, Inc. and Faber & Faber Ltd, 1962; Grove's *Dictionary of Music and Musicians*, edited by Eric Blom, 5th edition, Macmillan Publishers Ltd, London and St Martin's Press Inc., New York, 1954: articles by C. R. Halski, D. Heron-Allen, P. Donostia and Eric Blom; Ida Haendel, *Woman With Violin*, Victor Gollancz Ltd, 1970; Eduard Hanslick, *Vienna's Golden Years of Music: 1850-1900*, translated by Henry Pleasants III (Copyright © 1950 by Henry Pleasants III), Simon & Schuster, a Division of Gulf & Western Corporation.

Margaret Campbell

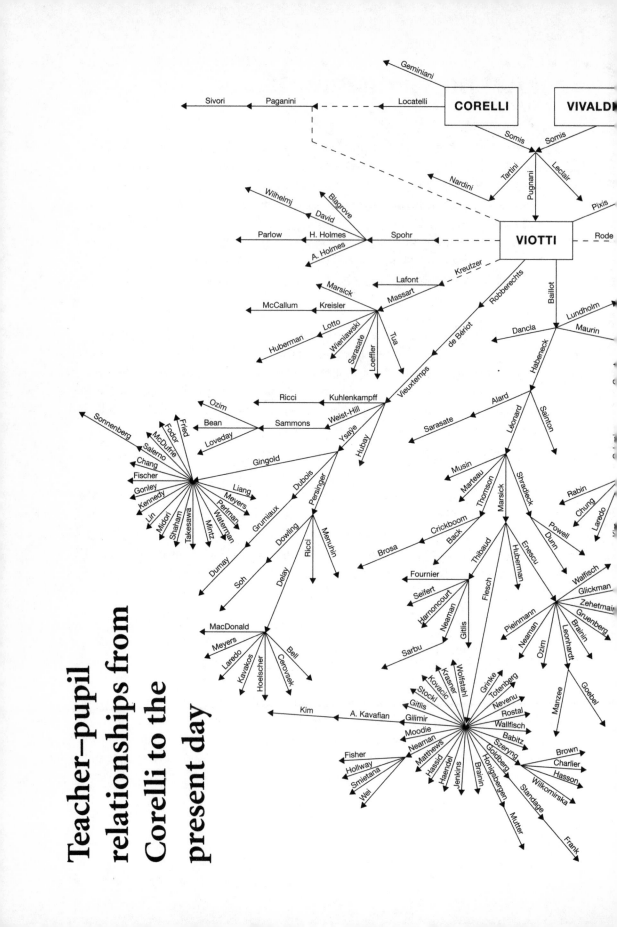

# Teacher–pupil relationships from Corelli to the present day

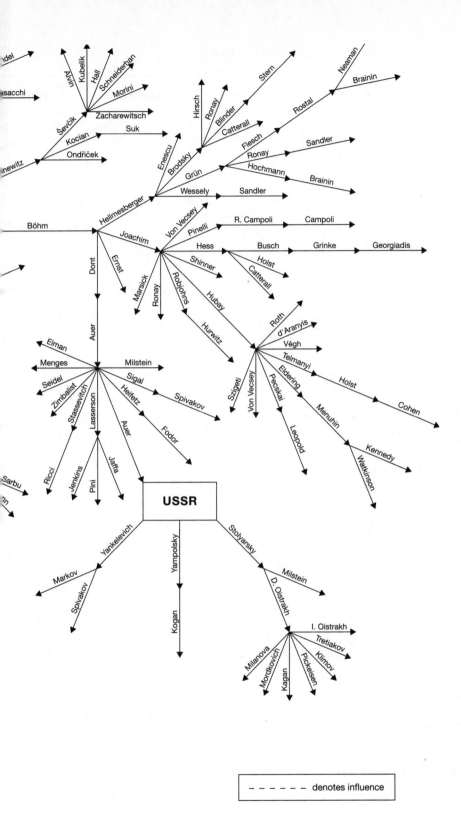

# Prelude

The history of the violin has long been associated with myth and legend, and antiquity holds the secret of its origins. The earliest and most primitive examples of stringed instruments played with a bow come from the Middle East and Arabia, and the pear-shaped, three-stringed medieval rebec is probably the violin's most likely immediate ancestor. This instrument was brought to Italy in the ninth century by the invading Arabs. From it stemmed the miniature form that survived to the end of the eighteenth century as the 'kit' or dancing master's fiddle, in France called *pochette*, a term derived from the habit of its being carried in a dancing master's tailcoat pocket.

In medieval times we have the fidel also known as *fidula*, *vythule* and a variety of related names. Three-stringed like the rebec, this instrument was played with a *fydelstyk*, a clear indication that it was bowed, not plucked. Since it was used by 'those who make a living from it through their labour',[1] by playing for dancing and at banquets and other social events, it was not considered respectable.

During the Renaissance a fairly short-lived but direct development of the medieval instrument was the *lira da braccio* ('arm-lyra'), a violin-shaped bowed instrument with seven strings, held low against the shoulder and supported by the upper arm. This distinguished it from the viols, which are held downwards between the knees of the player.

About the middle of the sixteenth century a fourth string was added to the medieval three-stringed instrument. The tuning was in fifths – g below middle c, d, a, e. Thus the violin had come into being.

Gasparo da Salò (*c.*1540–1609; real name Bertolotti, but he was called da Salò after his birthplace on Lake Garda), settled in Brescia in northern Italy, and is one of the first known craftsmen in the records of violin making. The instruments made by these early Brescian makers – of which there were a number – were generally robust, often on the large side and sometimes roughly built, with an extremely powerful tone. But the violins made by Gasparo da Salò's most famous pupil, Giovanni Paulo Maggini (1581–*c.*1632), are uncommonly elegant; they also have a distinctive large tone. The Belgian virtuoso Charles de Bériot (1802–70) owned two by this maker. After the death of Maggini the Brescian school went into a decline.

The most important centre of violin making was in the neighbouring city of Cremona, where it had flourished since the middle of the sixteenth century. The first of its celebrated makers was Andrea Amati (*c.*1511–80), who is believed to have worked there as early as 1550. He was followed by his two sons, Antonio (1540–?) and Girolamo (1561–1630), and they in turn by Nicolò Amati (1596–1684), the best known in what became the most powerful dynasty in the history of the instrument. It was in Cremona that the violin reached its peak of perfection.

In the second half of the seventeenth century, schools of composition and violin playing were emerging at centres all over Italy, the most important being at Bologna, Venice, Rome and Modena. This development was clearly linked with the growing popularity of the violin itself. Nicolò Amati experimented for many years to achieve a combination of the sweetness of tone and brilliance demanded by the new and proliferating breed of musician, the 'soloist'.

Amati had many famous pupils, some of whom settled in Cremona. Others set up workshops and took on pupils in other parts of Italy. Francesco Ruggieri (1620–95) and Giovanni Rogeri (*c.*1670–*c.*1705) had all been apprenticed to 'Old Amati', as had Andreas Guarneri (*c.*1626–98), founder of the other great Cremonese dynasty. And finally, there was Nicolò Amati's most celebrated pupil, Antonio Stradivari (1644–1737).

Stradivari is believed to have been a wood-carver before he entered Amati's workshop. After his training was over he continued to live and work with his master, and his first violin is dated 1666. In 1667 he married and in 1680 left Amati to start up on his own in the Piazza San Domenico in Cremona, where the craftsmen lived side by side in the 'violin makers' quarters'. These old three-storey houses were built with a seccadour, or 'drying room', on the top floor, exposed on all sides to the Italian sun. It was here that the women hung the linen and the fruit to dry alongside the maturing unvarnished violins and selected pieces of seasoning wood.

For some time Stradivari followed his master's design faithfully with only an occasional deviation, but after Amati's death in 1684 he began a series of experiments in his search for a richer tone. By the turn of the century he appears to have arrived at his ideal, and the instruments he completed between 1700 and 1725 are acknowledged to be his best. Although they can convey *pianissimo* with absolute clarity, they can also make their powerful voices heard over a large orchestra. At this time orchestras were gradually expanding their forces beyond the scope of the Baroque chamber groups, but the solo concerto as we know it today had not come into being. It was almost as if Stradivari could anticipate what would be asked of his instruments a hundred years hence.

Great players have, not surprisingly, always been attracted to Stradivari instruments. Mischa Elman played one dated 1721 which had once belonged to Joseph Joachim; David Oistrakh owned a Stradivarius made in 1706 and Nathan Milstein played the 'Goldman' dated 1716.

Many of these 'Golden Age' Stradivaris have been named after their owners. The 'Viotti' of 1709, for example, was played by the Italian virtuoso until his death in 1824. The most famous of all named instruments is the 'Messiah', which owes its nickname to an unusual set of circumstances.

Early in the nineteenth century, a young Milanese carpenter-turned-collector, Luigi Tarisio (*c*.1790–1854), travelled all over Italy driving hard bargains for forgotten treasures, and accumulated a valuable store of master violins, including one superb example from the estate of Count di Salabue, one of the most famous eighteenth-century collectors. The violin had been purchased in 1775 in perfect condition from Stradivari's son Paulo (1708–75). Tarisio went to Paris, offering some of his less valuable pieces for sale, which were immediately snapped up. Finally he approached Jean-Baptiste Vuillaume (1798–1875), the best-known Parisian dealer and violin maker of the nineteenth century, and found his most enthusiastic customer. He tantalised Vuillaume with descriptions of the Salabue Stradivarius which he 'would bring next time'. Tarisio frequently reappeared, but never with the promised instrument. On one occasion Delphin Alard, Vuillaume's son-in-law, overheard the conversation and exclaimed: 'Really, Monsieur, your violin is like the Jews' Messiah! We always wait, but he never comes!'

When Tarisio died, Vuillaume rushed to Italy and bought the entire collection from the unsuspecting heirs for a fraction of what it was worth. When he finally owned the 'Messiah', he fell victim to the same disease and could never part with it. Ironically, the 'Messiah' has always retained its unattainable image. Over the years it changed hands several times, but was never actually used by a performer: even when it was owned by Alard himself, he scarcely ever played it. Eventually it became the property of Hills of London, who gave it to the Ashmolean Museum at Oxford. The 'Messiah' can be seen there today in a glass case, immaculate and still unplayed.

The most brilliant of the younger generation of the Cremona School was Giuseppe Antonio Guarneri. Born about 1683, he was generally known as del Gesù because he inscribed his instruments IHS (Jesus Hominum Salvator – Jesus, Saviour of Mankind).

If Stradivari is seen as the refined aristocrat of his profession, del Gesù could be regarded as the drunken ruffian, the wayward genius who worked in fits and starts, especially towards the end of his short life. Del Gesù's instruments reflect the variation which was the natural outcome of his unpredictable and individual genius. He is the one maker who is considered the equal of Stradivari, and his instruments are celebrated for their ravishing beauty of both form and tone. His varnish, amber in colour, with a translucent red overlay, gives off a luminous effect which has been compared with the 'dying glow of the evening sun on the waves of the sea'.[2]

Many great players today prefer Guarneri instruments to any others, on account of their pungent tone. Fritz Kreisler owned a del Gesù of 1733, and Heifetz played on the 'Ferdinand David' of 1742. Kyung-Wha Chung plays a Guarnerius dated 1735. Paganini played a Guarnerius. He named it the 'Cannon' on account of its exceedingly powerful tone, and in his will he bequeathed it to his native city of Genoa, where it rests in a glass case, as mute as the 'Messiah'.

The only German-speaking master violin maker, Jacob Stainer (*c*.1617–83), came from Absam in the Austrian Tyrol. He was a wood-carver by trade and a first-class violinist. Stainer's work shows some influence of Amati and it is possible that he studied in Cremona. Musicians of the time were enthralled with the 'Stainer' tone, and in seventeenth- and eighteenth-century Germany he was considered the greatest of all makers. His instruments – distinguished by their high arching – then fetched far higher prices than those of Stradivari. In 1800, Count di Salabue placed Stainer's name at the top of a list that included all the most celebrated Cremona masters. J.S. Bach and Mozart both had Stainers. In his famous *Violinschule* (a tutor on violin technique), Mozart's father Leopold does not mention the existence of Italian violins.

During the Thirty Years War, Bohemian violin makers escaped across the border and settled in Saxony, where they set up a collective cottage industry. Similar methods were employed in Mittenwald, a small town in the Bavarian Alps, and made famous by the work of Matthias Klotz (1653–1743), who worked in Italy as a young man.

The first mastercraftsman in the French school was Nicolas Lupot (1758–1824) from Mirecourt; and from the same town came Jean-Baptiste Vuillaume, whom we know later set up in Paris and became famous both as a maker and dealer. Copying was Vuillaume's greatest strength and he successfully imitated the work of the greatest masters. When repairing the Guarneri 'Cannon' for Paganini, Vuillaume made a copy so perfect that at first sight it deceived its owner. Paganini was sufficiently impressed to offer a high price for it, but the astute Vuillaume presented the instrument as a gift on receiving Paganini's assurance that he would play on it at a public concert.

The phenomenal advances in violin making technique in the seventeenth century were not reflected in the development of the bow. The first performers on the violin used the bows already in use for viols, the principles of which had not changed since medieval times. A convex wooden stick strung with horsehair at a fixed, slack tension, slightly modified it came to be called the 'Corelli' bow, after Arcangelo Corelli (1653–1713), the Italian virtuoso-composer. Eminently suited to the Baroque performing style, the old bow could produce beautifully clear, short unaccented strokes. However, with the development of the Classical symphony and the solo concerto, new musical demands were made upon both composers and violinists. The emphasis on cantabile, or 'singing tone', especially in a long phrase, called for a longer bow and a wider spread of hair. The new accented *martelé*, or 'hammer-stroke', needed a greater tension than that of the old bow and staccato was difficult to achieve with the less perfectly balanced stick.

Tartini carried out intensive study of the bow resulting in certain modifications. But the solution to the problems just mentioned was provided by the Parisian Tourte family, culminating in the work of François Tourte (1747–1835). His standards for curvature of the stick and tapering of the head towards a fine point, so as to attain the correct balance together with the most desirable length, were established about 1780 and have been accepted as perfect right up to the present day. He justly earned the title 'Stradivari of the Bow'. Tourte never stamped his bows with his name, but to the connoisseur they are clearly recognisable by their finely tapering heads. They were frequently embellished with beautiful tortoiseshell nuts mounted in gold.

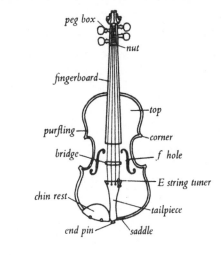

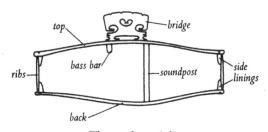

The modern violin

It is entirely logical that the bow should have been developed in France and not in Italy. The latter country brought the violin and its Baroque performing technique to a peak of perfection. But around the time of the deaths of Bach (1750) and Handel (1759), the Baroque style of playing declined. When Viotti went to Paris in 1782, he took with him a fusion of the past and future virtuoso styles. He passed on his ideas to pupils who became the leaders of the new French school of violin playing which was to dominate Europe for most of the nineteenth century.

**Notes**
1. Boyden, *The History of Violin Playing,* p. 32.
2. Farga, *Violins and Violinists,* p. 54.

# 1 Beginnings

Paganini is the name that naturally springs to mind as the archetypal virtuoso of the violin. But mountain peaks do not fall from the sky. Although they may not have reached such dazzling heights, there were many accomplished performers a century and more before Paganini was born. The explorations of these early violinists, who were also of necessity composers, laid the foundations on which all techniques of future generations were based.

The first known 'virtuoso' appears to have been the Italian Carlo Farina (c.1600–40) from Mantua. His reputation for performing tricks on the violin, from the mewing of cats to the imitation of fife and drum, earned him the contempt of serious musicians. Nevertheless, even at this early date he was employing advanced techniques such as double-stopping and pizzicato.

The French violinist Louis Constantin (c.1585–1657) was described by Marin Mersenne as being one of the great virtuosos of his time. In 1618 he became one of the Vingt-Quatre Violons at the Paris court of Louis XIII. In 1624, he was appointed *Roy des joueurs d'instruments*: this post entitled him to levy taxes from anyone entering the profession; in return, he was obliged to uphold the statutes of the guild and see that violators were punished.

The Florentine-born Jean-Baptiste Lully (1632–87), remembered today as an opera composer at the court of Louis XIV, was also a gifted violinist and dancer. Soon after his court appointment, in 1653, Lully persuaded the young Louis XIV to create a new, elite band of 16 players, known as the Petits Violons, which he led. As a conductor, he imposed a rhythmic discipline that gave his orchestra a distinctive precision and style that was the envy of every European monarch of the day. However, fame came at a price: Lully died of gangrene after having accidentally pierced his foot while marking time with his conducting cane. The tribute in the March 1687 *Mercure galant* declared that 'never did any man carry so far the art of playing the violin'.

In the entry for 4 March 1656, the diarist John Evelyn described as 'incomparable' the playing of Thomas Baltzar (1630–63), a native of Lübeck in Germany and at one time employed at the court of Queen Christina of Sweden; his 'wonderful dexterity' was greatly admired. 'There was nothing, however cross and perplexed, brought to him by other artists, which he did not play off at sight with ravishing sweetness and improvements to the astonishment of our best masters.' Baltzar's success earned him the coveted appointment of leader of the 'Twenty-four Violins of the King' under Charles II who, during his exile at the court of Louis XIV, had acquired a taste for everything French. But Baltzar's popularity encouraged him to 'drink more than ordinary',[1] the consequence of which brought him to an early grave, albeit in Westminster Abbey.

John Banister (*c.*1630–79), Baltzar's successor as leader of the King's Band, was required – like his counterpart at the French court, Lully – to 'make choyce of twelve drawn from our four and twenty violins to be a select band to wayte on us whensoever there should be occasion for musick'. He was given 'full power to instruct and direct them for better performance of service, without being mixed with the other violins unless the King orders the twenty-four'. Samuel Pepys mentioned Banister favourably in his diary, as both performer and composer. Banister gave the first public concerts in London at his house in White Friars off Fleet Street, on the site where the Guildhall School of Music and Drama stood until it moved to the Barbican. But he fell from grace when it was discovered that he had misappropriated funds entrusted to him for paying the musicians' wages.

The aristocratic patrons of music of the day also often employed their own private bands. The leader of the group was a violinist or a keyboard player, or both, and usually had to fulfil some additional household function, such as steward, secretary, or even valet. Musicians were regarded as servants and tradesmen who supplied a commodity – namely an endless stream of new compositions to divert their patrons and impress their patrons' rivals. There were special occasions, both sacred and secular, but mostly the music was provided as background for dining or card-playing: Richard Wagner later bemoaned 'the clatter of princely plates' and more than one musician was reprimanded by his patron for allowing the music to drown out the card-calling.

By the late seventeenth century, German violinists were already exploring the virtuoso potential of their instruments. The most important of them was Heinrich Franz von Biber (1644–1704) of Wartenberg, in Bohemia. Biber became Konzertmeister at the court of the Prince Archbishop of Salzburg. Charles Burney, the eighteenth-century music historian and commentator, wrote: 'Of all the violin players of the last century, Biber seems to have been the best, and his solos are the most difficult and the most fanciful of any Music I have seen of the same period.'[2] Biber's powers of execution must have been extraordinary and his knowledge of the violin considerable. He made extensive use of *scordatura* (re-tuning) to obtain special effects, with strings tuned in thirds and fourths instead of the usual fifths, thereby facilitating certain passages and the execution of chords. The different tension on the strings also brought about a change in tone colour which Biber highlighted in his music. His set of 'Mystery' or 'Rosary' sonatas (*c.*1676), depicting 15 episodes in the life of Christ, calls for a different tuning for each sonata.

Biber was not alone among seventeenth-century violinists to use *scordatura*. Johann Jakob Walther (1650–1717), first violinist and chamber musician at the Saxon Court, was renowned for his feats of virtuosity, including sustaining a melody with the bow while he accompanied himself with left-hand pizzicato. The German

Nikolaus Bruhns (1665–97) went one better: he used to astonish his audience with two-part improvisations on the violin while playing the bass with his feet on the organ pedals.

Of Nicolo Matteis (d.? 1707) who came to England in 1672, John Evelyn wrote in his diary on 19 November 1674:

> I heard that stupendous violinist, Signor Nicholao, whom I have never heard mortal man exceed on that instrument. He had a stroke so sweet – and made it speak like the voice of a man, and when he pleased, like a concert of several instruments. . . . he played such ravishing things as astonished us all.

Roger North remarks in his memoirs that although many gifted amateurs had heard Matteis play solos, yet none would attempt '... to do the like, for none could command that fulness, grace and truth of which he was the master', and that 'his staccatos, tremolos, divisions, and indeed his whole manner was surprising, and every stroke was a mouthfull'. Although poor when he arrived in England, Matteis amassed a fortune through his concerts and publications. North tells us that he 'took a great house, and after the manner of his country lived luxuriously, which brought diseases upon him of which he died'.[3]

### Notes
1. Van der Straeten, *The Romance of the Fiddle*, p. 68.
2. Burney, *A General History of Music*, iii, p. 462
3. Van der Straeten, *History of the Violin*, p. 151.

# 2 The Archangel and the Red Priest

The first important influence on violin playing, to say nothing of his impact on early eighteenth-century music in general, was that of Arcangelo Corelli (1653–1713). A native of Fusignano who spent most of his working life in Rome, he received his earliest musical training from a priest in Faenza. At the age of 13 he went to Bologna, where he had his first violin lessons from the two well-known teachers, Benvenuti and Brugnoli.

Corelli was fortunate in his Roman patrons, who included the former Queen Christina of Sweden and Cardinal Pietro Ottoboni, who engaged him as director of his household music and took him as a personal friend. Corelli lived comfortably in his own apartments in the cardinal's palace, composing, teaching and conducting the Monday Concerts that were attended by the elite of Roman society. George Frideric Handel, who collaborated with him between 1707 and 1708, recalled Corelli's frugality and that 'his favourite pastime was to look at pictures which cost him nothing'.[1] Corelli, in fact, amassed a fine collection of paintings (as did Handel) and became recognised as an authority on art.

Frequently asked to play for people of high rank, he was not above meeting them on equal terms. During a concert at the Ottoboni Palace, some of the guests began talking between themselves: Corelli put down his violin and seated himself among them; when questioned, he replied coolly that he was afraid his playing might interrupt the conversation.

In the early eighteenth century, it was difficult to find a violinist who did not claim to have studied with Corelli; Pietro Locatelli (1695–1764) was one of the most famous. Through his teaching and his music Corelli laid the foundations of violin playing, and his solos were seized upon immediately they appeared. Important enough in their own time, his compositions today remain a permanent influence on violin literature. He took the best ideas of his predecessors and synthesised them into a form which exploited the possibilities of the violin, both in ensemble and as a solo instrument, in an entirely new way. It was Corelli who first extensively exploited the violin as a melodic, singing instrument. Before the middle of the seventeenth century, composers appear to have been more concerned with writing violin music that contained scale passages, figurations and special effects. Corelli provided variety by the use of small ensembles in a dialogue with the larger body of strings, as exemplified in his 12 Concerti Grossi, Op. 6. Corelli's best known piece for violin is his 23 variations on the popular theme, 'La Folia di Spagna' contained in Op. 5.

The cornerstones of Corelli and violin playing were the production of a beautiful tone, variety and elegance of bowing, expressively interpreted slow movements and a well developed left-hand technique. He insisted that his pupils should not use the fingers of the left hand to stop the strings before they could master the slow sweep of the bow across the open strings, a practice still endorsed today. Indeed, Corelli's Op. 5 sonatas contain some of the best bowing exercises to be found anywhere.

As a performer, Corelli was said to be a serious and dignified artist, but occasionally, when carried away with the music, 'his countenance was distorted, his eyes red as fire, and his eyeballs rolled as if he were in agony'.[2] His sense of humour is manifest in an encounter with the brash German virtuoso Nicolaus Strungk (1640–1700). In the master's presence, Strungk is said to have performed well-nigh impossible feats of *scordatura* without difficulty, expecting the master's acclamation to follow. Instead, Corelli smiled and said quietly: 'I am called Arcangelo, but you one might justly call Archidiavolo.'[3]

When Corelli died he left a fine collection of master violins and a considerable fortune. His paintings went to Ottoboni, who showed his gratitude by placing Corelli's remains in the Pantheon near the tomb of Raphael.

If Corelli laid the solid foundations of violin playing, Antonio Vivaldi (1678–1741) decorated them with sparkling inventiveness which, through his pupils and imitators, provided later eighteenth-century virtuosos with stock-in-trade. The son of a Venetian violinist in the orchestra at San Marco, Vivaldi grew up in a city where music was ever-present and enjoyed by all classes of society. At the age of ten the young Antonio could play well enough to assist his father with the music at the cathedral. He entered the priesthood at 15, and his bright red hair inspired the nickname 'the Red Priest'. In line with prevailing custom, he combined his church duties with musical studies.

In 1703, Vivaldi was appointed violin master at the Ospedale della Pietà, where, apart from sporadic leaves of absence, he remained for almost 40 years. The Pietà was one of the four asylums in Venice established in the fourteenth century for the protection of orphaned and foundling girls. Apart from general education, the girls were given a good musical training and had their own choir and orchestra; their concerts raised funds for the Ospedale's running costs. During Vivaldi's time, the Pietà was known throughout Europe for its high standards of performance and some of the girls became professional musicians.

Vivaldi's fame and influence as a virtuoso violinist and opera composer during his lifetime had been immense, but the dimming of his reputation in his final years was followed by a neglect of almost a century. His name seldom appeared in the eighteenth-century violin tutors and, although there were sporadic efforts in Germany to play and publish his music, the great turn-of-the-century masters of the French School totally ignored him. Nevertheless, his ideas, like those of Corelli, survived in the music of his pupils.

Although we do not have precise accounts from those who studied with Vivaldi, many contemporary performers and players acknowledged his influence. 'La Chiaretta', one of his girls at the Pietà, is said to have been among the best Italian violinists of her day. A pupil of his later years, the violin virtuoso Santa Tasca was employed by the Emperor Francis I of the Holy Roman Empire. However, Vivaldi's most important pupil, the German Georg Johann Pisendel (1687–1755), was already a professional violinist with an established reputation when he was sent by his employer, the Elector of Saxony, to have lessons with the Venetian. Pisendel and Vivaldi became close friends and the composer dedicated many violin concertos – the most famous being the one in A major (RV 29) – to his pupil.

Vivaldi was a prolific composer whose ideas were so rapidly committed to paper that he said he could compose a concerto with all its parts faster than a copyist could write it out. Besides his 40 operas, he wrote almost 400 violin concertos. His violin music involves wide leaps from one string to another: many passages require a leap from the lowest string to the highest, a manoeuvre achieved by deftly pivoting the bow. His cantabile passages reveal his innate understanding of his violinistic craft, and yet he incorporates many effects that are vocal in origin. A man of great human contrasts, Vivaldi was, on the one hand, very devout – described as never having the rosary out of his hand unless it was to take up his pen – and, on the other, hot-tempered, easily irritated and as quick to regain tranquillity. His music magnificently reflects these contrasts.

Few accounts of Vivaldi's own performances as a violinist survive but it is clear from the music itself, and the post he held, that he must have been a virtuoso. In 1715, Vivaldi's German pupil, Johann von Uffenbach (1687–1769), wrote in his journal of a visit to the opera in Venice:

> Towards the end Vivaldi played a solo accompaniment admirably, adding at the end a free fantasy which quite frightened me, for it is scarcely possible that anyone ever played or will play this way, for he placed his fingers but a hair's breadth from the bridge, so that there was barely room for the bow, doing this on all four strings with imitations at incredible speed.[4]

Von Uffenbach was an amateur violinist, but nevertheless, in musical matters his journal is regarded as trustworthy. Even if a 'hair's breadth' was an exaggeration, it is sufficient to confirm Vivaldi's virtuosity and that he employed fingering positions quite unfamiliar to the informed observer. What is also interesting is that, if this account is correct, Vivaldi would have played in much higher positions than were possible on the short fingerboard of the time: the only logical explanation must be that he had a longer fingerboard fitted on his violin.

Johann Joachim Quantz (1697–1773), flautist and musician to the court of Frederick the Great, attributes the invention of the cadenza to Vivaldi. In the Dresden Library is a Vivaldi manuscript in which an improvisatory solo passage 39 bars long occurs just before the orchestra enters for the finale. It begins with rapid scale passages, frequently changes key and then soars into high positions, looking forward to the cadenzas of Mozart and Beethoven.

In England, the art of violin playing in the early eighteenth century was still primitive compared with that of the rest of Europe. Thanks to the arrival of Italians such as Francesco Geminiani (1687–1762), this situation greatly improved. Geminiani had been a pupil of Corelli in Rome and started his career as leader of an orchestra in Naples. But according to the eighteenth-century lexicographer John Busby, his sense of rhythm was so erratic that he '…disordered their motions, embarrassed their execution and, in a word, threw the whole band into confusion'.[5] The penalty for this crime was demotion to the viola section. It was a common saying at the time that no good music was written for the viola because there were no good viola players, and vice versa. Although Geminiani's talents may not have been suited to the orchestral ranks, he made a fine reputation for himself as a soloist by his brilliant style, which far exceeded anything previously heard.

Geminiani's greatest contribution was his treatise, *The Art of Playing the Violin*, published in 1740. It contains the essence of Corelli's teaching and was considered one of the best instruction books of the time. Geminiani was the first to advocate holding the violin as it is held today, with the chin to the left of the tailpiece. At the time the violin was held against the neck, with the chin resting upon the right side of the tailpiece and with little support from the chin itself (the chin-rest had not yet been invented). The main support came from the left hand holding the rather thick neck (modifications to the instrument came later). The hand itself was held much lower than it is today, so that the violin scroll was lower than the tailpiece. For accompanying simple dances this was adequate, but in more sophisticated music, requiring shifts up and down the fingerboard, bracing of the neck and bending of the head were unavoidable. Geminiani's reliance on the chin allowed the player to keep his head straight and made shifting easier. Interestingly, Leopold Mozart (1719–87) adhered to the established practice of the chin resting on the right of the tailpiece, in his tutor, *Versuch einer gründlichen Violinschule*, published in 1756.

A small but significant link between the classical and modern schools of violin playing was provided by the Italian Giovanni Battista Somis (1676–1763). A pupil of both Corelli and Vivaldi, he combined their teaching philosophies to form a style of his own, which took violin technique a step forward. Students from throughout Europe were attracted to the school he established in Turin. Among his most famous pupils were Jean-Marie Leclair (1697–1764), through whom Somis exerted a considerable influence on French violin playing, and Gaetano Pugnani (1731–98). A contemporary writer, Hubert le Blanc, reports that Somis '… had the most beautiful bow stroke in Europe' and that 'he can play a whole note in one bow [so] that it takes one's breath away when thinking of it'.[6]

## Notes

1. Van der Straeten, *History*, i, p. 143.
2. Ferris, *Great Pianists and Great Violinists*, p. 12.
3. Van der Straeten, op. cit., i, p. 139.
4. Kolneder, *Antonio Vivaldi: His Life and Works*, p. 116.
5. Busby, *Concert Room and Orchestra Anecdotes*, ii, p. 205.
6. Van der Straeten, op. cit., i, p. 153.

# 3    Master of the Nations

By the end of the seventeenth century the violin was capable of a brilliance of tone and range of expression that went hand-in-hand with its growing popularity. Consequently different styles of playing had begun to assert themselves. The fiddler who provided accompaniments for dancing could not be compared with the court soloist, whose playing was on a more sophisticated level. About the middle of the seventeenth century, playing styles had become associated with national characteristics and the differences between the Italian and the French styles became most apparent of all. Violin playing in other countries largely followed the lines of these two schools.

The virtuoso techniques of the Italian school were developed to suit the newest forms of composition, the sonata, the variation and later, the solo concerto. The Italians also favoured the *cantabile* style of playing – a logical development in a land where musical sound had always been associated with the human voice. The French perfected a highly sophisticated style of bowing which suited the clearly accented courtly dance rhythms with which they were preoccupied. The Germans created an advanced virtuoso style of playing, modelled on Italian principles, which exploited the extended range of the violin, double-stopping and *scordatura*. Their bowing techniques were correspondingly advanced.

This high degree of development is reflected in the music of Johann Sebastian Bach (1685–1750). As Kapellmeister of the court orchestra of Prince Leopold of Anhalt-Cöthen, he composed violin sonatas, two violin concertos (in E major and A minor) and the Double Concerto in D minor. It was also at Cöthen that he wrote his unaccompanied Partitas for violin, which remain today among the most demanding music ever written for the instrument. There are no contemporary accounts of Bach's violin playing, but in a letter dated 1774 to the German music lexicographer, Johann Forkel, Carl Philipp Emanuel Bach mentions his father's lifelong interest in the violin:

> In his youth, and until the approach of old age, he played the violin cleanly and penetratingly, and thus kept the orchestra in better order than he could have done with the harpsichord. He understood to perfection the possibilities of all stringed instruments.[1]

By the beginning of the eighteenth century, the violin was to be found in all classes of society and had finally shaken off its early 'rogue and vagabond' image. This new measure of respectability was largely due to the increase in amateur playing. Giuseppe Tartini (1692–1770) formed the most significant link between the Baroque and Classical periods, his style containing elements of both. He may be seen as 'the most important exponent of the violin concerto between Vivaldi and Viotti'.[2]

Tartini's family were rich Florentines who had settled in Istria on the Adriatic, and much of their wealth found its way into the church, which provided the young Tartini with his first lessons on the violin. When he reached the age of 17, his father was determined he should enter the priesthood; Tartini was equally convinced he would not, preferring law. Despite strong pressure from the Bishop of Istria, whose monastery had been promised a handsome donation if his persuasion was successful, Tartini won his point. In 1709 he entered the University at Padua as a law student, but it is doubtful whether he was ever over-zealous in his studies. From the beginning, fencing, art and music held greater claims on him, and for a time he seriously considered opening a fencing school to subsidise his career as a violinist.

In his final year at the university, Tartini fell in love with the 15-year-old Elisabetta Premazone, a dependant relative of an eminent Paduan cardinal. Their elopement and secret marriage inevitably caused family fireworks: Tartini's father stopped his allowance and the cardinal issued a warrant for his arrest. Tartini fled from Padua and, disguised as a monk, wandered from city to city, finally reaching Assisi where he stayed for two years under the protection of the Franciscan Friars. During this time he took instruction in theory and composition from Bohuslav Matěj Černohorský (1687–1769), a distinguished Bohemian composer and teacher. (In the Bohemian monasteries the violin was employed both as a solo instrument and in string ensembles, and the music composed there shows a high degree of technical development.)

It was at this time also, through scientific experiments with the violin, that Tartini first became aware of what he called *terzi tuoni*, or 'third sound'. It is what we recognise today as the phenomenon of 'differential' notes, which were later investigated and documented by acoustical experts such as Hermann Helmholtz. The differential note is heard as a 'third' sound (which is not being played) when two notes are stopped in perfect intonation. On his own admission, Tartini's mathematical calculations contained errors and, although he published a treatise on harmony in 1754, he was never able to prove his theory. Tartini also experimented with a thicker gauge of violin string to obtain a richer tone; this was later taken into general use.

At Assisi Tartini wrote the 'Devil's Trill' sonata. It is said that he was inspired by a dream he had in which he sold his soul to the devil in exchange for the most exquisite sonata imaginable.[3]

In exchange for his food and lodging, Tartini provided a valuable source of revenue to the Friars, as his playing attracted large audiences to the concerts in the monastery chapel. He was, of necessity, hidden behind a curtain and spoken of as 'the Mystery Violinist of Assisi'. But in 1715, on the annual Feast of St Francis when pilgrims came from all over Italy to worship at the tomb, a deacon accidentally moved the curtain and revealed the identity of the performer. Paduans in the congregation immediately recognised Tartini. The story ended happily when the cardinal dropped his original charges, and Tartini and Elisabetta were reunited.

Tartini's fame quickly spread throughout Italy. Socially, he and his wife moved only in aristocratic circles. This state of affairs may well have continued but for an invitation extended to Tartini and the great Florentine violinist Veracini in 1716 to compete at Venice in honour of the visit of the Elector of Saxony. It was common practice in the eighteenth century to invite artists to outdo each other for the benefit of eminent guests. But Tartini was never to meet this challenge. By chance he happened to hear Veracini play in Cremona, was immediately convinced of the Florentine's superiority, and withdrew from the contest.

Shaken by this eclipse, Tartini went into exile. He left his wife and installed himself in Ancona, vowing to stay until he had reached the perfection he desired. How long he resided there is uncertain, but the records show that he was appointed to the post of first violin at the Capella del Santo at Padua in 1721. He was described as an 'extraordinary' violinist and received an annual stipend of 150 florins, a handsome sum at the time. He was also excused from the need to show proof of his excellence, a singularly high honour since each member of the choir and orchestra was required to re-audition annually. The ultimate concession was that he should be allowed to appear elsewhere. He did not take advantage of this opportunity until 1723, when an irresistible invitation to play in Prague at the coronation of Charles VI came from Count Kinsky, the Chancellor of Bohemia, a passionate devotee of music. Tartini's performance caused a furore in Prague, and he accepted an offer to stay on and lead Count Kinsky's private band. But he was fated never to enjoy prosperity for long. Three years later, when his brother became involved in financial difficulties, Tartini left Prague, in the belief that 'the skin is nearer than the purse'.[4]

In 1728, at the age of 36, he set up his 'School of the Nations' in Padua. It became renowned for its excellence and Tartini became even more famous as a teacher than he had been as a performer. Many great violinists studied there, including Gaetano Pugnani (1731–98), who was also a pupil of Somis, and the legendary Maddalena Lombardini (1745–1818), the young girl to whom Tartini wrote a letter (dated 1760 and first published in 1770) on the art of bowing which has passed into musical history as the sole and classic example of Tartini's detailed instruction of his method. In it, Tartini stresses that at first practice should be confined to the 'use and power of the bow', in order to learn:

> . . . the true manner of holding, balancing and pressing the bow lightly, but steadily, upon the strings; in such a manner as that it shall seem to breathe the first tone it gives, which must proceed from the friction of the string, and not from percussion, as by a blow given with a hammer upon it. This depends on laying the bow lightly upon the strings, at the first contact, and on gently pressing it afterwards, which, if done

gradually, can scarce have too much force given to it, because if the tone is begun with delicacy, there is little danger of rendering it afterwards either coarse or harsh.[5]

Tartini also advocates that his pupil should master the art of the swell on an open string, from *pianissimo* to *fortissimo*, by exercising for an hour each day until perfection is attained. 'When you are a perfect mistress of this part of a good performer, a swell will be very easy to you; beginning with the most minute softness, increasing the tone to its loudest degree, and diminishing it to the same point of softness with which you began, and all this in the same stroke of the bow.'[6]

Tartini wrote some 200 violin concertos and an equal number of sonatas; few of these are ever heard today, with the exception of the 'Devil's Trill' and 'Didone Abbandonata'. But the 38 variations on a theme by Corelli, *L'arte del arco* (1758), constitute one of the best exercises for the right arm in the repertory. Tartini, far more than any of his predecessors or contemporaries, undertook an intensive study of the bow. He made the stick itself narrower and was the first to modify its outward curve. He also altered the shape of the head and discarded the fluting.

As a performer Tartini was considered to be one of the most accomplished virtuosos of the day, rivalled only by Francesco Veracini (1690–1768). Pierre Lahoussaye (1735–1818), the great French violinist and pupil of Tartini at Padua, wrote: 'Nothing could express my astonishment and admiration caused by the perfection and purity of his tone, the charm of expression, the magic of his bow, the all-round perfection of his performance.'[7] Tartini hated virtuosity for its own sake. Most contemporary accounts remark upon the beauty of his *cantabile* passages, not only for their depth of expression, but for a certain reserve which would seem to point more to the style that was later to be echoed in the playing of Spohr and Joachim. Tartini possessed both the talent and the physical equipment for a virtuoso and yet he was singularly unambitious. And fame, though readily accepted at the time, passed lightly over his shoulders. He rejected countless offers to play abroad: Sir Edward Walpole and Lord Middlesex both tried hard to tempt him to play in London – the latter, to the tune of 3,000 lire – and neither the Prince de Condé nor the Prince de Clérmont could persuade him to appear in Paris.

Tartini's Venetian *protégée*, Maddalena Lombardini, was less reticent. She was so musically advanced that, at the age of seven, she attracted the attention of the governors of the Mendicanti at an open audition to select young girls as apprentices to the music school of the Ospedale, to study one or two musical instruments, singing and solfeggio. She made such astonishing progress that at 14 she was promoted to the rank of violin teacher; the Mendicanti governors sponsored her journeys to Padua for advanced study with Tartini and others. The famous letter from Tartini shows to what extent her talent had developed by 1760.

In 1767 she married the violinist Lodovico Maria Gaspar Sirmen (1738–1812) and thereafter was known as Maddalena Lombardini Sirmen. The following year, they embarked on a two-year concert tour. Her playing won the heart of audiences everywhere and when the couple appeared in Paris at the Concert Spirituel, the *Mercure de France* reported that her violin was 'the lyre of Orpheus in the hands of a Grace'.[8] Many considered her a much greater violinist than her husband. A second tour took them to London where in 1771 she made her debut as a soloist at the King's Theatre in London. She was also a gifted and prolific composer and on this initial visit she gave no fewer than 22 performances of her own concertos in various concert series. Later she appeared over 200 times in London in the series produced by J. C. Bach and C. F. Abel and at the King's Theatre and Covent Garden. She also sang at Marylebone Pleasure Gardens.[9]

## Notes

1. Menuhin, *Violin and Viola*, p. 224.
2. Boyden, *The History of Violin Playing*, p. 344.
3–4. *Grove*, 5th edn., viii, p. 313.
5–6. Tartini, *Letter to Maddalena Lombardini*, 1760.
7. Van der Straeten, *The History of the Violin*, ii, p. 9.
8. *Mercure de France*, *c.*1814.
9. *New Grove Dictionary of Women Composers*, pp. 287–8.

# 4　Viotti and the French Trio

'Viotti, it is true . . . astonishes the hearer; but he does something infinitely better – he awakens emotion, gives a soul to sound, and leads the passions captive,' wrote a critic in the *Morning Chronicle* on 10 March 1794, after one of Viotti's London concerts. A pivotal figure in violin playing, linking the Corelli tradition through Pietro Locatelli to the nineteenth-century French school which he established, Giovanni Battista Viotti (1753–1824) was 'the most influential violinist between Tartini and Paganini'.[1] His playing was brilliant and romantic.

Viotti was born at Fontanetto da Po, the son of a blacksmith and amateur horn player. His first violin lessons were from a roving lute player and, as a boy, he was fortunate to come under the patronage of Prince Alfonso dal Pozzo della Cistema, who chose him as a student-companion to his son. Viotti lived with the family and the two boys became pupils of Pugnani, who had studied with Somis, thus forming a link with Corelli. In 1775, Viotti became a member of the orchestra of the royal chapel in Turin, occupying the last desk of the first violins for five years .[2]

At the end of this period Pugnani took Viotti on a concert tour of Europe, introducing him as his 'pupil'. They first visited Switzerland, then Dresden and Berlin, and – encouraged by their success – extended their itinerary to include Warsaw and St Petersburg. In the latter city, Catherine the Great showered gifts upon Viotti and tried to persuade him to join her court orchestra. But he declined the Empress's offer by saying he did not care for the Russian climate.

From St Petersburg Viotti travelled to London. Here his playing was well received and compared favourably with that of Geminiani, then considered the finest violinist to have crossed the Channel. But it was at a concert in Paris in 1782 that Viotti achieved his greatest triumph. It immediately established him as a leading virtuoso and he enjoyed this success for almost two years, acclaimed by critics and the public alike. During this time he set up house with his friend, the composer Luigi Cherubini (1760–1842), and their soirées became the centre of Parisian musical life. Then he suddenly retired from the concert platform without explanation. The mystery of this defection at the height of his powers remains unsolved.

A year later he entered the service of Marie Antoinette at Versailles and in 1788, under the patronage of the Comte de Provence, produced a brilliant season of Italian opera at the Théâtre de Monsieur. But this venture, too, was short-lived. The Revolution in 1789 disrupted all Viotti's plans for future productions. Employment in royal service did not curb Viotti's democratic ideas. Once, during a private concert at Versailles, when he was playing one of his own compositions, there was an interruption, followed by whispering among the guests. As murmurs of 'Make way for the Duke' heralded the late arrival of the Duc d'Artois, Viotti stopped playing, tucked his violin under his arm and left the salon. Moreover, unlike his venerated predecessor Corelli, when faced with a similar situation at the Ottoboni Palace, Viotti resolutely refused all entreaties to return.

On another occasion in 1790, Viotti accepted an invitation to play in a charity concert which was arranged to take place on the fifth floor in the house of a friend. 'I will play', said Viotti, '. . . but only on one condition . . . that the audience shall come up here to us – we have long enough descended to them; but times are changed.'³ When the aristocrats had climbed the stairs, they found that the only ornament on display was a bust of Jean Jacques Rousseau, whose democratic ideas were so feared that his remains, together with those of Voltaire, were removed from the Panthéon and secretly disposed of when the Bourbon monarchy was restored some 23 years later. However, in 1792, on the eve of the arrest of the King and Queen, Viotti decided, democrat or not, that his views could be open to question. He fled without a sou to England.

In contrast to the turbulent events in France, Viotti's life in England was tranquil, and he earned a reasonable living. His success on the concert platform – especially at the Hanover Square Rooms – attracted an ever-widening circle of influential and cultured friends, and he took on a number of pupils, many of whom were from the upper echelons of society. The Duke of Cambridge was one of the most celebrated. It was through one of his young pupils, Walter Chinnery, that he became acquainted with the family who were to become his life-long friends. Chinnery was an employee of the Treasury, and his wife Caroline a gifted pianist. In 1794 Viotti took over the post of acting manager of the Italian Opera at the King's Theatre (now Her Majesty's) in the Haymarket.

In 1798 the British government, unjustly suspecting Viotti of involvement in a revolutionary plot, ordered him to leave the country. In exile he was given the use of the country house of a friend at Schoenfeld, near Hamburg, and spent the time composing and corresponding with his beloved Mrs Chinnery. It was here that he wrote the duets for two violins, Op. 5, which bear the inscription: 'This work is the fruit of leisure which misfortune procured for me. Some of the pieces were dictated by Pain, others by Hope.'

Viotti took on a few pupils, one of whom was the young Friedrich Wilhelm Pixis (1786–1842) of Mannheim, a brilliant young violinist who was himself to become a significant figure when the Prague Conservatory opened in 1811. This institution has since played an important part in the history of violin playing and given to the world many who have influenced the development of their art: Antonin Bennewitz (1833–1926), Otokar Ševčík (1852–1934), Jaroslav Kocián (1883–1950) and František Ondříček (1857–1922) who gave the first performance of Dvořák's Violin Concerto in Prague in 1883, are among the most prominent.

The Czechs have always possessed a natural instinct for music. Charles Burney, when travelling in Bohemia in 1773, was amazed to find in simple village schools throughout the country, children of both sexes from six to eleven years old, 'reading, writing, playing on violins'[4] and other instruments. Pixis brought to Prague the traditions of the Mannheim school allied to Viotti's teaching. The Mannheim traditions stemmed from the group of virtuoso musicians who formed the court orchestras during the reign of Duke Carl Theodor, in the third quarter of the century. The founder and leader of this school of violinists and conductors was the Czech Johann Stamitz (1717–57). The main features of their style of playing have been described as 'perfect team-work, fiery and expressive execution, uniform bowing, exciting dynamic effects and accuracy in phrasing in orchestral performance'.[5] Burney called them 'an army of generals'. Through Viotti Pixis would have learned that violin playing was not only concerned with technical brilliance but must also emphasise tonal beauty, power and expression.

With Napoleon firmly in power in France, it was seemingly safe in 1801 to allow Viotti to return to England. But he had temporarily lost interest in concert giving and, acting upon Mrs Chinnery's encouragement, reinforced by her financial support, he opened a shop in London as a wine merchant. Many of Viotti's Italian contemporaries had similar commercial interests: Geminiani bought and sold pictures; Muzio Clementi (1752–1832) made a fortune out of making pianos. The parsimonious Clementi and his pupil John Field (1782–1837) would wash their own shirts and socks when on tour in St Petersburg. At first Viotti probably made a living from his business for he declined at this time to take on any pupils. He even refused Louis Spohr (1784–1859), who had long held Viotti as his model. In his autobiography Spohr bitterly laments the fact that he was denied the chance to study with the master. Spohr always maintained that no better test existed for a fine player than the execution of Viotti sonatas or concertos. Spohr relates the tale of a friend who, by chance, entered Viotti's shop and was surprised to find the great man behind the counter. He reproached him for denying the public the pleasure of hearing him play. Viotti replied: 'My dear Sir, I have done so simply because I find that the English like Wine better than Music.'[6]

Unfortunately, the wine shop never prospered sufficiently to keep Viotti out of financial difficulties and, in consequence, he later made several attempts to re-establish himself in the musical world. In 1802 he visited Paris to present some of the works he had composed at Schoenfeld. Viotti's pupil, the celebrated Pierre Baillot de Sales (1771–1842), wrote of this particular performance: 'Everything seemed to flow without effort, softly yet powerfully. With the greatest *élan* he climbed the heights of inspiration. His tone was magnificent, sweet, but metallic, as though the tender bow were handled by the arm of Hercules.'[7]

Later Viotti was appointed director of the Opéra in Paris at a high salary but, as in previous years, misfortune dogged every undertaking and he returned to London in 1822. The previous year he had made his will, a pathetic document revealing the underlying sadness in a life that once held so much promise:

> If I die before I can pay off this debt [he still owed Madame Chinnery 24,000FF] I pray
> that everything I have in the world may be sold off, realized, and sent to Madame
> Chinnery or her heirs . . . .[8]

He died at the Chinnerys' house in Upper Berkeley Street, London, in 1824.

Viotti seems to have been a man of extreme sensitivity and too vulnerable for the hazards of a public career. He was liked by his contemporaries and remained unspoiled by the decadence of the French court. According to a friend, 'No one ever attached so much value to the most simple gifts of nature. Everything struck his imagination; everything spoke to his soul and his heart overflowed with warm and affectionate feelings.'[9]

The critics were unanimous in their praise of Viotti's handling of the bow. The *Allgemeine musikalische Zeitung* of 3 July 1811 described the hallmarks of Viotti's school: 'A large, strong, full tone is the first; the combination of this with a powerful, penetrating, singing *legato* is the second; as to the third, variety, charm, shadow and light must be brought into play through the greatest diversity of bowing.' Viotti was one of the first violinists to use the Tourte bow, which had a lightness, firmness and elasticity that the older bows lacked. He would therefore have had a considerable advantage over his predecessors. According to the nineteenth-century Belgian musicologist, François-Joseph Fétis, during his time in Paris from 1782 or thereabouts, Viotti gave advice and guidance to François Tourte in his efforts to perfect the bow.

Although Viotti abandoned his career so unaccountably at such an early age, his influence on tone production and expression has remained one of the most important of the eighteenth century. As a violinist, Viotti was not only regarded as the greatest player of his day in the classical Italian style, but as the founder and originator of the modern school of violin playing. As a composer he was prolific, though not remarkable for his originality. He was one of the first violinist-composers to expand the violin concerto by adopting, as far as possible, the symphonic form of Haydn, with well-contrasted themes. In our own time there has been a welcome revival of his music.

One of Viotti's most prominent pupils was the Belgian violinist André Robberechts (1797–1860), who in turn became teacher of Charles-Auguste de Bériot (1802–70), father of the great nineteenth-century Belgian school. Through his trio of French disciples – Pierre Baillot de Sales, Pierre Rode and Rodolphe Kreutzer – Viotti's influence on performing style was firmly established early in the nineteenth century. All three became professors at the newly established Paris Conservatoire (1795). Their jointly produced *Méthode de Violon*, first published in Paris in 1803, was based on the principles of Viotti's teaching in its insistence on refinement, excellence of bowing, and power and beauty of tone. The level of attention paid to detail in left-hand technique looks forward to the late nineteenth and twentieth centuries. The usual range of three octaves and tone known to Geminiani and Mozart was increased to over four, and in addition, the directions for holding the instrument were considerably advanced from earlier methods. Baillot mentions the 'Tourte' grip and his bowing directions are near to our own. It is also clear that the violin was by now universally held with the chin to the left of the tailpiece. On the production of a good tone, he advised: 'Aspirants should search no further than their own sensitivity, which they should try to draw out of the depths of their soul, for it is there that they will find its source.'[10] The *Méthode* subsequently developed into *L'Art du Violon* (1834), and remained the standard violin text of the conservatoire during its greatest era.

Pierre Baillot de Sales was born in Passy, a suburb of Paris, the son of a schoolmaster. He first learned to play the violin with a pupil of Pietro Nardini (1722–93). He heard Viotti play in Paris when he was only ten and, although 20 years elapsed before he heard him again, the experience was cataclysmic. Viotti remained his model for all time.

Viotti helped Baillot secure a place in the orchestra at the Théâtre Feydeau, but he abandoned the post to become a government official. However, he continued to play in private. In 1795, Baillot decided to return to the music profession and studied theory and composition with Cherubini. He then travelled extensively as a soloist throughout Europe, achieving considerable success. Baillot was last in the line of the classical French School. After him, Paganini's style dominated the scene. Paul David writes: 'His playing was distinguished by a noble, powerful tone, great neatness of execution and a pure, elevated, truly musical style.'[11]

Baillot was said to have been one of the few players who retained his skill and freshness to the end of his career. Felix Mendelssohn considered the performance of his octet led by Baillot the finest he ever heard. Hiller wrote in 1831 that, at a Conservatoire concert, Baillot (then 60) 'still played with all the fire and poetry of youth'.[12] Spohr also spoke admiringly of Baillot's technique as being 'unrestricted by the narrow limits of mere virtuosity'.[13] As a teacher, he was greatly respected, and of his many pupils the most celebrated were Charles Dancla (1817–1907) and François Habeneck (1781–1849), the latter being the teacher of Hubert Léonard (1819–90), François Prume (1816–49) and Prosper Sainton (1813–90).

Pierre Rode (1774–1830), the second of the French trio, was born in Bordeaux. In 1788, his teacher sent him to Paris with an introduction to Viotti, who, struck by the 14-year-old boy's exceptional talent, taught him for two years. Rode toured as a virtuoso and held leaderships in a number of theatre orchestras including that of the Paris Opéra where he remained until 1799; in 1800 he was appointed solo violinist to Napoleon.

In 1803, Rode went to St Petersburg as principal violinist to the Tsar Alexander at a salary of 5,000 silver roubles, with the sole obligation to play at court and at the Imperial Theatre. He met Spohr en route at Brunswick and enchanted the German virtuoso with his playing. The constant pressures and intrigues of five years at the Russian Court had a harmful effect both on Rode's playing and his health. He became increasingly nervous in disposition and when he returned to Paris, his playing was said to have deteriorated. Rode never succeeded in re-establishing himself as an artist, and he died of a stroke in 1830.

In his better days Rode was a true artist. His profoundly musical nature shows itself in his compositions which are particularly suited to the violin and are of a higher standard than those by most of his contemporaries. He published a considerable number of concertos, quartets, sets of variations and duos for two violins. The 24 Caprices remain today indispensable for serious students of the violin. He also had many pupils. Although his wandering life was not conducive to teaching for long periods, there were those who benefited greatly from sporadic instruction from him, the most famous being Josef Böhm, teacher of Joseph Joachim.

The third of Viotti's great pupils, Rodolphe Kreutzer (1766–1831), was born at Versailles, where his father was a member of the Royal Chapel; he was also his first instructor. Later Kreutzer studied with Anton Stamitz (1750–*c.*1789–1809), son of the famous Johann Stamitz (1717–57) of Mannheim. Anton was also a pupil of Viotti. At the age of 13, Kreutzer played one of his own compositions in Paris and, before he was 16, was regarded as equal to the greatest virtuosos of the day. Following the death of his father the same year, Kreutzer took his place at the Royal Chapel. Through Viotti's influence he became first violinist at the Théâtre Italienne. Later he undertook a concert tour of Europe with great success and was subsequently appointed professor of violin with Baillot and Rode at the conservatoire. He also was a soloist in Napoleon's private band. At the height of a brilliant career Kreutzer broke his left arm and retired from the concert platform, but continued to compose, conduct and teach. His music includes 19 violin concertos and 42 studies, which address all aspects of technique.

As a man Kreutzer was arrogant and unpopular with his colleagues; as a performer, he was an artist in whom warmth, feeling and liveliness were well blended. Often compared to Viotti, he was said nearly to equal him in the sweetness of his cantilena and broad full tone. His playing had more impetuosity and fervour than Rode's, but it lacked Rode's elegance of style.

To most people his name is known in connection with Beethoven's Kreutzer Sonata, Op. 47. Beethoven originally composed it for the mulatto George Bridgetower (*c.*1779–1860), whose training in Vienna had been sponsored by the Prince of Wales. Bridgetower created a great impression there, not only because of his eminent patron but on account of his stylish playing. At the premiere on 24 May 1802, Beethoven accompanied Bridgetower on the piano. However, when the composer later fell out with Bridgetower, he re-dedicated the sonata to Kreutzer. Unfortunately, this most passionate of Beethoven's sonatas was not to Kreutzer's taste, and he never performed the work. (At the time, Beethoven's music was certainly not popular in Paris. Most music from the other side of the Rhine suffered a similar neglect. When Kreutzer heard a rehearsal of Beethoven's Second Symphony in progress, he is alleged to have rushed away with his hands over his ears.)

François Antoine Habeneck (1781–1849), a contemporary of the French trio and pupil of Baillot at the conservatoire, is principally remembered as a great conductor, but he started his career as a brilliant violinist at the age of ten. As director of the Concert Society at the Paris Conservatoire in the 1820s, he gave accomplished performances of Beethoven. He taught many gifted violinists such as Hubert Léonard, François Prume and Prosper Sainton (who brought his art to England). Habeneck's most celebrated pupil was Delphin Alard, who was, in turn, the master of the great Spanish virtuoso, Pablo Sarasate.

So began the renowned French school of violin playing which stood for elegance and grace in bowing as well as brilliance of left-hand technique. Rode, like his master Viotti, excelled as a performer and demonstrated his influence through his playing, while Kreutzer and Baillot consolidated his principles through their writing and teaching. Kreutzer's pupil, Lambert Massart, was the teacher of Fritz Kreisler.

## Notes

1–2. *Grove*, 6th edn., 19, p. 864.

3. Ferris, *Great Pianists and Great Violinists*, p. 29.

4. Adrienne Simpson, 'An Introduction to Czech Baroque Music' *The Consort*, 34, (1978), p. 288.

5. *Grove*, 5th edn., v, p. 554.

6. Spohr, *Louis Spohr's Autobiography*, i, p. 13.

7. Farga, *Violins and Violinists*, p. 150.

8. *Grove*, 5th edn., viii, p. 827.

9. Souper, *The Strad*, May 1930, p. 25.

10. *Méthode de Violon*, 1803.

11. *Grove*, 5th edn., i, p. 356.

12. Blunt, *On Wings of Song*, p. 144.

13. Spohr, op. cit., iii, p. 278.

# 5   Nightingale of Violinists

A giant of a man, well over six feet in height, and of herculean constitution, Ludwig – he preferred the French 'Louis' – Spohr (1784–1859) dominated the violin world of Germany at the beginning of the nineteenth century and his reputation spread throughout Europe. When the 20-year-old Spohr made his debut in Leipzig, the critic Friedrich Rochlitz wrote: 'Perfect purity, security, precision, the most beautiful finish, every type of bowing, all varieties of violin tone, the most natural ease in the execution of all such things, even in the most difficult passages – these render him one of the most skilful of virtuosos.'[1]

The English composer Charles Villiers Stanford, who died in 1924, could recall the time when Spohr was considered a better composer than Beethoven. Spohr's output was voluminous; yet except for the F major Nonet, Op. 31, for string and wind ensemble, his violin music is rarely heard. And as a virtuoso violinist he is virtually forgotten. Spohr's posthumously published autobiography (1860–1), although exasperatingly egotistical, is a valuable account of contemporary social conditions for the musician. His own achievements are recounted in pompous language, but when he turns to travel, self-aggrandisement gives way to evocative description.

Louis Spohr was born in Brunswick, the son of a physician and amateur flautist; his mother sang and played the piano. At the age of four, he taught himself to play a small fiddle bought at a local fair, and had his first lessons from a French amateur musician. As a child, he also showed a natural gift for composition which led to study with a member of the Duke of Brunswick's band.

The rigid discipline of a strict father may have influenced Spohr's struggle for identity. If Dr Spohr saw his son crossing out to re-write, he would shout to his wife: 'The stupid boy is making windows again!' Spohr remembered this all his life: 'That is perhaps the reason why I acquired early the habit of writing a clean score straight off without erasing anything.'[2]

When he was 15, Spohr was taken on as Kammermusikus (chamber musician) to the Duke of Brunswick at a salary of 100 Thalers. The band gave weekly concerts in the duchess's apartments. As the music disturbed her card playing, the duchess ordered a thick carpet to be spread underneath the musicians to deaden the sound. Spohr tells us that the words 'I play' or 'I stand' were often louder than the music. When the duke was present, the carpet was discreetly removed. One evening, when playing one of his own compositions, Spohr got carried away, and a lackey took hold of his sleeve: 'Her Highness sends me to tell you not to scrape away so furiously.'[3]

The enraged Spohr played even more loudly and was reprimanded by the court marshal.

But Spohr's truculence earned him the duke's approval. He offered to give him a proper musical education, and asked Spohr to name his choice of teacher. Unfortunately, his first choice, Viotti, was then running his wine shop in London, so Franz Eck (1774–1804) agreed to take him on tour to Germany and Russia and give him lessons en route.

Eck was born in Mannheim and probably came under the influence of Anton Stamitz's brother, Carl (1745–1801). At any rate he would have been well grounded in the Mannheim school with its emphasis on clean bowing and expressive execution. Of Eck, Spohr wrote that his style was 'powerful without harshness, exhibiting a great variety of subtle and tasteful *nuances*, irreproachable in his execution of difficult passages, and altogether possessing a great and peculiar charm in performance'.[4]

Eck and Spohr set out in April 1802, just after Spohr's 18th birthday. The first lesson left Spohr discouraged, when he found he could not play a single bar to his teacher's satisfaction. He practised for ten hours each day and within two weeks was confident that for him 'nothing in the violin literature of the time was too difficult'.[5] In St Petersburg, although he did not appear in public, Spohr met all the visiting celebrities, among them the famous pianist Muzio Clementi and his pupil John Field. Less exalted was his teacher's involvement in a scandal with the daughter of a member of the Imperial Band. Eck was deported, went insane and eventually died in a lunatic asylum in Strasbourg. Spohr returned home by sea, alone.

In 1803, Spohr made his debut in Brunswick as a violinist-composer and was given a place in the first violins in the duke's band at twice his previous salary. It was at this time that Spohr first heard Rode play and, greatly affected by the experience, he modelled himself on the master's style. He considered himself to be one of the most faithful imitators of Rode among the young violinists of the day. Spohr gradually developed his own individuality, but the playing of Viotti and Rode always remained the main sources of his inspiration.

From this time onwards, Spohr achieved the kind of success we associate with present-day virtuosos, while lacking the advantage of modern transport. Journeying by road or water, Spohr visited almost every important city in Europe and made a number of trips to London. After his marriage in 1806 to the harpist Dorette Scheidler, he designed a special passenger coach to accommodate their music, instruments and personal belongings.

In 1812, Spohr fulfilled a lifelong ambition to visit Vienna, the city where Mozart and Haydn had lived and worked and where their successor, Beethoven, in the full strength of his creative powers, still lived. To succeed here, at the centre of the musical world, was the ultimate test. Spohr took Vienna by storm. One musical journal described him as 'unquestionably the nightingale of all the living violinists and noted that 'in fast tempi he masters difficult passages including the most extended reaches with incredible ease, thanks partly, no doubt, to the size of his hand'.[6]

A year later Spohr was appointed leader of the orchestra at the Theater an der Wien, and moved to Vienna with his wife and family. Shortly after his arrival, Spohr was approached by Johann von Tost, a wealthy Moravian textile merchant who was also a passionate music lover. They entered into an agreement whereby von Tost would purchase everything that Spohr wrote and retain the manuscripts for three years; after this time they would be returned, unconditionally. A sliding scale of payment according to the number of instruments involved was agreed upon: thus 30 ducats for a quartet, 35 for a quintet, and pro rata for further combinations. (It was for von Tost that Spohr wrote his nonet.) In return, von Tost would supply the music for parties or concerts, but only if he were present. It was a clever plan, for as a mere manufacturer von Tost would never otherwise have been admitted. The hosts had no option but to invite him. He would arrive with his portfolio, quietly place the music on the stands and sit silently throughout the performances. When it was over, he picked up the music and retired. Eventually, he became such a familiar figure in musical circles that he was automatically invited, even when Spohr's music was not being played.

At the Theater an der Wien Spohr became acquainted with Franz Clement (1780–1842), the violinist and director of the orchestra. His style of playing – known for its gracefulness and tenderness of expression – would have appealed to Spohr, who was opposed to virtuosity for its own sake. Beethoven thought so highly of Clement that he wrote his violin concerto for him, inscribing his manuscript to that effect. Clement played it at the first performance on 23 December 1806, but Beethoven, having only just completed the work a few hours before the concert, left no time for rehearsal and Clement was obliged to sightread the entire solo part. Nevertheless, 'on account of its originality and manifold beauties', the critics received the piece well enough, but thought that the 'endless repetition of some trivial phrases may become tedious'. As for Clement, his 'proven skill, his grace, his power of [tone] and absolute power over his violin, which is indeed his slave, called forth the ringing cheers of the audience'.[7] In the second half, by way of ludicrous contrast, equal praise was meted out to Clement for performing a set of variations while holding the violin upside down!

Spohr counted Beethoven among his friends, and his impressions of the composer are among the most vivid on record. Although a champion of Beethoven's early quartets, he reacted against the later works, particularly the late quartets, seeing them as full of 'aesthetic aberrations', which he attributed to Beethoven's deafness he considered the Ninth Symphony 'monstrous', 'tasteless' and 'trivial'. As for Beethoven himself, Spohr writes: 'He was a little blunt, not to say uncouth; but a truthful eye beamed from under his bushy eyebrows.'[8]

In 1815 Spohr left Vienna and visited Switzerland and Italy. When he made his debut at La Scala, Milan, the Italians loved his 'singing' tone. But Spohr had a poor opinion of the Italians as musicians. He thought them good singers, but even so, criticised their penchant for ornaments. 'Italian *virtuosi* and *dilettanti* direct their whole attention to the acquisition of mechanical skill, but as regards a tasteful style of execution, they form themselves very little after the good models which their best singers might be to them, while our German instrumentalists generally possess a very cultivated style, and much feeling.'[9]

It seems entirely appropriate that Spohr and Paganini should have met for the first time in Venice. Spohr notes that the connoisseurs of his day 'admit the wizard to be of great dexterity with the left hand in doublestops and in passage-work of every kind, but that the very thing by which he fascinates the crowd debases him to a mere charlatan'.[10]

Spohr was unwittingly involved in the pro- and anti-Paganini controversy when, without his knowledge, a letter appeared in the press comparing him favourably with the Genoese maestro. Spohr's playing reminded the writer of the style of Pugnani and Tartini, whose ' . . . grand and dignified manner of handling the violin has become wholly lost in Italy, and [who] had been compelled to make room for the petty and childish manner of the virtuosos of the present day'.[11]

Once, when Spohr was entertaining some friends, Paganini called to offer congratulations on his last concert. Spohr asked him to play, but Paganini declined, saying he had fallen and his arm was affected. When the friends had left, Spohr repeated the request but Paganini protested this time that his style of playing was for the great public only, and that he would have to adopt a different manner for private performance. Spohr almost despaired of ever hearing him, but in 1830 his wish came true: after Paganini's performance in Kassel, Spohr wrote down his impressions. 'His left hand, and his consistently pure intonation, were to me astonishing. But in his compositions and his execution I found a strange mixture of the highly genial and childishly tasteless, by which one felt alternately charmed and disappointed.'[12]

Spohr rapidly became one of the most sought-after musicians in Germany. He held a number of leaderships in theatre orchestras in succession and undertook some 53 concert tours, travelling by horse and carriage, even in the Russian winter. At this time, festivals were becoming a regular feature of musical life in all the important German capitals, and few of them would be considered successful without Spohr as director. In 1820, at the invitation of the Philharmonic Society, he made his first trip to England. Not only was he well received, but he even managed to get the autocratic governing body of the society to waive rules supporting their role in selecting the programme. The music of Mozart, Haydn and Beethoven was traditionally preferred, but Spohr established a precedent at his opening concert by playing his own Violin Concerto No. 8 'in modo di scena cantante' (1816). Shortly after Spohr arrived in England, he decided to make an early call on his friend Ferdinand Ries, the great German violinist, pianist and composer, and one of the most important figures on the London musical scene. Spohr made himself very smart, donned a bright red Turkish patterned silk waistcoat, and set out towards his destination. As he walked along he found everyone looking at him, and urchins shouting abuse, which, fortunately, through his lack of English, he did not understand. But by the time he arrived at Ries's house he had a trail behind him. Ries then explained that George III had just died and official mourning had been decreed. Ries assured Spohr that only his great height and serious bearing had protected him from a crowd who would certainly have tackled him had he been shorter and less formidable in appearance. Spohr was immediately taken back to his lodging, to exchange the offending waistcoat for one of the appropriate hue.

Spohr's most important appointment was that of director of the theatre at Kassel from 1822. It was here that he founded his school of violin playing which spread its influence so widely. Through Eck he had inherited the solid basic principles of the Mannheim school; with his adherence to the purity of Rode's example, together with his own individuality, he became the most important influence of his day. Spohr had close on 200 pupils, who came from all over Europe and America. They included Henry Holmes (1839–1905), one of the most distinguished English violinists and Ferdinand David, who was a close friend of Mendelssohn, and the dedicatée of Mendelssohn's violin concerto.

Possessed of exceptionally sized hands, Spohr was easily able to execute double stops and stretches. His breadth and beauty of tone and refinement of expression were said to be almost unequalled. Spohr treated the violin as a singing instrument and his music is proof of this, particularly the slow movements of his concertos. Spohr condemned the use of artificial harmonics daringly exploited by Paganini, and his light, free style of bowing, which has been adopted by modern players. Nevertheless, Spohr's staccato was said to be brilliant, every note firmly marked by a movement of the wrist. This manner of bowing – exemplified in the salon piece, *Hora Staccato* – is achieved by a single stroke of the bow drawn in one direction as the notes are stopped. The result is that any number of notes can be sounded articulately without change of bow direction. When Mendelssohn heard Spohr play his own Concerto in E minor and introduce, by way of novelty, a staccato passage in one long stroke, he remarked to his sister: 'See, this is the famous Spohrish staccato which no violinist can play like him.'[13]

Spohr was also interested in the construction of the violin itself and experimented with stringing and tuning. His most important contribution was the 1820 invention of the chin-rest. He disapproved of the earlier method of holding the violin on the right side of the tailpiece. As early as 1803, in St Petersburg, he found the playing of Ferdinand Fränzl (1767–1833) pure and clean but had reservations about his posture. 'He still holds the violin in the old manner, on the right side of the tailpiece, and must therefore play with his head bent.'[14] It is interesting that when Spohr heard Fränzl again in 1815, he found his playing 'antiquated' and wanting in purity of intonation. This is perhaps not so much a criticism as proof of the advance made in technique in one decade of the nineteenth century.

Spohr wrote over 200 works, which include no fewer than 15 violin concertos. His *Method*, completed in 1831, served successive generations of nineteenth-century musicians. His democratic attitude towards the nobility was no mean achievement at the time, and his insistence that a musician deserves to be given the hearers' full attention helped to establish a new respect for both musicians and musical performance in society.

## Notes

1. Pleasants, *The Musical Journeys of Louis Spohr*, p. 53.
2. Spohr, *Louis Spohr's Autobiography*, i, p. 4.
3. Ibid., p. 13.
4. *Grove*, 5th edn., ii, p. 879.
5. Pleasants, op. cit., p. 16
6. Ibid., p. 85.
7. *Wienertheaterzeitung*, December 1806.
8. Sonneck, *Beethoven: Impressions by his Contemporaries*, p. 95.
9. Spohr, op. cit., i, p. 302.
10. Ibid., p. 280.
11. Ibid., p. 281.
12. Spohr, op. cit., ii, p. 168.
13. Ibid., p. 189.
14. *Grove*, 5th edn., ii, p. 219.

# 6    The Catalyst

'**B**efore we can hope to see clearly into the mystery of this man's art, we shall have to remove from our imagination all the preconceived notions that have been placed there by a couple of generations of gossips,' Jeffrey Pulver writes of Niccolò Paganini.[1] This legendary figure was the quintessence of eccentric genius. Strange in physical appearance, brusque and often even rude in manner, mean in his financial dealings, with a fatal attraction for women, he was thought by some to be in possession of satanic powers. Such a combination, allied to playing powers without parallel among his contemporaries, could not fail to make him both famous and notorious.

A twentieth-century doctor has put forward the suggestion that Paganini was suffering from a connective tissue disorder now known as Marfan's syndrome (not diagnosed until 1896). Symptoms include a tall, thin build, long arms, spider-like fingers, exceptionally extensible joints and a transparent skin. The description fits all the known accounts of Paganini's appearance.

Niccolò was born in Genoa in 1782, the son of a ship's chandler, a delicate child of nervous disposition. When he was five, his father gave him lessons on the mandolin and violin; recognising his son's talent, his father exploited it to the limit. At the age of 11, he successfully appeared in public for the first time, playing not only pieces by Corelli and Tartini but also one of his own compositions, the 'Carmangole' variations on a popular air.

At the age of 13, having received the best instruction available in Genoa, Paganini, accompanied by his father, went to Parma to play to the distinguished violinist and composer, Alessandro Rolla (1757–1841). When they arrived, they were told the maestro had been taken ill and could not see them. While waiting in the vestibule, Paganini's father spotted Rolla's latest composition lying on the table. He made a sign to his son, who proceeded to play the piece at sight. Rolla was so astonished that he rose from his sickbed to investigate. Realising that he could teach the boy nothing, Rolla recommended Paganini to take lessons in counterpoint. After some study with the Neapolitan Gasparo Ghiretti, Paganini's musical education was deemed complete. 'Under his direction,' wrote Paganini, 'I composed, as an exercise, 24 fugues for four hands, without any instrument – just with ink, pen and paper.'[2]

This example apart, Paganini gives little credit to any of his teachers, claiming that he was 'self-taught', and that 'great ideas sprang spontaneously from the inner flame that animated him'.[3] However, there would appear to be another influence. According to Fétis, Paganini told him that some time in 1794 or 1795, he had an experience that 'revealed to him the secret of everything one could do on the violin'. He had heard the Polish Auguste Durand (1770–1834), a pupil of Viotti in Paris. Durand, whose natural gifts were said to be of an exceptional order, attracted attention solely by the execution of brilliant *tours de force*. Paganini confided to Fétis that 'many of his most brilliant and popular effects were derived to a considerable extent' from this artist. Certainly many contemporary accounts confirm Durand's virtuosity: 'His technical facility was prodigious and he invented a multitude of technical tricks and devices that no-one but himself could play.'[4] Paganini would certainly have imitated those tricks.

Accompanied by his father, Paganini made his first concert tour of northern Italy in 1797, but for the next few years there are no records of any sensational appearances. His father kept him on a tight rein, supervising every minute of his daily practice and when he was 18, Paganini told J.M. Schottky (his friend and biographer), 'My father's excessive severity now seemed more oppressive than ever as my talent developed and my knowledge increased. I should have liked to break away from him so that I could travel alone; but my harsh mentor never left my side.'[5] However, at the age of 19, he did break free.

In the autumn of 1801, Paganini and his brother Carlo went to play in the festival at Lucca. On the Feast of San Croce during High Mass, Paganini was invited to play a concerto after the Kyrie and he was audacious enough to play one lasting 28 minutes. A member of the cathedral orchestra gives an eye-witness account of Paganini's 'unusual and unprecedented virtuosity. He imitated on his strings the songs of birds, the flute, trombone and horn. And though everyone admired his astounding bravura . . . such mimicry . . . aroused laughter even in church.'[6] Paganini's unashamed playing to the gallery on such an occasion did him no harm: he was asked back to play, and a few months later he was appointed first violin to the newly formed Republic of Lucca.

Although there are few accounts of his public appearances at this time, there are many stories of love affairs. In later life, Paganini invented and perpetuated a number of such tales, always emerging as the hero. He was never able to admit failure and seems to have been under the impression that all women were 'mad about him'.

The wildest accounts of gambling excesses date from his youth. Paganini had inherited from his father a love of gambling, and would frequently risk the entire proceeds from a concert before it had taken place. The story of how he came by his famous 'Cannon' Guarneri del Gesù is the classic instance. On the eve of a concert in Leghorn, Paganini had gambled away his Amati violin. A rich merchant named Livron loaned him an instrument from his private collection. After the concert, Livron rushed up to Paganini begging him to keep it as a token of appreciation, making one proviso: that the violin should be played only by Paganini himself. The artist kept his word and used it for the rest of his life. He was once offered a high price for it and was tempted to accept the offer to settle a gambling debt but, instead, he staked his last 30 francs and won; he never sat at the tables again.

In 1806 Paganini entered the service of Elisa Bacciochi, Napoleon's sister and Princess of Lucca and Piombino. At this time he wrote his famous *Scena Amorosa* for the violin's two outer strings. Paganini described it to Schottky:

> The first string represented the girl, the second the man, and I then began a sort of dialogue, depicting little quarrels and reconciliations between my two lovers. The strings first scolded, then sighed, lisped, moaned, joked, expressed delight, and finally ecstasy. It concluded with a reconciliation and the two lovers performed a *pas de deux* closing with a brilliant coda.[7]

Paganini said he directed it to an unknown lady in the audience who rewarded him with 'the most friendly glances'. The princess challenged him by saying that if he could compose for two strings, why not one? In response, Paganini composed his Military Sonata for the G string, entitled 'Napoleon'.

During his leave of absence from court, Paganini gave public concerts. He finally broke with the princess in 1813 and promised never again to become dependent upon a single patron. As a free agent, Paganini decided to try his luck in Milan and found his first overwhelming success. In the space of six weeks he gave eleven concerts at La Scala and other theatres and had the audiences at his feet. He then toured northern Italy, Venice, Rome and Naples, scoring triumphs everywhere he went. In response, he demanded and received higher fees than those asked by any other violinist of his day.

In 1824 Paganini met the singer Antonia Bianchi. She became his mistress and bore him a son, Achilles, in 1826, but her possessive and jealous temperament caused them to part: two years later, after much wrangling, a final settlement was made in Bianchi's favour in exchange for the custody of Achilles, who turned out to be profligate and lazy, and remained for the rest of his life a constant source of anxiety to his devoted father. Exploited and ill-treated by his own father, Paganini was in turn tyrannised by his own son.

The other tyranny that overshadowed Paganini's life was recurrent ill health which frequently prevented him from undertaking concert tours. If it was not the rages of tuberculosis – which eventually attacked his larynx – it was the effect of taking mercury for syphilis, which he had contracted at the age of 27. In addition, he suffered from a recurring stomach complaint. Poor health prevented Paganini from appearing abroad until he was 46. By then, stories of his fame had reached every European capital and made audiences impatient to hear him. On 4 April 1828 he played in Vienna and the audience went mad with excitement. Next day the *Allgemeine Theaterzeitung* reported:

> To analyse his performance is sheerly impossible and numerous rehearings avail but little. When we say that he performs incredible difficulties with as clear and pure an

intonation as another, when we say that in his hands the violin sounds more beautiful and more moving than any human voice. ... when we say that every singer can learn from him, this is still inadequate to give a single feature of his playing. He must be heard, and heard again, to be believed.[8]

For months 'this god of the violin'[9] was the main topic of conversation across all classes of the population. Fashion followed: shirts and neckties were 'à la Paganini', snuff-boxes were enamelled with his portrait, and Viennese dandies carried walking-sticks with his head carved on the handles. A skilful stroke at billiards was called a 'coup à la Paganini'. One enterprising cabman who had once conveyed the virtuoso for a short ride placed a notice in his cab that read 'Cabriolet de Paganini' (so remunerative was his warrant that eventually the cabman was able to set himself up in business as a hotelier).

From Vienna, Paganini toured Europe. On 9 March 1831 he gave his first long-awaited concert at the Opéra in Paris. An account of this concert comes from the artist Amaury Duval, who had been invited to attend by his master, Jean-Auguste Dominique Ingres, who had painted Paganini's portrait in Rome. Duval tells us that the curtain rose on an empty stage without scenery or furniture. Then a tall, thin man dressed entirely in black entered, with features that were almost diabolical. The whole hall experienced a moment of sharp astonishment, bordering on a shudder. At the first notes he drew from his instrument, he captivated every person in the theatre, including Ingres, who expressed his pleasure with little gestures of admiration. But when Paganini suddenly abandoned himself to exercises in virtuosity – 'those *tours de force* that have given birth to such a ridiculous school'[10] – Ingres' face flushed with anger, and as the audience became increasingly delighted, he became more and more enraged by Paganini's exhibitionism. Finally, he stood up and cried out: 'It isn't him! Heretic! Traitor!'[11] Ingres saw in Paganini the antithesis of his own ideals, rooted in purity of line and intellectual application to art. However, Ingres' most deadly enemy, the arch-romantic painter, Eugène Delacroix, was in the same audience and reacted quite differently. In his memoirs he described his reaction: '*There* is the inventor! There is the man who is truly fitted for his art!'[12]

From Paris, Paganini went on to London, where he repeated his phenomenal success. The first concert took place on 3 June 1831 at the King's Theatre in the Haymarket. 'The house was full, though not fashionably attended; very few ladies were present, ... the orchestra pit and gallery were crowded, while a large proportion of the boxes remained unoccupied.'[13] For *The Times* critic, Paganini was 'not only the finest player perhaps that has ever existed on that instrument, but he forms a class by himself'.[14] Henry Chorley, the most celebrated critic of the day, wrote: 'There is a relation between a unit and a million – none between him and his fellow men.'[15] Mary Shelley, wife of the poet, wrote to a friend that Paganini 'threw me into hysterics' and that 'his wild ethereal figure, rapt look – and the sounds he draws from his violin are all superhuman'.[16] Paganini went on to play at Norwich, Bath, Cheltenham, Liverpool and Dublin. Altogether, he netted £16,000 from his appearances in the British Isles.

Over the years, Paganini amassed a considerable fortune, and in 1833 he purchased the Villa Gaione, a large estate at Vigatto, about four miles from Parma, where the soft air was beneficial to his respiratory condition. His fame was now worldwide but, although he still appeared in concerts from time to time, his periods of retirement became more prolonged. He had hoped to publish his compositions, but having demanded too high a price from the publishers, he failed ever to come to terms with them. Paganini exercised very astute control over the distribution of his music. At his concerts he provided orchestral parts, but no one ever saw the solo part because he always played from memory.

Paganini died at Parma on 27 May 1840, in his 58th year. In his last days a priest had called to give him the Last Sacrament, but Paganini refused, saying he was not ready to die. When death came he had still not received absolution. As no mortuary chapel could receive an excommunicated sinner, his coffin was placed in the cellar of the house in which he died. There followed a bizarre series of events in which the coffin was shunted from place to place, and was once taken out to sea and back again. Meanwhile, a war between relatives and authorities raged for 36 years. In 1876 the body was finally transferred to consecrated earth at the cemetery at Parma.

Paganini left about 2,000,000 lire (£80,000), mostly in estates and securities. He also left a valuable collection of master stringed instruments, including: 15 violins by Stradivari, Amati, Tononi and Ruggeri, and the 'Cannon' Guarneri del Gesù, which he bequeathed to the Civic Museum at Genoa; four cellos, two by Stradivari, an Andréas Guarneri and a Rogeri; a Stradivari viola and a Guadagnini guitar. The whereabouts of most of these instruments today is unknown, but a quartet of his Stradivari instruments have remained together and are played by the members of the American Paganini Quartet. (Paganini himself loved to play chamber music and he composed quartets for violin, viola, guitar and cello.)

For the most part, Paganini performed only his own compositions and comparisons with contemporary virtuosos are largely irrelevant. A law unto himself, Paganini often employed scordatura to facilitate the playing of certain intervals. When performing works with orchestra, he frequently tuned his G string up half a tone (or even a minor third), in order to play difficult passages with greater ease; this tuning was not only well-suited to harmonics, but also produced a more brilliant sound on open strings. An eye-witness, Carl Guhr, wrote of his bowing: 'His ordinary staccato, played with a very tight bow, was prodigiously loud and firm, like the strokes of a hammer, whilst his method of dashing the bow on the strings, and letting it leap through an infinity of tiny staccato notes with unerring precision, was wholly his own invention.'[17] In his Op. 11 *Moto perpetuo* in C (after 1830), he played whole passages staccato on one bow up and down – with perfect articulation and intonation. (This is what we know today as 'saltato' or 'ricochet' bowing.) Except when playing heavy broken chords near to the heel, he held his bow arm very close to his body. All the elasticity seemed to be controlled by the wrist. Paganini's way of holding the violin was also extraordinary. His shoulder was so wide, the bone structure almost horizontal, that the violin rested upon it as if it had been designed for the purpose. Paganini was the last virtuoso violinist to play without a chin-rest.

His 24 Caprices for solo violin remain today some of the most brilliant virtuoso music ever written for the instrument. The product of his youth (they were composed between 1801 and 1807), they are the work of a genius. The devices involved – double-stopping, octaves, tenths, trills in thirds, sixths and harmonics of every variety – brought technique to its zenith. The twentieth century added nothing that is not already embodied in these caprices.

In her biography *Paganini the Genoese* (1957), Geraldine de Courcey shows some significant links between the caprices and Locatelli's Op. 3 *Arte de nuova modulazione* (1733), which fell into Paganini's hands during his student days. Fétis reports that Paganini told him that 'this work opened up to him a world of new ideas and devices that had never had the success they deserved owing to their excessive difficulty'.[18]

Paganini's 'miracles' of harmonics, double- and treble-stopping and left-hand pizzicato are now common practice among virtuoso performers. Consequently many great players today perform his works. Arthur Grumiaux, Henryk Szeryng, Ruggiero Ricci and Itzhak Perlman have all made recordings of the Paganini concertos; Ricci was the first to record all 24 of his caprices. Of those who sneer at the 'mere virtuosity' of his music, one famous violinist remarked: 'The only violinists who denigrate Paganini are those who can't play him.'[19]

### Notes

1. Pulver, *Paganini the Romantic Virtuoso*, p. 44.
2. De Courcey, *Paganini the Genoese*, i, p. 44.
3. Ibid., p. 27.
4. Ibid., pp. 34–5.
5. Ibid., p. 56.
6. Ibid., p. 67.
7. Ibid., p. 99.
8. *Allgemeine Theaterzeitung*, 5 April 1828.
9. De Courcey, ii, p. 265.
10–12. Open University Course A202 'The Age of Revolutions'.
13. De Courcey, ii, p. 55.
14. *The Times*, 4 June 1831.
15–16. De Courcey, ii, p. 55.
17. Haweis, *My Musical Life*, p. 383.
18. De Courcey, i, p. 47.
19. Norbert Brainin, quoted from interview, M.C.

# 7    Disciples of Paganini

Paganini, by his example, unquestionably revolutionised the art of violin playing. But because of his obsessive control over his manuscripts, his contemporaries had little chance to perform his music. The only works published in his lifetime were the 24 Caprices, Op.1, 12 sonatas for violin and guitar – an instrument of which Paganini was very fond – and six quartets for strings and guitar.

The one link between Paganini and the next generation of violinists was through his solitary pupil, the Genoese Camille Sivori (1815–94). A virtuoso of considerable gifts in his own right, Sivori received lessons from Paganini when he was six. As a young artist he travelled extensively in Europe and North and South America, and in 1846 he came to England, where he gave the first British performance of the Mendelssohn Violin Concerto. *The Times* was unstinting in its praise of Sivori, but noncommittal in its assessment of the concerto: 'It is a great work, but we must listen to it again ere we venture on a detailed analysis.'[1]

Sivori enjoyed a long and successful career and naturally specialised in performing Paganini's music. His master had written several works for him and the first two concertos were published soon after Paganini died. Edmund van der Straeten, writing in 1933, says that he heard Sivori in the 1870s playing Paganini's B minor Concerto and 'Le Streghe' at Cologne. He still recalled 'the wonderful impression his superb technique, faultless intonation and beauty of tone' made.[2]

Paganini and Sivori were life-long friends, although, according to Sivori, not because of Paganini's pedagogic gifts (he was probably the worst teacher in the world). During lessons he was sarcastic and rude to his pupil: he would scribble a few manuscript exercises, place them on the stand and expect Sivori to execute them at sight. While Sivori struggled with the difficulties, Paganini paced up and down like a caged lion, a sardonic smile on his face; then, 'seizing the violin like a lion seizing a sheep [Paganini] would play the study again without reference to the manuscript on the stand'.[3]

The Moravian from Brno, Heinrich Wilhelm Ernst (1814–65), heard Paganini in Paris and immediately became a devoted admirer. A pupil of Josef Böhm, Ernst went on tour as a fully-fledged virtuoso at the age of 16. He met Charles-Auguste de Bériot in Paris and studied with him for a further six years. By observing Paganini perform, Ernst took on many elements of his technique, such as staccato runs and the use of harmonics and left-hand pizzicato. His playing was described by Berlioz as a 'fascinating display of virtuosity put to consistently tuneful ends, and performed with almost careless ease'. Of Paganini himself Berlioz wrote: 'He is like a juggler whose counters are diamonds.'[4]

On the concert platform, Ernst – apart from his moustache – even looked like Paganini, with cadaverous features, high cheekbones and long, dark hair. But in character he was altogether different. Berlioz considered him to be 'the most delightfully humorous man I know' and 'the complete rounded artist, profoundly and predominantly expressive in everything he does, yet never neglectful of the craft, the disciplining art of music'.[5] Today Ernst is remembered mainly as a composer. Leopold Auer commented on the idiomatic qualities of his music: 'His compositions have far more than mere technique to recommend them, his expressive *Elegie*, his incredibly difficult transcription of Schubert's 'Erlkönig', his 'Otello' fantasy, no violinist can afford to ignore.'[6]

Another virtuoso who modelled himself on Paganini was the Brescian Antonio Bazzini (1818–97). Auer admired his playing, particularly the singing quality of his tone, and considered Bazzini to have been 'a virtuoso in the true sense of the word'.[7] Bazzini once played to Paganini, who encouraged him to tour as a virtuoso. As a result, his fame spread throughout Europe and he was hailed as Paganini's successor. He made considerable efforts to popularise the works of Bach and Beethoven in his own country: a difficult task since Italians were never well disposed towards German music. Bazzini's own music was frequently performed in the church and in the theatre. Today he is remembered for 'La Ronde des Lutins' ('Goblins' Dance'), a popular showpiece employing every possible virtuoso technique, including the lavish use of harmonics and left-hand pizzicato.

Perhaps the most colourful figure among Paganini's disciples was the Norwegian Ole Bull (1810–80), whose virtuoso playing gained him the nickname 'the flaxen-haired Paganini'.[8] Bull was born in Bergen, the son of a physician who was also a good amateur musician; his earliest memory was of listening to his family playing string quartets. When Ole was five years old he taught himself to play the violin, and probably also received some instruction from the peasant fiddlers at the family's country home at Osteroy. The Norwegians had had little contact with European music until the Romantic movement touched them in the middle of the nineteenth century. But they possessed a rich store of folk music and accompanied themselves on indigenous instruments. The most popular of these was the *hardingfele* or 'hardanger' fiddle, an eight-string violin with sympathetic strings (placed under the playing strings and which vibrate in sympathy when the upper strings are bowed or plucked).

Ole had his first music lessons from a Dane with an inordinate passion for brandy. As long as there was a drop in the bottle he was happy to teach or join in family music-making. But when it was empty he would stagger on to the house of the next patron. One night he became too inebriated to continue playing string quartets and the eight-year-old Ole took his place.

In 1822 a visiting Swede named Lundholm, who had studied with Baillot, gave Ole some thorough training in violin technique. A stickler for posture, he insisted that his pupil should stand upright when playing, with his head against the wall, a practice advocated by Viotti and his school. In later years, Bull was noted for his poise and graceful bearing on the concert platform.

Bull's family opposed his ambition to become a performing violinist. His father wanted him to become a clergyman, but when Ole failed his university examination, he immediately set out for Kassel to consult Spohr, then the most famous violin teacher in Europe.

The mighty Spohr was unimpressed, and declined to take on this wild, self-taught youth as a pupil. To make matters worse, Bull heard Spohr and his quartet play and was so overcome with their style and musicianship that he temporarily gave up all idea of becoming a professional violinist. Five years later, Spohr admitted having been hasty in his original assessment of Bull's playing, albeit with some Spohrish reservations! 'His wonderful playing and the sureness of his left hand are worthy of the highest admiration, but unfortunately, like Paganini, he sacrifices what is artistic to something that is not quite suitable to the noble instrument.'[9]

In 1831 Bull went to Paris with two objectives: the first was to hear Paganini and the other to enter the Conservatoire. He failed in the latter but succeeded in the former. From this time on he took the master for his model. There is plenty of evidence to show that Bull attained a great deal of Paganini's technical facility and had a vast repertory of similar inventiveness, which later gained him a tremendous public following.

At first, life in Paris for Bull was adventurous. He suffered the inevitable poverty of the penniless artist, and once tried to commit suicide by jumping into the Seine, but was rescued by a passer-by. On another occasion, through an absconding landlord, he lost all his possessions, including his violin. He had a fiery and impulsive temperament, ill-suited to regular employment in, for example, an orchestra. Eventually, he met a violin maker who exploited his virtuosity to sell his fiddles; he was engaged to play at a soirée given by the Duke of Riario, the Italian *chargé d'affaires* in Paris. Ole Bull is reported to have played magnificently, despite being nearly overcome by the pungent smell of the instrument's new varnish. His performance so impressed the Duke of Montebello, Marshal Ney's son, that he invited him to breakfast the following day; this introduction, in turn, brought Bull into contact with Chopin, Ernst and other celebrated artists. Under the duke's patronage, he gave his first public concert in Paris and was again received with much enthusiasm.

Buoyant on this wave of success, Ole Bull travelled to Italy, and in Milan was warmly received by the audience at La Scala, although one journalist was critical:

> M. Bull played compositions by Spohr, Mayseder, and Paganini without understanding the true character of the music, which he marred by adding something of his own. It is quite obvious that what he adds comes from genuine and original talent, from his own musical individuality; but he is not master of himself; he has no style; he is an untrained musician. If he be a diamond, he is certainly in the rough, and unpolished.[10]

Ole Bull's reaction is revealing: he sought out the critic, listened to more of his advice which he found invaluable, and for the next six months devoted himself to study under the guidance of good teachers.

Bull's fortunes changed, almost by chance, in Bologna; the Belgian violinist Charles-Auguste de Bériot, and the Spanish singer, Maria-Felicita Malibran, had refused, at the last minute, to appear at a concert because of a dispute over fees. Someone who had passed Ole Bull's window and heard him practising suggested that he might fill the bill. So that night, Ole Bull was woken up and brought to the theatre to play before a distinguished audience that included the Duke of Tuscany and his friends. Ole Bull's virtuosity caused a sensation and his charming personality captivated the audience. After supper he reappeared and asked for a theme on which to improvise. He was given three and proceeded to use all of them, combining them in a brilliant display that had his audience cheering loudly. He was escorted back to his lodgings by a torchlight procession in a carriage drawn by his admirers.

Bull repeated these triumphs all over Italy, and in London the audiences responded with equal enthusiasm. Like Paganini, he asked high fees for his performances. In Liverpool he received £800 for one concert, and if that fee was representative, he must have accumulated a fortune from the other 273 appearances he made in Britain in the space of 16 months.

Ole Bull now repeated these successes in all the principal cities of Germany, where Spohr reigned supreme, and continued to Vienna and Budapest. At St Petersburg, he gave a number of concerts to audiences of over 5,000 people. When he finally arrived in the Scandinavian countries he was fêted like a victorious monarch returning from battle.

Americans first heard Ole Bull in November 1843. He stayed for two years and gave 200 hundred concerts, playing in every important city, and his programmes were often printed on silk. He amassed a considerable fortune, making about $100,000, a fifth of which he donated to charity.

Although away from Norway much of the time, Ole Bull always maintained a great feeling for his native country and was much concerned with the poverty existing there. On his second visit to the USA he tried to set up a colony for Norwegian immigrants and purchased a tract of land of some 125,000 acres in Potter County, Pennsylvania. Here he hoped to found a 'New Norway, consecrated to liberty, baptised with independence, and protected by the Union's mighty flag'.[11] Three hundred houses, stores and a church were soon built. A splendid castle for his own use was set on the top of a mountain. Hundreds of immigrants flocked to the new colony to take up residence. But during a concert tour he was summoned to Philadelphia with the news that he had been swindled by a confidence trickster who had sold him land owned by somebody else. Many years of litigation followed. The real owner agreed to let Bull have the land at a low price, but his fortune was already dissipated.

Travelling the length and breadth of the American continent over the next five years, Bull gave concerts to regain the money he had lost. Along the way he became a victim of yellow fever, was caught in the cross-fire of a riot in California, and had his violin stolen when crossing the Isthmus of Panama. When he made his last appearance in New York, in 1857, he was so ill he had to be assisted in getting on and off the platform. On his return to Europe, all his debts honoured, he was restored to health and resumed concert-giving.

In appearance Bull was tall and athletic, with large blue eyes: the typical Viking. Like Paganini, his personal magnetism attracted a large following. He never missed an opportunity to make full use of theatrical gestures. At the suggestion of the King of Sweden, he celebrated his 66th birthday in Egypt, ascending to the pinnacle of the Pyramid of Cheops to play one of his own compositions, *Saterbesog*. An account of the proceedings was duly telegraphed from Cairo to the king next morning.

Ole Bull may have been criticised for his eccentricity but he never pretended to belong to the modern cultivated school of violin playing. Henry Lahee makes an apt point: 'He was a minstrel rather than a musician in the broad sense of the word, but he held the hearts of the people as few, if any, minstrels had previously done.'[12]

## Notes

1. *The Times*, 30 June 1846.
2. Van der Straeten, *History*, ii, p. 353.
3. Laurie, *Reminiscences of a Fiddle Dealer*, p. 61.
4. Berlioz, *The Memoirs of Berlioz*, pp. 538–9.
5. Ibid., p. 538.
6. Auer, *Violin Playing as I Teach It*, p. 91.
7. Ibid., p. 5.
8. Lahee, *Famous Violinists of Today and Yesterday*, p. 200.
9. Ibid., p. 183.
10. Ibid., p. 188.
11. Ibid., p. 193.
12. Ibid., p. 203.

# 8    Age of Transition

The beginning of the nineteenth century saw a decline in private patronage. Although a few of the nobility still maintained their own orchestras, there was little support for the solo performer. An artist had either to find someone with money, or depend on personal resources. Apart from exceptions like Spohr and Paganini, artists were a poverty-stricken lot. At the Paris Conservatoire there was never any question of anything as vulgar as a fee being paid to a soloist, however eminent. In his memoirs, Carl Flesch reveals that things were only slightly better there in the 1890s.

Orchestras also suffered from a similar impecuniosity. They were under-rehearsed, seldom consisted of more than 30 players and were led by the first violin in lieu of a conductor. Standards of performance were generally low. Inevitably, the implications of the system were reflected in the box office. The complete indifference of the early nineteenth-century public to anything but virtuoso tricks on the violin meant that concert-giving was a hazardous occupation. Concerts were by subscription only, so the appropriate sponsor had to be sought out before tickets could be purchased.

The popularity of the virtuoso was synonymous with a continued striving after brilliance and power. Paganini had used thinner strings to obtain his effects. When a' was raised a semitone to 435 cycles per second, the violin itself had to be modified to meet the new demands placed upon it. The pressure of the bridge on the belly increased, and the bass-bar (a strip of pine, glued to the left side of the belly, to spread the vibrations to the back by the soundpost) was made longer and thicker.

One other change – by far the greatest since Stradivari – took place at the beginning of the nineteenth century. It concerned the proportions and position of the head and neck of the violin. Until the late eighteenth century, few players exceeded the fifth or sixth positions (we have already seen that Vivaldi and Locatelli may have done so, but they were exceptional). The fingerboard was lengthened and the neck tilted back to accommodate the extra tension. Stradivari's longest fingerboard in 1715 was 21.5cm – the modern fingerboard is about 26.5cm.

When a player uses a Stradivarius or a Guarnerius today, the instrument will certainly have undergone modifications to the neck and bass-bar. The necks of Stradivari's instruments were approximately 0.4cm thicker and, when modified for the modern player, were narrowed for the comfort of the left hand. Since the revival of playing Baroque music on period instruments, there has been a return to

Stradivari's dimensions and proportions.

It was inevitable that the modified violin, with its greater carrying power, and Spohr's chin-rest (allowing greater freedom of the left hand), would affect playing techniques. Consequently, the nineteenth century witnessed some of the greatest teachers in the history of the instrument. One of the most important of these was Josef Böhm (1795–1876), a Hungarian who, through his teaching at the conservatory in Vienna attracted much Hungarian talent. His most prominent pupil was Jenö Hubay (1858–1937), who put his principles into practice at the conservatory in Budapest.

Hungary's long history of violin playing stems from the gipsy virtuosos. Böhm was the first Hungarian violinist to pursue more formal studies. Born in Pesth, he received his first instruction from his father, and in 1808 became a pupil of Rode, who was on his way home from a Russian tour. Böhm enjoyed considerable success as a soloist and toured Europe with the pianist Johann Peter Pixis, brother of the violinist who had studied with Viotti in exile.

When Böhm first played in Vienna in 1815, he met with such a warm reception that he decided to settle there. In 1819 he was appointed professor of violin at the conservatory and, in 1821, he also became a member of the Imperial Chapel. He took over the leadership from Ignaz Schuppanzigh (1776–1830) – Beethoven's famous quartet player – in the quartet matinées at the Erste Kaffeehaus.

From 1827, Böhm played less and taught more. His technique, tone and style were above reproach, but he was temperamentally unsuited to performance. His exceptional talent as a teacher placed him as one of the most important links in the chain forged by Viotti and Rode from the classic to the modern school of violin playing. Through his pupil Joseph Joachim (1831–1907), a fellow Hungarian, the line remains unbroken to the present time since Joachim's pupil, Leopold Auer, was the master of Sascha Lasserson (1890–1978), who was teaching in Britain right up to his death. Virtuosos of the same line are Nathan Milstein, Mischa Elman and Jascha Heifetz. Jacob Dont (1815–88), a Böhm pupil at the conservatory, is another example of a fine soloist and chamber musician who is remembered as a gifted teacher. Dont's best-known pupil was Auer.

Spohr's pupil, Ferdinand David (1810–73), was another important link. David trained a number of young violinists at the conservatory in Leipzig, including Joachim and August Wilhelmj. David was born in Hamburg, but moved to Kassel in 1823. Two years later, he made his first appearance at the Gewandhaus in Leipzig. In 1827, he first made the acquaintance of Mendelssohn, while serving as a member of the Königstädter Theater in Berlin. They became life-long friends, and each exercised a considerable artistic influence upon the other.

In 1835 Mendelssohn became conductor of the Gewandhaus Orchestra and a year later offered the post of Konzertmeister to David, who also deputised as conductor. Although Dresden was then the capital of Saxony, Leipzig was an important city. During his time there, Mendelssohn strove to improve the working conditions of musicians. Through his efforts their wages were increased and a pension fund established. The Gewandhaus Orchestra became a model for all Europe, as had the Mannheimers under Carl Stamitz a century before him.

In the summer of 1838, Mendelssohn wrote to David: 'I want to write a violin concerto next winter. One in E minor is running in my head, and the beginning of it never gives me a moment's peace.'[1] Frequent letters passed between the two friends during the process of composition: the finished work reveals Mendelssohn's deference to David's taste and practical knowledge, especially from the violinistic point of view. David premiered it with the Gewandhaus Orchestra on 13 March 1845. When Mendelssohn opened the conservatory in Leipzig in 1843, he appointed David professor of violin. David was one of those who sat at the composer's bedside in his last hours and served as one of the pall-bearers at Mendelssohn's funeral in Leipzig on 6 February 1847, along with the pianist Ignaz Moscheles (1794–1870), Robert Schumann, and others.

David was also responsible for reviving the works of the eighteenth-century masters at a time when mostly contemporary salon music was played. He collected, edited (with accompaniments and marks of expression) and published works by eminent Italian, German and French composers: his arrangement of Tartini's 'Devil's Trill' is the popular version still used today. He also wrote a violin tutor.

André Robberechts (1797–1860), from Brussels, is one of the two significant links between Viotti and the Belgian school of violin playing, the main influence in nineteenth-century violin playing; the other was through Baillot and the Liège branch. In Paris, Robberechts studied privately with Baillot and, for many years, with Viotti. His playing was distinguished by a combination of technical brilliance and beauty of expression. He became one of the most respected teachers of his time, and among his many pupils was Charles-Auguste de Bériot, who is recognised as the founder of the Belgian school of violin playing.

Bériot was born in 1802 at Louvain, into a noble but impoverished family, and was orphaned at the age of nine. That same year he made his debut in public, playing a Viotti concerto. Bériot had already met Viotti in Paris, where the master told him: 'You have a fine style. Give yourself up to the business of perfecting it. Hear all men of talent, profit by everything, but imitate nothing.'[2] It was this piece of advice that Bériot was later to give to the seven-year-old Henri Vieuxtemps.

On the concert platform, Bériot enjoyed continuing success. He first appeared in London in 1826 at a Philharmonic Society concert playing a Rode concerto. The English audiences loved him, not only for his beautiful playing but for his aristocratic good looks. Nevertheless, it was fortunate that he made his debut before Paganini arrived on the scene, for it is doubtful if he could have competed successfully with the eccentric Genoese maestro.

Bériot's style was elegant rather than showy, and distinguished by its pristine intonation. But it was in terms of bowing that he was considered a master. Critics frequently praised the neatness and facility of his bowing, aspects that were helped considerably by the extra lightness and elasticity of the Tourte bow, by then in universal use. Unlike many virtuoso performers, Bériot was uncomplex in character and equable in temperament; he also had many interests outside music. He was a talented painter and sculptor, wrote poetry, and was also interested in violin making and repairing.

While in Paris in 1828, Bériot first met the beautiful opera singer Maria-Felicita Malibran. She was already married to (albeit separated from) an elderly, but supposedly rich, French merchant, who had wedded her with the idea of restoring his own failing fortune. Singers, in contrast to instrumentalists, earned very high fees. In one London season of 40 appearances at Drury Lane, Malibran received more than Bériot could have earned in a year.

The Bériot–Malibran love affair was one of the great romances of the day. They toured together with much success and, from about 1830, they set up house together in a villa on the outskirts of Brussels, in the fashionable Ixelles district. Malibran obtained a divorce in 1836 and the couple were married. But six months later, Malibran fell from her horse and died from her injuries at the age of 28.

Bériot retired from public life for four years, after which he was persuaded to return to the concert platform. He resumed his European tours and regained his former success. When Baillot died in 1842, Bériot was offered his post at the Paris Conservatoire, but he refused it, preferring to teach in his own country; and, in 1843, he was appointed professor of violin at the Brussels Conservatoire, a post he held until 1852, when he resigned owing to failing eyesight. However, he continued to teach a few special pupils privately, one of whom was Émile Sauret (1852–1920). By 1858 he was totally blind and paralysed in one arm; he died in 1870.

Bériot published seven concertos and many books of technical studies. His *Grande Méthode*, published in 1858, has been widely used by students ever since. His music was known in his day for its pleasing melodies and the way it brings out the most characteristic effects of the violin as a 'singing' instrument. It was often said that in his compositions his wife's singing could be heard.

### Notes
1. Blunt, *On Wings of Song*, pp. 241–2.
2. Van der Straeten, *History of the Violoncello*, p. 134.

# 9    The Hot-bed of Liège

At the close of the eighteenth century, Flanders, allied to the Dutch, had been incorporated into France, and in 1815, Belgium and Holland were united, incorporating most of Flanders and the French-speaking Walloon districts. Considerable antipathy existed between the two peoples, and even after the revolution of 1830 brought independence to Belgium, the dichotomy persisted.

In music, the Walloon influence predominates. From the eighteenth century onwards, the Walloons have excelled in musical performance, particularly in violin playing. A tradition of amateur violin playing and violin making had existed in Liège for almost three centuries – not among the aristocracy, but among the artisans. It was the weavers and the barbers who had kept the tradition alive, culminating in the foundation of the Conservatoire Royal de Musique de Liège in 1826. Most of the great violinists of the nineteenth-century Belgian school were born in or around Liège: Lambert Massart, Hubert Léonard, Henri Vieuxtemps, Martin Marsick, César Thomson and Eugène Ysaÿe. At the beginning of the nineteenth century it was reckoned that most of the string players in the Paris orchestras were of Walloon birth and training.

Lambert Joseph Massart (1811–92) from Liège, who once performed the Kreutzer Sonata with Liszt, was a violinist of considerable talent, but lacked the desire to excel on the concert platform. He was awarded a municipal scholarship to study at the Conservatoire in Paris, but Luigi Cherubini, then director, refused him a place without explanation: a chauvinistic attitude prevailed at the time, and doors were kept tightly closed to foreigners. Fortunately, Kreutzer took him on as a private pupil.

Massart was received by audiences with the greatest enthusiasm, but shyness and nerves dogged every performance, and he decided to devote himself to teaching. In 1843, he was appointed professor of violin at the Paris Conservatoire, where he gained a worldwide reputation, renowned for his vigour, and for his infinite care and thoroughness in considering the individual needs of each pupil. Few teachers of the time can boast as many celebrated pupils as Massart, either in direct line or second generation: Izydor Lotto (c.1842–1936), Henryk Wieniawski, Teresina Tua, Pablo Sarasate and Fritz Kreisler.

Hubert Léonard (1819–90) was born at Bellaire in Belgium, and studied as a child under Rouma at Liège. He entered the Paris Conservatoire in 1836 as a pupil of Habeneck, and subsequently toured successfully throughout Europe. When Bériot retired from the Brussels Conservatoire on account of ill health, Léonard succeeded him. His most famous pupils were César Thomson, Henri Marteau, Martin Marsick and Ovide Musin. He was also an avid promoter of performances of music by contemporary composers, particularly that of Johannes Brahms and César Franck.

Martin Pierre Marsick (1848–1924) was born at Jupille, near Liège. He was a pupil of Léonard at the Liège Conservatoire and also studied at the conservatories in Brussels and Paris; at the latter he was in Massart's masterclass. In 1870, he was awarded a scholarship to take a final year with Joseph Joachim at the Hochschule in Berlin, and was greatly influenced by the poetic quality of Joachim's playing. Carl Flesch described Marsick's bow arm as 'an absolutely perfect instrument'; Flesch found his tone 'enchanting', and considered that he played with 'great imagination, constantly engaging one's interest without falling into mannerisms'.[1] In 1892, Marsick became professor of violin at the Paris Conservatoire and gained a reputation both as a teacher and string quartet player. During one five-year period, Marsick had three pupils whose names will always be synonymous with the development of their art: Carl Flesch, Jacques Thibaud and Georges Enescu. A first-class, all-round musician, Marsick was also a gifted organist and pianist.

Marsick's exceptional good looks made him irresistible to women and, unfortunately, womanising overtook his teaching and performing career. After a disastrous affair with a married woman, Marsick, then in his 50s, tried unsuccessfully to re-establish himself in Paris. He went to New York where he died in poverty in 1924.

The Liège-born Ovide Musin (1854–1929) gained a reputation for both solo and quartet playing of a high order. He toured extensively throughout the world, and in 1874 formed a quartet, mainly with a view to popularising Brahms in Paris. After several successful appearances in New York, he returned in 1908 to make it his home and establish a school of violin playing there.

César Thomson (1857–1931) was also born in Liège, and studied with Léonard at the Conservatoire. He spent some years as leader of Bilse's orchestra (which later became the Berlin Philharmonic), for a short time sharing the leadership with Ysaÿe, then at the beginning of his career. From 1883 to 1897, Thomson taught sporadically at Liège Conservatoire, fitting his teaching in between extensive concert tours. In 1898 he settled in Brussels, where he succeeded Ysaÿe at the Conservatoire. At the height of his fame, Thomson seems to have been considered one of the most brilliant performers of the Belgian School. His good taste and excellent musicianship were assets in themselves, but by all accounts it was his extraordinary technique that 'fills the listener with wonder'.[2] He was particularly celebrated for his almost magical 'fingered octaves', which Flesch tells us 'rolled up and down under his fingers at the pace of a simple scale'. His performances are variously described as 'big, but inflexible and cold'[3] by Flesch, and by Henry Lahee: 'His command of all the technical resources of the violin is so great that he can play the most terrific passages without sacrificing his tone or clearness of phrasing, and his octave playing almost equals that of Paganini himself.'[4]

Thomson took his teaching seriously. He was ruthless in his attempts to right a bad habit; particularly efficacious was his method of correcting faulty *vibrato* with gymnastic exercises. This was the germ of an idea that was further developed by Achille Rivarde and perfected by Flesch.

In the early nineteenth century, the Belgian and French branches of violin playing developed independently, although their roots were common. Many violinists considered it important to study in both schools, perfecting their bowing according to Bériot's principles in Brussels while developing a virtuoso technique in Paris.

Delphin Alard (1815–88) stepped into the professional post Bériot declined at the Paris Conservatoire in 1843. A product of the classical school of Viotti through Baillot and François-Antoine Habeneck, Alard was the foremost representative of the French school of his day. He had many pupils, the most distinguished being Pablo Sarasate. Alard's edition of collected classics, 'Les Maîtres Classiques', a valuable collection of sonatas, and his tutor, are still in use.

Prosper Philippe Catherine Sainton (1813–90) from Toulouse was another important product of the French school. A pupil of Habeneck, he pursued a distinguished career, touring Europe, and played for some time in the orchestra of the Paris Opéra. In 1844, he went to London, where he was appointed professor of violin at the Royal Academy of Music, leader of the Queen's Band, Chamber Musician to the Queen and leader of the orchestra of Her Majesty's Theatre. In 1860 he married the singer Charlotte Dolby, who became known as Madame Sainton-Dolby. She was a great favourite in the 'Pops' – a series of chamber music concerts founded in 1858. Sainton was highly respected in Britain, where he considerably raised the standards of violin playing. Robin Legge, writing about the last Birmingham Festival before Sainton's death, remarked that 'every violinist in the orchestra had been either a direct pupil of Sainton's or a pupil of a pupil'.[5]

## Notes

1. Flesch, *The Memoirs of Carl Flesch*, pp. 65–6, 143.
2. Lahee, *Famous Violinists of Today and Yesterday*, p. 269.
3. Flesch, op. cit., p. 44.
4. Lahee, op. cit., pp. 268–9.
5. Van der Straeten, *The History of the Violin*, ii, p. 180.

# 10 'He Holds You in a Magic Circle'

O
f the wealth of musical talent that existed in the mid-nineteenth-century Belgian School, one name is outstanding: that of Henri Vieuxtemps. As a virtuoso violinist, Vieuxtemps was one of the greatest in modern times. His staccato, both up- and down-bow, was acclaimed and his intonation considered to be perfect. His use of strong dramatic accents and contrasts brought a new dimension to the art of violin playing. Paganini had shown the public how virtuosity as an end in itself could capture an audience. Vieuxtemps applied a more musical approach to virtuosity.

Vieuxtemps was also one of the first modern players to take a comprehensive approach to his art. Many of his predecessors and contemporaries had studied composition and were violinist-composers of considerable talent, but Vieuxtemps, like Spohr, investigated every possible aspect of his art.

The son of poor weavers, Henri Vieuxtemps was born in 1820 in Verviers, the centre of the wool trade in Belgium. His father played the fiddle and made musical instruments to earn extra money to feed his family (besides Henri, there was another brother who later became a cellist in the Hallé Orchestra in Manchester).

Henri had his first lessons from his father and, before he was five, had exhausted his father's knowledge. A benefactor financed further lessons from a local music teacher and Henri made such rapid progress that he appeared with success in his first public concert at the age of six playing Rode's Fifth Concerto and Fontaine's Variations with Orchestra.

A year later, Vieuxtemps and his father embarked on a concert tour of Belgium, Holland and the Netherlands. Bériot heard him in Brussels and, convinced of his genius, agreed to teach him without a fee for a period of four years. In 1828 Bériot took him to Paris where the eight-year-old child appeared in a number of concerts and was well received. When Bériot left Paris to settle in Italy, he passed on the same advice to his young pupil that he had himself once received from Viotti – that he should go his own way and imitate no one. Vieuxtemps heeded that advice.

Vieuxtemps returned to Brussels, where he took lessons in harmony and immersed himself in studying chamber music. Even as a young boy, he had had a predilection for this music, and even established his own quartet. When he was 12 he met Pauline García, a contralto singer and pianist of considerable skill, and sister of Maria-Felicita Malibran. Together the two young musicians undertook an intensive study of works by Mozart, Schubert and Beethoven, so that by the time Henri was 14, he was not only a fully fledged virtuoso, he was equipped with a mature repertory. Robert Schumann heard him in Leipzig and wrote of his playing: 'When we listen to Henri, we can close our eyes with confidence. His playing is at once sweet and bright, like a flower . . . . From the first to the last sound that he draws from his instrument, Vieuxtemps holds you in a magic circle traced round you, and you cannot find the beginning or the end.'[1]

In Vienna he came into contact with other great musicians of the day. Here he took lessons in counterpoint with Simon Sechter (1788–1867), Anton Bruckner's teacher. Despite his extreme youth, Vieuxtemps performed the Beethoven concerto there in 1834, the first to do so since the composer's death in 1827. Vieuxtemps was praised not only for his style and the beauty of his powerful tone but, even more significantly, for the degree to which he reflected the spirit of Beethoven. From Vienna, Vieuxtemps went to London where he took part in a Philharmonic concert. There he first met Paganini, who encouraged him.

On Vieuxtemps' return to Paris, he studied composition with Antonin Reicha (1770–1836) – teacher of Gounod, Franck, Berlioz and Liszt – while maintaining a hectic schedule of solo appearances. After 1835 he began composing and, during a tour of Holland the following year, he first included his own compositions in his programmes. His pieces were first published in Vienna in 1836. Even so, Vieuxtemps did not feel that he yet fully understood orchestration. To remedy this, he returned for some months to Brussels, where he attended rehearsals of the orchestra of the Théâtre de la Monnaie. Sitting among the players, he absorbed every detail of the individual orchestral parts; he discussed the music with the players. The colourful music he composed from this time reflects this greater understanding of instrumental idioms. Berlioz was particularly interested in his compositions and observed that: 'Beethoven was the first to find a successful solution to the problem of how to give the solo instrument full scope without reducing the orchestra to a minor role, whereas the plan adopted by Ernst, Vieuxtemps, Liszt and one or two others … seems to me to strike the balance exactly.'[2]

In 1846 Vieuxtemps took up employment in Russia as director of violin studies at the conservatory in St Petersburg and as solo violinist to the imperial court. His six years in St Petersburg are important because through his pupils there he exercised considerable influence on what became the Russian School. Vieuxtemps brought to his pupils the lightness and elasticity of Bériot's bowing and the perfection of his staccato. He also instilled in them the need to look into the music for the composer's intentions. The subsequent work of Henri Wieniawski and, later, Leopold Auer in the same city formed a direct link between Vieuxtemps and the Soviet School, which produced David and Igor Oistrakh, Leonid Kogan, Gidon Kremer and Vladimir Spivakov. Auer was himself heir to Vieuxtemps, the line strengthened through his own additional links with Jacob Dont, Böhm and Rode back to Viotti.

In 1871 Vieuxtemps was invited to take over the post vacated by the now blind Bériot at the Brussels Conservatoire. In 1873 he suffered a stroke, which left him paralysed down the left side, but his determination to continue teaching became a source of both pity and amusement. He was quite unable to demonstrate how he wanted his pupils to play certain passages and frequently lost his temper. If a student did not heed his advice, he would prod them with his iron-shod stick. When important visitors were brought to his class to observe him at work, he would turn and smile sweetly to them, but scowl and grimace on facing his pupils.

In his memoirs, David Laurie, the nineteenth-century violin dealer, tells of his encounter with Vieuxtemps in Paris. He had been invited to the home of a M. Jansen, who was giving one of his regular musical afternoons. One of the late Beethoven quartets was being played. While the performance was in progress, Laurie observed a stocky, clumsy-looking little man enter. He bowed in greeting to certain members of the audience and sat down next to Laurie. The leader of the quartet immediately became nervous, began to make mistakes, and began casting frightened glances towards the new arrival, who made signs in return. He shook his arm to suggest more vibrato and threw his right arm up and down as if to demonstrate how each passage should be bowed. He grimaced at every mistake and made wild gestures to indicate a preferred tempo. Laurie was so thoroughly incensed that when the music was over and the young leader ran towards the little man, he expected a confrontation. He was disappointed. The violinist apologised to the visitor, who proceeded to play the passages to perfection and then demanded why the leader could not play them like him. The embarrassed violinist retorted: 'Because I am not M. Vieuxtemps!'[3]

Vieuxtemps was an inveterate traveller. In 1881 he went to Algiers for a period of convalescence. When travelling in his carriage he was struck by a stone hurled by a drunken Arab, and died from his injuries. On 28 August 1881, Vieuxtemps' remains were brought back to his birthplace at Verviers. The scowls and the grimaces so characteristic of the man in life were forgotten as pupils and friends turned out, lining the streets in their thousands. The cortège was drawn by four magnificent black horses and followed by Vieuxtemps' favourite pupil, Eugène Ysaÿe (he had travelled from St Petersburg to pay his last respects), who carried the black velvet cushion with silver tassels on which rested the master's violin and bow.

**Notes**
1. Schumann, *Gesammelte Schriften.*
2. Berlioz, *The Memoirs of Berlioz,* p. 538.
3. Laurie, *Reminiscences of a Fiddle Dealer,* p. 112.

# 11   The Slavonic Wizard

The Slavs have always made a significant contribution to the history of violin playing. A virtuoso who lent considerable colour to international concert platforms in the latter half of the nineteenth-century was the Polish-born Henryk Wieniawski (1835–80). His warm, impetuous Slavonic temperament was evident to his audience from the minute he stepped onto the platform, and the fascinating, individual quality of his tone went straight to their hearts. He had a miraculous technique: his fellow violinists claimed that for him difficulties were virtually non-existent.

Wieniawski's compositions, idiomatic and possessing great charm, include 24 published works with opus numbers, four without and about a dozen unpublished pieces. His Op. 22 Concerto No. 2 in D minor became one of the most popular violin compositions of the day. Although Wieniawski's music was intended mainly to show off his own dazzling technique, this concerto (1870), along with the Opp. 4 and 21 polonaises (1853, 1870) and the Op. 17 *Légende* (*c.*1860), is still indispensable and greatly loved by present-day violinists.

Born in Lublin, Wieniawski was fortunate to grow up in a cultured musical background. His father was an army surgeon and his mother the sister of the pianist Edward Wolff. When he was five, Henryk had lessons on the violin from Jan Hornziel, later leader of the Warsaw Opera Orchestra, before becoming a pupil of Stanislaw Serwaczyński (1791–1859), who also taught the young Joachim.

Henryk's success was phenomenal, even at a time when prodigies seem to have been abundant. When he was eight, he was immediately accepted into J. Clavel's class at the Paris Conservatoire and soon afterwards became a pupil of Lambert Massart. At 11, Henryk carried off the much-coveted first prize for violin playing: this, for a foreigner, was exceptional.

As a fully fledged virtuoso the 13-year-old Henryk toured Poland and Russia, meeting with success everywhere. Two years later, in 1850, he and his pianist brother Józef conquered audiences in the Netherlands, France, England and Germany. In 1860 Wieniawski was appointed solo violinist to the tsar at St Petersburg, a post he held for 12 years. During this time he considerably influenced the development of the Russian School.

By the mid-nineteenth century, it was essential for great artists to visit the USA. Not only were they likely to be well received, but the financial rewards were tremendous. In 1872, Wieniawski crossed the Atlantic for the first time, travelling with his close friend, the world-famous pianist Anton Rubinstein, and a group of ensemble instrumentalists. The tour was a historic one for a number of reasons. They contracted to play in 200 performances at $200 a concert, and gave no fewer than 215 concerts in 239 days. According to the *New York Times* critic, Harold Schonberg, Rubinstein complained that an artist becomes 'an automaton' under such conditions: 'May Heaven preserve us from such slavery!' But in spite of being 'a man of extreme nervous temperament', who because of recurrent ill health had habitually missed engagements in St Petersburg, Wieniawski never cancelled a single concert on the tour. 'However ill he might be, he always contrived to find strength enough to appear on the platform with his fairy-like violin.'[1] It seems that the reason for this uncharacteristic punctuality was a penalty clause in the contract.

The pressure on Wieniawski and Rubinstein took its toll on their friendship. Tempers were often frayed and heated arguments were followed by long periods of icy non-communication. One of the main bones of contention – as far as Wieniawski was concerned – was that Rubinstein insisted that his name be billed in larger type. Although they played Beethoven's Kreutzer Sonata on some 70 occasions, giving superb performances which reduced the audience to tears, they privately maintained an acrimonious silence which neither was prepared to break.

After his first appearance in the USA, a critic wrote: 'In Wieniawski we have the greatest violinist who has yet been heard in America. . . . Of all now living Joachim alone can claim superiority over him.'[2] In private life, Wieniawski drank heavily and gambled, often sitting up all night playing roulette. Quite often he gambled away his earnings before the concert had taken place. Although this high living did not detract from the quality of his playing, it had a disastrous effect upon his health, which was not improved by extreme corpulence. When Vieuxtemps became ill in 1873, Wieniawski took over his post at the Brussels Conservatoire for two years, proving himself to be a valuable teacher. The regular regime also led to an improvement in his health, but when Vieuxtemps had recovered sufficiently to take over again, Wieniawski resumed his former lifestyle. In his thirties, he was already found to be suffering from heart disease and he died, impecunious and alone, in a Moscow hospital at the age of 44.

There is a touching story concerning Joachim and Wieniawski. Always his ungrudging admirer, it appears that Joachim encouraged his pupils to attend a concert that Wieniawski was giving in Berlin. It was to be the first performance of his Second Violin Concerto. When Wieniawski walked onto the platform he looked very ill and after playing for only a few minutes, he stopped and asked for a chair. As he continued to play, he was overcome by an attack of asthma that almost suffocated him, and he had to be carried off the platform. Joachim rushed backstage and, after a short delay, returned carrying Wieniawski's violin. He apologised for being in morning dress and also for his inability to play his friend's wonderful concerto. Instead, he would give them Bach's Chaconne for unaccompanied violin. The applause was tumultuous, and when poor Wieniawski staggered onto the stage, with tears of gratitude pouring down his face, and embraced Joachim, the enthusiasm of the audience knew no bounds.

In his memoirs, Joachim said that 'no-one who had not witnessed Wieniawski's playing could imagine the feats of his left hand'.[3] This was praise indeed from one who was not overgenerous in extolling the merits of his fellow artists. Wieniawski was said to perform double harmonics, swift passages in tenths, left-hand pizzicato and flying staccato, crystal clear and always with perfect intonation. His bowing was considered to be flawless. According to C. R. Halski, he was 'one of the first, if not the first, to discover an important factor in the rational production of tone by means of a special grasp of the bow, in which the stress was laid on the function of the fore-finger and its ability to balance the weight of the bow'.[4] This would seem to be the earliest indication of a move towards the new 'Russian' method of holding the bow as advocated much later by Carl Flesch and which is still used today. Wieniawski also perfected the rapid, stiff-arm, bowed staccato.

Wieniawski owned two exquisite violins, both of which sadly he was forced to sell to pay gambling debts. One was the 'Wieniawski' Strad, made in 1719, when the maker was 75 and still at the height of his powers. Otakar Ševčík, who heard Wieniawski play the instrument, said that of all the virtuosos and instruments he had heard in his long lifetime, none could compare with the 'Wieniawski'. In his last years, Wieniawski acquired a magnificent Pietro Guarneri violin. All who heard him play it said that his dazzling genius was admirably matched to the rare qualities of this instrument. Eventually, it came into the possession of Jenö Hubay, who played on it for many years.

### Notes

1. Schonberg, *The Great Pianists*, p. 260.
2. Lahee, *Famous Violinists of Today and Yesterday*, p. 224.
3–4. *Grove*, 5th edn., ix, p. 288.

# 12 Servant of Art

It was on 28 March 1844, at Drury Lane Theatre in London, at a benefit for the manager, Alfred Bunn, that the 'Bohemian Girl' and the 'Hungarian Boy' appeared together on the same bill. The 'Girl' was Michael William Balfe's operetta *The Bohemian Girl*, then all the rage, and the 'Boy' the 12-year-old Joseph Joachim, making his 'first appearance before an English audience'.[1] Sandwiched, as was customary, between the first and second acts of the operetta, the young performer played Ernst's *Grand Variations* on a theme from Rossini's *Otello*, and brought the house down. Two months later, at a Philharmonic Society concert conducted by Mendelssohn, Joachim gave his first performance of the Beethoven Violin Concerto, with his own cadenzas. Mendelssohn wrote enthusiastically to Joachim's family of his 'unparalleled success'. As soon as Joachim stepped onto the platform, so great was the excitement that the audience started applauding. He played the opening bars 'so splendidly, with such certainty and pure intonation' that the public frequently interrupted him. At one point he had turned to Mendelssohn and admitted, 'I really am very frightened.'[2] At the end the audience would not let him go and he had to return again and again to acknowledge the applause.

The seventh of eight children of a poor Jewish family, Joachim was born in the Hungarian village of Kitsee. When he was five, he took lessons with Stanislaw Serwaczyński, the best violinist in Pesth, and within two years he was playing duos with his master in public. A critic described him as 'a living marvel', 'a second Vieuxtemps, Paganini or Ole Bull'.[3] Years later, when asked what he could remember of the occasion, he replied that it was his 'sky-blue coat with its mother-of-pearl buttons'.[4]

Later he studied in Vienna with the greatest teacher in that city, Joseph Hellmesberger the elder. Unfortunately, Serwaczyński's neglect of bowing exercises had produced what Hellmesberger considered insurmountable problems; a second opinion was sought from Ernst, who recommended his own teacher, Josef Böhm. Apart from improving his bowing, Böhm introduced Joachim to the chamber music repertory.

Paris would have been the natural choice for further training, but he opted instead for Leipzig, then an important centre of music, because he had relatives there. The Gewandhaus Orchestra had been thriving under Mendelssohn's direction since 1834, and there was the newly opened conservatory. In 1843, Joachim was auditioned by Mendelssohn, who suggested that he study counterpoint with Moritz Hauptmann (1792–1868), but considered that no further lessons in technique were necessary. 'Let him work by himself and play occasionally to [Ferdinand] David [then violin professor at the conservatory] for the benefit of his criticism and advice. . . . I myself will regularly play with him and be his adviser in artistic matters.'[5]

In a letter written in April 1844, Hauptmann remarked that young Joachim hardly needed to practise:

> The other day he played Spohr's 'Gesangsscene' [the Violin Concerto No. 8, Op. 47 in A minor], which he had only read through with David for the first time a few days before. It was an impromptu performance and, as the solo part was mislaid, he played it by heart, and in such a way that even Spohr would have been satisfied. The singing quality of his tone was of touching beauty, his intonation clear as a bell, and the most difficult passages unfailing in precision.[6]

The following year saw Joachim's great success in England, and on his return to Leipzig he took part in a performance at the Gewandhaus of Ludwig Maurer's Sinfonia Concertante for four violins, Op. 55, along with Ernst, Antonio Bazzini and David, world-famous and all very much his senior. At 13, Joachim was now clearly on equal terms with the greatest artists of the day. But his family feared he would be exploited like other child prodigies, so he completed his general education and continued to study with David.

Mendelssohn's powerful influence on the young Joachim was of much benefit and many of his later attitudes stemmed from this association. Mendelssohn introduced him to the music of Bach. Every Sunday the two would play duos and sonatas at the composer's home for hours on end. The social advantages of mixing with the musical elite at Mendelssohn's house must also have been enormous. It was here, crucially, that he met Robert Schumann and his wife Clara, one of the greatest pianists of the day. Joachim became closely associated with them and, later, he and Clara undertook highly acclaimed recital tours.

Standards in Leipzig declined after Mendelssohn's death in 1847, and Joachim felt the need for a change. The opportunity came by way of a suggestion from Liszt, who had ceased to give solo performances and was seeking a quieter life as Kapellmeister at the Weimar court. Liszt offered Joachim the post of Konzertmeister, which he accepted with enthusiasm. Until this time he had been rather over-protected and, being of a naturally serious disposition, had experienced little outside his sheltered world of study. At Weimar, where he remained for three years under Liszt's powerful personality, his transition from boyhood to maturity was undoubtedly effected. Joachim's compositions at Weimar show the strong influence of Liszt. He dedicated his Op. 3 Violin Concerto in G minor to Liszt, who returned the compliment by dedicating his Hungarian Rhapsody in C sharp minor to Joachim.

Joachim's Weimar period was one of inner conflict. Although an admirer and friend of Liszt, he held strongly independent views of his own. For him the 'classics' predominated, whereas Liszt and the classics were like oil and water. Furthermore,

Joachim felt increasingly ill at ease in Weimar, where the fashion for Wagner's music was gaining momentum, and with which he had little sympathy.

When the opportunity came to move on, he relinquished his post, although loath to leave Liszt and his other friends. He would have been even more distressed had he known the part he was to play in the dramatic battle between the progressive 'New German School' and the conservative opposition. The 'new' movement represented the 'music of the future', with Liszt and Wagner as their idols. The opposition condemned all post-Beethoven music (except that of Mendelssohn), holding the classics as their models. But it did not stop there: music began to take on an ethical significance. A composition with chromaticism or striking effects of orchestral colour was considered depraved, whereas work adhering more closely to the rules of Classical harmony represented high moral purpose.

When Liszt published in 1857 what Joachim considered to be an arrogant preface to his *Symphonic Poems*, Joachim wrote politely severing their relations but thanking him for his past friendship. This was followed by depositions in Robert Schumann's *Neue Zeitschrift für Musik*, after which the opposition to the New German School published the now famous manifesto of 1860, disagreeing with the 'new and unheard-of theories which are contradictory to the innermost nature of music'.[7] It was signed by Brahms, Joachim, the pianist Julius Otto Grimm and the conductor Bernhard Scholz.

When Joachim left Weimar in 1853, he took up an appointment as 'royal court and state violinist' to the blind King George of Hanover, a great patron of music. Although he was on intimate terms with the king, Joachim's affairs did not always run smoothly. A perfectionist in everything he undertook, he was unhappy with the prevailing standards of orchestral playing, but had minimal success in raising it. He frequently grumbled that musically he was preaching to the deaf and was obliged to make his own music at home. He remained in his post until 1866, when Hanover became part of Prussia and the king went into exile.

In 1863, Joachim married Amalie Weiss, a beautiful contralto from the Hanover Opera. Six years later, when he was appointed director of the newly opened Hochschule in Berlin, they moved there with their young family. After Prussia's emergence as the leading German state following her defeat of Austria in 1866, Berlin played an increasing part in European politics and, as a result, the musical life of the city improved. Clara Schumann, Brahms and Wagner all visited Berlin with far greater frequency than before.

When Joachim arrived it was rightly sensed that a new era in the musical life of the city had begun. The Hochschule went from strength to strength, and within three years the number of pupils had increased from 19 to 100. Joachim inaugurated public students' concerts, which were attended by the press and soon became major events in the musical life of the city, and in which Joachim himself took part. In 1869 he founded a string quartet, establishing the medium as a specialised field and raising it to a high peak of achievement.

Joachim's violin teaching is best described by one of his most famous pupils, a fellow Hungarian, Leopold Auer, who had lessons with him in Hanover in 1862. Because of the busy life of their master, students never had fixed lessons and were summoned by a servant at short notice. Auer says that Joachim rarely addressed technical details and never made suggestions as to how to achieve technical facility; this was supposed to be taken care of at home. But he always had his violin in his hand throughout the lesson, and whenever he saw fit to criticise, he 'would draw his bow and play the passage or phrase in question himself in a manner truly divine'.[8] Divine or not, Carl Flesch – also a Joachim pupil – was highly critical of his master's bowing. He tells us that Joachim played with the upper arm in such a low position that a right angle was formed between the arm and the forearm at the nut. He held the bow by the fingertips, the index finger touching the stick at the line of the top joint with the little finger remaining on the stick. When a change of bow at the nut was required, it could only be accomplished by a horizontal jerk of the wrist, due to the stiffness of the fingers. Nevertheless, Flesch considered that 'Joachim's bowing was a purely personal affair, an intuitive motional translation of a thoroughly expressive need'. It was only when his followers tried to establish a 'school' based on wrong and 'unnatural' principles that the trouble started. Flesch claimed that the majority of Joachim's pupils, as violinists, were 'cripples for life' and, for this reason, Joachim 'never trained a single violinist who achieved world fame'.[9]

But in other respects Flesch agreed with Auer that Joachim was no ordinary teacher. Since he seldom made his meaning clear in detail, it was absolutely essential that the student have considerable technical training before approaching the master. For those who understood him and could follow his inarticulate directions, there was much benefit to be gained; the less gifted were left unenlightened.

Joachim had tremendous reserves of mental and physical strength, and retained the buoyancy of youth well into his later years. His capacity for work was almost inexhaustible. After a 20-hour journey he was quite likely to be at the Hochschule within an hour, ready to give three or four lessons. After lunch he would probably conduct an orchestral rehearsal and then get into a carriage, drive to the Mendelssohns for dinner, and spend the remainder of the evening playing quartets with the other guests.

One of the most significant associations in Joachim's life was his friendship with Brahms, whom he first met in Hanover in 1852. Brahms had heard Joachim play the Beethoven Violin Concerto in Hamburg four years before, and the performance had left a deep impression. The friendship lasted over 40 years. Their extensive correspondence shows that they frequently sought one another's opinion and exchanged musical sketches for criticism. In fact, Brahms considered Joachim to be a better composer than himself.

When Brahms turned to writing a violin concerto, it was naturally with Joachim in mind. He made the first sketches of the work while spending the summer of 1878 at the Wörthersee, and sent the solo part to his friend for comment. Joachim found it difficult to judge from an incomplete score. However, he must have envisaged some of the problems for he wrote: 'Some of it is quite original, violinistically, but whether one can comfortably play all this in an over-heated hall is another matter.'[10] The extended duration of solo passages in this concerto has always been a test of stamina for the soloist.

Their letters highlight the disadvantages suffered by the keyboard player writing for an instrument he knew little about. Curiously enough, Brahms was more willing to accept Joachim's advice on the composition itself than that relating to matters of technical difficulty in the solo part. It was only in the writing of the cadenza that Joachim had a free hand. One of the main points of disagreement concerned directions for *legato* phrasing where Brahms insisted upon pianistic slurs rather than bowing directions. Joachim writes: 'With so many notes on the same stroke [of the bow], it is better to divide the notes by several strokes. It can still sound as if it is played with one.'[11] On another occasion Brahms was quite put out. 'With what right, and since when, and on whose authority do you violinists write the sign of portamento where it doesn't mean anything? So far I've never given in to violinists and not accepted their damned slurs!' Stubbornly maintaining his stance, Brahms asked: 'Why should [the slur] mean something else with us than it did with Beethoven?'[12] However, in a passage where 'the basses should play pizzicato, not sustained',[13] Brahms seemed happy enough to accept Joachim's suggestions for making the solo part less taxing by providing a 'lighter' accompaniment. In another instance, Brahms was persuaded by Joachim to reduce the strength of the woodwind so that the soloist would not be overpowered.

Brahms completed the Violin Concerto by December 1878 and it was given a first reading before an audience at the Hochschule. Almost without exception, Berlin critics condemned it as 'a barren production' and attacked Joachim for having compelled a student orchestra to accompany 'such unmitigated rubbish'.[14] On New Year's Day 1879, the first public performance took place in Leipzig at the Gewandhaus and the critics were no kinder. For the early performances, Joachim carried the entire manuscript score and orchestral parts from city to city. At the first five performances he played with the music: only at the sixth – a Philharmonic concert in London – did he feel confident enough to play from memory. The concerto was published in the autumn of 1879. Brahms knew Joachim's technique and musicianship to be superior to any other living violinist's and at first resisted publication because he feared it would be too difficult for other violinists.

Over the years Brahms and Joachim had occasional minor disagreements. Mostly these concerned the performance or non-performance of one of Brahms's compositions and did not greatly disrupt the course of friendship. But when Joachim brought an action against his wife, accusing her of an illicit relationship with the publisher Fritz August Simrock, Brahms took Amalie's part, writing her a long personal letter confirming his belief in her innocence. When the letter was read out in court, Joachim lost his case.

For a year all contact between the two men ceased. Then they corresponded on purely musical matters, addressing each other without intimacy. Brahms appears to have suffered most and sought ways in which to patch up the quarrel. For his part, Joachim continued to play Brahms's music.

In the summer of 1887 when Brahms was in Switzerland, he began work on the Double Concerto for violin and cello. This was composed for Joachim and Robert Hausmann (1852–1909), cellist of the Joachim Quartet, and represented an attempt at reconciliation. When Brahms sent the solo parts to Joachim and Hausmann, they seized upon them excitedly. All three musicians came together at Clara Schumann's house at Baden-Baden in September, where they rehearsed together before trying it out with the Kursaal orchestra. The first public performance took place on 18 October 1887, with Brahms conducting. At a later performance in Leipzig, with the same artists and the Gewandhaus orchestra, Tchaikovsky said: 'In spite of the excellent performance this concerto did not make the slightest impression on me.'[15]

The concerto succeeded in its purpose, for Clara Schumann noted in her diary that Joachim and Brahms were again on speaking terms. The two string players offered a number of suggestions for improvement, and many of Joachim's pencilled modifications remain on the manuscript score. But Brahms, intransigent as always, never fully gave way to their wishes until the work was finally published in 1888. Even then, in the Rondo finale, where the cellist has the main theme and is called upon to play a lively passage, the bowings in the score are Brahms's, not Joachim's.

The impressions of Joachim left by his contemporaries range from idolatry to blunt criticism. After a concert in Vienna in 1861, when Joachim was 30, Edward Hanslick wrote:

> After the first movement [of the Beethoven concerto] it must have been clear to everyone that here was no stunning virtuoso but rather a significant and individual personality. For all his technique, Joachim is so identified with the musical ideal that he may be said to have penetrated beyond the utmost in virtuosity: anything suggestive of vanity or applause-seeking has been eliminated . . . What a flood of strength there is in the tone which his large, sure bow draws from the instrument![16]

Joachim's efforts to improve standards of musicianship had immeasurable influence throughout Europe. Although artists like Ernst and Vieuxtemps had made the public aware that virtuosity could be successfully allied to musicianship, it was Joachim who established it as a fact of performing life. He was the first of the nineteenth-century violinists to revive the unaccompanied sonatas of Bach and his programmes invariably included works by Scarlatti, Tartini and Spohr. Before his introduction of the classics into his own programmes, the usual violinists' repertory contained an abundance of short, contemporary items, *potpourris* and transcriptions. Other artists soon followed Joachim's example, and although there were sporadic bursts of empty virtuosity, the seriousness that Joachim brought to the concert platform has remained. Flesch, although critical of Joachim's bowing, considers that it is 'thanks to the high ethical ideals of Joachim's art' that 'the virtuoso developed, within a mere 30 years, from his early nineteenth-century position of an entertainer to that of an artist who wished to be primarily regarded as a mediator between the work and the listener'.[17]

Joachim was not an avid promoter of performances of new music, yet Brahms might never have had a hearing without him. His own composing gifts were considerable, and Carl Flesch regarded his *Concerto in the Hungarian Style* as 'a work of genius' and 'the most outstanding creation that a violinist has ever written for his own instrument'.[18] His cadenzas, worked out before the Berlin period, have stood the test of time rather better than his concerto, which is rarely played.

Joachim was a complex character: outwardly very serious and a man of high ideals – some thought too high; inwardly containing depths of feeling that he seldom revealed even to his closest friends. But his response to an erring pupil could be fiery, and when competition emerged from an unexpected quarter, he could be witheringly sarcastic. When the 23-year-old Fritz Kreisler, who had scored a sensational success in Berlin in 1898, was brought by a friend to Joachim's class, he was greeted by the master with cold formality. When the accompanist failed to appear, Kreisler (also an accomplished pianist) offered to take his place and played perfectly. When he took his leave, Joachim said curtly, 'You certainly are a ready pianist.'[19] Yet in later years, Kreisler admitted that Joachim had been one of the great influences in his life: 'He was a queer mixture of generosity and jealousy. He wanted everybody to do exactly as he desired it to be done and was very pedantic about it.'[20]

Joachim was honoured and fêted everywhere. In 1899, at his Golden Jubilee on the concert platform, a festival concert in the Philharmonic Hall in Berlin was mounted in his honour. An elite orchestra was formed from his most prominent pupils and he was presented with a Stradivarius violin to add to his collection, which already included the 'De Barrau', the 'Alard' and the 'Dolphin'.

In a letter to his brother 50 years earlier, he had written of his struggles with a work he had composed for his next London concert:

> It seems as though I were fated to do no good in music. And I do mean well with my art, it is a holy thing to me . . . But in spite of that I accomplish practically nothing; it seems as if some tragic fate hung over me, with which I am powerless to battle! Will this fate pursue me all my life? . . . I shall yet conquer it. I should so like to be of some great service to art![21]

Although he was not a direct pupil of Joachim, Adolf Busch (1891–1952) was considered his natural successor through his teacher, Willy Hess (1859–1939) and his later personal contact with Joachim. Born in Siegen, Busch was the son of a cabinet maker and amateur musician who also made and played violins. Busch studied at the Cologne Hochschule, first under Hess and then under Bram Eldering (1865–1943).

(The Dutch Eldering had studied with Hubay in Brussels and had followed him to Budapest, to play in the Hubay-Popper Quartet. It was not until 1888 that Eldering renewed his studies with Joachim at the Hochschule in Berlin, so that when Busch became his pupil about 1904, the latter would have benefited from the fusion of teaching elements present in his master.)

Busch played the Brahms concerto at his London debut in 1912. According to the *Strad* critic, 'No-one short of Kreisler could approach him for purity of style and intense beauty of phrasing.'[22] At 21, Busch took over the leadership of the Konzertverein Orchestra in Vienna, where he formed the first Busch Quartet. In 1917, when only 26, he succeeded Henri Marteau as chief professor of violin at the Hochschule in Berlin, where ten years earlier Joachim had held the same post. It was then that Busch founded the string quartet which was to become famous throughout the world.

Busch's solo career also continued to flourish and in 1931 he made his American debut. He caught the attention of Arturo Toscanini, who was so impressed that he invited Busch to tour the USA with him. This close contact bred a friendship between these two great opposites that lasted until the violinist's death in 1952.

Flesch called Busch 'a character', 'a thoroughly sympathetic figure in every respect' and 'the greatest purely German violinist of his age'.[23] This view was borne out by Yehudi Menuhin, who acknowledged a great debt to Busch, with whom he studied: 'He presented me with German culture; in after years the people and the literature would improve my acquaintance with it; but to him I owe the entry through music, and music expressed in a sensibility which combined scholarship and passion and was never dry.'[24]

To many, Busch had one of the finest bow arms in existence and his 'elastic' cantilena and faultless phrasing can be heard in his numerous recordings, many of which are of the quartet. When he and Rudolf Serkin performed all the Beethoven sonatas at Carnegie Hall in the 1937–8 season, the critic from the *New York Times* declared that the highest ideals of ensemble playing had been realised. One of the features of their playing was that they 'never use their magnificent technical equipment save as a means to express the full power and beauty of the music'.[25]

Apart from his undeniable musical contribution, Busch is also remembered as one of the few non-Jewish musicians who stood out against Hitler and the Nazi regime. In 1927 he left Germany for Switzerland and, from 1933, refused all concert dates in his native country, which not only halved his income but virtually ended his career as a soloist, chamber musician and composer. Hitler always referred to him as 'our German violinist', and made many unsuccessful attempts to lure him back. In 1938, in protest against Mussolini's anti-semitic laws, he cancelled all his concerts in Italy where he had always been very popular. He finally settled in the USA in 1939, where he was never as fully appreciated as he had been in Europe.

In complete contrast to Busch, Willy Burmester (1869–1933), a pupil of Joachim in at the Berlin Hochschule, spent the rest of his life denying any benefit derived from his training under the great man. We know that Joachim could be very cruel when he took a dislike to someone, and Burmester was a typical victim. Ironically, he turned out to be one of Joachim's most brilliant students.

Burmester was born in Hamburg, the son of a musician who taught him to play the violin when he was four years old. At eight he was auditioned by Joachim, who offered words of encouragement to the father but said nothing to the boy, causing him bitter disappointment. However, four years later Burmester was accepted by the Hochschule and given a place in Joachim's class. Invariably his instruction was left to Joachim's assistant and when he had completed his four years of study, Joachim denied him a certificate, resulting in permanent animosity between the two.

Burmester took a job in Finland, with an orchestra in Helsingfors and later became leader. During this time he devoted himself to an intensive period of study, which often involved some ten hours' practice each day. In order to develop his own way, he worked alone, making a special effort to unlearn everything he had been taught at the Hochschule. He emerged with a brilliant technique which stood him in good stead for the rest of his performing life. However, it was probably at this time that he wore his first finger down to the nerve; he was condemned to suffer constant pain, which surgery failed more than once to alleviate.

From 1886, Burmester toured frequently, meeting with enthusiasm everywhere he went. In 1890 he was appointed leader of the orchestra at Sonderhausen and, subsequently, at Bremen and Weimar. Then, at Hans von Bülow's request, he became leader of his orchestra at Hamburg; von Bülow had taken Burmester under his wing when he was 16 and had always tried to help him with his career. Much later, when von Bülow experienced his own difficulties in putting on a series of concerts in Berlin that interfered with the Philharmonic series, Burmester was one of the few to defy the ban forbidding Hamburg musicians to play for von Bülow.

In October 1894, Burmester became famous overnight when he gave a Paganini evening at the Singakademie in Berlin; one critic wrote: 'Mr Burmester comes from an obscure town, unheralded and, in the face of indifference, prejudice, jealousy conquered the metropolis off-hand, and for nearly half an hour recall followed recall.'[26] Another described his technique as 'marvellous, almost diabolical':

> Difficult pizzicato passages and runs in thirds and tenths at top speed are but child's play to him. His left hand pizzicato is marvellous and he makes runs in single and artificial harmonics as quickly as ordinary violinists can play an ordinary scale. He plays harmonics with a vibrato and his staccato volente is developed to an astounding degree of perfection.[27]

Burmester bitterly resented that his subsequent triumphs were immediately attributed to his being a product of the Joachim School, since he considered he had narrowly escaped musical suffocation. He had previously refuted the assumption in Berlin and stressed that he had chosen to go abroad in order to develop in his own way. To his surprise, the announcement brought forth a deluge of letters from 'pupils of Joachim'; Burmester replied that he had no idea that there were so many 'Joachim' pupils, and added that if any 'known' pupils of the great man would be prepared to discuss the matter, he would be happy to meet them. But not a single pupil, known or unknown, seemed willing to accept the challenge. Time justified the grudge that Burmester held against his teacher and his outstanding musical talent and technical facility earned him universal acclaim. He made a number of recordings which have been reissued on CD.

A second-generation Joachim student, Shin'ichi Suzuki (1898–1998), who died just short of his hundredth birthday, was not a great violinist *per se*. However, as a teacher he made an immense and important contribution to the musical world: many youngsters around the world would never have played a musical instrument but for his pioneering method of class-teaching of very small children. Suzuki was born in Nagoya, Japan, son of the founder of the largest violin-making factory in the country. He had violin lessons from two Joachim pupils, Ko Ando in Japan and Karl Klingler in Berlin.

He formed his own string quartet in 1928 and later was founder and conductor of the Tokyo String Orchestra. He was elected president of the Teikoko Music School, and during this time Suzuki began to study the way in which children develop language skills; he came to the conclusion that, irrespective of nationality, they could communicate in their mother tongue, regardless of their intelligence, by the age of five. He also studied the effect of the environment on children and decided that if conditions were conducive to learning speech, the same conditions could apply to learning an instrument.

Suzuki believed that there is no such thing as inborn talent, a concept with which many musicians disagreed. Nevertheless, his success in teaching children from the age of three was indisputable; he later applied the same method to general education, in subjects ranging from languages to drawing and gymnastics, and proved his method to be just as effective. His aim was to find the easiest way for children to learn in a completely natural way. When showing them how to move the bow over the strings correctly he would kneel on the floor so as to be the same height; he devised games which would achieve the best results with as little effort as possible. Another of the controversial aspects of Suzuki's method was that he recommended the parents should sit in on the lessons so they would know how to guide their children when practising. 'Our goal is to have them understand the unique life-force which their child possesses, and to realise their power to nourish that life force.'[28]

From 1964 he travelled abroad, giving lectures and demonstrations. The British violinist Helen Brunner-Spira, who trained with Suzuki in Japan and pioneered the movement in the UK, recalls that: 'Once I had read his book *Nurtured by Love*, I was totally convinced of his premise that each human being is innately musical and this musical ability is trainable, not inherited.'[29]

Even in his own country, Suzuki was regarded as being too unorthodox because his ideas challenged traditional methods of teaching. But criticism never bothered him. His main concern was that he could not hope to reach everyone in a normal life span: 'I'm trying to reach as many people with my ideas, writing as much as I can, fighting for what I believe in. But I think that if I hope to see some of my hopes fulfilled, I'll have to live at least to a hundred and ten.'[30] He also claimed he never felt weary, because there was still so much to be done. He would rise at 3 a.m. and he would work until late afternoon. He felt it was his duty to continue working as long as possible because the world was in a state of crisis. When he spoke about this and the threat of weapons of mass destruction in New York in the late 1960s, he received a standing ovation for his suggestion that the world should become one family: 'I have faith that children can become better human beings and create a better world. I am here for every child.'[31]

## Notes

1–2. Moser, *Joseph Joachim*, p. 57.

3. *Honmuyesz*, 21 March 1839.

4. Moser, op. cit., p. 7.

5. Ibid., p. 39.

6. Ibid., pp. 51–2.

7. Ibid., p. 173.

8. Auer, *Violin Playing as I Teach It*, p. 6

9. Flesch, *Memoirs*, p. 34.

10. Joachim to Brahms, 24 August 1878.

11. Ibid., 20 May 1879.

12. Brahms to Joachim, May 1879.

13. Joachim to Brahms, end of March 1879.

14. Moser, op. cit., p. 263.

15. Hill, *Brahms: A Study in Musical Biography*, p. 152.

16. Hanslick, *Music Criticisms 1846–99*, pp. 78–91.

17. Flesch, op. cit., p. 32.

18. Ibid., p. 36.

19. Ibid., p. 37.

20. Lochner, *Fritz Kreisler*, p. 50.

21. Moser, op. cit., pp. 286–7.

22. Schwarz, *Great Masters of the Violin*, p. 325.

23. Flesch, op. cit., p. 265.

24. Menuhin, *Unfinished Journey*, p. 97.

25. *New York Times*, 2 January 1938.

26–27. Lahee, *Famous Violinists of Today and Yesterday*, p. 288.

28. *The Strad*, December 1989, p. 1067

29–31. Letter from Helen Brunner-Spira to M.C.

# 13 Lady of the Bow

In King Henry VII's accounts, there is an item dated 2 November 1495: 'For a womane that singeth with a fidell, 2s', whereas the queen's male 'fideler' of the period, 17 February 1497, was paid 'in rewarde' £1.6s.8d![1] The 'womane' would have been exceptional for her time, since we know that the fiddle was not thought to be respectable. Nevertheless, the existence of amateur women violinists can be traced throughout the history of the instrument.

The earliest professional would seem to be a Mrs Sarah Ottey, born about 1695 who performed 'solos on the harpsichord, violin and bass viol'[2] at concerts around 1721–2. Another was 'La Diamantina', born around 1715, who was described by the poet Thomas Gray in 1740 as 'a famous virtuosa who played on the violin divinely, and sung angelically'.[3] We have already learnt of Maddalena Lombardini Sirmen through the letter she received from Tartini (see pages 11–13).

Regina Strinasacchi (1764–1823), a product of the Pièta in Venice, where the standards were high, has also been mentioned previously; a highly successful soloist in her own right, she is immortalised by her association with Mozart in the historic performance of his Sonata in B flat major (K.454), when the composer accompanied her from a blank sheet of paper, having notated only the violin part.

Around the turn of the eighteenth century there are an increasing number of women violinists, some of whom were child prodigies, well known in their own time. Among the best known were the Milanollo sisters. Natives of Savigliano in Piedmont, they caused a furore wherever they appeared. Nicknamed Mlle Staccato and Mlle Adagio, they travelled extensively through France, Belgium, Holland and England. Teresa, elder of the two, went to Paris in 1836, when she was only eleven, to study with Charles Lafont. Afterwards, she took some lessons from Habeneck, and finished under Bériot in Brussels.

Despite these isolated success stories, the violin was still not considered to be fit for ladies. Spohr, for example, discouraged his wife from playing it. Only two women born during the mid-nineteenth century are remembered today. One was the French Camilla Urso (1842–1902), who travelled extensively throughout the world as a virtuoso before finally settling in New York. The other was the Moravian Wilhelmina Neruda, who became better known as Wilma Norman-Neruda, and later as Lady Hallé, wife of Sir Charles Hallé.

Wilhelmina Neruda (1839–1911) was born in Brno into a distinguished family of violinists and musicians dating back to the seventeenth century. She was taught by her father, Josef Neruda, a violinist and organist. She later had further instruction from Leopold Jansa (1795–1875), a Bohemian violinist and imperial court chamber virtuoso in Vienna. In 1849, Wilhelmina made her debut in Vienna with her pianist sister Amalie, and impressed the critic, Edward Hanslick, who declared: 'The little Neruda is wonderful indeed in bravura music, in musical intelligence, and finally in her remarkable accuracy.'[4]

Josef Neruda caused a stir when he brought his trio of talented children to London in April 1849 – nine-year-old Wilhelmina and Amalie, aged 12, were joined by Victor, their 11-year-old brother. Wilhelmina was the star. *The Times* music critic wrote warmly of her performance of Vieuxtemps' *Arpeggio* and Ernst's *Carnaval de Venise*. The juvenile trio, booked originally for two nights only, were re-engaged for a further 16 performances.

The following month, Wilhelmina was invited to play a Bériot concerto at a Philharmonic Society concert, an account of which comes from William Bartholomew (English librettist and violinist), who wrote to a friend the next day:

> A little girl, a child in years and person, but a perfect miniature Paganini, played last night to the Philharmonic audiences a concerto of de Bériot's on the violin. Her tone, her execution, especially with the bow hand, were all perfect – the latter is beautiful: her graceful and elastic wrist produced some of the most sparkling staccatos by up and down bowing that I have ever heard.[5]

In 1864, Wilma (as she now preferred to be called) made a great success in Paris, where she played in the Pasdeloup (a famous series of popular concerts founded by the composer, Jules Pasdeloup) and Conservatoire concerts. In musical circles she was dubbed 'The Queen of Violinists'. Wilma Neruda favoured the 'classic' style of playing and, consequently, was considered by many to be the female counterpart of Joachim. She was a child prodigy who, unlike so many others, fulfilled the promise of early talent. Her performances were always considered to be synonymous with all that is good in musical art. Also a fine quartet player, she was for many years first violin of the Philharmonic Quartet in London and played in the Joachim Quartet. In 1896 she appeared with Joachim playing the Bach D minor Concerto for two violins. Indeed, it was Joachim who, after having heard her as a child, first recognised her talent. He remarked to Charles Hallé, who had not then met her, 'I recommend this artist to your careful consideration. Mark this, when people have given her a fair hearing, they will think more of her and less of me.'[6]

In 1864 she married the Swedish Opera conductor Ludwig Norman, and took up a post as professor of violin at Stockholm Royal Academy of Music. When they separated, in 1869, she came to London and appeared in both Philharmonic Society and the Monday 'Popular' concert series. Her first husband died in 1885 and, three years later, she married Sir Charles Hallé.

The bassoonist Archie Camden and Sir Robert Mayer could recall hearing Lady

Hallé in their youth, and both remarked upon her fine presence and beautiful tone. She also possessed a sense of fun. Alfred Gibson (1849–1924), an English violinist who played occasionally with the Joachim Quartet, reported that Lady Hallé used neither chin-rest nor shoulder-pad. When she was in the artists' room with Joachim, she would tease the members of the quartet by saying 'Now put on your little pincushions.'[7]

There is no doubt that Lady Hallé's success encouraged other women to take up professional violin playing, a field which until this time had been virtually dominated by men. But the struggle was to remain uphill for some time to come.

### Notes

1. Haweis, *My Musical Life*, p. 296.
2. Lahee, *Famous Violinists of Today and Yesterday*, p. 302.
3. Thomas Gray, 1740.
4. *The Strad*, August 1897, p. 107.
5. Scholes, *The Mirror of Music*, ii, pp. 834–5.
6. Lahee, op. cit., p. 315.
7. Gibson, *A Musician's Life*, p. 50.

# 14  Incomparable Charmer

By the middle of the nineteenth century, Spain was one of the most musically backward countries in Europe. It was not until the end of the century that Spaniards finally had the opportunity to hear all the Beethoven symphonies. Few therefore sought a career in music, and those who were gifted enough to try were obliged to train in Paris. One of Spain's most famous émigré musicians was Pablo Sarasate, the favourite pupil of Alard at the Paris Conservatoire, whose 'Spanish Dances' perpetuate his memory with music lovers the world over.

'Pablo' – his real name was Martin – Sarasate was born in Pamplona in 1844, the son of a bandmaster, who gave him his first violin lessons at the age of five. He later studied with Manuel Rodriguez Saez in Madrid and played for Queen Isabella. She not only gave him a magnificent Stradivari violin, dated 1724, but also provided the means for him to study at the Paris Conservatoire. He was then 12 years old. After only three years' study, Sarasate carried off the first prize for violin playing. When asked by Alard what he would like as a personal gift from him, the boy replied without hesitation, 'a box of tin soldiers'.[1] This direct simplicity was characteristic of the man who was to become Joachim's most serious rival.

After completing his studies, Sarasate undertook several concert tours, but achieved very little success other than as a salon virtuoso. His style of playing was somewhat affected, and his programmes consisted mainly of variations on opera themes arranged for the violin. Then, in 1867, there came about a complete change both in his playing and in his choice of programme. At the age of 20, Sarasate fell deeply in love with the pianist, Maria Lefébure-Wély, daughter of Louis Lefébure-Wély, organist at Saint-Sulpice in Paris. Three years later, their wedding planned, Sarasate returned from a concert tour to find Maria was marrying another. Sarasate never recovered from the shock. Although throughout his life he was followed everywhere by women (they even fought over his cigarette stubs), he remained a lifelong bachelor. He had also experienced a great tragedy in his childhood that could have been linked with this later event: when he was 11, he and his mother set off for Paris, stopping overnight in Bayonne; entering his mother's room to kiss her goodnight, he found her dead from cholera.

From this time, he started playing the standard repertory and his style took on a seriousness which had hitherto been totally absent. His expanded repertory included the concertos of the German masters and those of the French and Belgian schools. Edouard Lalo composed both his Violin Concerto, Op. 20 (1873), and 'Symphonie

Espagnole' for Sarasate. Camille Saint-Saëns had already written his First Violin Concerto (1859) for him. While on tour in Germany, Sarasate met the pianist Max Bruch, at the beginning of his career. They toured together with great success and Bruch dedicated both his Op. 44 Violin Concerto no.2 (1878) and his Op. 46 *Scottish Fantasy* (1880) to Sarasate. However, Sarasate generally avoided the music of Paganini, partly because he had little taste for it, and also because he had very small hands and could not manage the long stretches that these compositions demanded.

In Leipzig, Sarasate caused a sensation. He quickly followed this with tours in Germany, Austria, England and Belgium, which were not only financially rewarding but earned him a reputation as a virtuoso. It was Sarasate's 1876 debut in Vienna that won him celebrity at the age of 32. Hanslick wrote: 'There are few violinists whose playing gives such unalloyed enjoyment as the performance of this Spaniard. His tone is incomparable – not powerfully or deeply affecting, but of enchanting sweetness.' Praising his 'infallible correctness' and purity of tone, Hanslick declared that: 'He is distinguished, not because he plays great difficulties, but because he plays with them.'[2]

Sarasate had first appeared in London in 1861, when he was 17, at one of the series of Opera Concerts at the Crystal Palace, and also at St James's Hall, but the press failed to comment. Even when, 13 years later, he played Lalo's Violin Concerto at a Philharmonic Society concert, the critic of the *Musical Times* was singularly unimpressed: '. . . neither the composition nor the performer excited any special sensation'. The writer conceded only that Sarasate 'has an agreeable but thin tone and executes with neatness'.[3]

But in 1879, at another Philharmonic Society concert, it was quite another matter. This time he was 'positively overwhelmed with applause and thrice recalled'.[4] When, in 1883, he played the Mendelssohn concerto with the same society, the room was crowded to its limit. One critic remarked upon Sarasate's 'emotional style' and compared it with Joachim's 'highly refined and intellectual interpretation',[5] but agreed that two distinct readings of a great work may be permitted. One dissenting voice bemoaned the excessive speed at which he played the last movement – a criticism that was to be repeatedly levelled at Sarasate during his performing life.

Archie Camden recalled that at the age of 11 in 1899, he was taken by friends to a concert in Manchester given by the Hallé Orchestra, with Sarasate playing the Mendelssohn concerto under Hans Richter. Camden's already acute ear detected a discrepancy between the speeds at which soloist and orchestra were playing, an impression firmly put down by his parents. Many years later, discussing the matter with Arthur Catterall, who had been on one of the back desks in the violin section of the Hallé at the time, Camden learned that he had been right. Apparently, a row had erupted because Sarasate claimed that he, as the soloist, could choose his own tempo and that the orchestra should follow. Richter maintained that Sarasate's tempo was still too fast. After much wrangling (recounted in amusing detail in Camden's memoirs), they agreed on an alarming compromise. When performing the solo sections, the orchestra would play in his time: when it was the turn of the tutti, they would obey the conductor. Carl Flesch tells us, incidentally, that Sarasate was the only violinist whom he ever heard playing the flying staccato of this movement at the extreme point of the bow rather than at the frog.

Flesch maintained that when Sarasate visited the USA he was literally 'a flop', but the American Henry Lahee considered: 'He won great favor, for his playing is of the kind which appeals to the fancy, graceful, vivacious, and pure toned, and he plays Spanish Dances in a manner never to be surpassed.' Lahee went on to make a telling comparison with other eminent violinists of the day: 'Vieuxtemps was an artist with an ardent mind, and a magnificent interpreter of Beethoven; Joachim towers aloft in the heights of serene poetry, upon the Olympic summits inaccessible to the tumults of passion; Sivori was a dazzling virtuoso; Sarasate is an incomparable charmer.'[6]

Sarasate was striking in appearance. Flesch admitted that he and his contemporaries held the small, black-eyed Spaniard with the well-trimmed coal-black moustache and eyes, and black, curly, over-carefully arranged hair in awe: 'It was a unique experience to see this little man stride on to the platform, with genuine Spanish *grandeza*, superficially calm, even phlegmatic, to witness how, after some stereotyped movements, he began to play with unheard of sovereignty and, in a rapid climax, put his audience into astonishment, admiration and highest rapture.'[7] The poet and critic Arthur Symons wrote of that pallid 'strange, attractive, contradictory face. . . . The eyes are passionate and stormy even when the jaded indifferent face breaks into a smile of unaffected pleasure as the enthusiasm of a whole audience mounts in applause.'[8]

Sarasate lived on the Left Bank in the rue du Bac, not far from his friend James Whistler, the artist. Whistler painted a magnificent portrait of the violinist. After seeing it, Symons wrote:

> The man who holds the violin in his hands is a child pleased to please; not a student or a diviner. And Whistler has rendered all this, superbly. Note how Sarasate dandles the violin. It is a child, a jewel. He is already thinking of the sound, the flawless tone, not of Beethoven. Whistler has caught him, poised him, posed him, another butterfly, and alive.[9]

What Symons saw as a virtue, others considered a shortcoming. Flesch once described Sarasate as intellectually in 'the lower income brackets',[10] and Ferruccio Busoni dismissed him as having 'neither brains nor temperament'.[11] But irrespective of his intellectual ability, he had a ready wit and could be disarmingly candid. When he was in Bucharest, the Queen of Romania invited him to be the guest of honour at a party, for which she had ordered the finest gipsy band to entertain them. When asked what he thought of the performance, Sarasate replied abruptly, 'It's pretty bad!'[12]

As a composer, Sarasate contributed some of the most popular pieces in the violin repertory, and when he performed them, they usually brought the house down. Even in the 1930s, Flesch thought that the Spanish Dances were too little considered by virtuosos who preferred 'perfumed . . . pot-pourri-like arrangements'.[13] He correctly prophesied that Sarasate's compositions would dominate the virtuoso repertory much longer than those of any of his more learned colleagues. Today, these pieces, along with those of Kreisler, are finding renewed favour.

Whatever other criticism was levelled at Sarasate, there was never a murmur against his technique. Hanslick, Flesch, Sir Adrian Boult and Sir Robert Mayer, all of whom heard him in the flesh, bear witness to his incomparable tone, immaculate phrasing and incredible left-hand technique over which he had the most perfect command.

Flesch studied and recorded his impressions of Sarasate's technique at close range.

> With the precise and effortless function of both his arms he represented a completely new type of violinist. The finger-tips of his left hand were quite smooth and ungrooved; they hit the finger-board in the normal fashion, without excessive raising or hammering. His vibrato was rather broader than had hitherto been customary. Following an absolutely correct if unconscious principle, he considered his bowing first and foremost a means of producing the kind of tone which he regarded as ideal and which was of a pleasant and elegant smoothness . . . The label of 'sweet' tone which hung round his neck all his life was not so much the result of an inner need as of a technical peculiarity.[14]

According to Flesch, Sarasate's bow made contact with the strings exactly halfway between the bridge and the fingerboard, and hardly ever near the bridge.

Sarasate influenced his contemporaries for a quarter of a century by his absolute purity of intonation, which resulted in considerable raising of standards of technique. However, his influence was both good and harmful: good, because those who heard him had living proof of his excellence; bad, because he attracted so many imperfect imitators. They tried to copy Sarasate in the same way that everyone had tried to copy Paganini, with the result that everything was magnified and inevitably coarsened. What Flesch called 'passionless, smooth, eely tone production' became very fashionable until Ysaÿe came along to set the course in quite another direction. Even so, he considered Sarasate to be 'the ideal embodiment of the salon virtuoso of the greatest style'.[15]

Sarasate never took pupils; he was essentially a performing artist. He received very high fees for playing: in Germany, he was said to have received 3,000 Marks per concert, when Joachim was paid only 1,000. In his later years, he was inclined to play sharp and his vibrato was less secure, but the old magic never left him, and he always filled a concert hall without difficulty. He died suddenly in 1908 in Biarritz from a collapse of the lungs.

## Notes

1. Van der Straeten, *The History of the Violin*, ii, p. 419.
2. Lahee, *Famous Violinists of Today and Yesterday*, p. 229.
3–5. Scholes, *The Mirror of Music*, i, p. 347.
6. Lahee, op. cit., p. 231.
7. Flesch, *Memoirs*, p. 38.
8. Symons, *Illustrated London News*, 21 November 1891, p. 658.
9. Symons, *Double Dealer*, November 1921.
10. Flesch, op. cit., p. 42.
11. D. C. Parker, *The Strad*, January 1966, p. 323.
12. Flesch, op. cit., p. 43.
13. Ibid., p. 42.
14. Ibid., pp. 38–9.
15. Ibid., p. 43.

# 15 The Great Teachers

Two of Sarasate's contemporaries profoundly influenced the development of violin playing. They were the German August Wilhelmj and the Hungarian Leopold Auer.

August Wilhelmj (1845–1908) is one of the comparatively few great violinists to have been born into a wealthy family. His father was a distinguished lawyer and the owner of important vineyards on the Rhine; his mother was a pianist who had studied with Chopin. She encouraged early signs of talent in her son, sending him to the Wiesbaden court Konzertmeister, Conrad Fischer, with whom he made swift progress. He was brought to the attention of Prince Emil von Wittgenstein, who sought the blessing of Liszt. Liszt took the boy to Ferdinand David at Leipzig, who immediately accepted him as a pupil at the conservatory.

There is a story concerning Joachim, who happened to be passing through Leipzig late one night and called in on his old master. David was full of enthusiasm for his clever pupil, Wilhelmj, and told Joachim that he could play his Hungarian Concerto in his sleep. Joachim insisted David make good his claim: 'Wake him up and let me hear him.'[1] It was two o'clock in the morning but the sleepy student, clad in his dressing gown and slippers, apparently gave a faultless performance of the work. Wilhelmj made his debut, playing this concerto, at the Gewandhaus in November 1862 at the age of 17.

In later years, Joachim was less kindly disposed towards Wilhelmj. In many respects, Wilhelmj's powerful and beautiful tone and 'racy virtuosity',[2] made him a serious rival to Joachim. But more important was Wilhelmj's early involvement, through Liszt at Weimar, in the neo-German Wagnerian movement. It was he who persuaded Wagner to visit London in 1877. Wilhelmj also made paraphrases of Wagner's music and 'arrangements' of many of the classics. The one for which Joachim never forgave him was the still popular Air from the Bach Suite in D major, which he transposed to C major, and played entirely on the G string. Once, when the French violinist Lucien Capet unwisely played this 'Air on the G string' to him, Joachim flew into a rage, reducing the Frenchman to tears. With typical arrogance, he considered that Bach was his province and rejected such travesties of the master's work.

For some time Wilhelmj travelled widely as a virtuoso violinist in Europe, America, Australia and Asia. He made his American debut in New York in 1878, but although he achieved success for his playing in the grand manner, Americans didn't take to him in the same way as they had to Ole Bull and Ede Reményi (1828–98) before him. In 1885 Wilhelmj was invited by the sultan of Turkey to perform to the ladies of the harem, a unique privilege never before accorded to a violinist. What the houris thought of him is not recorded, but the sultan decorated him with the Medjidie Order (second class), and presented him with diamonds.

On the concert platform Wilhelmj cut a splendid figure, rather like a Greek statue. He was 'tall, broad-shouldered, with a massive forehead surrounded by a mass of long wavy hair, the picture of dignified repose', writes Edmund van der Straeten, who remembered hearing him at the height of his powers. 'His notes issued from his violin like clarion notes, scintillating with extraordinary brilliance, always beautiful, never forced and rarely equalled in purity of intonation.'[3] A well-known London violin dealer once said: 'He tried some violins [in my shop] – I think he could make a cigar box sound like a Cremona fiddle.'

At his peak, Wilhelmj was certainly one of the greatest players of the late nineteenth century, but his career as a performer was short. He was only 40 when he retired from the concert platform to devote himself to teaching. A variety of reasons are given for this decision; some say he suffered from ill health, others that he was over-fond of good Rhenish wine. Nevertheless, his reputation as a teacher is unblemished. His equable temperament was eminently suited to teaching, and in 1894 he was appointed principal professor of violin at the Guildhall School of Music, where he remained until his death in 1908. The English violinist, Dettmar Dressel, who studied with him, tells us that his methods were highly personal and that he had infinite patience. He trained a large number of first-class professionals, greatly raising standards of violin playing in Britain.

It was not until after the Russian Revolution of 1917, that the musical world became fully aware of the significance of the Hungarian-born Leopold Auer (1845–1930) as a teacher. He had been violin professor at the Imperial Conservatory in St Petersburg for 48 years before making his American debut, at the age of 72 at Carnegie Hall in 23 March 1917. Kreisler and many of his pupils were in the audience. Richard Aldrich, then critic of the *New York Times*, commented on the 'fluent ease' with which he played a programme of 'Old Masters', including Handel, Locatelli, Nardini, Vitali, unaccompanied Bach, 'his own arrangements of a Haydn Serenade … and a *vivace* that would have been a task for younger fingers'.[4] And yet this was the violinist who, when Tchaikovsky dedicated his Violin Concerto to him in 1878, refused to tackle it because it was too difficult. Although he later revised this opinion, the first performance was given in Vienna in 1881 by Adolph Brodsky (1851–1929), to whom Tchaikovsky re-dedicated it. (On hearing the première, Hanslick wrote: 'The violin is no longer played. It is yanked about, it is torn asunder, it is beaten black and blue . . . .').[5]

The son of a house-painter, Leopold Auer was born in the small town of Veszprem. He played the violin from the age of six and took his first lessons with the local church organist. When he was nine, he entered the Budapest Conservatory under Ridley Kohne, who was also concert master at the Budapest National Opera House. (Kohne's colleague on the first desk was Carl Huber, whose son, Eugen, later became famous as Jenö Hubay.) Paris dominated the violin scene at this time and was a magnet for aspiring performers. In his book *Violin Playing as I Teach It*, Auer tells us that despite the importance of the conservatory at Leipzig, neither this nor the one at Vienna were well known outside the German-speaking countries. But as his parents could not afford to send him to Paris, Auer went to Vienna, where he studied with Jacob Dont (1815–88) at the conservatory. He completed his course in 1858, aged 18, having won the coveted medal and diploma, which served him as a musical passport in the provincial towns in which he played. In 1862, he continued his studies with Joachim at Hanover. Afterwards, Auer toured as a virtuoso, playing at the Gewandhaus in Leipzig and at other leading concert halls in Germany, Holland, Scandinavia and England.

A key factor in Auer's development had been the training with Dont in Vienna. Dont, who had been taught by Böhm, was one of the most influential figures in the development of the Viennese School, represented over several generations by Auer's pupils: Mischa Elman, Efrem Zimbalist, Toscha Seidel, Isolde Menges, Nathan Milstein and Jascha Heifetz.

In 1868 Auer succeeded Wieniawski as professor of violin at St Petersburg Conservatory. He served under three tsars, Alexanders II and III, and the ill-fated Nicholas II, who knighted him in 1894. While there, he founded the famous St Petersburg Quartet. Although Auer's influence in St Petersburg was considerable, it was Wieniawski who founded the Russian School. Milstein, who studied with Auer at St Petersburg, considered Auer's great strength to have been that he did not know too much: 'If you asked him a specific question about the playing of a certain passage, he would say, "Go away and think it out for yourself." In the long run it was the best way because you develop your own style and do not copy anyone else.'[6] This is borne out by the widely diverging performing styles and personalities of his pupils.

Auer incorporated into his teaching many of the highly individual characteristics of Joachim, Wieniawski and Sarasate, and his insistence upon sonorous tone and a strong mental approach to study brought violin playing into a new era. He placed the greatest importance on purity of intonation and tone, neatness of execution and good taste. But it was the dynamic force of his personality that inspired his pupils and thus enabled him to wrest the best results from them. Disliking the excessive vibrato which came into vogue in the last two decades of the nineteenth century, he advised his students to use it sparingly, and then only on sustained notes. Like Corelli, he was adamant about bow technique and recommended practising bowing exercises for a whole year before addressing the left-hand technique. He was also against the use of either shoulder pad or rest. He considered that the presence of any extra body destroyed the vibrations of the violin, and maintained that if the instrument is held properly, no such support is necessary. Needless to say, Auer's most famous pupils avoided shoulder rests.

One of the best descriptions of the Auer 'sound' comes from Carl Flesch: 'it seemed to possess a roundness and mellowness not easily to be found elsewhere'.[7] Flesch made a particular study of bowing, and concluded that the Russians placed the index finger slightly higher (*c*.1cm) on the stick towards the wrist than was customary in the Franco-Belgian School. Flesch himself adopted this manner of holding the bow and described it in great detail in the first volume of *Die Kunst des Violon-Spiels* (1923). Many modern players use the 'Russian' hold.

The latter half of the nineteenth century proved a vintage period for great teachers. Auer, the first important influence of his time, was closely followed by two more Hungarians and a Czech: Jenö Hubay, Carl Flesch and Otakar Ševčík.

With Hubay's appointment at the Budapest Conservatory in 1886, there came into being a specifically Hungarian School. Flesch brought together three important streams of violin playing – the Viennese, the Franco-Belgian and the Russian – in his teaching. Ševčík was the first to analyse the fundamentals of violin technique and devise a system which could reliably produce a Paganini-like facility.

When Ševčík was over 80, he was asked how he managed to remain energetic throughout a day which began at 5 a.m. and ended at 1 a.m. the next morning. 'A vegetarian diet, no strong liquor and long walks'[8] was the instant response. Had he been less modest, he might have added that simplicity of nature, innate generosity and a love of work were also contributory factors. His enthusiasm was such that in order to attend a pupil's concert, he would travel for hours, third class, in the icy carriage of a branch line train.

The son of a schoolmaster, Ševčík (1852–1934) was born in the Bohemian hamlet of Horažd'ovice and entered the Prague Conservatory at the age of 14, having twice failed the entrance examination. One learned adjudicator rejected him as hopeless and entirely without talent; fortunately, a rich patron intervened and he was placed with Antonin Bennewitz (1833–1926), a pupil of Moritz Mildner (1812–65) who had studied with a Viotti pupil, Friedrich Wilhelm Pixis (1785–1842).

Following the completion of his studies, Ševčík toured successfully as a soloist and held a number of leaderships in important orchestras, including that of the Mozarteum at Salzburg. While he was professor of violin at the Imperial School of Music at Kiev (1875–92) he completed his work on his system of study. He left Russia to take up the post of principal professor at the Prague Conservatory, and devoted himself to teaching for the rest of his life.

The loss of the sight of his left eye and increasing attacks of shyness on the concert platform merely confirmed his own belief that his true vocation lay in teaching. During his 14 years at Prague, he put his system into practice. The 12-year-old Jan Kubelík was one of his first pupils. Ševčík produced a generation of virtuosos who were living proof of the brilliance of his teaching, from the Russian Michael Zacharewitch (1879–1959), and later another Russian, Efrem Zimbalist, to the Viennese Erica Morini.

As Ševčík's fame spread, he was invited to hold classes throughout Europe and in the USA. From 1909 to 1919 he was principal violin professor at the Vienna Music Academy, after which he returned to Prague. In 1933, he organised the first English Masters' School to be held in Britain, at the Guildhall School of Music. But it was at Pisek, a picturesque, sleepy little town in southern Bohemia, that Ševčík founded a summer school that drew violinists from all over the world. After the First World War, Ševčík resigned from his post in Prague in order to devote himself totally to his school.

Simplicity ruled Ševčík's personal life, and the room in which he taught in Prague reflected his personality. One student said it resembled a railway station waiting room, with neither carpets nor furniture; the austerity was relieved by hundreds of photographs which lined the drab walls. Lessons were held daily, from seven in the morning to ten at night, except Sunday. On Saturday evenings Ševčík would join his students in a little restaurant run by a Czech who had lived in New York; here he would converse on any subject and in almost any language. He extorted high fees from those who could afford them, but he could be generous to those who could not. He gave free lessons to a number of poorer students and, if they ran short of money on the course, he would invite them to eat 'on the house' and invariably slipped them a little extra cash to help with the journey home.

Ševčík could not tolerate laziness in his pupils, nor the slightest lapse in intonation. In a *bravura* passage he would interrupt a pupil to announce: 'Your 1st, 3rd, 9th and 15th notes were flat, your 8th and 12th were slightly sharp!'[9]

Ševčík's candour was sometimes acutely embarrassing. On one occasion, Kubelík, at the height of his fame, interrupted a world tour to visit Pisek. He had agreed to play the Beethoven and Paganini concertos with a students' orchestra (conducted by his son, the young Rafael Kubelík, then at the start of his career), in the old man's honour. The Paganini held the audience spellbound. Then, halfway through the first movement of the Beethoven, Ševčík got up from his seat in the front row and left the room. The soloist gave no sign of having noticed, but as a student remarked: 'If Kubelík had not been as embarrassed as the audience, he must have been a great actor.'[10]

Ševčík's method is based on the semitone system. In his treatise, he wrote: 'The semi-tones are produced on all the strings with the same fingers, thus giving rise to the same fingering on all the strings, so that the beginner experiences no difficulty in finding the intervals, because all the stoppings are the same on each string, and this materially helps him in acquiring pure intonation.'[11]

His guiding maxim was that 'slow practice is the basis of technical perfection'[12] and he allocated a greater part of each lesson to teaching his students 'how to practise'. He knew the disastrous results of mindless repetition of mistakes, and he was also aware that it is often the talented pupil who has the greatest difficulty with technical problems. Paradoxically, Ševčík's genius lay in the fact that he despised pure technique and yet devoted his life to the perfection of it. His favourite teaching pieces were by Paganini, Ernst, Wieniawski and Vieuxtemps.

His method has endured because it is based on scientific principles. 'Let us consider the universe which is ruled by the eternal laws. Symmetry, number and logic prevail everywhere and each phenomenon is subject to the universal rhythm.'[13] He maintained that the same cause and effect logic could be applied to learning the technique of a musical instrument. 'Whosoever carries within himself an ideal that he wishes to express, must have as his prerequisite, absolute mastery of his means of expression. Art must not tolerate any mediocrity and that is why technical perfection plays a prime role in matters of musical aesthetics.'[14]

Jenö Hubay (1858–1937) had his first lessons from his father, a professor of violin at the Budapest Conservatory. Although he made his first highly successful public appearance at the age of eleven, it is much to his father's credit that he waited until his son was 13 before sending him to Berlin for five years to study with Joachim at the Hochschule. Hubay subsequently embarked upon a highly successful solo career. His playing was a mixture of Magyar, German and Franco-Belgian elements, individual and appealing in style. The normally highly critical Flesch remarked that, although he heard him only once, he considered him to be 'a noble violinist with outstanding technical and musical qualities'.[15]

In 1878 Hubay met Vieuxtemps in Paris, and for the remaining three years of the older man's life the two were close friends. Vieuxtemps dedicated his Seventh Violin Concerto to Hubay and, through his influence, Hubay succeeded him at the Brussels Conservatoire in 1882. Hubay had found his true vocation. Four years later, his father died, and the Budapest Conservatory offered his post to the son. He accepted because, like most Hungarians, he had a fierce streak of patriotism, and saw the post as the opportunity to consolidate his own teaching ideas in their natural, national setting.

Hubay never had the large following of Ševčík or Flesch, but indisputably he raised the standards of violin playing in Hungary, and three of his star pupils later achieved phenomenal success on the concert platform: Franz von Vecsey (1893–1935), Joseph Szigeti and Emil Telmányi (1892–1988). Eugene Ormandy was also a Hubay pupil in Budapest, starting his performing life as a concert violinist before turning to conducting. Flesch tells us that the Hubay students could be relied upon to have a very well developed left-hand technique and that they had 'a natural feeling for tonal beauty', but he criticises their vibrato as too slow and too wide; and he bemoans a 'lack of dynamic differentiation'.[16]

Looking back, Joseph Szigeti was struck by 'the lack of solid musical foundation and outlook' during his studies with Hubay. It seemed to him that he had played the Beethoven concerto 'without awareness of its place in the microcosm that Beethoven's scores represent for us'. In the classroom, an atmosphere of 'puerile technical rivalry' prevailed; his students were completely absorbed in the externals of their craft. But Szigeti does not consider that this diminishes Hubay's authority, and placed the blame more on the parents, who 'generated such an unhealthy impatience'.[17]

A generation later, Nicholas Roth (1903–90), was a pupil in Hubay's masterclass; aged 17, he took his place alongside half a dozen boys aged between 12 and 14. Hubay was always addressed as 'your Excellency' and his morning entrance involved almost pontifical ritual: they would all stand to attention while Hubay led a procession of younger professors, one of whom carried his violin case. He would solemnly remove the fiddle, tune it, and hand it ceremoniously to the master. In Roth's opinion Hubay was a first-class violinist. He heard him when he was 72, playing the Bach Chaconne from the Partita in D minor, and said that the chords were just as articulate as if they had been played with the out-curved bow.[18]

Carl Flesch (1873–1944) was born in Moson in Hungary, the son of a doctor. He studied with Jakob Grün (1837–1916) in Vienna from the age of seven, and later, under Martin Marsick, at the Paris Conservatoire. Not only did Flesch admire Marsick's playing, but he found an affinity with his perfectionist principles. 'It was he who taught me to think logically without endangering the spirit of the living world of art; and to him I owe the development of what later made me realise that teaching was the noblest of artistic activities.'[19]

Despite early struggles with the chauvinism prevalent at the conservatoire, Flesch carried off the first prize in 1894 and, after a stint of orchestral playing, enjoyed a successful solo career. One of his most significant undertakings was a series of five concerts in Berlin in 1905, when he covered the entire violin repertory chronologically from Corelli to Reger.

Unlike Ševčík and Hubay, Flesch did not forsake concert-giving for teaching; for him they were parallel pursuits. He played with most of the world's leading orchestras and under the greatest conductors, who included Arthur Nikisch, Hans Richter, Richard Strauss, Wilhelm Furtwängler, Willem Mengelberg, Bruno Walter and Leopold Stokowski. Flesch had a built-in aversion to conductors as a breed – a fact he never tried to disguise. He also had a distinguished international career in chamber music, most notably in partnership with the pianist Artur Schnabel. They formed a trio with Hugo Becker and, later, with Gregor Piatigorsky.

Flesch's first teaching post was in Romania in 1897, when he became professor of violin at the Bucharest Conservatory. He considered that it had a decisive influence on his 'human and artistic development'.[20] At the time he rarely made solo appearances and, when prevailed upon to do so, he walked onto the platform with reluctance. He brooded over his solo career and 'slid into the muddy channel of self-tormenting, hypochondriac fussiness'.[21] Flesch's opinion of himself did improve, and he went on to teach or play in almost every major musical centre.

Flesch made his first highly successful visit to the USA in 1914 and, ten years later, he was engaged as principal violin teacher at the newly-formed Curtis Institute in Philadelphia. From 1926 to 1935 he lived in Baden-Baden, where, in his own home, he established a school, attracting pupils who would become some of the greatest violinists of the day, including Henryk Szeryng, Thomas Matthews, Ida Haendel and Ginette Neveu.

Ida Haendel recalled that his method of teaching was, for the time, unconventional, but later developed into the masterclass as we know it today. There was always a small audience of celebrated musicians, pupils and guests, as Flesch considered this made the transition from lesson to concert platform a less painful journey. He would always allow a pupil to play through without interruption, and when he or she had finished, he would 'slowly rise from the chair upon which he sat like a Caesar'[22] and read from the notes he had jotted on the score. First came the good points and then the onslaught from his merciless tongue. Although pupils cringed, they seldom bore resentment. Haendel never personally feared Flesch, but instead, liked and respected him: the 'head-washings'[23] as Flesch himself called them, were just as acceptable to her as the praise.

Flesch's book of studies was published in 1911, and the first of his two volumes of *The Art of Violin Playing* in 1923, the second following in 1928. Of these Professor Ševčík wrote to him: 'With your work you have provided violinists with a bible. . . . nothing connected with the violin and violin playing has been left out of account, and to every question you have found a convincing answer.'[24]

Flesch encouraged the development of each pupil's individuality and established sure methods of overcoming technical problems. His treatment of bowing is of the greatest importance. Norbert Brainin, who studied with both Carl Flesch and Max Rostal (himself a pupil of Flesch), says: 'His own bowing was of the Franco-Belgian style, but he taught his pupils in the Russian manner. He believed that the Russian school of Leopold Auer was the most advantageous for good violin playing.'[25] In the first volume of his classic work, Flesch wrote: 'Personally, I am firmly convinced that just as today, after centuries of slavery, the theory of necessity for the unimpeded freedom of movement of the upper arm has been accepted, so the Russian manner of holding the bow will be exclusively taught in 50 years' time, because of the energy saving and exceptional tonal qualities inherent in it.'[26] This prediction was not far out. Although some use a combination of Russian and Franco-Belgian techniques, most great players today favour the Russian hold.

As a man, Flesch was highly complex. His posthumously published memoirs give an acutely observed and remarkably objective picture of his times. He reveals his own weaknesses with as much frankness as those of his friends. He was obviously something of a dual personality. There are instances of the dedicated teacher who spared no part of himself to reach a certain goal, and occasional glimpses of the frustrated virtuoso locked inside a pedagogic hair shirt. When describing his early days in Paris, the exacting professor identifies himself with Bohemian Montmartre, and seems to have been as happy in the company of pimps and tarts as with musicians, painters and penniless aristocrats.

The number of Flesch pupils is said to be in the region of a thousand. Flesch had boundless energy and, in spite of a heart condition, taught up to within a few days of his death. His last physical action was to write several postcards to his pupils informing them of the dates of their next lesson. He died while the cards were in the post. The Carl Flesch Medal 'for excellence in violin playing', instituted at the Guildhall School of Music in 1945, is a fitting memorial to a great man.

A pupil of Hubay, Ilona Feher (1901–88), was one of the best-loved teachers of her day. She specialised in the teaching of young children, who seemed to stay with her until they were adult. Among them were Shlomo Mintz, Shmuel Ashkenasi and Pinchas Zukerman. She was born in Budapest, the daughter of a well-known Jewish author and playwright, and had her first lessons on the piano when she was seven. Two years later she took up the violin and, after lessons with several local teachers, she completed her studies with Hubay at the Franz Liszt Academy. Her concert career took her all over Europe, but was soon curtailed at the outbreak of the Second World War. When the Nazis entered Hungary, most of her possessions were confiscated and she and her daughter were taken to a concentration camp outside Budapest. In 1944, with the help of some peasants, they escaped and Feher immediately formed a small orchestra of 20 women who played light music in restaurants. She later returned to the concert platform but could not accept the authoritarian restrictions prevalent in Hungary at the time, and in 1949 she emigrated to Israel.

She had always enjoyed teaching children and she now had the opportunity to train the young talent she encountered in her new country. She looked upon it as a small way of compensating for the terrible destruction of a whole generation and culture in Europe.

Feher accepted only 'pure beginners' and preferred to take them when they were about eight. She presided over classes of 15 twice a week and expected them to work hard in between times. An unashamed perfectionist, she stretched her pupils to the limit. She did not subscribe to a 'method' as such, considering every student to be different, and devising fingerings in keeping with the size and shape of their hands. She believed that bowings should be adjusted throughout an artist's life to suit their personal expression.[27]

Optimism and generosity were just two of Ilona Feher's many endearing qualities. She encouraged her more talented pupils to further their studies with other great teachers abroad. In a more practical way, she gave all of the fine instruments she had collected over the years to her more talented students in order to help their careers.

Sandor Végh (1905–97), also a Hubay pupil, was not only a fine solo violinist in his own right, but had a great gift for teaching; he held professorships at numerous conservatories in Europe, including the Franz Liszt Academy of Music in Budapest and the Mozarteum in Salzburg. He also made a tremendous impact on the musical life of the UK when, together with Hilary Behrens, he founded the International Musicians Seminar (IMS) at Prussia Cove, Cornwall in 1972.

Végh was born in Koloszvar in Transylvania and studied at the Liszt Academy Budapest with Hubay for violin, Leo Weiner for chamber music and Zoltán Kodály for composition. In 1931 he made his debut with the Hungarian Trio, touring with them for many years in addition to his solo appearances. He was leader of the Hungarian String Quartet from 1935 to 1938, and in 1940 he formed the Végh String Quartet, which he led for 38 years. They travelled the world and made many recordings, including complete cycles of the Beethoven and Bartók quartets. Végh was a close friend of Pablo Casals, and for some 15 years he appeared as a soloist in the festivals at Prades, playing under many famous conductors.

Throughout his performing life Végh devoted a considerable time to teaching, both at musical institutions and masterclasses throughout the world. His masterclasses at Prussia Cove were riveting. He could pinpoint problems exactly and then demonstrate how to remedy them – accompanied by groans and sighs, with arms waving windmill-like in every direction.

When in his sixties Végh was asked if he hoped to remain active in old age, he contended that everything to do with music retarded the process of ageing. He would reel off the names of famous musicians who had lived well into their late eighties or nineties, Pierre Monteux, Artur Rubinstein, Felix Weingartner, Leopold Stokowski and many others, and would retort: 'Have you ever seen a senile musician?'[28] Happily, he was still *compos mentis* and making music to the end of his life.

Toronto-based Lorand Fenyves (*b*.1918) is another stalwart who seemingly ignores the confines of age. He is still teaching at three institutions, the University of Toronto, the Royal Conservatory in Toronto and the University of Western Ontario in London, Ontario. Fenyves was born in Budapest and took his principal studies with Hubay and Kodály at the Franz Liszt Academy, where he graduated at 16. He wasted no time in mounting the concert platform and achieved considerable success; a meeting with Bronislav Huberman in 1936 brought about a solo engagement with the Israel Philharmonic Orchestra under Toscanini, and the following year he was offered the leadership of the orchestra. He became interested in teaching and was one of the co-founders of the Israel Academy of Music and the Israel String Quartet in Tel Aviv. But, in 1957, he was invited by Ernest Ansermet to lead the Suisse Romande Orchestra in Geneva. During his 20 years in Switzerland he also taught the 'classe de virtuosité' at the Geneva Conservatoire. In 1963 he emigrated to Canada and took Canadian nationality in 1971.

That year he became associated with the Banff Centre for the Arts. At his jubilee concert there in 1996, he performed the Beethoven concerto with the Winnipeg Symphony Orchestra. The leader of the orchestra, Gwen Hoebig, said: 'None of us will ever forget the demonstration in proper technique of pizzicato he gave at the end of the first movement cadenza. His performance of both the "Kreutzer" Sonata and the Concerto were a reflection of his life as a musician and educator – noble, at times both profound and exquisitely beautiful, but always with a twinkle in his eye. Towards the end of the concerto his E string broke and wrapped itself round the A string – rendering both A and E useless – just in time for the arpeggios in the Coda! Somehow he managed to finish climbing up the D string, and seeming to convey that he was completely unaware that something could be wrong!'[29]

**Notes**

1. Dettmar Dressel, *The Strad*, February 1952, p. 296.
2. Flesch, *Memoirs*, p. 33.

3. Van der Straeten, *The History of the Violin*, ii, p. 264.

4. *New York Times,* 24 March 1917.

5. Hanslick, *Music Criticisms 1846–99,* 1881.

6. Quoted from interview, M.C.

7. Flesch, op. cit., p. 253.

8. Reid Stewart, *The Strad*, June 1933, p. 59.

9. Ibid., p. 58.

10. Granville Case, *The Strad*, October 1966, p. 207.

11. Schule der Violine-Technik Op. 1 (1881), Ševčík treatise.

12. Stewart, *The Strad*, June 1933, p. 58.

13–14. Andrée Alvin, *Monde Musical*, 28 February 1934.

15. Flesch, op. cit., p. 153.

16. Ibid., p. 154.

17. Szigeti, *With Strings Attached*, pp. 87–8.

18. Quoted from interview, M.C.

19. Flesch, op. cit., p. 66.

20. Ibid., p. 161.

21. Ibid., p. 174.

22–3. Haendel, *Woman with Violin*, p. 73.

24. Flesch, op. cit., p. 371.

25. Quoted from interview, M.C.

26. Flesch, *The Art of Violin Playing*, i.

27. *The Strad*, September 1985, p. 343.

28. Quoted from interview, M.C.

29. *The Strad*, June 1997, p. 627.

# 16  'As the birds sing'

Joachim and Sarasate emerge as the last representatives of the two opposing forces that dominated violin playing in the second half of the nineteenth century, Joachim representing seriousness and Sarasate, wizardry. Inevitably, as the powers of these two poles of genius diminished, there arose a need for something new – a synthesis of the two approaches to violin playing, which would unite intensity of feeling with technical perfection. In the last two decades of the nineteenth century the need was largely fulfilled by the Belgian Eugène Ysaÿe (1858–1931), who 'played the fiddle as the birds sing'[1] and whose personal magnetism was second only to Paganini's.

Ysaÿe's family had been humble nailmakers since the sixteenth century, but his father ignored tradition by becoming a tailor. A good amateur violinist, he was also musical director at the cathedral church of Liège. Eugène had lessons on the violin at the age of four from his father. Ebullient and self-willed, he would have preferred the boisterous company of his friends to the interminable practice regime imposed by his parents. Nevertheless, he entered Liège Conservatoire in 1865, won a second prize after his first year, but was expelled in 1869 for failing to 'work'. For the next few years, Ysaÿe accompanied his father in local musical activities, during which time he was briefly, and unsuccessfully, apprenticed to an armourer.

One day, in 1873, a chance encounter with Henri Vieuxtemps changed the direction of his life. The virtuoso was passing Ysaÿe's house, heard someone playing the Adagio from his own Fourth Concerto rather well and knocked on the door to ask the name of the performer. The meeting was fortuitous for all concerned: Vieuxtemps became greatly attached to the boy, whom he was to regard as his spiritual successor, and Ysaÿe in turn became devoted to his mentor and friend for the remaining years of the old man's life. When Vieuxtemps heard the story of Ysaÿe's dismissal from the conservatoire, he had him reinstated immediately, this time into Rodolphe Massart's masterclass. His efforts were amply rewarded when Ysaÿe carried off both the first prize and the gold medal.

Vieuxtemps invited Ysaÿe to study with him at Brussels, but, when he arrived, he found the master had suffered a stroke and had lost the use of both hands. When Vieuxtemps went to Algiers in search of a cure, Henryk Wieniawski, who succeeded him at the conservatoire, was entrusted with his protégé for the next two years. (Here there is an interesting dual link with Viotti, who had taught both Robberechts and Kreutzer, whose pupils, Bériot and Massart, had in turn been the teachers of Vieuxtemps and Wieniawski.)

When Vieuxtemps returned to Paris, he sent for 'the young violinist with the marvellous E string',[2] and Ysaÿe, sponsored by a grant from the authorities at Liège, joined him for three years. During the summer vacations, the young student earned extra money as a solo violinist with the Kursaal Orchestra at Ostende. His beautiful 'line' attracted much attention, and it was here that the German conductor Benjamin Bilse heard him and offered him the concertmastership of his own orchestra in Berlin. Ysaÿe held this post for two years; his playing aroused so much interest that eminent visiting musicians attended concerts especially to hear him. In 1881 Ysaÿe left Berlin for Paris, where he joined the coterie of young composers centred round César Franck, Ernest Chausson and Claude Debussy – all three of whom later dedicated works to him.

Although acknowledged at an early age by fellow musicians, Ysaÿe was in his twenties before he achieved anything like the public acclaim received by Joachim when still in a velvet suit. His first important concert was in Paris in 1883 under Edouard Colonne, when he played Edouard Lalo's *Symphonie Espagnole* and Camille Saint-Saëns' *Introduction and Rondo Capriccioso*. One critic wrote: 'This was a triumph of execution, style and presentation.'[3]

Ysaÿe appeared in England for the first time in the spring of 1891, but did not win hearts as easily as he had in Paris. George Bernard Shaw, then writing for *The World*, did not care for his playing and, characteristically, made no bones about it. While admitting that his technical mastery made him Sarasate's only serious rival, Shaw abhorred 'his readiness to sacrifice higher artistic qualities to the speed of a dazzlingly impossible presto'.[4] When Ysaÿe played at a Philharmonic Society concert at St James's Hall in March, Shaw was scathing: 'His determination to cap feats impossible to other violinists and his enormous self-assertiveness, really broke up and destroyed the Beethoven Concerto.' The cadenzas were Ysaÿe's own; Shaw castigated them as 'monstrous excrescences on the movements, nailed on, not grafted in', and maintained that they 'have no form, being merely examples of madly difficult ways of playing the themes that have been reasonably and beautifully presented by Beethoven. One comfort is that since Ysaÿe can hardly play them himself, nobody else is likely to be able to play them at all.' Shaw also found Ysaÿe's personality offensive. He accused him of 'elbowing aside the conductor, eclipsing the little handful of an orchestra . . . and all but showing Beethoven the door', continuing: 'The fact is he has created himself so recently that he is not yet tired of his consummated self.'[5] A few weeks later, however, Shaw wrote more favourably after hearing Ysaÿe in a recital. He was particularly impressed with his interpretation of chamber music. Later, in the eyes of English music lovers, Ysaÿe could do no wrong, and in 1901 he was awarded the Philharmonic Society's gold medal, an honour he shared with Joachim.

Arthur Symons wrote in the *Saturday Review*:

You see the music in the great black figure [Ysaÿe stood over six feet four], that sways like a python: in the eyes that blink, and seem about to shed luxurious tears; the face like an actor's mask, enigmatic, quivering with emotion. . . . The lips suck up music voluptuously . . . the tones . . . are pleasure, not joy; the soul is not in them, but a luxury which becomes divine because it is an ecstasy, even if a carnal ecstasy. A marvellous passage of double-stopping in one of the cadenzas in Beethoven was played as if one's teeth met in a peach. . . . He floats on the surface of a river of pure sound, and dreams; every note like drops of water. . . . His technique, unclassical, romantic, though finished in perfection, is part of his unconscious revelation of himself.

Symons closes with some interesting discussion on the musician's approach to the 'sound' of each individual composer. 'Ysaÿe listens for that sound in the depths of Beethoven and on the heights of Mozart; it comes to him living and naked, and he clothes it with silken garments, as if it were a woman.'[6]

If this description of Ysaÿe's playing and personal magnetism seems exaggerated, we have only to consult the hypercritical Flesch, who, characteristically, cannot allow Ysaÿe to enjoy unmitigated praise, but still finds plenty of good things to say. Flesch called him 'the most outstanding and individual violinist I have ever heard in all my life'.[7] He described his tone as 'big and noble', and capable of responding to his wishes like 'a horse to its rider'. His vibrato was 'the spontaneous expression of his feeling' and very far removed from the restrained quiver 'only on expressive notes' which had previously been accepted as correct. His left-hand agility and intonation was 'of Sarasate-like perfection', and 'there was no kind of bowing that did not show tonal perfection as well as musical feeling'. Flesch also extolled Ysaÿe's interpretation, 'the impulsive romantic . . . concerned not so much with the printed note values . . . as with the spirit that cannot be reproduced graphically'.[8] Another endorsement came from the late Josef Gingold, professor of violin at Indiana University, who had been a pupil of Ysaÿe: 'His *rubato* was indescribable. You could set a metronome and whatever happened in the duration of that bar, would come out, metronomically correct. He was on the beat every time.'[9]

Ysaÿe's first trip to the USA in 1894 was considerably more rewarding than his British debut. When he arrived on the American continent he was a mature artist and the respected leader of the Belgian school; he was also founder and conductor of the Ysaÿe Orchestral Concerts in Brussels, at which many famous artists appeared. He was principal professor at Brussels Conservatoire, a position he had held since 1886, and had been decorated by all the crowned heads of Europe. The Americans were utterly charmed by him, the women were almost hysterical in their admiration. He was showered with critical acclaim. 'He plays with a bold and manly vigour, and yet with exquisite delicacy . . . "he creeps up under your vest". He disarms criticism, and he seems to be more completely part of his violin and his violin of him than . . . any other player. . . . He combines Sarasate's tenderness of tone and showy technique with more manliness and sincerity than Sarasate gives.'[10]

One of Ysaÿe's greatest triumphs was when he played the Bach E major concerto under Arthur Nikisch in Berlin in 1899. The Berliners had reservations about

Belgians who play the classics and, like the British, were misty-eyed in adoration of their great Joachim, but Ysaÿe won them over. The audience were deeply moved by the dignity and poetry of his reading and recalled him 15 times to acknowledge their emotional ovation.

During the First World War, all three of Ysaÿe's sons fought at the front while he and his wife Louise (the daughter of a high-ranking army officer) escaped to England. They left behind all their possessions, with the exception of Ysaÿe's violin – a beautiful Guarneri del Gesù, dated 1740 (later owned by Isaac Stern). In London, they lived at 49 Rutland Gate, in Kensington, where Ysaÿe was lionised by a great circle of pupils and admirers. His soirées were major events in London musical life, and he counted among his many English friends Edward Elgar, Ralph Vaughan Williams, Henry Wood and Thomas Beecham, among others. At this time he also gave recitals with the young Artur Rubinstein, Vladimir Pachmann, Frederic Lamond and Lionel Tertis. In 1918, Ysaÿe returned to the USA, accepting the conductorship of the Cincinnati Symphony Orchestra and the chair of music at the conservatory. He promoted the works of contemporary Belgian and French composers, and produced a generation of American performers. Always a strong advocate for performances of modern music, he gave many performances of the now famous Violin Sonata dedicated to him in 1886 by César Franck, when that composer was still completely unknown.

A few days before Ysaÿe's wedding in September 1886, a celebration banquet was held in Luxembourg, to which the Paris coterie came, headed by Charles Bordes, the French scholar and composer. After the speeches had been made, Bordes presented a manuscript to Ysaÿe with greetings from 'le père Franck', who had composed a sonata especially for his marriage. Overcome with emotion, Ysaÿe said he would like to perform it there and then. He asked Léontine Bordes-Pène, the distinguished pianist and sister-in-law of Charles, if she would consent to be his partner in this unique première. The two proceeded to sight-read the sonata, moving the guests to tears. Madame Bordes-Pène also joined Ysaÿe in the first public performance in Brussels on 16 December the same year.

Ysaÿe returned to Belgium in 1922. His wife died in 1924 and, four years later, he married Jeannette Dincin, one of his American pupils who had come to study with him in Brussels. Ysaÿe was then 70 and his bride only 24, but it would appear to have been one of those happy marriages for which elderly maestros seem to have a flair. Ysaÿe's health was already problematic, but his young wife persuaded him to maintain a strict diet to combat the diabetes from which he suffered for many years. He was never able to overcome the attacks of cramp and the ever-present tremors which by then affected his hands.

As a teacher, Ysaÿe's skill lay in his ability to demonstrate. He always taught with his fiddle in his hand. When the American Louis Persinger (1887–1966) first heard Ysaÿe at the Gewandhaus in Leipzig, he did not rest until he had secured the opportunity to study with him in Belgium in 1905. Josef Gingold, another pupil, gives us valuable first-hand evidence of Ysaÿe's skill as a teacher. He was auditioned at 'La

Chanterelle' (literally 'E (top) string'), the magnificent summer home Ysaÿe built for himself at Le Zoute in Belgium.

> I had prepared the first movement of the Brahms concerto and arrived, full of enthusiasm. Ysaÿe said very calmly in that deep voice of his, 'Will you please play a G major, three-octave scale for me?' Momentarily I was stunned, but I did what he asked. This was followed by my having to play scales in every conceivable manner of bowing, and finally I was allowed to play the Brahms.[11]

Gingold was accepted as a pupil, with the stipulation that he learn to speak French.

The first technique that Ysaÿe corrected in Gingold's playing was string crossing (moving the bow from one string to another without a break), by demonstrating the Franco-Belgian method of using the forearm stroke to develop a more powerful and sustained tone connecting one string with another. It was two months before Ysaÿe was satisfied with Gingold's bow arm. Only then did they begin on repertory, the first work being Vieuxtemps' Fifth Concerto.

Ysaÿe's dry sense of humour was an outstanding aspect of his personality. Once, when the 18-year-old Gingold was preparing the Beethoven concerto for his first important solo engagement in Antwerp, he had some extra lessons. The closing bars of the solo part in the last movement are marked *pianissimo* on the score, with the final cadence from the full orchestra, contrasting, *fortissimo*.

> I played it and tried to observe the composer's intentions, but Ysaÿe shook his head, 'No, no, it's too soft. Play it like *this*,' and he took up his own fiddle and what he gave was a good forte. Normally, I was a good student. I never argued with him, but this time I was a little worried. I knew that if Ysaÿe himself played it loud, everybody would say, 'What an innovation', but if I, an unknown, would do so they would say, 'The boy can't read music!' So I ventured to say, 'Maître, do you not think that if one plays this passage softly and then when the orchestra comes in fortissimo, it is rather a nice surprise?' He smiled and answered me slowly. . . . My boy, if you have not surprised them until then, it's too late!'[12]

Ysaÿe had a heart of gold and his generosity extended to all kinds of people. Success brought him riches and distinction, but although he had a sense of grandeur which he could summon as the occasion demanded, he remained essentially an 'ordinary' man of the people. In fact, the artificial trappings of success occasionally disgusted him so much that he was prone to fits of melancholia, in sharp contrast to his normally ebullient disposition. At these times he took refuge in his magnificent library at 'La Chanterelle', for despite his initial lack of education, he had acquired a wide knowledge of various subjects, including fluency in several languages.

An inveterate pipe smoker, Ysaÿe would delight his students at the conservatoire by lighting up right under the 'No Smoking' sign. Once he was smoking while waiting to go on stage, when the duty fireman approached him politely. 'Excuse me, Monsieur, there is no smoking here.' Ysaÿe continued to puff away and, between his teeth, calmly replied, 'Don't be stupid. You can see perfectly well that there is.'[13]

A virtuoso in every sense, Ysaÿe brought a magical individuality to every performance. His platform manner was easy, his movements relaxed. For Gingold, his lasting memory of Ysaÿe's artistry was his rendering of a long phrase, the *grande ligne*. His memory was phenomenal. Ernest Chausson dedicated his famous *Poème* to Ysaÿe in 1898. When he played the work for the first time, he had only had time to run through it with a pianist and study the score on the train; after only one orchestral rehearsal, he had memorised it for a perfect performance. As a composer, Ysaÿe contributed some of the most attractive and, for his time, the most advanced solo sonatas in the violin repertory. They incorporate almost every technical gymnastic for the performer and are fiendishly difficult. In many ways, both as composer and performer, he was ahead of his time, although strangely enough he deferred playing the Brahms concerto until he was over 40. Joachim's equivocal comment on that occasion had been that he had 'never heard it played like that before'.[14]

Ysaÿe fought for many causes. He was an avid protagonist of the movement to bring about copyright laws in favour of the composer. He was a staunch defender of Paganini and collected much evidence to disprove the legends of his empty acrobatics. He maintained that without the technical innovations of virtuosos, the development of the symphonic genre would have progressed more slowly. Ysaÿe would tell his students that compositions by virtuoso-performers are necessary to instrumental art because it is only by practical demonstration that the composer can be sure that a work is playable. Gingold recalls that in the 1920s, when he was preparing for his first recital in Brussels, he planned to perform the Paganini D major Concerto in the Wilhelmj version, in which only the first movement (a fashionable showpiece of the time) is played. But Ysaÿe insisted that he play the entire concerto and, furthermore, directed him to tune the violin up a semitone, as Paganini had, in order to adhere properly to tradition.

When Ysaÿe was dying, he was visited by the young violinist Philippe Newman, who decided to play for him. He chose Ysaÿe's Solo Fourth Sonata, which he had dedicated to his great friend Fritz Kreisler. When Newman finished playing, the barely conscious Ysaÿe, who wrongly assumed that it had been Kreisler playing, gave a final benediction: 'Splendid … but the finale … a little too fast.'[15]

## Notes

1. Ysaÿe, *Eugène Ysaÿe*, p. 21.
2. Ibid., p. 29.
3. Ibid., p. 47.
4. George Bernard Shaw, *The World*, 1 April 1891.
5. Ibid., 20 May 1891.
6. *Saturday Review*, 28 December 1907.

7. Flesch, *Memoirs*, p. 78.
8. Ibid., p. 79.
9. Quoted from interview, M.C.
10. Lahee, *Famous Violinists of Today and Yesterday*, pp. 272–3.
11–12. Quoted from interview, M.C.
13. Ysaÿe, op. cit., p. 154.
14. Van der Straeten, *History of the Violoncello*, p. 145.
15. Ysaÿe, op. cit., p. 90.

# 17   Symbol of an Epoch

In the entire history of violin playing there is probably no performer who was more universally loved and admired than Fritz Kreisler. He was the first of the twentieth-century violinists to anticipate the fashion for emotional expression in playing. He appealed to the hearts of his listeners, not only by his virtuosity but by the subtle vitality, humour, sweetness and pathos with which he endowed all his performances.

The young Szigeti was 'bowled over' when he first heard Ysaÿe, Kreisler and Elman in 1905. Although there was disparity in their ages, and their roots were in three different schools, for Szigeti they formed an entity, 'the opening of a door'.[1] The advent of these three, together with Jacques Thibaud and, later, Jascha Heifetz, brought together a group of distinctly individual violinists whose playing nonetheless possessed a common denominator: a new concept of beauty. Kreisler was the high priest of this school.

Born in Vienna in 1875, Kreisler read music before he had learnt his alphabet. His father, a doctor of moderate means and a passion for string quartet playing, gave him his first lessons when he was four. Further instruction from Jacques Auber, concert-master at the Ringtheater, prepared him for his first public performance at the age of seven, when he appeared as supporting artist to the singer, Carlotta Patti, sister of the better-known Adelina. His fee was a box of sweets. The same year he became the youngest pupil ever to be accepted at the Vienna Conservatory under Joseph Hellmesberger for violin and Anton Bruckner for harmony. At the age of ten young Fritz carried off the gold medal.

Endowed with a scholarship to the Paris Conservatoire, he entered Massart's class and was placed with the amiable, if promiscuous, Léo Delibes for composition. This time, in the face of heavy competition from older students, the 12-year-old Kreisler was awarded the *ne plus ultra*, the Prix de Rome. Two years later he toured the USA with the brilliant Ukrainian pianist Moritz Rosenthal (1862–1946). In a velvet suit with knee-breeches, 'Master Fritz Kreisler' performed in 50 concerts for which he was paid $50 a performance. Despite the phenomenal success of the tour, he returned to Vienna, quietly finished his normal education, studied two years at medical school and completed his national service. But, in 1896, at the age of 21, he decided that music was the only career for him.

It came as a shock, when Kreisler auditioned for a place in the Hofoper Orchestra, at the second desk of the first violins, to be turned down by the leader, Arnold Rosé

(1863–1946), because his sight reading was supposedly inadequate. Apart from being a gold medallist at two of the most important musical institutions in Europe, Kreisler had been composing since he was a child. Although self-taught, he was a superb pianist. (Maybe Rosé recognised a superior talent and felt threatened.)

It took almost five years before Kreisler gained due recognition, but the intervening time spent in the Vienna cafés and the famous Tonkünstlerverein (Musicians' Club) afforded him a stimulus he needed. Here he met Brahms, who became his idol and with whom he often played, and Joachim with whom he could seldom agree but enormously admired.

On 23 January 1898, Kreisler made his Viennese debut. With the Vienna Philharmonic Orchestra under Hans Richter, he played Max Bruch's Second Concerto. The critics were impressed with his 'brilliant virtuosity'[2] and 'the sweetness of his tone'.[3] But the opportunity which was to prove decisive came a year later on 1 December 1899, when Nikisch presented him as the soloist at a Berlin Philharmonic Society concert, playing the Mendelssohn concerto. Afterwards, Ysaÿe, who happened to be present, rose to his feet, applauding loudly. The inspired audience followed suit and Fritz Kreisler, virtuoso violinist, became a reality. These two great fiddlers later became close friends.

An amusing sequel to the Berlin triumph came in 1901, when Ysaÿe, engaged to play the Beethoven concerto with Nikisch and the Philharmonic, was taken ill after the morning rehearsal. Kreisler stepped in without rehearsal and played magnificently on a borrowed fiddle (his own had been pawned to pay for the extravagant tastes of 'Mimi', his current lady-love).

When Kreisler appeared at Carnegie Hall in New York on 7 December 1900, he scored a tremendous success. His own orchestration of Tartini's 'Devil's Trill' Sonata, with a brilliant cadenza, inspired rave notices extolling his astonishing violinistic powers. He then completed a twelve-month, coast-to-coast tour that had audiences flocking in their thousands to attend.

On the return voyage to Europe, Kreisler met the beautiful red-headed Harriet Woerz, whom he married the following year. Harriet has been described as powerful and controlling, but she was also generous and quite without fear. No doubt she could be overbearing at times, but she protected the vulnerable Fritz from over-zealous admirers and saw to it that he arrived on the platform, ready to perform. Kreisler never suffered from nerves on stage, but was very retiring in private life.

Kreisler made a disappointing London début in 1902. The *Musical Times* critic, cool and inaccurate in describing him as 'yet another Hungarian', noted that 'although failing to give the impression of being a great executant, he played with intelligence, tenderness of expression, and skill which excited attention'.[4] A few years later, when Kreisler played at one of Henry Wood's concerts at the Queen's Hall, it was quite another matter. Arthur Symons, writing in the 4 May 1907 issue of the *Saturday Review* of Kreisler's interpretation of the Beethoven concerto, said that he 'played it as if Beethoven had revealed it privately, over again, to him . . . His soul seems to confide in his fiddle, and the fiddle tells us the secret … His playing has that energy which comes to flower in grace, with a supple concealed agility, a skill which is never allowed to tell for itself, to mean anything apart from what it expresses.'[5]

On 10 November 1910, the historic world première of the Elgar Violin Concerto, dedicated to Kreisler, took place at the Queen's Hall, in the opening concert of the 99th season of the Philharmonic Society, with Elgar conducting. The critics were unanimous in their praise for all concerned. The *Musical Observer* critic commented that 'the composer was determined that no ordinary violinist should attempt the work, for the solo part is of great difficulty'.[6]

Harriet served as Kreisler's business manager. Some said that she prevented her husband from making his own decisions; others said that, since they were opposites, they complemented each other. Nevertheless, Kreisler adored her, was totally dependent upon her and miserable when they were apart. However, he seldom suffered this deprivation, for wherever Fritz went, Harriet went. Even when he was called up to serve in the Austrian Army in 1914, she became a nurse and got herself assigned to a nearby field hospital.

Later that year, Kreisler was invalided out of the Austrian Army, whereupon he and Harriet returned to the USA. As soon as his health was restored, he resumed his career. He was now a highly successful artist, earning large fees (since 1903) and receiving considerable royalties from his recordings. When he donated a large part of his income to Austrian war orphans and the wounded in Europe, the gesture caused havoc in the USA. He was castigated to such an extent that in 1917, when America entered the war, he was forced to withdraw from all public engagements, at a loss of some $85,000 in broken contracts. Resourceful as ever, Kreisler spent the time composing an operetta called *Apple Blossoms*, which ran for over a year on Broadway.

In 1919, Kreisler returned to the concert platform in a high profile charity concert at Carnegie Hall. He received a five-minute standing ovation before he played a note, and after the concert the audience became almost hysterical in their appreciation of this modest artist who, in the name of patriotism, had been forced off the platform two years earlier. However, this did not signal the end of hostilities: a new militant organisation, the American Legion, was represented at every subsequent Kreisler appearance. At Cornell University, in upstate New York, they cut the electric light cables in the middle of a concert, but Kreisler – unperturbed as always – simply continued to play in the dark.

Kreisler reappeared in Britain in May 1921 and his reception at the Queen's Hall was overwhelming. Nellie Melba presented him with a laurel wreath after the first concerto, and after the second, the great English violinist Albert Sammons presented him with another. But Kreisler waited until the autumn of 1924 to return to Paris. In the event, he was given a heart-warming reception and the audience 'cheered him for hours'.[7] It proved a highly emotional experience for Kreisler. The French acknowledged him as the greatest violinist of his time and, two years later, they made him an officer of the Legion of Honour.

Kreisler now had the world at his feet. He had toured China and Japan in 1923, Australia and New Zealand in 1925. His recordings were bestsellers on every continent, and his renewal contract in 1925 with the Victor Company of USA (HMV in UK) guaranteed him royalty earnings of $750,000 over a period of five years – the largest sum paid to any artist at the time.

But he became weary of travelling. He was welcome everywhere but domiciled nowhere. Over the years he had amassed a valuable collection of violins, rare books, manuscripts and *objets d'art* from all over the globe, but had nowhere to keep them. In 1924 the Kreislers bought a property set in several acres of woodland in the quiet residential area of Grünewald in western Berlin. Harriet and Fritz settled there with all their treasures, until 1939, when they returned to the USA. They transferred the book collection to safe keeping in England, a wise move since the Grünewald house was bombed in the course of the Second World War. When the news reached Kreisler, his first question, typically, was to ask if there had been any human casualties.

Kreisler was probably the most happy-go-lucky violinist of all time. He had a strong gambler's streak, which manifested itself at the tables whenever he had the chance, and also permeated his attitude to the occupational hazards of a virtuoso's life. He never practised and seldom took up his violin between performances, insisting that to wash his hands in warm water before playing was sufficient to keep them flexible.

The double-bass player Horace Green recalled an incident from 1933, when Kreisler made his historic recording of the Brahms concerto with the London Symphony Orchestra under John Barbirolli. At the rehearsal, Kreisler opened his violin case and found that his top three strings had gone. He sighed 'Oh dear' in a voice quite untouched by concern and proceeded to fit new ones. With no more than a few minutes' delay, the rehearsal began.

The rank and file musicians adored Kreisler. He had no side about him, and never put himself above others. He would sit and chat to the players as if he were one of them. Kreisler could count among his personal friends most of the great musicians of his time, but perhaps his closest was Sergei Rachmaninov, with whom he recorded the beautiful Schubert Duo in A major, D. 574, and the Beethoven Op. 30 Sonata No. 3.

It is generally claimed that, owing to his own lack of practice (which he could scarcely recommend to a pupil), Kreisler did no teaching. But, like Paganini, he did have one pupil: David McCallum (1897–1972), who for many years was leader of the BBC Symphony Orchestra and a fine soloist in his own right, studied with Kreisler whenever he was in Britain.

Kreisler died on 29 January 1962, four days before his 87th birthday. All over the world, newspapers carried tributes to this great artist. (In Britain, *The Times* and the *Guardian* perpetuated the error [finally corrected in the *New Grove Dictionary of Music and Musicians*, 1980] that Kreisler was a pupil of Auer.) *The Times* praised his 'sweetness of tone', but criticised him for taking '. . . the easy course marked out for him by his great popularity, choosing his programmes from attractive and musically trivial pieces, which delighted the audience, and playing them with an ease that became almost mechanical'.[8]

Sadly, no obituarist thought to mention the humane side of Kreisler. We have already learned of his generosity to the war orphans of the First World War. During the second, he donated all royalties from his record sales in Britain to the British Red Cross Fund, and made similar gestures in the USA. In 1947, he put up his collection of rare books and manuscripts, amassed over 40 years, for auction, because he felt it wrong to hold onto such possessions when people all over the world were in need. The sale realised $120,000, which Kreisler donated to charity.

Kreisler played all the classic concertos. Before he was 20, he composed cadenzas for the Beethoven concerto which Nathan Milstein described as 'epoch-making',[9] and the famous American critic Henry T. Finck as summing up 'the essence of Beethoven's music as a few drops of attar of rose do the fragrance of an acre of flowers'.[10] Kreisler played the Brahms concerto superbly. He not only knew Brahms personally, but later acquired (for $7,000) the original manuscript of the concerto, with all Brahms's own markings. Kreisler also played chamber music, with Jacques Thibaud, Pablo Casals and Harold Bauer not only to a cheering audience, but for pleasure – a luxury for which he never had enough time. In 1910, he told the *Musical Courier*: 'I look forward to every summer, when Ysaÿe, Thibaud, Casals, Raoul Pugno and I meet in Paris. Ysaÿe and I alternate in playing viola, but the queer thing about it is that we all want to play second violin.'[11]

The critics were never able to accept Kreisler's own charming salon pieces – the so-called 'trivia'. But these were the pieces with which he conquered the world. Audiences wanted to hear them and purchased his recordings by the millions. Far from trivial, some are little masterpieces in their own right; some are extremely difficult to play. Today they are firmly established in the solo repertory, but their wide variety shows just how subtle these pieces are. They can be tender, musicianly and beautifully phrased, but ruined with excessive vibrato and sliding. Tambourin Chinois was considered by Thibaud to be one of the greatest salon pieces ever composed. It is fiendishly difficult and full of traps for the performer who assumes that it is 'light' or 'easy'.

Kreisler's greatest sin was the famous hoax for which the eminent critic Ernest Newman never forgave him. In his youth, Kreisler had found the solo violin repertory limited. When he needed more short pieces for his recitals, he wrote them in the style of composers completely unknown at the time (Vivaldi, Porpora, Pugnani, Dittersdorf, Stamitz and Couperin) and presented them as 'arrangements'. They were an instant success and the critics congratulated him on his researches. It so happened that Heifetz, George Enescu and other close friends knew about the deception, and Kreisler himself hinted at the truth many times, but no one believed him. Eventually he decided to admit that these were originals and not transcriptions, and instructed his publishers to print an announcement to this effect in their next catalogue. Olin Downes, then chief music critic of the the *New York Times*, wrote a very fair article accepting Kreisler's justification for what he had done. The critics were taken aback, but none quite so much as Ernest Newman, who took the view that anyone could, if they tried, write in the style of Handel or Vivaldi, so therefore Kreisler's achievement in that respect was nil. But it was the deception that most incensed Newman. In an excellent letter which was published in *The Sunday Times* on 10 March 1935, Kreisler maintained that the critic's prestige was not endangered simply because a piece that had been pronounced good was later found to be composed by someone else. 'The name changes, the value remains.' The last word in the argument came from Olin Downes: 'Mr Kreisler has added to the gaiety of nations and the violinist's repertoire. Shall we begrudge him that? Should the man who kissed the wrong girl in the dark condemn the practice of kissing?'

An incident which took place in Antwerp before the First World War is typical of the esteem in which Kreisler's playing was universally held. Browsing round an antique shop, he came across a nondescript fiddle and asked the price. The answer did not satisfy Kreisler, so as a test, he took out his own priceless Guarneri and asked the dealer if he was interested in buying it. The old man caressed it with reverence and said he had an Amati at home that his customer might like to see. He then vanished and returned somewhat flustered, without the Amati and accompanied by a policeman. 'That man is a thief; he's stolen Fritz Kreisler's violin,' he shouted. 'Arrest him!' Kreisler unfortunately could not prove his identity because his passport was at his hotel. Suddenly he smiled, picked up the fiddle and played. The antique dealer beamed and then blushed with shame. 'Nobody else can play Schön Rosmarin like *that*.'[12]

Josef Gingold, in a speech given at the Kreisler Centennial Concert at Indiana University on 2 February 1975, summed up Kreisler by quoting Flesch. 'He will live not only as an artist whose genius stimulated and expanded the art, but also as a most valuable symbol of a whole epoch.'[13] The 'epoch' was that of the individualist.

Whether playing virtuoso or classical compositions, Kreisler's phrasing was never glib. Every note had a meaning and was an integral part of the composition. He was an orator on the violin and could sway his audience, lay or professional, whichever way he wanted. His playing was imbued with the Italian–French influence via the Massart–Kreutzer–Viotti link. Through Hellmesberger, Böhm, Rode, Robberechts and Viotti, he had inherited something from the Viennese, Belgian and Italian Schools. Whatever he had drawn from these influences he transformed into a style of playing which combined a strength and sweetness distinctly his own. 'Even in his most brilliant technical feats there was never anything of the steely, machine-like perfection which has become common today,' wrote Martin Cooper in the *Daily Telegraph* obituary.[14]

Kreisler's so-called 'continuous' vibrato was criticised by the purists – followers of Joachim who insisted upon no vibrato except in the most expressive passages. Yet Kreisler's vibrato was not 'continuous', neither was it the sentimental oscillation of the teashop fiddler. Kreisler was the first to use vibrato in a more highly developed way.

It was very fast, highly centralised, with his fingers firmly on the string. It produced the vibrant golden tone that every violinist tried – mostly without success – to imitate. Today, violinists aim at a vibrato that is capable of gradation, so that it can be applied to the varying moods of the music. Kreisler did this as naturally as breathing.

Gingold, who never missed a Kreisler concert, is allowed the last word.

When he made his stage entrance his majestic bearing demanded attention even before he played a single note. However, once he put his violin under his chin he was completely transformed. A certain modesty and humility were evidenced as he seemed to say, 'I would love to play for you.' I felt that Kreisler played personally for each listener in the audience, so personable was his magnetism.[15]

## Notes

1. Szigeti, *With Strings Attached*, pp. 88–9.
2. Hanslick, *Neue Freie Presse*, 25 January 1898.
3. *Neues Wiener Journal*, 26 January 1898.
4. *Musical Times*, 1 June 1902.
5. *Saturday Review*, 4 May 1907.
6. *Musical Observer*, 11 November 1910.
7. Lochner, *Fritz Kreisler*, p. 196.
8. *The Times*, 30 January 1962.
9. Lochner, op. cit., p. 365.
10. Ibid., p. 38.
11. *Musical Courier,* January 1910.
12. Lochner, op. cit., p. 353.
13. Flesch, *Memoirs*, p. 125.
14. *Daily Telegraph*, 30 January 1962.
15. Josef Gingold, speech given at the Kreisler Centennial Concert at Indiana University, 2 February 1975.

# 18 The French Phenomenon

With a few notable exceptions, such as Wieniawski, most of the top-rank violinists from the Belgian School were natives. With the French school it was exactly the reverse. Apart from Émile Sauret, a century had passed since France had produced an outstanding violinist. Then suddenly, with Jacques Thibaud, France produced her greatest violinist. His bewitching tone, technique and ebullient and individual style of playing, so emblematic of French music, gained him a lasting reputation. His colourful personality endeared him to all who knew him, and his tall, slim figure and devastating good looks won an immediate response from his audiences.

Thibaud was born in Bordeaux in 1880, into a family where music was taken for granted. His father was a violinist and local music teacher; his brothers played cello and piano, and in later years they worked together as a professional piano trio. Thibaud originally intended to be a pianist. In fact, he was so skilled on the keyboard that he made his first public appearance as a piano soloist at the age of five. Two years later he was taken to a concert where he heard the Beethoven Violin Concerto and was moved to tears. He gave his father no peace until he agreed to give him some lessons on that instrument. His progress was so remarkable that when Ysaÿe heard him at the age of nine, he encouraged him to take further study and predicted a bright future.

Thibaud entered the Conservatoire in Paris under Marsick when he was 13, and, three years later, carried off the first prize. To supplement his modest allowance, Thibaud played in the band at the Café Rouge where he was spotted by Edouard Colonne, founder of the popular Concerts Colonne, who immediately took him into his orchestra. One day, when the leader was unwell, Thibaud deputised. His exquisite playing of the violin solo in the Prélude to Saint-Saëns' 1875 Oratorio *Le Déluge* caused a sensation, and soon he was so inundated with solo engagements that he was obliged to give up his orchestral job. He made his solo début in Angers in 1898 and subsequently appeared in over 50 concerts with the Colonne Orchestra.

In 1899, Thibaud made his first appearance in London at one of the 'Pop' concerts under Henry Wood. He returned frequently thereafter to play in this same series and became a favourite of English audiences. In Berlin in 1901, barely 21, he took Germany by storm. As 'the long-awaited exponent of the French type of violin playing', Flesch tells us that 'above all, it was his tone which, though not big in itself, fascinated the listener by its sweet and seductive colour, literally unheard of at the time'.[1]

In 1903, New Yorkers heard Thibaud for the first time, playing the Mozart E flat and the Saint-Saëns B minor concertos with the Wetzler Symphony Orchestra at Carnegie Hall. While the critics made no wild claims for Thibaud's greatness, they fully appreciated that they were hearing something remarkable. The critic of the *New York Times* wrote that Thibaud's temperament was 'poetic and gracious rather than impassioned and impetuous' and praised his warm, pure tone.

In 1905, Thibaud's love of chamber music led him to form the remarkable Cortot-Thibaud-Casals Trio, perhaps the greatest combination of musical talent ever seen or heard. From the beginning, they were in constant demand and achieved universal acclaim. Fortunately for posterity, their recordings of works such as the Beethoven 'Archduke Trio' remain as evidence of their artistry.

During the First World War, Thibaud served in the French Army and saw active service at many of the historic battles before being slightly wounded and discharged.

During the period between the two wars, Thibaud travelled the world and established a reputation for his unique interpretations of French music. His playing of the concertos of Bach, Mozart and Beethoven was always well received but it was in the music of Lalo, Chausson, Saint-Saëns and Franck that he excelled. His travels brought him into close contact with many diplomats and others in high places, many of whom became his personal friends. This had a sequel during the Second World War when Thibaud retired, ostensibly to write his memoirs; in reality he was serving as a valuable member of the French Intelligence.

According to Flesch, 'It is always an artist's character that provides the master key to an understanding of his art'. In Thibaud's case, it was simple. He was French, he loved life and he loved women – for him the eternal feminine was an absolute necessity. His playing 'was imbued with his yearning for sensual pleasure, with an unchastity that was all the more seductive for its refinement'.[2] Though never vulgar or over-expressive, his playing was always virile. The caressing quality unique to his playing evoked the image of a lover wooing his mistress.

Thibaud was a close friend of both Kreisler and Ysaÿe. At one time he studied with the great Belgian and his playing showed a great deal of the master's influence. Although he did not actually suffer from platform 'nerves' as such, Thibaud was a temperamental artist who could be disturbed by the slightest distraction. For this reason he always allowed 15 minutes of silence in which to concentrate on the music before going onto the concert platform.

The social value of music was very important to Thibaud. He believed that music had a special mission to distract people from the pressures of everyday life. He was impatient with those who insisted that modern music should depict the realism and ugliness of the present. 'People do not want to have their miseries and worries reflected in music; they want to get away from them.'[3] Nicholas Roth, a former musical director of radio in The Hague, heard him many times in Holland and also in London, at a Wigmore Hall recital when he was over 70. 'There was a wonderful French charm in everything he did. I heard him play the Introduction and Rondo

Capriccioso [Saint-Saëns] and he made mistakes; he was out of tune and he scratched. But the audience gave him a standing ovation and the mistakes were washed out as soon as they were made.'[4] One of Thibaud's influences on violin playing was his introduction of a levelling up of flat intonation on sustained or expressive notes. An integral part of his playing, it never failed to come off; unfortunately, when it was copied by less accomplished performers, the result was disastrous.

At the age of 73, Thibaud was still performing all over the world, but on 1 September 1953, the plane in which he was travelling crashed into one of the highest mountain peaks in France. There were no survivors.

Following closely on the steps of Thibaud was Zino Francescatti (1902–91), one of the last and most distinguished exponents of the old French School; but because he did not seek the limelight, he was not as well known as some of his contemporaries. An obituary in *The Strad* notes: 'He had both personality and individuality, and both shone through his playing in the same bow stroke which was at once elegant and brilliant with immaculate intonation'.[5]

He was born in Marseilles, into a family of professional musicians. His father, Fortunato Francescatti, a student of Camille Sivori, gave him his first lessons when he was a child. A taskmaster, he was never content with imperfection. His mother, also a violinist, supervised his daily practice. When he was 11, he and his mother secretly arranged for him to take part in a concert, performing both the Wieniawski D minor Concerto and the Polonaise in D, for which he received rapturous applause and, from his father, recognition that he was, after all, ready for a public concert. In later years Francescatti acknowledged the value of his early training, which he believed had benefited both his playing and his teaching.

At 20 he was sent off to Paris where he earned his living as an orchestral player. He made his solo début at one of the Conservatoire concerts, attracting the attention of Thibaud, who helped him considerably to further his career as a soloist. He also met Maurice Ravel, with whom he later enjoyed a close friendship and a long and successful professional association. In 1926 they toured Britain, performing Ravel's Tzigane (1924) and Berceuse (1922) with resounding success. Francescatti once said: 'Most people don't realise he [Ravel] made a close study of the violin and its literature before attempting to write his Tzigane. We played it many, many times. It has a special meaning for me – a truly magnificent piece.'[6]

Meanwhile Francescatti was steadily gaining recognition as a soloist and captivating audiences everywhere with the Paganini Concerto No. 1, which his father had taught him, passing on what he himself had learned from Sivori (Paganini's only pupil). He made his American debut in 1939, playing this concerto with the New York Philharmonic Orchestra, and was recalled again and again by a rapturous audience; shortly afterwards, he settled in New York and also bought a house at Tanglewood, in the Berkshire Mountains of western Massachusetts.

Although closely identified with Paganini, his repertory was vast, and he championed the works of many twentieth-century composers, including Igor

Stravinsky, Paul Hindemith, Darius Milhaud, Leonard Bernstein and William Walton. Also a fine recitalist, he formed a partnership with the pianist Robert Casadesus, with whom he toured for many years. They also made a number of recordings, of which the sonatas of Claude Debussy, César Franck and Gabriel Fauré were outstanding.

Despite his own strict upbringing, he never inflicted this rigorous approach on his own pupils. He taught at the Ecole Normale de Paris for a short time, but for the most part his teaching was private; when the need arose, he would give lessons without charge. He devoted a great deal of time and energy to nurturing promising young talent and encouraged individuality in playing, which he associated with the great violinists of the past, and which he felt needed to be revived.

Admired for his refined musicianship and limpid tone, he had developed an impeccable technique that gave the impression of coming as naturally as breathing. In later years he achieved a richer tone which may be attributed to his acquisition in 1942 of the 1727 'Hart' Strad. However, during a pre-recording rehearsal of the Brahms concerto, with Ormandy and the Philadelphia Orchestra, the 'Hart' became unplayable. Kreisler happened to be in the studio and lent Francescatti his Guarnerius del Gesù. Casadesus arrived during the rehearsal unaware of the change of instrument and in the break said to Francescatti: 'You know, I could have sworn it was Kreisler playing!' Francescatti later sold the 'Hart' to his friend, Salvatore Accardo, who now plays it almost exclusively, and people have said that *he* now sounds like Francescatti.

In 1973, after 34 years in the USA, Francescatti returned to his native Provence. In 1987, the Zino Francescatti International Violin Festival was founded in his honour at Aix-en-Provence. Sadly, on 16 September 1991, he died at his villa in the small Mediterranean port of La Ciotat, just a week before the opening of the third of these highly successful events.

Maurice Hasson was born in Berck-Plage in 1934 and, because of the Second World War, did not take up the violin until he was 11. Despite his late start Hasson made swift progress and at 13 he was accepted at the Paris Conservatoire to study with Line Talleul, Ginette Neveu's teacher. Two years later he graduated with a Premier Prix for violin, a Grand Prix for chamber music and the first Prix d'Honneur to be awarded for 60 years. The following year he made a successful Paris debut with the Lamoureaux Orchestra, playing the Mendelssohn concerto. There followed a period of crisis, in which he began to question his whole approach to playing; he abandoned the violin for two years and completed his general education.

At 19, he began playing again and, impetuous as always, he entered the Long-Thibaud International Competition, taking the fifth prize. However, Henryk Szeryng was on the jury and although he recognised in Hasson outstanding talent, he was brutally honest about his deficient sense of style. He ordered him to put away his violin for a while, after which he would take him on as a pupil. This was a watershed in Hasson's career. Szeryng's cool, logical teaching, the fruit of both his own temperament and his studies with the rigorous, analytical Carl Flesch, was the perfect tool for tempering Hasson's impulsive playing. Everything was questioned: why this bowing or that fingering? Hasson describes the lessons as 'marathons'; nonetheless they worked together for nine years, always under the same terms.

In 1959, Hasson took up a violin-teaching post at the University of Venezuela, remaining there for 11 years. Despite idyllic conditions, Europe eventually beckoned, and in 1972 he undertook a tour which opened with a debut recital at the Wigmore Hall in London. The concert was well received and Richard Kaylan, writing in *The Times*, called him an 'aristocrat among violinists'.[7] During that visit he was invited by EMI to make some recordings. So over the next three years, he commuted between South America and Europe before finally settling in London.

In 1975, he stepped in at short notice to play the Paganini Concerto No. 1 at a Promenade concert at the Royal Albert Hall, deputising for Ruggiero Ricci, who had suddenly been taken ill. After receiving a tremendous ovation, he was introduced to Lorin Maazel, who had come to hear Ricci. Maazel promptly engaged him for several concerts in the UK and the USA.

Hasson has been a professor at the Royal Academy of Music in London since 1986:

'I try to get my students to think logically and intelligently about what they are doing. However beautiful the sound you make with your violin, if you do not understand why or how you are making music, you are not getting the best out of yourself or your instrument. I find that young people respond to this approach and it is very gratifying to see them grow in consequence.[8]

Jean-Jacques Kantorow was born in Cannes in 1945, into a family of Russian origin. As a child he had his first lessons on the violin with Jean Hubeau (1917–92) in Nice. At 13, he entered the Paris Conservatoire to study with René Benedetti (1901–75) and, a year later, won the Premier Prix and made his solo debut at the Théâtre des Champs Elysées. By this time he had become interested in chamber music and re-entered the Conservatoire for a further period of study with Joseph Calvet (1897–1984).

In 1962, Kantorow won the Carl Flesch Competition, but it was winning the Paganini Competition in Genoa two years later that set him thinking. In common with many violinists, Kantorow had never given serious regard to Paganini; but when he began to look closely at the music, he revised his opinions: 'At first the writing appears very correct and square without any surprises, but when you examine it in more detail you find there are many ways in which you can interpret it … . For example, the sonatas [for violin and guitar] seem much easier than the concertos … but in fact they are not.'[9] Kantorow and the guitarist Anthea Gifford formed a duo in 1984.

Kantorow's initial career as a soloist brought him many glittering successes. He has also been concertmaster of several well-known chamber orchestras and is a member of the Paganini Ensemble. At present, he is principal conductor of three orchestras and holds professorships at the conservatories in Paris and Rotterdam. When asked about his method, he replies: 'My teaching is absolutely instinctive. No two students are alike, so I improvise for each one. Even after studying with me for some time, there is no JJK "stamp". What interests me is the person, their targets and how to find a way to make each student enjoy what he is doing.' An observer at his summer schools over several years concurs: 'People respond to him because he treats them as individuals and coaxes them to bring out that individuality. He is also very kind and encouraging, and can demonstrate marvellously.'[10]

Another French violinist of this generation is Augustin Dumay, born in Paris in 1949. He was taken to a recital given by Nathan Milstein when he was three and would not rest until he was given violin lessons. At ten, he was accepted at the Paris Conservatoire to study with Roland Charmey and stayed for two years. When he was 14, he gave a recital at the Montreux Festival. Henryk Szeryng was in the audience; a week later, he contacted Dumay to invite him to take his place on a South American tour. Dumay was stunned, but accepted what was a golden opportunity to gain experience on the concert platform.

Eventually Dumay met his idol, Milstein, in Paris and was fortunate to have some lessons with him. He also studied for five years with Arthur Grumiaux in Brussels and found the contrast between the two teachers fascinating. Grumiaux, it seems, was very strict, whereas Milstein was more flexible, 'more Romantic, in the good sense, more virtuoso'.[11]

## Notes

1. Flesch, *Memoirs*, p. 196.
2. Ibid., p. 197.
3. Brook, *Violinists of Today*, p. 178.
4. Quoted from interview, M.C.
5–6. *The Strad*, December 1991, p. 1117.
7. *The Times*, 12 April 1972.
8. Letter from Maurice Hasson to M.C.
9. *The Strad*, June 1993, p. 559.
10. Quoted from interview, M.C.
11. *The Strad*, September 1987, p. 638.

# 19   To Dance in Chains

'I am a son of the soil, born in a land of legends. My whole life has been spent under the eyes of my childhood deities,'[1] wrote the Romanian George Enescu (1881–1955), one of the last of the great teachers born in the nineteenth century. And yet, Flesch described him as towering 'above his musical compatriots like a solitary rock in a sea of mediocrity'.[2] It was impossible to know which of the versatile Enescu's gifts were the greatest: he seemed to be equally accomplished as teacher, composer, conductor, violinist and pianist. He also played the cello and mastered eight languages with equal fluency.

As Yehudi Menuhin pointed out in his autobiography, *Unfinished Journey*, Enescu never lost contact with the soil, although his 'childhood deities' sent him far afield, and by the turn of the century he was a highly successful virtuoso, always on the move. He made his home in Paris but also had a mountain retreat in Romania appropriately called 'Villa Luminiş,' (House of Light).

Enescu was born in Liveni, near Dorohoiu, a Moldavian village where the inhabitants were of mixed Turkish, Greek, Magyar and Ukranian blood. He was admitted to the Vienna Conservatory under Joseph Hellmesberger at the age of seven. Two years later he was taken into the adult class and graduated, carrying off the highest award for violin playing, at the age of 12. Composition was already of the greatest importance to the young Enescu; he had written his first four-voice fugue at the age of ten. Hellmesberger – then leader of the Vienna Opera Orchestra – smuggled him, night after night, into the opera house and hid him behind the drums. Here he would sit, absorbing the variety of sounds and colours of the orchestra, learning the capabilities of each instrument first-hand. After his first Wagner opera Enescu came away intoxicated. He later said of the experience: 'I didn't want to look at the sky because I had seen all the stars there were in Wagner's music.'[3]

From Vienna Enescu went to Paris where he entered the Conservatoire as a pupil of Martin Marsick and studied harmony and composition with André Gédalge and Gabriel Fauré. Again, in 1899, he took away the Premier Prix for violin. But his was success with a difference. He had no desire to be a virtuoso, he did not even want to be a violinist. He much preferred the piano, which he played superbly, and nursed an even greater ambition to be a composer. He had his first work, Poème Roumain (1897), performed by the Colonne Orchestra in Paris while he was still a student which seemed a good start. When Enescu was only 15 he played for Joachim in Berlin. The elder violinist was suitably encouraging with regard to his talent and his playing.

Enescu then produced his own Sonata No.1, Op. 2 (1897), written when he was in his early teens, and timidly asked whether Joachim would play through it with him, Enescu taking the piano part. When they had finished, the old man looked horrified. 'Why,' he retorted, 'it is even more modern than César Franck!'[4] Sir Adrian Boult later wrote of his famous Rhapsody (1901) that 'however impossible, musically, [it] showed off finely the virtuosity of the orchestra'.[5] While still a young man, Enescu decided that he would play the violin solely to make himself enough money to buy a piece of land in Romania. He planned to retire early and compose to his dying day:

> Mad about composing, I grudged every minute I had to give to my violin, and although I had no delusions about what I was writing, I very much preferred my own humble attempts [at composition] to the persistent study of an instrument that gave me so little satisfaction in return for all my efforts. I have so often looked at my fiddle in its case and said to myself: You are too small, my friend, much too small.[6]

His view was an isolated one. The *New York Times* critic wrote on 23 January 1923: 'He is first and last a musician and an interpreter, devoted solely to expounding music and not at all to the display of his technical powers. These are indeed remarkable but they are employed entirely as a means to an end. . . . his playing is notable for its exquisite purity of intonation, especially in double-stoppings.' Enescu was also commended for choosing to play the entire Bach Partita in D minor – 'delivered . . . with a remarkable repose and apparent freedom from effort' – instead of selecting, as most violinists do, only the Chaconne.

The 'apparent freedom from effort' was helped, no doubt, by an intensive study and love of Bach from early childhood. While Enescu was in Paris, he returned to Romania for his summer holidays. When at the royal resort at Sinaia, Queen Carmen Silva presented him with a set of the complete Bach Gesellschaft edition that became a source of study and joy for the rest of his life. Many of Enescu's pupils have confirmed that he knew at least 120 of the cantatas from memory.

He often pointed out to pupils that the bulk of Bach's music was vocal, composed with a text, and that only a small portion was written solely for instruments. He suggested that they took the time to study a few of the cantatas, so that they could begin to feel the 'pull' of the harmonic structure in relation to the words. This close emotional relationship between words and music was for Enescu the key to the performance of Bach's instrumental works. The late Helen Dowling (1916–87), a close associate of Enescu who studied with him for four years, said: 'It was a revelation to study Bach with Enescu. Gradually the music began to speak to you, and you in turn had to find the way of communicating this to your audience.'[7]

Enescu held master classes every summer in Paris. He hardly ever concerned himself with technique since he felt that was the job of the pupils' regular teachers. He tried to give them a newer and deeper understanding of music. He never insisted that they should play his way, but he gave them a general musical concept from which they could find their own way. 'You must learn to dance in chains,' he would tell them. By this, 'He meant that one should learn to move freely and yet remain within the framework set by the composer. . . . His universe was music, and he felt himself its very humble servant. Nothing else in life mattered. It was this single-minded devotion to music that left its mark on all those who came within his orbit!'[8]

Today, it is as a teacher that Enescu is remembered best. Ida Haendel, then a child but already a virtuoso performer, had been temporarily dismissed by Flesch from his class, in one of his bursts of anger. She had always wanted to study with Enescu, and was taken to Paris by her father to have a few extra lessons. Though still so young, she knew she was in the presence of 'the most inspired and uplifted of human beings'. She recalled that his 'shortness of stature, his rounded spine [in later years Enescu suffered from a terrible crippling disease], indifferent attire, seemed almost to enhance his greatness and spiritual quality'.[9] In a lesson on Bach, she found Enescu 'firm and uncompromising; he removed all the frills … so allowing the true form and anatomy to be exposed'. When the music had been freed of all embellishments it sounded strange but she realised that his emphasis on purity of line served to reveal the real grandeur of its structure. 'I seemed to hear Bach the giant for the first time.'[10]

Much later in her career, Haendel visited Enescu in Paris and played the Bach Chaconne to him. It was Enescu's birthday and she had brought him a cake. When she had finished playing, Enescu asked 'Have you studied the Chaconne with me?' 'No, maître, but I heard you play it in New York.' She waited anxiously for the verdict. 'By playing the Chaconne the way you did, you brought me a much bigger present than the cake.'[11]

Haendel drew an interesting comparison between Flesch and Enescu. The latter never tried to impose his ideas on a pupil; his remarks were more like suggestions than advice. Flesch's approach was more methodical and clinical. With Enescu, a pupil seldom had the chance to perform a work without interruption, and he very rarely demonstrated a point on his violin. Instead, he would teach from the piano.

Menuhin also studied with Enescu as a youngster and always cherished the infinite value of that encounter:

> A lesson was an inspiration, not a stage reached in a course of instruction. It was the making of music much as if I were his orchestra . . . for while he accompanied me at the piano he also sang the different voices of the score . . . . What I received from him by compelling example . . . was the note transformed into vital message, the phrase given shape and meaning, the structure of music made vivid. . . . Music was hardly dead for me; it was a fierce passion, but I had never known it to have such clear and vital form before.[12]

Ion Voicu (1923–97) was one of the last surviving exponents of the old school of violin playing and his studies with Abram Il'ich Yampol'sky (1890–1956) and Enescu place him in a direct line to Leopold Auer and Viotti. He was born in Bucharest into a family of musicians who had an unbroken line of professional string players and pianists for almost 400 years. He had his first violin lessons from Constantin Niculescu when he was six years old, and at 14, he entered the Royal Academy of Music in Bucharest. He studied with Georg Enacovici and graduated at 17, having completed the seven-year course in three.

His first employment was as a rank-and-file violinist with the Bucharest Radio Orchestra. His first rehearsal was a disaster. The guest conductor, Willem Mengelberg, noticed that Voicu was not paying attention. He shouted to him to get out and the blushing new member retreated in shame. During the interval the musical director asked Mengelberg to listen to one of his violinists, whom he thought very gifted. But when Voicu entered, Mengelberg exploded: 'This boy can't even pay attention to the conductor. How can he be gifted ?' The director pleaded and Mengelberg listened – at first reluctantly and then with increasing interest. When Voicu stopped playing, the conductor admitted that he now understood. 'This young man is not meant to be sitting in an orchestra. He should be *standing* – as a soloist!'[13]

Once, at a concert in which Voicu was the soloist, Enescu was in the audience. He was so impressed that he offered to give him an audition. Voicu recalled that just as he was about to play, he realised he had left the piano parts at home. Enescu was unconcerned and simply asked: 'Which pieces?' and seated himself at the piano. One after another, Enescu, whose memory was infallible, accompanied him perfectly throughout. Voicu recalled: 'He was a wonderful teacher and had an innate understanding of the music – he knew how to bring out all the subtleties . . . . If I were asked to sum up his influence, I would say his mastery of the instrument, his skill in every possible technique, his sensitivity and his unique sonority.'[14]

In 1946 Voicu won first prize in a national competition organised by Menuhin and Enescu; with the prize money he was able to travel to the West. On his return to Romania he was much in demand as a soloist and in 1949 became the official soloist of the George Enescu Philharmonic Orchestra. Nonetheless, Voicu still felt he had much to learn. He had always wanted to study with Yampol'sky, who was then 90. ('The idea of studying the classics with such a master was very exciting.') So in 1954 he went to Moscow for a year to study with his idol, of whom he said: 'He somehow managed to combine a mastery of the instrument with his own musical feelings. He had a wonderful tone, perfect intonation and a nobility of style. But above all, he encouraged us to think for ourselves.'[15]

When Yampol'sky died in 1956, Voicu continued his studies with David Oistrakh in order to complete a doctorate at Moscow University. Voicu recalled that the lessons would often take all day and he would almost always end up eating with the family. So the teacher–pupil relationship soon grew into a close friendship that endured right up until Oistrakh's death.

On his return to Romania in 1957, Voicu joined the international circuit and made his highly successful American debut at Carnegie Hall in 1965; he followed this with a coast-to-coast tour that delighted the audiences and inspired the critics to write about his 'magic fingers'[16] and 'a poet's mind and a dexterity that makes one think of a conjuror'.[17]

In the intervening years before his untimely death in 1997, Voicu participated in almost every field of his profession. Besides his solo work, he was an excellent conductor, having founded the Bucharest Chamber Orchestra in 1969. He was also a fine teacher and gave masterclasses worldwide. He sat on the jury of many major competitions including the Carl Flesch, the Sibelius, the Enescu and the Tchaikovsky in Moscow (for which he was many times vice-president). At the time of his death he was in the process of setting up a foundation to assist young Romanian musicians in the early stages of their careers.

## Notes

1. Menuhin, *Unfinished Journey*, p. 68.
2. Flesch, *Memoirs*, p. 178.
3. Quoted from interview, M.C.
4. Quoted from interview, M.C.
5. Sir Adrian Boult, *My Own Trumpet*, p. 141.
6. Menuhin, op. cit., p. 69.
7–8. Quoted from interview, M.C.
9–10. Haendel, *Woman with Violin*, p. 90.
11. Ibid., p. 172.
12. Menuhin, op. cit., p. 71.
13–14. Quoted from interview, M.C.
15. *The Strad*, May 1994, p. 473.
16–17. Voicu's brochure.

# 20　The Unbridled Individualist

When Ida Haendel was a small child, she played for Bronislav Huberman (1882–1947) at a banquet in Warsaw. Recalling the incident some 40 years later, she said: 'I looked at him, the idol of thousands, and I could hardly believe it. He smiled at me gently and he was beautiful to me. I saw none of his defects – the famous cross-eyes, the protruding lower lip and the over-large head. All I saw was a great spirit shining in that powerful, determined face, which for a moment made me think of Beethoven.'[1]

This perceptive child was near to the truth. Huberman felt an affinity with Beethoven which went further than the music itself. He shared the composer's love of mankind and firmly believed that a united Europe was the only solution to world peace. As one of the leading musical personalities of the era, he was able to influence the furtherance of the Pan-European Movement, to which he gave both time and money. Like Beethoven, he saw music as a unifying force, 'a lofty reconciling spirit . . . seeking to unite all listeners'.[2]

Huberman refused to play in Nazi Germany, even though the conductor Wilhelm Furtwängler wrote begging him to change his mind. A decree had been drawn up to allow any artist 'no matter what his race or nation' to perform. Furtwängler pleaded with him: 'Someone must make the first move to break down the barrier.' Although Huberman appreciated Furtwängler's efforts to overcome the difficulties, he could not excuse 'the menaced destruction by racial purgers'[3] and the deposition of Mendelssohn, Rubinstein and Joachim because they were Jews. He held to his decision and never appeared in Hitler's Germany. There were others who also took this view: Arturo Toscanini refused to go to Bayreuth, and Thibaud, a non-Jew, also declined Furtwängler's invitation.

Huberman was born in the small Polish town of Częstochowa, the son of a barrister, who gave him every encouragement when he showed early talent on the violin. He studied in Warsaw, first with Mieczyslaw Michalowicz, a pupil of Auer and teacher at the School of Music, and then with Izydor Lotto (c.1840–1936), who had studied with Massart. At the age of seven, the child performed Spohr's Second Violin Concerto at a public concert, also taking the part of leader in a quartet by Rode.

When the chance came for the ten-year-old Huberman to study in Berlin with Joachim, he stayed with him only nine months. At the time it was not understood why he threw away the opportunity to study with one of the great teachers. In later years he revealed that not only was he more often taught by Joachim's pupil, Carl

Markees, than by the master himself, but that he felt stifled by the atmosphere of pedantic academicism then infecting Berlin. The individualism that was the hallmark of his personality was already manifest: he sought tuition elsewhere.

After short spells with Hugo Heermann (1844–1935) in Frankfurt and Marsick in Paris, Huberman sought no further training and instead embarked upon his solo career at 11. He toured the main cities in Europe – Amsterdam, Brussels, Paris and, a year later, London, where he was heard by the singer Adelina Patti. The prima donna took him to Vienna and presented him at her farewell concert in 1895.

In 1896, Huberman performed the Brahms concerto for the first time. Many famous musicians, including the composer himself, sat in the management box waiting to hear what this child could make of a work which had frightened off so many leading violinists, even in their riper years. Brahms's biographer Max Kalbeck tells us that Brahms was overwhelmed from the first stroke of the bow and when Huberman began the Adagio, tears came to the composer's eyes. 'At the end of the Finale, he embraced the young boy whose musical genius had found the exact mode of interpretation of the concerto.'[4]

In Poland he was treated as a god. Strangely enough, he was never truly appreciated in England. In Menuhin's view, 'Such artists reflect a certain culture, temperament, mixture of races, and they thrive most happily in home soil.'[5] When Huberman first appeared as an adult performer in the USA (he had given concerts as a child prodigy in New York in 1897), Richard Aldrich, of the *New York Times*, wrote that his 'talent is manifested with a certain crudeness'.[6] Aldrich acknowledged that Huberman's focus on the music itself was more important that the impression he was making as a player. But he was disturbed by Huberman's 'back-bending' and straining to produce certain effects. His tone is 'powerful, but it is not notable for warmth or appealing quality'.[7] However, in 1936, *The Strad*'s correspondent in Alexandria, Alexander Ruppa, found Huberman to be 'endowed with the rare power of portraying the whole gamut of human emotions from the most exquisite tenderness to the most brutal violence'.[8]

Huberman would seem to have been one of the first of the modern violinists to sense the links between psychology and music. Thibaud had recognised the effects of music as an antidote or escape, but his approach was both more conscious and more emotional. For Huberman, Beethoven was the supreme example of what he most admired in music, and he placed Brahms next, as the composer who spoke to him most intimately. He saw Brahms as a synthesis of human and transfigured sensuality, as revealing a conscious renunciation of impulsive longings, not so much rejection as resignation, expiation and forgiveness.

Huberman held strong views on the role of the interpretative artist. He did not see the performer as a passive mediator. For him, two important elements determined the approach to a performance: first, in the interpretation of a work, the artist must invoke in the listener a personal experience; secondly, 'he must make the listener aware of the inner storms and birthpangs which buffeted the composer in the act of creation'.[9] To bring this about, the artist is obliged to study every minute detail of tempo, dynamics, harmonisation and orchestration. Huberman was adamant in his view that the composer's intentions must always be observed. He often took a long time to learn a work. 'I must live the piece before I can play it beautifully. That moment may come when I am playing it upon the stage for the first, the fifth or the tenth time. But if it does not come, I discard the composition, no matter what pains its mastery may have cost.'[10]

One of Huberman's most severe critics was Carl Flesch. He deplored his lack of training, his vibrato, his holding of the bow in an outmoded style, his self-willed personality and his habit of adjusting the 'tone of the work to the pitch of his own ego'. In Flesch's opinion, Huberman will survive only 'as the most remarkable representative of unbridled individualism, a fascinating outsider'.[11]

Hans Keller, editor of Flesch's memoirs, took another view. 'Huberman was one of the greatest musicians I have ever come across. . . . a long line of artists has testified to his towering stature as an artist, violinist and man.' He conceded that his technique was always individual and depended greatly upon the prevailing mood, but 'when he was "on form", both hands evinced a virtuoso technique of the utmost brilliance and an almost uncanny verve'. Keller rebutted all Flesch's accusations regarding Huberman's vibrato and manner of holding the bow. As for his intonation, Keller did not know 'of another violinist who adjusted his intonation so consistently to harmonic and melodic requirements.'[12]

Perhaps Huberman's most enduring achievement was his musical pioneering on behalf of displaced Jews. In 1936, assisted by Toscanini and other leading musicians, he founded the Palestine Philharmonic Orchestra, which later became the Israel Philharmonic.

**Notes**

1. Haendel, *Woman with Violin*, pp. 30–1.
2. Arthur Herman, *The Strad*, February 1932, p. 531.
3. Ruppa, *The Strad*, March 1934, p. 464.
4. Ruppa, *The Strad*, February 1936, p. 439.
5. Menuhin, *Unfinished Journey*, p. 97.
6–7. Aldrich, *New York Times*, 8 December 1922
8. Ruppa, *The Strad*, February 1936, p. 438.
9–10. Arthur Herman, *The Strad*, February 1932, p. 530.
11. Flesch, *Memoirs*, p. 178.
12. Hans Keller, Appendix I in Flesch, *Memoirs*, p. 368.

# 21 Our Own Albert

For well over 200 years, extending until the 1930s, foreign musicians dominated British musical life. For the public, native performers lacked the charisma that surrounded the imported artist. Violinists were particularly affected by this prejudice. Spohr, Paganini, Ysaÿe and Kreisler were all names with magical connotations. The only strategy open to the British artist was to study abroad for a couple of years, and return with a 'ski' or an 'ini' added to his name.

One of the artists who, by his own example, did much to elevate the status of the British performer was the London-born Albert Sammons (1886–1957) – 'Our own Albert' to his colleagues. Sammons was born into a musical family. His father, a good amateur musician, gave him his first lessons on the fiddle. As a boy of 11 he attended school by day and spent his evenings playing in the orchestra of a Piccadilly restaurant. When he left school a year later, his West End experience of playing the light classics enabled him to become a freelance professional, at the palm court of a Harrogate hotel and at a hunt ball in the Shires. The authentic 'Hungarian band'[1] with whom he frequently played were ordered to keep a trappist silence, lest it be discovered that the only language they spoke was Cockney.

Sammons's first great breakthrough came in 1908, when he was leading a small orchestra at the Waldorf Hotel in London. Thomas Beecham had heard that they had a violinist of uncommon dexterity and had dined there in order to hear him. Beecham put in a request for a solo and was rewarded with the finale of the Mendelssohn concerto, played at a speed which flabbergasted the conductor, who had a reputation for some fairly rapid tempos himself. He scribbled on a card: 'Splendid, but the right tempo is so and so,'[2] indicating by a metronome mark what he thought it should be. Sammons's response was to play it again at the requested tempo.

Beecham immediately offered Sammons a place in his own orchestra. A few months later he became leader, a position he held for five years. Beecham never flagged in his enthusiasm for Sammons and he wrote of him in his memoirs, *A Mingled Chime*: 'This gifted and resourceful youth developed into the best all-round concert-master I have ever met anywhere, uniting in himself a technical facility equal to any demand made upon it, a full, warm tone, a faultless rhythmic sense, and a brain that remained cool in the face of any untoward happening.'[3]

Sammons had a few isolated lessons from John Saunders (1867–1919) and Frederick Weist-Hill, a pupil of Ysaÿe. But, like his eminent predecessors, Paganini and Ole Bull, he was largely self-taught. Nonetheless, his technique lacked nothing.

By assiduous application to the study of all the important aspects of technique he acquired a mastery of the instrument which led him to become outstanding both as a soloist and a teacher.

In 1909, Sammons's love of chamber music prompted him to form the quartet which later became famous as the London Quartet. Their association lasted until 1919, when Sammons regretfully gave it up so that he could devote himself to his solo engagements.

Sammons's career as a virtuoso began with an outstanding performance of the Bruch G minor Concerto under Stanford at a concert at the Queen's Hall in 1911. A few days later, a letter arrived from Sir Landon Ronald, saying that he had never heard a finer performance and asking whether Sammons could play for him at the Albert Hall. That same year, Sammons was appointed Musician-in-Ordinary to King George V, and in 1912 was chosen to perform the Saint-Saëns B minor Concerto in the presence of King George V, Queen Mary and the ageing composer, at the Queen's Hall.

In 1913, Sammons was invited to lead the Dieppe Symphony Orchestra under Pierre Monteux; when war broke out the following year, he returned to England. It was during the First World War, when so many of the foreign virtuosos were not readily available, that the British musical public began to realise they had a remarkable native talent in Albert Sammons. When Ysaÿe heard him play for the first time, he exclaimed: 'At last, England has found herself a great violinist!'[4]

Sammons was closely associated with the Elgar concerto. It had been sadly neglected since its first performance by Kreisler in 1910. Sammons performed it for the first time on 23 November 1914, at the Queen's Hall, with the London Symphony Orchestra under Vassily Safonov. At the time, Sammons was one of the very few violinists capable of tackling the work, to which he devoted a considerable period of study. After this performance, the critic of the *Star* wrote:

> It has for some time been clear to musicians that Mr Albert Sammons is a violinist of quite uncommon gifts, who only needed a few chances to convince the public at large of his powers; but the chance never came. It apparently needed a European war to give it to him. He had it last night, and made splendid use of it. His performance of the difficult solo part put him in the front rank of violinists, and the public cheered him with as much enthusiasm as if he had had a foreign name.[5]

Later, through countless performances, Sammons became one of the world's finest exponents of the work. Elgar himself admitted that no-one seemed to get to the heart of the piece as Sammons did. John Barbirolli wrote to the violinist after a performance with the Hallé: 'We felt privileged to be associated with you in the performing of the Elgar, which will live long in our memories.'[6] It has often been said that it was the 'Englishness' of Sammons's playing which made him such a sensitive interpreter of national composers.

Frederick Delius dedicated his concerto to Sammons in 1919. It is an elusive work which even today tends to be neglected. Sammons made a careful study of it when it came to him fresh from the composer's pen, and found much to amend. Although Delius himself played the fiddle, some passages were violinistically impossible. Grateful for Sammons's suggestions, Delius prepared a revised version. It received its first performance on 30 January 1919 in a Philharmonic Society concert conducted by Adrian Boult at the Queen's Hall. The next day *The Times* critic wrote: 'The work has two moods rather than sections, one of agitated inquiry followed by one of happy trover. It was the latter that suited Mr Sammons, as if written for him: he can play poetical, throbbing cantilena like practically no-one else.'[7] Delius was much moved by the performance. He considered there were only three musicians who could properly interpret his music: Thomas Beecham, Eugène Goossens and Sammons.

However, there was a background drama to this first performance that almost resulted in its cancellation. At the time Sammons was serving as a private in the Grenadier Guards, leading the string section of the military orchestra and doubling on the clarinet in the band: he had not previously played the clarinet, but was forced to double out of necessity. At the last moment he found himself ordered to play at a grand ball at the Albert Hall on the night before the final rehearsal and concert at the Queen's Hall. Knowing how difficult it would be to do justice to a new work after a late night of continuous dance music, he asked for leave of absence from the ball. When his bandmaster refused his request, two panic-stricken directors from the Royal Philharmonic Society rushed to Wellington Barracks to plead with the colonel and the adjutant of the Grenadier Guards. The officers were sympathetic and overruled the bandmaster's decision, so the situation was saved.

Sammons's interpretation of the Brahms concerto was said by critics to rank with the best from abroad, and he played the Beethoven over 100 times, 70 of them during the Second World War. He considered the Mendelssohn, which he loved, to be a difficult work to play well, and most violinists today share that view. He also had reservations about the Bartók concerto, which he thought wasn't successful as a violin concerto *per se*, for reasons of balance between the violin and the orchestra. He considered the Bloch concerto entirely suitable in this respect.

As a man, Sammons remained simple and unassuming. 'Our own Albert' had no time for the snobbish upper echelons of the musical world. He was adored by the orchestral players, with whom he would often sit down and chat after a rehearsal. More often than not their conversation revolved around sport rather than the latest piece of musical gossip. His great hobby was golf, and in his prime he was a match for anyone. On one occasion, Sammons won a championship at Bognor and gave a recital the same evening. A reporter asked if his golf interfered with his fiddle playing. Sammons chortled: 'No! On the contrary, my fiddle playing is apt to interfere with my golf!'[8]

A connoisseur of master violins, Sammons owned a number of beautiful instruments by celebrated makers. For many years he used a Guadagnini and later a Stradivari, but his favourite fiddle, and one he used to the end of his performing life, was a superb Gofriller, dated 1696. Once, in the Cobbett Competition for Violin Makers, he played, behind a screen, a violin made by the Englishman Alfred Vincent and one by Stradivari. The majority of the judges were in favour of the sound of the modern instrument and Sammons aquired it for himself and used it for many years.

The outstanding feature of his solo playing was the searching power and depth of tone that enriched every phrase, be it light and lilting or intense and emotional. Hugh Bean (1929–2003), for many years leader of the Philharmonia Orchestra, recalled Sammons's warm, rich sound. 'His great sincerity and dignity as a man came over in his playing.'[9] According to Bean, his recordings do not do him justice. (The reissue on LP of the 1944 Delius recording had to be taken from a good set of 78 rpm discs because the matrices of the original recordings were destroyed in an air-raid.)

Composition was yet another of Sammons's accomplishments. In addition to a number of attractive solo works for the violin, he published three volumes of a concentrated form of exercises entitled *Secrets of Technique* (1916). This project was the result of many years' diligent research into the technical aspects of the instrument, and the studies illustrate his novel approach, especially with regard to the way to practise. Hugh Bean was reared on these exercises and considered them to be of vital importance:

> Sammons worked out what matters most and put it down in a concise and logical way. He taught me precisely how to use ten minutes in the best possible way. For example, you arrive late for a concert because the train is late. The hall is cold and there is no hot water. You have ten minutes to prepare yourself. He taught me how to overcome these hazards and it is all there in these little books.[10]

These exercises are at present out of print, despite the fact that many teachers use now-tattered copies and swear by them.

Sammons was a painstaking and flexible teacher. Not affiliated to any school, he had gained his experience by many years as an orchestral player. He realised that a musician never stopped learning and such humility stood him in good stead with his pupils. From 1939 to 1956, he was a professor of violin at the Royal College of Music, and among his many pupils were Thomas Matthews and Alan Loveday as well as Hugh Bean, who studied with Sammons for a period of some 20 years. Bean recalled Sammons's ability as a teacher:

> His wonderful directness and simplicity of character enabled him to communicate with his pupils. Since he was virtually self-taught himself, his problems had to be worked out in a matter-of-fact, thoroughly down-to-earth manner. He was not one for sophisticated phrases. He would either describe what he wanted in a straightforward way that everybody could understand, or demonstrate – not to show how brilliant he was, but how the problem could be analysed in a way that would be relevant to the particular pupil. But he was very suspicious of any slick way of solving a technical

problem. It had to be founded on rock-like foundations. Anything that resembled a gimmick or streamlining for effect would be absolutely alien to him. But even then if he saw that such a course came naturally under a student's fingers and that it worked for him, then he would not oppose him.[11]

For all his students Sammons had one unbreakable rule: 'Concentrate upon perfect intonation. You will never distinguish yourself until your intonation is perfect, for it is this and artistic interpretation that marks the difference between the work of the great violinist and the mediocre.'[12]

## Notes

1. Brook, *Violinists of Today*, p. 145.
2–3. Beecham, *A Mingled Chime*, p. 81.
4. Brook, op. cit., p. 148.
5. *Star*, 24 November 1914.
6. Brook, op. cit., p. 148.
7. *The Times*, 31 January 1919.
8. Brook, op. cit., p. 156.
9–11. Quoted from interview, M.C.
12. Brook, op. cit., p. 155.

# 22   The Russian Vanguard

wo of the first important violinists to emerge from the Auer School were the Russians Efrem Zimbalist and Mischa Elman. Regarded as competitors for many years, there was a time when Zimbalist achieved even higher public acclaim than his distinguished rival.

Efrem Zimbalist (1889–1985) was born at Rostov-on-Don, the son of a professional conductor. Naturally, he received a first-class grounding in music from his father and by the age of nine, he was leading the orchestra at the Rostov Opera House. He was 13 when he entered Auer's class in St Petersburg and, three years later, he left with the gold medal and the Rubinstein scholarship, worth 1,200 roubles.

The next few years brought the young Zimbalist success on every side. At 18, he made his Berlin début with the Brahms concerto to impressive reviews and, in London, he thrilled audiences with his brilliant performance of the Glazunov concerto at the Queen's Hall in 1908 under the baton of a young conductor also making his debut, Leopold Stokowski. As a fully-fledged virtuoso, he toured Europe, receiving rave notices everywhere he played, and was invited by the Leipzig Gewandhaus to play on New Year's Day, continuing the Joachim tradition, unbroken for 50 years.

In 1911, Zimbalist crossed the Atlantic. When he played the Glazunov concerto with the New York Philharmonic Orchestra under Josef Stransky at Carnegie Hall, the *New York Times* critic wrote: 'He is already a virtuoso in the best sense of the word, of the first rank, a mature artist who can stir feelings that it is not given to many to touch.' In the more decorative and brilliant passages the critic praised not only a 'technique of perfect security, but his power of transmuting a perfunctory work into something more noble than it merits' and declared that: 'Few artists are more unassuming than Mr Zimbalist, more absorbed in the music they are playing.'[1]

In a recital at the same hall in New York a few days later, Zimbalist again compelled admiration as 'an artist of truly remarkable powers'.[2] In a programme of music by Brahms, Paganini and Tchaikovsky, he also included pieces by York Bowen and Cyril Scott, two comparatively unknown English composers. Zimbalist reached the highest point of his achievement in the prelude and fugue from the solo sonata in G minor by Bach, which 'he interpreted with magnificent breadth and dignity of style, and with that tone which, the oftener it is heard, seems more astonishing in its power, virility and beauty'.[3]

Zimbalist was a genial and modest man, much admired by his fellow musicians.

An avid collector of books and rare manuscripts, he was also a connoisseur of vintage wines and cigars. He loved social life, and an invitation to one of his dinner parties promised a varied evening of entertainment. A sumptuous meal would be followed by string quartet playing, but that was not all. Donald Brook, the author of *Violinists of Today*, wrote that: 'An evening with Zimbalist generally concludes with bridge or poker, but unless you are an exceptionally good player, it is better to think of some ingenious excuse for an early departure.'[4]

Zimbalist composed a considerable amount of music for his instrument, although none is played today. But he should be remembered for his painstaking researches into the early violin repertory at a time when the works of composers such as Giacomo Torelli, Marco Uccellini and Giovanni Battista Bassani were largely unknown to violinists.

At the Royal Festival Hall in London in October 1961, a portly, short-legged, bald-headed little man played both the Brahms and the Mendelssohn concertos to a rapt audience who gave him a standing ovation. The next morning the press was also unanimous in its praise of this great artist who had first appeared (in an ill-fitting suit) before a British audience 56 years earlier. The violinist was Mischa Elman (1891–1967) and the concert took place nine months after his 70th birthday. Pianists and conductors would appear to be indestructible. But throughout the history of violin playing, there are few soloists who have maintained perfect accuracy into old age. Ysaÿe, Thibaud and Kreisler all declined towards the end of their careers, but Elman retained his glorious tone and perfect intonation until the close of his career. In fact, he died in action at the age of 76: he was practising for a forthcoming concert when his heart failed.

Elman was born in Tolna, a village near Kiev, the son of a Jewish schoolmaster who played the violin. When Mischa was four, he received some preliminary instruction from his father. His phenomenal progress prompted his parents to send him to the Imperial School of Music at Odessa, where he studied with Alexander Fidelmann. One day, Leopold Auer was visiting the school and heard young Mischa play; he was so taken with the boy's talent that he immediately offered him a place at the St Petersburg Conservatory. Since it was not possible for a Jew to attend a school outside his own domicile, the authorities raised objections until Auer threatened to resign his post if permission was not granted for this, the most talented boy he had ever encountered. The battle won, the entire Elman family moved to St Petersburg.

From the outset, Elman was Auer's favourite pupil; so astounding was his progress that in 1904 Auer presented him before a critical Berlin audience, who gave him a stupendous reception. He was immediately offered a number of further engagements in Berlin and in other German cities. Elman's St Petersburg debut came about as the result of a ruse. Auer himself had been invited to play the Paganini Moto Perpetuo and the Mendelssohn concerto, but at the last moment he feigned illness and pushed his prodigy onto the stage. The audience was astonished by the exquisiteness of his playing and would not let him go until he had given half a dozen encores.

Elman was 13 when he made his triumphal British debut at the Queen's Hall on 21 March 1905. *The Strad* critic wrote: 'From the moment he stepped onto the platform until he had played his last encore at 11.20 p.m. (and even then the public seemed to want some more) his success in this country was an assured thing.' In particular, the critic praised the way that he 'tackled the terrific difficulties of Tchaikovsky's D major Concerto as though they were a mere bagatelle' (Auer, it will be remembered, thought this work unplayable) and 'literally "waltzed round it", made light of its technical pitfalls, and gave a rendering of it so thoroughly in accord with the spirit in which it was written, that the audience literally rose to him'.[5]

A year later, Elman gave his first performance of the Brahms Concerto with the London Symphony Orchestra. The *Musical Times* reported that he interpreted 'the solo part with astonishing depth of expression and technical mastery'.[6] This was one of the works that many of his eminent predecessors had tackled only in their prime and some had avoided altogether. In an interesting article on the merits and drawbacks of infant prodigies in general, which appeared in the *Saturday Review*, Harold E. Gorst referred to Elman:

> His genius is as robust as that of a musician who has developed and matured slowly by natural stages . . . . I found in him not a young boy precociously proficient on the violin, but a musical giant, standing head and shoulders above most of his contemporaries . . . The dryest technical passages are phrased with such masterly conception that everything he plays is galvanized into life, and is made to convey some meaning, in the form of musical ideas, to the listener . . .

Gorst's summing up is revealing. 'Mischa Elman has survived the ordeal of the infant prodigy stage because his genius is spontaneous, not the imitative cleverness of a precocious child.'[7]

Elman was 17 when he made his first American appearance in New York, on 10 December 1908, playing the Tchaikovsky concerto with the Russian Symphony Orchestra. After his first New York recital, at Carnegie Hall a week later, the *New York Times* reviewer was critical of Elman's playing, citing 'serious defects' and rather too much 'temperament'. More specifically, it lacked 'poise and restraint'.[8] Many writers criticised him for his tendency to force the note of pathos and sentiment which resulted in a lack of breadth and simplicity. Elman's own response was simply 'I play how I feel'.

But the critical voices didn't reflect popular opinion, and Elman continued to pack the concert halls on both sides of the Atlantic. He returned to Britain soon after his American success, having decided some years before that he preferred to live in that country. Londoners flocked in their thousands to hear him and the only place large enough to accommodate them was the Albert Hall. He was commanded to appear at Buckingham Palace on several occasions because Queen Alexandra was especially fond of his playing. On one occasion, when playing to the royal family,

Elman appeared with two distinguished fellow artists, Nellie Melba and Enrico Caruso. A friendship developed between the great tenor and Elman and they made a number of bestselling recordings together. Elman lived in New York for a couple of years at the Knickerbocker Hotel, where Caruso also had a suite.

When the First World War broke out, Elman received a message from Nicholas II granting him dispensation from military service, on account of his great value as an artist, and saying that 'Russia would not wish harm to come to one of her great geniuses'.[9] Elman never returned to his native country, but like all Slavonic expatriates became misty-eyed when talking about it. When, after the Second World War, the Russians began the restoration of the Tchaikovsky Museum at Klin, he lost no time in making his contribution by way of a complete set of his recordings of the composer's music.

Elman went to America in 1914 and in 1923 he took US citizenship. Two years later, he married a wealthy American, Helen Katten. His wife's wedding gift to him was the superb Madame Recamier Stradivarius (1717), said to have been presented to the famous beauty by Napoleon. It was purchased in Paris while on their honeymoon, and was said to be worth £10,000, an extremely high price for the time.

Elman's long career experienced several ups and downs, but his tremendous resilience stood him in good stead. A world celebrity at 16, he had to compete at 25 with the phenomenal Kreisler, who stole much of the limelight on the American concert platform. At the same time, Heifetz was emerging as the most formidable rival of all. Ten years later the 12-year-old Menuhin took the world by storm. Also emerging at this time was the young Nathan Milstein (from the Auer School) and, by the 1930s, another Russian, David Oistrakh, joined the galaxy.

Elman's survival through all this fierce competition was largely due to his innate sense of purpose and a stability that many other artists lacked. Auer tells a story about this quality, which he already exhibited as a boy. Auer had a theory that a pupil with great talent and unusual physical advantages will rise above the general level if he is set a task well beyond his power. He decided to experiment with Elman when he was only 12 years old by setting him the first movement of the Tchaikovsky concerto for a public examination. At a rehearsal the boy was struggling with a passage in thirds in the cadenza. Having told him to repeat the passage several times, Auer said it was obvious Elman could not play the Tchaikovsky and he should therefore prepare another piece. 'With eyes filled with tears, and a voice full of determination, he assured me that at the examination the passage would go well.'[10] Auer insisted that he doubted it, and he should find an alternative piece for the examination, but that he should also perfect the concerto. When the dress rehearsal came round, Elman played the Tchaikovsky faultlessly.

Perhaps as an insurance against the abundance of talent on the solo side, Elman founded the successful Elman Quartet in 1924. The performance of the Mozart B flat Quartet at their first concert was described as 'positively thrilling'[11] and the recording they made of the Andante Cantabile from the Tchaikovsky Quartet in D major, Op. 11, No. 1, was a bestseller on both sides of the Atlantic.

Like Kreisler, Elman was equable in temperament and not given to rages when things went wrong. There is a story of the boy who reappeared regularly after a number of concerts, always to collect his autograph. Elman asked him why so many. Nonchalantly the boy replied: 'Oh, I'm trading my pal five Elmans for one Kreisler.'[12] Elman took it all in good part and would tell the story against himself.

But there were things Elman felt strongly about. He was highly critical of the mania for speed, which was beginning to develop during his career. Something was radically wrong with teaching methods that allowed talented students to become obsessed with the idea that speed was the most important element. He also regretted the trend to place too much importance on sheer mechanics. Sam Applebaum discussed this problem with Elman, and in his book, *With the Artists*, reports him as saying: 'Students are prone to lose sight of the nature of their instrument as a medium second only to the human voice as expressive of tonal beauty. I would place strong stress on impressing pupils with the fact that the violin is a singing instrument – appreciation of its musical function should be cultivated and they should not be carried away by dazzling technical display.'[13]

Elman was the first of Auer's pupils to spread his master's fame abroad, and it was through him that the 'Russian' bow grip was made known. Flesch describes it thus: 'The index finger touches the stick at the line separating the second from the third joint, and in addition embraces it with its first and second joint.'[14] When this hold is correctly employed, the index finger guides the bow and the little finger only touches it at the lower half while playing. David Oistrakh was a perfect example of a player who used the Russian grip in its 'classic' form.

Elman is best remembered for his superb dark, mellow tone, as individual and unmistakable as that of Kreisler or Heifetz. Flesch described it as 'overflowing', 'with a sensuous mellifluence, an Italian *bel canto* in oriental dress'. He praised his intonation, which he said was 'as clear as a bell'.[15] And yet Elman's hands were small and his fingers short and thick. Like Sarasate, he was unable to play certain works by Paganini. However, his repertory was extensive. He played Handel and unaccompanied Bach superbly, but equally, he could turn to the Lalo *Symphonie Espagnole* and project quite another mood. The salon pieces of Józef Wieniawski, Jules Massenet and Saint-Saëns became masterpieces in his hands. But above all, he made the Tchaikovsky concerto his own. Many consider Elman's performance the best of his time, and his recording of the work is lasting proof of it. Donald Brook aptly sums up the Elman phenomenon. 'The outstanding feature of his playing is not the technical mastery of his instrument . . . nor yet the satisfying breadth of tone, but that spiritual Hebraic quality that artists of Jewish ancestry seem to be able to put into music of a sombre mood.'[16]

**Notes**

1. *New York Times*, 3 November 1911.
2. Aldrich, *Concert Life in New York*, p. 338.

3. Ibid., p. 339.

4. Brook, *Violinists of Today*, p. 191.

5. *The Strad*, April 1905, p. 367.

6. *Musical Times*, July 1906.

7. *Saturday Review*, 9 June 1906, p. 718.

8. *New York Times*, 18 December 1908.

9. Brook, op. cit., p. 37.

10. Auer, *Violin Playing as I Teach It*, pp. 42–3.

11. Brook, op. cit., 37

12. Gaisberg, *Music on Record*, p. 207

13. Applebaum, *With the Artists*, p. 4.

14. Flesch, *The Art of Violin Playing*, p. 51.

15. Flesch, *Memoirs*, p. 254.

16. Brook, op. cit., p. 38.

# 23 The Scholarly Virtuoso

When Joseph Szigeti's *With Strings Attached* was published in 1947, a reviewer commented: 'As a writer of personal reminiscences he has one serious fault; he dislikes talking about himself.' As a soloist, he didn't seem 'to have the virtuoso soloist temperament at all'. On paper, Szigeti appears to be 'more interested in other people and in music as an art than he is in his own personality'.[1] The same writer also draws attention to the time and energy that this remarkable man spent on the promotion of new music. Szigeti (1892–1973) probably holds the record for first performances of new works by living composers, many of them dedicated to him.

Szigeti was born Joska Singer, in Budapest, where the gipsy fiddler was part of everyday life; he could not recall a time when music was not present in his consciousness. Everyone in his family played a stringed instrument; his uncle, who stood nearly 2 metres, was appropriately put on the double bass. His father, who gave him his first lessons, was the leader of a café orchestra.

Szigeti's mother died soon after his birth, so his childhood was divided between the city of Budapest and the home of his grandparents in a little village in the Carpathian mountains called Maramaros-Sziget, hence the name Szigeti. Joska was taken at an early age to study at a private preparatory conservatory in Budapest. His tutor, a rank-and-file member of the opera orchestra, was kindly but inadequate as a teacher. Nevertheless, when he played for Hubay at the Music Academy, Szigeti was placed straightaway in his masterclass.

Szigeti always remained grateful for his studies with Hubay, but equally was aware that there were certain aspects of the Hungarian school that attracted criticism. Hubay, epitome of the establishment, did not care for the music of either Béla Bartók or Zoltán Kodály and was surprised when his young pupil showed enthusiasm for it. Although Hubay was an excellent teacher and a fine musician, he was in many ways still under the spell of Joachim. At the same time he was pulled in quite another direction by the insatiable demands of parents that he should turn their children into prodigies. Szigeti's formative years must have been influenced by this situation, especially when the violin-playing world was being inundated with a host of brilliant players with an entirely new concept of sensuous sound and emotional projection, such as Elman and Zimbalist. As if this were not enough, the young Szigeti had also to compete with Kreisler.

Szigeti's debut in Budapest, playing the Viotti A minor Concerto, did not automatically ensure the instant success stories associated with so many of his contemporaries. At the time, Budapest was one of the favourite places in Europe for talent scouting. Szigeti recalled the 'cigar-chewing, fur-coat-sporting' impresarios who hovered around their prodigies, Franz von Vecsey and Jan Kubelík, and were frequently photographed with their 'wards', as if to show that they had a share in the 'almost occult hair-raising accomplishments of those they promoted'.[2] Szigeti himself decided early on that it was better to avoid such offers of 'management'.

Szigeti made his Berlin debut at the small Bechstein Saal in 1905 when he was 13. For economic reasons this took place in the morning. Despite a programme which included the Bach Chaconne, the Ernst Concerto in F sharp minor and the Paganini Witches' Dance, the only response from the press was an honourable mention in the *Berliner Tageblatt* of 10 December, by way of a photograph captioned 'A musical prodigy, Josef Szigeti'.

The 13-year-old soloist spent the next few months with a fourth-rate summer theatre company in a small resort in Hungary where he made solo appearances between acts of Hungarian folk operettas. All the music had to be orchestrated by the pianist conductor to suit the seven- or eight-piece ensemble. If this experience did little to further Szigeti's musical education, it probably taught him a great deal about the facts of life.

An even more unlikely engagement for the violinist who was to become known as 'the Scholarly Virtuoso' was a few months' employment at the Zirkus Albert Schumann Theatre in Frankfurt-am-Main. At first Szigeti's father refused to let him go, but when a large fee was proffered he agreed, on condition that his son should take a *nom de plume*. As 'Szulagi', Szigeti, made his debut in the music halls, appearing with acrobats, a trained dog act and Abbie Mitchell, a black American singer, with her group of 'shuffledancing, spiritual singing, banjo-playing young negroes' called the 'Tennessee Students'.[3] In later years, when Abbie Mitchell was asked what she remembered of the young boy who played the Mendelssohn concerto so beautifully in between the circus acts, she said he was intensely serious and isolated, but when he played his face lit up and a complete metamorphosis took place. His father, who always watched from the wings, hovered over him 'like a mothering hen'.[4]

In the winter of 1906, Szigeti made his London debut at the Bechstein (now the Wigmore) Hall. Owing to a rather unorthodox dual management consisting of a former music critic and a backer of stage plays, he appeared with a pianist for the salon pieces and a small orchestra for the Ernst and Mendelssohn concertos. Szigeti recalled his embarrassment at being ordered to wear an alpaca sailor suit with short trousers, which necessitated having his legs shaved.

However, the experience was successful enough to bring in engagements to play throughout the country, especially at the seaside resorts. These concerts were sponsored by the National Sunday League in an effort to brighten the gloom of the Victorian Sabbath. Ostensibly, they were confined to religious music only, but not surprisingly secular items were slipped into the programmes whenever possible.

The efforts of the League were opposed by the Salvation Army and other religious organisations. On one occasion, the Army played a brass band relentlessly outside the hall in protest while Szigeti attempted to convey the sensuous charm of the Wieniawski concerto within.

When Szigeti was 14, Hubay took him to play for Joachim in Berlin. The gout-crippled master was sufficiently impressed to suggest he should finish his repertory studies with him. Szigeti and his father were invited to attend one of Joachim's classes at the Hochschule, where the old man sat on a small platform in the middle of the room. Although he listened to his students and criticised verbally, Joachim had no violin in his hand. Young as he was, Szigeti felt that this distance symbolised the absence of rapport between master and pupil. Szigeti declined Joachim's offer and remained loyal to Hubay.

For the next six years, Szigeti made his home in England, having been adopted by a musical family who lived in Surrey. Besides fulfilling engagements all over the country, in 1908 he gave the first performance of Hamilton Harty's Violin Concerto, which the composer dedicated to 'Joska Szigeti, in Friendship'. It was also during this time that Szigeti toured with the legendary Nellie Melba and the 25-year-old John McCormack. With either Ferruccio Busoni or Wilhelm Backhaus as pianist, and the French virtuoso flautist, Philip Gaubert, to provide obbligatos to some of the prima donna's coloratura arias, they formed an interesting and diverse company.

In 1913 Szigeti had his first serious setback when it was discovered he was suffering from tuberculosis. He spent the next three years in Switzerland, at Davos, undergoing treatment, after which the cure was fortunately complete, enabling him to resume his solo career in 1917. That same year he succeeded Henri Marteau as professor of violin at the Geneva Conservatory, a post he held for seven years. During this time he appeared in all the principal cities of Europe under leading conductors, and was a great favourite of Arthur Nikisch for his concerts in Berlin.

A chance meeting with Leopold Stokowski in Geneva in 1925 brought Szigeti his first invitation to play in the USA. Stokowski, then conductor of the Philadelphia Symphony Orchestra, engaged the young violinist to play the Beethoven concerto in December of that year. Szigeti recalled the first rehearsal as he stood waiting for his entry, becoming weaker and weaker at the knees, 'as the silken sheen of that orchestral introduction enveloped me'.[5] The performance was praised for his musicianly interpretation, but it did not attract the hysterical acclaim that other artists received. And when Szigeti gave his first recital in New York, on 19 December, the popular journalists did no better. However, Olin Downes, music critic of the *New York Times*, wrote: 'Mr Szigeti appears to be most himself, and to show most effectively the different phases of his artistic personality when he can get close to his audience and discourse the music of different composers.' Astonishingly, by today's standards, he played a programme that included selections by Tartini, Bach, Mozart, Bloch, Prokofiev, Veracini, Dvořák, Kreisler and Paganini. 'There was lightning change from the radiant Mozart to the savage rhapsodic orientalism of Ernest Bloch. His two pieces Vidui and Nigun are masterly in their brevity and intensification of mood ... Hebraic in the emotional force and the jagged contour of the melodies. They were given their true character, their utmost significance by Mr Szigeti ....'[6]

Apart from Carnegie Hall recitals, where the programmes favoured the 'classics', the musical hotch-potch presented in other places caused Szigeti much concern. The public lapped up programmes composed entirely of salon pieces. Once, during a heated argument on the subject with an executive of one of the country's leading concert circuits, the promoter retorted: 'Well, let me tell you, Mr Dzigedy – and *I* know what I'm talking about – your Krewtser sonata bores the pants off my audiences!'[7] Another zealous impresario was known to crouch on the platform camouflaged by the potted palms and train opera glasses on the audience to note their reactions. The measure of their approval was not rapt silence but a variety of nods and nudges conveyed to their companions.

Despite the demands of commercial-orientated promoters, Szigeti took pains to build up his reputation as a scholarly interpreter of the great composers, so that by the early 1930s he had achieved world fame. His concert tours took him twice round the world and it is almost impossible to name a country in which he did not play. He made many visits to the Soviet Union and regarded the audiences in that country as some of the most cultured in the world. He was amazed by the way an unknown performer could fill a hall, which was half empty when the concert began. When an artist shows himself to be out of the ordinary, the enthusiasts slip out, one by one, and telephone their friends. The news is passed on and gradually the newcomers arrive. When the concert is over, the hitherto unknown player finds he has a packed house, all loudly applauding his performance. (Clearly, a bad performance could spark the opposite effect.)

Szigeti's polish and style appealed to the discriminating music lover. Alexander Ruppa, *The Strad*'s critic in Egypt, writing about a concert at the Alhambra Theatre in Alexandria on 21 March 1935, said: 'Szigeti has the technical equipment of Heifetz plus musicality.' Ruppa described his tone as 'satisfyingly full, woody, elastic, and extraordinarily equal on all four strings'. He praised Szigeti's varied choice of programme, above all his Mozart: '... his crowning feat was decidedly the exquisite D major Mozart Concerto which became a scintillating jewel in his hands'. Szigeti's recital partner on this occasion was Prince Nikita Magaloff, who played the piano parts from memory 'with the utmost competence and restraint'.[8]

Carl Flesch admired Szigeti both as man and musician, although he criticised what he called his 'archaic' bowing technique. Szigeti held his arm closer to the body than any other violinist, a position condemned by others besides Flesch. Nonetheless, the result was a wonderful elasticity of bowing, prompting one critic to declare that 'he had the most elegant right arm of living violinists'.[9]

Flesch was probably nearer the truth when he said that Szigeti's real significance was his feeling for contemporary music and progressive programme building, rather like Joachim in the nineteenth century. And in common with his eminent predecessor, Szigeti had few rivals in this art. He spent much time organising his pieces, not only in chronological order but with special consideration for their 'mood and density'.[10] He believed that the order in which pieces are played can be just as important as the way an artist displays paintings on a wall.

Szigeti's repertory of both classical and contemporary works was enormous. Ernest Bloch composed his Violin Concerto for Szigeti, who gave its first performance under Beecham in 1939, because he felt that in his hands it would receive sympathetic treatment. Earlier in his career, Szigeti gave the first performance of the Busoni concerto in Berlin in 1912, with the composer conducting.

Sergei Prokofiev always regarded Szigeti as one of his finest interpreters and dedicated his First Violin Concerto to him. Béla Bartók, with whom Szigeti enjoyed a close friendship, also spoke highly of his readings; in 1939, Szigeti, Benny Goodman and Endre Petri gave the first performance in New York of his Rhapsody for clarinet, violin and piano, which Bartók dedicated to Szigeti and Goodman. The following year they performed it in its final three-movement version, re-named 'Contrasts', with Bartók at the piano.

There were recordings made of Szigeti as early as 1908 but techniques had been vastly improved a decade later when he was regularly making recordings. The number he made from the end of the First World War is considerable and ranges from Bach, Brahms and Mozart to Bartók (many with the composer at the piano), Berg and Ives. His recording with Claudio Arrau of the ten Beethoven sonatas is particularly memorable.

Flesch used to say that Szigeti was better 'canned' than live.[11] The English violist Frederick Riddle was a member of the orchestra when Flesch and Szigeti made their famous recording of the Bach Double Concerto in 1937, under Walter Goehr. Before the rehearsal the two artists were feverishly practising virtuoso exercises, each trying to outdo the other. When the actual recording took place, 'it was more like a competition than a concerto'.[12] Flesch was difficult as always, and it would seem that Szigeti also for once abandoned his cool approach, with the result that in the Vivace the homogeneous spirit of the music was lost. But in the slow movement, Bach becomes the mediator and all sense of rivalry dissolves.

Apart from such isolated incidents, Szigeti was popular with his fellow musicians and greatly respected for his interests outside music. He was a voracious reader and a witty, lively conversationalist who could tackle subjects ranging from science, art and literature to sport – cricket being one of his passions. He held the view that sport, allied to a good background of general culture, was indispensable to any musician and he frequently deplored the one-track mind of so many of his colleagues.

On Szigeti's 80th birthday, the American critic Henry Roth wrote a tribute in *The Strad*: 'Szigeti offered new vistas of imagination, breadth of vision, grandeur of spirit, sincerity of purpose, ineffable sensitivity and the exhilaration which accompanies daring new musical explorations. And he played with an intense visceral power which somehow always radiated his own humanism.'[13]

Sixty-six years earlier, the 14-year-old Szigeti had received an autograph from one of the great figures of the day which read:

My wish is:

May your art satisfy you – others will then rejoice in it, but the former is more important.

Ferruccio Busoni[14]

It was advice that Szigeti heeded throughout his life.

## Notes

1. *The Strad*, April 1951, p. 432.
2. Szigeti, *With Strings Attached*, p. 29.
3. Ibid., p. 46.
4. Ibid., p. 48.
5. Ibid., p. 245.
6. *New York Times*, 19 December 1925.
7. Szigeti, op. cit., p. 250.
8. *The Strad*, May 1935. p. 41.
9. Brook, *Violinists of Today*, p. 172.
10. Ibid, p. 170.
11. Flesch, *Memoirs*, p. 292.
12. Quoted from interview, M.C.
13. Roth, *The Strad*, December 1972, p. 413.
14. Szigeti, op. cit., p. 83.

# 24 'King of Violinists'

When Jascha Heifetz made his London debut in 1920, George Bernard Shaw was sitting in the audience. In his days as a music critic, Shaw had been an astute judge of musical sheep and goats, and many of his prophecies came to pass. He was moved by the performance of the 19-year-old and wrote to him, making a forecast which has an uncanny veracity about it:

> My dear Heifetz,
> Your recital has filled me and my wife with anxiety. If you provoke a jealous God by playing with such superhuman perfection, you will die young. I earnestly advise you to play something badly every night before going to bed, instead of saying your prayers. No mortal should presume to play so faultlessly.
> G. Bernard Shaw[1]

In an article in *Time* magazine of 31 October 1969, Roger Kahn took up this idea in a moving and perceptive article that suggests that Shaw was right in that Heifetz 'presumed' and has 'paid for his genius with his humanity'. The significance of Heifetz's influence on violin playing throughout the world is tremendous. Three generations of players have murmured his name with reverence and he remains their model, still unsurpassed. The American writer-violinist Henry Roth summed up the situation perfectly: 'Had Heifetz never lived, violin playing might never have attained the pinnacle of perfection on the instrumental level that it enjoys today – a fact freely admitted by his colleagues everywhere!'[2] But in his latter years, the most famous violinist in the world no longer played in public, and lived alone in a large luxurious house in Beverly Hills, California, separated from the outside world by four acres of grounds and an electrified gate.

Jascha Heifetz (1901–87) was born in Vilnius, Lithuania, the son of the leader of the Vilnius Symphony Orchestra. From infancy, Jascha responded to music and at the age of three he was given a quarter-size fiddle, which he mastered within a week. He received his first lessons from his father but soon surpassed his knowledge and entered the Imperial School of Music. He was not quite five when he made his first public appearance in the crowded auditorium of the Music School. A year later he played the Mendelssohn concerto to an audience of over a thousand.

Heifetz graduated from the Music School at the age of seven and was taken to St Petersburg to play for Auer, but was not accepted immediately into his masterclass, as is generally believed. However at nine, he became the youngest child ever to have been admitted to the St Petersburg Conservatory.

According to Heifetz, 'Auer was a wonderful and incomparable teacher. I do not believe that there is any teacher in the world who could possibly approach him. Don't ask me how he did it, for I would not know how to tell you, for he is completely different with each student.'[3] Heifetz studied with Auer for about six years, both privately and in his masterclass; he never played exercises or technical works of any kind, and apart from concertos and sonatas, the professor allowed him freedom to choose his repertory.

Auer's pupils were supposed to be sufficiently technically advanced for him to concentrate on interpretation: 'Yet there were all sorts of technical finesses which he always had up his sleeve; any number of fine subtle points in playing, as well as in interpretation, which he would disclose to his students as it became necessary.'[4] The more interest and ability a student showed, the more Auer could give in response. A glimpse of the inside workings of the Auer school is furnished by the American violinist Albert Spalding (1888–1953), who attended an Auer class in 1913 when on a concert tour of Russia. He recalled that 'the other "star" pupils were eclipsed by this miniature wizard in his early teens', and went on to describe Heifetz's rendering of the difficult Ernst concerto: 'The first flush of fingered octaves was attacked with a kind of nonchalant aplomb. The tone was firm, flowing and edgeless, the intonation of fleckless purity. A kind of inner grace made itself felt in the shaping of the phrase.' Auer strode nervously up and down, casting a periodic glance in Spalding's direction to note his reactions. 'His dark, restless eyes danced with delight as the wonder boy threaded his effortless way through the tortuous technical problems. . . . he would turn away with a helpless shrug of the shoulders as if to say, "Was there ever anything like it?"'[5]

Even while studying at the conservatory, young Jascha was giving public recitals in St Petersburg and many other Russian cities. He once played at an open-air concert at Odessa, where 25,000 people gave him a standing ovation. Reports began to circulate throughout Europe long before he set foot outside his native country. He was only 11 when he made his Berlin debut under Nikisch, playing the Tchaikovsky concerto. Nikisch, one of the few conductors who had originally trained as a violinist, admitted that he had never heard anything to equal the playing of this child. Heifetz subsequently performed under Nikisch in Vienna and Leipzig, where he took the audiences by storm. When he played the Bruch concerto at the Gewandhaus in Leipzig in 1913, he was told that Joachim was the only other violinist as young as himself to have appeared as soloist with the orchestra. It was at this particular concert that Kreisler first heard him and made the legendary remark to Zimbalist: 'You and I might as well take our fiddles and break them across our knees.'[6]

The jest was not far off the truth. Although Kreisler never suffered personally, there were many established violinists who were overshadowed by this rising star. We know that Jan Kubelík was one of the casualties whose career was damaged by the young Heifetz. According to Flesch, violinists at the turn of the century tended to copy Kubelík's way of playing rapid passages – clearly, but not too fast. After Heifetz appeared on the scene, 'young fiddlers are possessed by the devil of speed and are trying to establish records'.[7]

The outbreak of the First World War brought international concert-giving to a halt, and when strong rumours of impending revolution in Russia presented an additional hazard, Heifetz's father decided to risk a wartime crossing of the Atlantic in order for his son to make his American début. This took place at Carnegie Hall in New York on 27 October 1917. Heifetz was 16 years old, slim, blue-eyed, with fair curly hair. He astonished an audience that included all the top string players in the city – not only by his brilliant playing but by his cool platform manner. His programme included the Wieniawski D minor Concerto, Paganini's 24th Caprice and Tartini's Variations on a Theme by Corelli. The *New York Times* critic remarked on his unassuming manner and praised him for the 'remarkable beauty and purity' of his tone, which was characterised by 'power, smoothness and roundness. . . . His bowing is of rare elasticity and vigour, excellent in many details as is his left-hand execution, which is accurate in all sorts of difficulties.' There then followed the understatement of the century: 'In his technical equipment, Mr Heifetz is unusual.'[8]

The musicians who had witnessed this miracle were all members of 'The Bohemians', the New York Musicians' Club. They decided unanimously to give a dinner in Heifetz's honour on Saturday, 29 December 1917 at the Biltmore Hotel. Everybody who was anybody was there, including Kreisler, Zimbalist, Franz Kneisel (1865–1926) and a host of others. It was The Bohemians' recognition that placed Heifetz firmly on this throne as 'King of Violinists', although with such a talent he would probably have risen to the top regardless. He became a member of this exclusive club and reciprocated their gesture by playing at a concert on 2 February 1940 at The Bohemians in honour of Fritz Kreisler's birthday, which was also his own.

As Heifetz's fame spread, his earnings soared. In the USA in December 1919 he received a fee of $2,250 per concert, making him the highest paid classical artist of his day. (Kreisler, for example, collected only $2,000 per concert that year.)

Heifetz made his debut in London on 5 May 1920 at the Queen's Hall. Through the phenomenal success of his gramophone recordings (70,000 of which had already been sold in the UK before he ever set a foot on British soil), the hall sold out well before the day of the concert. The *Musical Times* critic described him as 'the greatest sensation of the musical world so far'.[9] Heifetz was offered engagement upon engagement, playing always to packed houses. He repeated this success all over the world and his name became known on every continent.

Eventually, Heifetz found himself playing some 200 engagements a year, for which he usually received rave notices. They praised his impeccable playing, his superb left hand, his wonderful bowing arm, his phrasing, his musicianship. There were simply no words which could adequately proclaim his genius. After a recital at the Queen's Hall in London in 1930, a critic wrote of Heifetz winding up his programme with the

Moto Perpetuo of Paganini, which he took at a seemingly impossible speed. Turning to his neighbour, he exclaimed 'Good Heavens, he'll never keep up that speed!' He did; and each note shone like a glittering diamond. What execution. The audience literally rose to its feet and shouted its approval.[10]

But Heifetz was also accused of gimmickry – such as recording the Bach Double Concerto, playing both parts himself. But is it gimmickry that disturbs his critics? Is it perhaps their inability to believe that one virtuoso can play two parts with such artistry and expression? Do they not echo Shaw's concern? His recording of the slow movement is not only ravishing in tone but profound in its depth of feeling.

Nonetheless, there have also been critics who persistently accused Heifetz of coldness. 'How frigid is this dazzling playing,'[11] wrote Henri Prunières after a recital at the Paris Opéra. Another commented: 'His command of the mechanics of the fiddle is still what it was, well-nigh impeccable. But is he broadening and developing in other respects?' That particular critic found that during the course of the years Heifetz was 'beginning to appeal to the emotional as well as to the intellectual'.[12]

But perhaps a remark made by an old lady, who was overheard as she left a concert in 1922, holds the most significance: 'That young man only needs some great sorrow, some terrible disappointment to make him really wonderful, because he will then be more human. Today he suggests a disembodied spirit.'[13]

For Flesch, Heifetz represented 'a culmination in the contemporary development of our art'. He likened his finger and bow functions to a machine that runs at maximum capacity as soon as the button is pressed. 'His tone has a noble substance and is of a magical beauty, and there is not the smallest flaw in his technical equipment.' However, Flesch could not, in the end, allow this perfection to go unsullied, and maintained that Heifetz took the Russian grip of the bow to 'its utter extremes, exaggerating it, in fact, in a way that would render it useless for ordinary mortals'. He also criticised his bad habit of playing *diminuendo* on down-bows and *forte* on the up-bows which 'he shares with most Auer pupils'.[14]

Flesch wrote his memoirs in 1940, just as Heifetz was approaching 40 and at the height of his career, but the enigma was already present. Flesch puts forth the argument that Heifetz, like Mozart, was born with gifts from heaven. He never had to struggle to perfect his technique – it just happened. It is hardly surprising that he fell into the habit of playing with his hands and allowing his mind to rest. Flesch cites as the exception the superb Heifetz recording of the Sibelius concerto, whose transcendental qualities bear witness to a different mood. Flesch could be right when he says that the infallibility of Heifetz's technical approach is his worst enemy.[15]

Heifetz was often described as being a man with a mask. His flat, tartar features assumed a supercilious expression when he was displeased. But his friends of earlier years tell stories of his great sense of humour and the wicked mimicry he exhibited at parties. In his day a great raconteur, he would also tell jokes against himself with gusto. There was the time when he took a rather good-looking black valet with him on a European tour. They were passing through Switzerland early in the morning, and Heifetz was still asleep when the porter knocked and asked: 'At what hour does His Highness wish breakfast?'[16] Heifetz thought that he had been mistaken for a nobleman travelling incognito, but it transpired that the entire train staff were under the impression that his valet was a Maharajah and Heifetz a member of his entourage.

Heifetz always had a wide range of interests. As a young man he was 'camera crazy' and took pictures of everything. He played an excellent game of tennis at one time and was also known for his skill at ping-pong. He was an avid collector of rare books and would occasionally take a special guest on a conducted tour of his library. Here, Heifetz's voice would soften and his expression relax as he fondled his first edition Dickens and his Kelmscott Chaucer. He would apologise for having only a fourth folio Shakespeare.[17]

He made the last of his rare public appearances in Los Angeles on 27 October 1972. After that, his music-making was confined to occasional chamber music with a select group of friends. His self-imposed, hermit-like existence was open to much debate. Some say that Heifetz had everything in life – wealth, success and the adulation of millions, that he was now bored and, because he was bored, he could not be bothered to perform in public. Yet until his death he still practised diligently for concerts that were never intended to take place.

Heifetz's formidable but effortless execution, his tone, his accuracy of intonation and his ability to bring an infinite variety of nuance into his bowing were unique. On the interpretative side, he had a sensuality of expression that never spilled over into sentimentality. Here again, he was unique. As a man Heifetz remained an enigma, but as a violinist his influence will continue to reverberate for centuries to come.

Heifetz had another side – as a teacher – and two of his most celebrated pupils, his first regular students, were Erick Friedman and Pierre Amoyal. Erick Friedman was born in Newark, New Jersey in 1939 and had his first lessons on the violin with Samuel Applebaum; at the age of ten he went on to study with Ivan Galamian at the Juilliard School for six years (but was one of the few Galamian pupils who did not enthuse about his teaching). Friedman was only 15 when he made his New York debut as a soloist with the Little Orchestral Society, and his Carnegie Hall recital debut followed in 1956. This was the year that he left Galamian to study with Milstein, whose methods were in complete contrast; his lessons (which often went on for hours) were of immense value to Friedman. 'I would sit back and watch him [play] and probably learned more that way.'[18]

Meanwhile, Friedman had come under the wing of Arthur Judson, doyen of US concert managers, and, as a result, relinquished a place at Cornell University which he had already accepted. With his future virtually assured, he began giving a series of successful concerts throughout the USA. Then, in 1957, he met Heifetz – an encounter that changed his life. It seems that Heifetz had heard him play and offered him a half-hour audition. The 18-year-old was very nervous, but, to his surprise, he was allowed to play for over two hours, after which Heifetz offered to teach him himself. Friedman became Heifetz's first regular pupil.

Naturally, Judson was opposed to the idea because Friedman's concert diary was already full, but Friedman cancelled all concerts for a period of three years and moved to Los Angeles. He had private lessons two or three times a week, for which Heifetz never charged a cent. Without doubt, the years with Heifetz transformed his playing, and those who heard him recognised the hand of the master. Lessons consisted mostly of coaching on interpretation when Heifetz – a fine pianist – would accompany him at the piano. Heifetz was never doctrinal where technique was concerned and every technical point was addressed to a specific musical idea.

> For Heifetz, phrasing a musical line was the most important aspect of violin playing. He told me that he often went to the opera as a young boy with his mother, and you could characterise his musicianship as strongly vocal influenced. You might say that he emphasised the horizontal rather than the vertical, or structural dimension of music.[19]

Friedman recalls that because of his 'fierce honesty', Heifetz was never effusive with compliments. However, he paid Friedman the greatest compliment of all when, in 1960, he invited him to record the Bach Double Concerto with him in London – the only recording in which he is partnered by another violinist.

Friedman's career gained momentum over the years until, in 1985, he was involved in a car accident that injured his left arm and hand. As a result, he was obliged to give up performing and concentrate on teaching. He has been artist-in-residence at the Southern Methodist University in Dallas, Texas and holder of the Mischa Elman Chair at the Manhattan School of Music in New York. Friedman is a dedicated teacher. Having had the rare privilege of studying with Heifetz, he tries to impart the same principles and ideals to his students. 'One of the great stipulations that Heifetz imposed upon me was that I would teach and thus carry on the little bit of tradition that he gave me... . Maybe I was in some way anointed to carry on a tradition that goes from Heifetz and Milstein through Auer back to Joachim. Because I know what it is.'[20]

Pierre Amoyal was born in Paris in 1949. When he was seven, he heard a recording of Heifetz playing the Tchaikovsky concerto and begged for a violin. After some initial instruction from a local teacher, he had lessons with Roland Charmey and the following year entered the Paris Conservatoire. He graduated at twelve, carrying off the Premier Prix (a feat only previously achieved by Kreisler). At 16 he was accepted as a pupil of David Oistrakh, and was about to leave for Moscow when he met Heifetz personally for the first time.

Due to his demanding and intimidating manner, Heifetz did not attract many pupils, so on one of his tours, he auditioned would-be students in a number of capital cities worldwide. Someone organised an audition for Amoyal, who, with considerable trepidation accepted the challenge. Afterwards, he admitted it was a nightmare. Heifetz asked each violinist which of the Paganini Caprices they knew and then commanded them to play a different one – without music. 'My ordeal lasted over two hours as I hacked away at caprices I knew only partly. Thoroughly ashamed of my performance, I was miserable . . . . Then, believe it or not, Mr Heifetz accepted me as a pupil.' At first it was difficult to switch from Charmey's French school approach to that of Heifetz and the Auer school; he had to make many mechanical adjustments. 'Mr Heifetz never insisted that technical details like the position of the bow grip or matters of fingerboard manipulation be styled in his image. But the things he demanded of me could only be negotiated in the Heifetz manner. Consequently my technical development became strongly fashioned by his methods of holding the instrument.'[21]

Amoyal studied with Heifetz for five years. One day Heifetz came to the class carrying a case containing a beautiful Vuillaume violin and asked Amoyal to try it. He was at the time playing on an inferior French instrument and loved the sound made by the Vuillaume. Heifetz said that, if he liked it, it was his. Amoyal was 'profoundly moved by his generosity'.[22] Heifetz also gave him a piece of advice: 'It doesn't matter how long it takes to get to the top. It's how long you stay there that counts.'[23] Amoyal has stayed firmly at the top for over 20 years.

## Notes

1. Letter from George Bernard Shaw, 5 May 1920.
2. Axelrod, *Heifetz*, p. 33.
3. Ibid., p. 126.
4. Ibid., p. 128.
5–6 Ibid., p. 46.
7. Flesch, *Memoirs*, p. 337.
8. Richard Aldrich, *New York Times*, 28 October 1917.
9. *Musical Times*, June 1920.
10. A. Bryan, *The Strad*, July 1930, p. 148.
11. Axelrod, op. cit., p. 280.
12–13. Ibid., p. 263.
14. Flesch, op. cit., pp. 335–6.
15. Ibid., p. 337.
16. Applebaum, *With the Artists*, p. 38.
17. Axelrod, op. cit., p. 277.
18. *The Strad*, January 1990, p. 48.
19. *The Strad*, February 1986, p. 791.
20. *The Strad*, January 1990, p. 54.
21–22. *The Strad*, April 1986, p. 929.
23. *The Strad*, January 1995, p. 31.

# 25 Child of the Revolution

When Szigeti was on a concert tour of Russia in 1924, Auer's daughter, Nadine, invited him to her house to hear a young up-and-coming violinist, 'a fabulously gifted young man who seemed diffident about his impending trip across the borders to Berlin'.[1] Szigeti reassured him that Western Europe was waiting for such artists with enthusiasm. His forecast was not exaggerated. The budding virtuoso was Nathan Milstein (1904–92).

He was born in Odessa into a music-loving family, but no previous history of professional musicians; as the middle child of seven, he confessed that he was by far the most aggressive. 'I think my mother wanted me to play the violin because she hoped it might stop me from doing grievous bodily harm to my brothers and my friends.'[2] At the age of seven Nathan went to the Music School in Odessa to study under Pyotr Stolyarsky and at 12 he was accepted into Auer's class at St Petersburg.

Milstein remained grateful to Auer because he allowed his pupils to develop within their own personalities:

> I knew others who were better musicians than Auer, who knew much more. But this is not always a good thing. They dictate every point of technique and impose their own style upon their pupils, with the result that they've not produced a single soloist at international level. At a certain stage it is not enough just to practise. You must develop your technique, of course, but violin playing is what you do with your technique. If you have a teacher who knows too much, you will never find your own way. When you are concertising on your own, you must know yourself where you are going.[3]

When the Revolution broke out in Russia, and Auer fled the country, the 13-year-old Milstein had the opportunity to put these ideas into practice. Despite the chaotic social and political upheaval, he was engaged for concerts arranged by the Ministry of Education in and around Odessa. (The Greeks, Turks, Italians, Jews and Russians who populated this city, all loved music.)

In 1922 Milstein met the young pianist Vladimir Horowitz, fresh from Kiev Conservatory. As solo artists, they gave a series of highly successful concert tours in Russia, eventually appearing in Moscow. The respected and cultured Anatoly Lunacharsky was at this time Commissar of Fine Arts and Education. Following one of the young players' concerts he wrote a review in a Moscow newspaper and headed it 'Children of the Soviet Revolution'. It provided excellent publicity and brought the two many further engagements. 'We made a great deal of money, but there was nothing to spend it on, so we gave it to the beggars who sat on every corner. They soon got to know us and waited for their money.'[4]

On the strength of Lunacharsky's review, the young musicians were allowed to leave Russia to undertake a European tour. Milstein recalled the occasion as a landmark in his life. 'It was on Christmas Eve, 1925, that I left. It was a wonderful feeling. I didn't know then that I would never go back: there was something in the back of my mind. But I didn't run away. I left officially with a Soviet passport. It was just that I never returned.' Their first call was at the Russian Embassy in Paris. When they asked when they would return to Moscow, the Cultural Attaché told them: 'Stay as long as you like. Look around and learn, and let the capitalists see what gifted young performers we have in our country.'[5]

The two took his suggestion to the letter. Although their concerts in Paris and elsewhere were well received, it was in Spain that they achieved their first triumph. A highly successful trial concert in Madrid produced a further 15 engagements, followed by a tour of South America, where they gave some 56 concerts, performing every two days. Milstein reflected: 'It was a very good life. In the late afternoon we would play bridge and sometimes spend a whole day in the mountains, returning to the hotel half an hour before the concert. We never worried about performances. Today I can't even eat *lunch* if I have to play in the evening.'[6]

In two years Milstein had earned himself an international reputation which was further enhanced by his American debut. He had had the good fortune to meet Leopold Stokowski, who gave him his first opportunity to play with a top-flight American orchestra. On 28 October 1929, Milstein played the Glazunov concerto in Philadelphia. The *Evening Bulletin* critic wrote that the soloist was 'a young, dark, vibrant Russian capable of magical things upon a violin', and that 'above and beyond his prodigious technical equipment is a brilliant mind moulding the music into a coherent and symmetrical whole'.[7] For the next ten years Milstein toured the USA and Canada, repeating his successes everywhere; in 1943 he took US citizenship.

In the meantime, Milstein continued to pursue a successful international solo career. When he appeared in Egypt for the first time, in January 1935, Ruppa, *The Strad*'s critic in Alexandria, called him 'a star of the first magnitude' and praised his wonderful bowing technique, especially his 'scintillating *spiccato* at all speeds, which he calls *une cascade de perles*'. As for his left hand, 'its dexterity and precision are amazing, even in the most rapid and exacting passages, the intonation remaining throughout of a crystalline purity'. But Ruppa warns: 'As a violinist you will be dazzled. As a musician you will be disappointed.' He considered that Milstein's temperamental fervour lacked conviction and that he 'fails to emotionally grip his audience'. Ruppa also considered that Milstein was far better suited to the music of Ernst, Wieniawski and Paganini than to that of Corelli, Bach and Beethoven.[8]

Milstein made his first appearance before a British audience at the Queen's Hall on 14 November 1932, playing the Brahms and Tchaikovsky concertos conducted by

Malcolm Sargent. Next morning *The Times* correspondent wrote of 'his clear cantilena, his organ-like double-stopping, his impeccable octaves in the finale'. While praising him as a violinist of a high order, he questioned Milstein's musicianship, particularly in the Brahms concerto, for 'while he was playing his cadenza we wondered whether he had forgotten all about Brahms'.[9]

Four years later, after a recital at the Wigmore Hall in London on 22 October 1936, the *Musical Times* critic wrote that: 'He gave Vivaldi's sonata in A major with a fire and precision that fairly caught one's breath, just because it breathed life into music that until now had seemed to be dry bones. This was the Vivaldi whom Bach admired: not the pedagogue in whose likeness most people present the old Venetian.' But this critic seemed less happy with his Beethoven (Sonata in G major, Op. 30), not because his execution left anything to be desired, but because 'some of Beethoven's thoughts . . . are still to Milstein a closed book'[10]. This is an interesting observation considering that Milstein came to be regarded as one of the great interpreters of the Beethoven Violin Concerto.

Milstein was still playing superbly well into his late 70s. If there ever was any substance to the criticisms of his artistic ability, he had long ago transcended them. His recording of the Goldmark concerto is one of the many living examples of his integrity in playing that is stylish yet scrupulous in attention to detail. Immaculate phrasing, perfect intonation: with Milstein there were no gimmicks, no tricks, and yet the music became exceptional on account of his innate musicianship and honest playing. It is the music that predominates, not Milstein's personality.

He tried never to play a work in quite the same way twice. A good example is his recording of the Brahms concerto under Eugen Jochum with the Vienna Philharmonic Orchestra. In his opinion, this was a more romantic interpretation than his previous recordings. He also felt that his Bach had changed. 'I played the Bach sonatas 20 years ago . . . but the approach was less improvisational, more playing. Bach is always improvisational.' Milstein held that it is of vital importance to try to build some sort of contact with the composer before attempting to stand up and play the work. Here, then, is the heart of Milstein who passed on to his pupils the sage advice that Auer had given to him: 'Don't practise with your fingers – practise with your head!'[11]

Milstein held firm views on the past and its relation to our musical present: 'In my opinion London is not, as so often quoted, "the most active music centre in the world", but like New York it is an enormous musical supermarket.' He felt that today too many people participate so that music and art are no longer 'special', and suffer in consequence. 'Not everyone who goes to concerts is so devoted to the music. It is often more of a social occasion. In the eighteenth and nineteenth centuries they listened to music because they loved and understood it.' He illustrated his point with Beethoven:

He went to people's houses to play quartets – which is how the music came to be written. When you had an élite, you had an example for the people who looked up to those who provided the works of art. All the artistic treasures we admire today were brought about by these people; the popes and the Medicis. If it were not for them we would have no idea of what happened in the past. In order to recapture this love of music and the need for great artists, we must bring back the kings and princes. We must have an élite. Today we have no group whom we can respect spiritually, and we are losing ground all the time.[12]

Milstein died peacefully at his London home on 21 December 1992.

## Notes

1. Szigeti, *With Strings Attached*, p. 221.
2–6. Quoted from interview, M.C.
7. *Evening Bulletin*, 29 October 1929.
8. *The Strad*, February 1935, p. 462.
9. *The Times*, 15 November 1932.
10. *Musical Times*, November 1936.
11. Simon Collins, *The Strad*, August 1976, p. 267.
12. Quoted from interview, M.C.

# 26 The Bel Canto Virtuoso

Alfredo Campoli was probably unique among British virtuoso violinists in that he successfully walked the tightrope between the light and classical fields of music and achieved a consummate balance. In his seventies he was still playing in public with elegance and style. In an age when an almost uniform virtuosity abounds, the sweet purity of his cantilena was immediately identifiable.

Alfredo Campoli (1906–91) was born in Rome, the son of a professor of violin at the Accademia di Santa Cecilia and leader of the orchestra at the Teatro Massima. His mother, Elvira Celi, was a well-known dramatic soprano who toured with Caruso and Antonio Scotti and sang many times at La Scala. In 1911, when she was engaged for a season at Covent Garden, the Campoli family came to England. They never returned to live in Italy.

Alfredo had shown interest in the violin from the age of four, and was taught from the beginning by his father, who remained his sole instructor. He made such rapid progress that he was already giving public performances in his adopted country before he was ten. Campoli recalled being dressed in a sailor suit and playing to troops and wounded soldiers during the First World War.

By his 12th birthday Alfredo had won several first prizes, two gold medals and a silver cup in music competitions. In fairness to the other candidates the authorities then asked him to abstain from entering any further competitions. However, he was allowed to enter the London Music Festival at Central Hall, Westminster in 1919, and carried off the gold medal for his performance of the first movement of the Mendelssohn concerto.

When the 16-year-old Campoli made his Wigmore Hall debut on 18 May 1923, a footnote in the programme read: 'Birth certificate can be verified in the vestibule.'[1] Even as a boy he was heavily built, and looked older than his years. Certainly the programme, which included concertos by Bruch and Wieniawski and the Nardini Sonata in D major, might have been chosen by a veteran. The *Morning Post* declared that he played 'not as a prodigy but as a mature artist'.[2] Others mentioned his brilliant execution and 'breadth of style'.[3] Perhaps the most significant comment was that 'his talents seem to be of an enduring kind'.[4]

All seemed set fair for a distinguished solo career when the effects of the mid-1920s slump pervaded music and the other arts. In spite of the economic depression, the gramophone business boomed, and radio broadcasting increased in popularity. The cumulative effect of these competitive elements made concert-going a luxury.

Halls everywhere were closing down, and even Kreisler and Heifetz were hard put to draw capacity audiences. Some musicians opted out of the profession altogether.

Campoli was fortunate in being engaged for a series of celebrity concerts touring with Melba and Clara Butt, and assisted his father with his teaching. Then in 1926 Edward Lewis asked Campoli to form a small orchestra to record a few popular classics for Decca. 'We recorded a piece called "Serenade" by Heykins and sold half a million copies in a few months.'[5] Within two years, Campoli and his Salon Orchestra became known throughout Britain. He also had a trio, and worked for at least half a dozen ensembles at film studios and in the light entertainment sector. When the Dorchester Hotel opened in 1931, Campoli and his Salon Orchestra moved in to provide the musical entertainment. He proved himself an excellent conductor as well as a superb violinist. He said: 'I always tried to make the orchestra sing.'[6] But, the warmth of his personality also drew the crowds to hear him play. Sadly, Campoli's father was unimpressed by his son's success. He thought he had not managed his career properly. Nonetheless, Campoli had no regrets: 'I am not ashamed of having worked in light music. I think I am a better musician *because* of it.'[7]

Despite his phenomenal populist following, Campoli never relaxed his hold on his aspirations as a classically trained violinist. He continually practised the classic repertory and appeared concurrently in recitals and as soloist with orchestra. In 1938 he played the Paganini Concerto No. 1 in his first Promenade Concert under Sir Henry Wood.

The Second World War brought additional hazards for Campoli, who narrowly missed being interned. Professor Campoli had never taken British naturalisation: 'He had the idea that it was almost immoral to sign away your birthright.'[8] But unknown to his father, his son had applied for British citizenship, which was due to be legalised a few weeks after the Italians entered the war on the German side. Campoli had to surrender both his car and his radio – possessions forbidden to an 'enemy alien'. The problem was resolved when invitations came to tour Britain, giving concerts at military bases and factories. Campoli was allowed to own a car again and his radio was returned.

After the war, Campoli turned exclusively to classical music and was rewarded with international fame. He made his American debut in 1953 with the New York Philharmonic Orchestra under Georg Szell, playing the Lalo Symphonie Espagnole at the beginning of a tour of the USA and Canada. Subsequently, Campoli performed in almost every country in the world. He made many tours of Canada, Australia and New Zealand and twice visited Russia and Japan, where he also made recordings. He gave the first performance in Moscow of the concerto that Sir Arthur Bliss had dedicated to him, and was warmly received by one of the most discriminating audiences in the world. David Oistrakh attended several of his Russian concerts and went backstage to offer his congratulations.

An unashamed lover of music of the Baroque, Classical and Romantic periods, Campoli played the Mendelssohn concerto almost 900 times. He had been taught by his father to regard the violin as a singing instrument. 'From the very beginning I was taught the *bel canto* singing style of playing. My father believed that the violin is the finest man-made instrument because it is nearest to the human voice.'[9] Professor Campoli would illustrate by playing recordings made by the leading singers of the day; the voices of Mattia Battistini, Giacomo Lauri-Volpi and Beniamino Gigli rang in Alfredo's ear when he was making his own first attempts at a 'singing' tone.

Campoli explained how this has affected his own playing in a positive way: 'You must learn how to control your sliding so that each phrase has a natural sense of breathing – just like a singer.' As an example, he took the octave leap: 'You have to imagine yourself singing. You wouldn't then make the jump in a jerky staccato manner. You must take the slur smoothly. When you come down again, you make up your mind as to whether the up-bow or the down-bow is the correct one.' He further illustrated the point by saying that Toscanini 'could make a whole orchestra sing'. Campoli bemoaned the fact that the British know so little about *bel canto*. 'English composers never write in this style. You have Vaughan Williams using the great effects of English choral music, but not quite *bel canto*. It is the Latin element in every Italian that comes naturally to him long before he has had a single lesson.'[10]

Campoli had strong views on the use of a shoulder rest. He maintained that any form of pad or rest ruins the vibrations of the violin, an opinion he shared with Erica Morini, Milstein and Heifetz. On the platform, Campoli was an undemonstrative player. One critic, commenting on his performance of the Tchaikovsky concerto, wrote: 'Unlike other violinists Mr Campoli played the fast and furious finale in a standing position instead of on all fours.'[11] He held the violin high and well to the left. He considered that in this position the player could move freely and rapidly into the high positions without muscular strain. Certainly Campoli gave the impression that he was at one with his instrument. His shimmering, singing tone and an elegant and relaxed bow arm were hallmarks of his playing. It is not difficult to understand why, when once asked which violinists he most admired, he replied 'Kreisler, Szigeti and Grumiaux'.[12]

At a recital at the Wigmore Hall in 1978, Campoli opened his programme with Tartini's 'Devil's Trill' sonata, playing his own cadenza, and followed it with the Bach unaccompanied Chaconne. He was then joined by a pupil, Belinda Bunt, for what was probably the first performance in Britain of Vivaldi's virtuoso Variations on La Folia, for two violins and continuo. The couple then played Sarasate's dazzling Navarra as an encore, bringing the audience to its feet. The concert took place only a few weeks short of Campoli's 72nd birthday. In a long and distinguished career, Campoli showed that whether the music is light or serious, the singing tone so beloved of Viotti and Spohr and their followers is the quality most admired by the public.

### Notes

1. Quoted from interview, M.C.
2. *Morning Post*, 19 May 1923.

3. *Westminster Gazette*, 19 May 1923.
4. *Daily Express*, 23 May 1923.
5–10. Quoted from interview, M.C.
11. *Daily Mail*, 4 September 1945.
12. Quoted from interview, M.C.

# 27  The Entertainers

In considering 'great' violinists, it is important not to underrate the performers who have attracted millions of music lovers to the violin not by unaccompanied Bach, but by the popular classics well played. Much of the serious violin repertory is fiendishly difficult, but so are most of the entertainers' show pieces. Sarasate's Zigeunerweisen or Bazzini's Ronde des Lutins are prime examples. These, and dozens more, all have to be memorised by the violinist, who must be ready to perform them at a moment's notice. In the Palm Court Trio and similar ensembles, unusual requests are regular occupational hazards. If asked, for example, for Paganini's Moto Perpetuo or a Liszt transcription, the player can scarcely protest that he must first go home and work out the fingering.

Campoli went into entertainment purely for financial reasons. One of the great violinists who intentionally followed the lighter field was the London-born Albert Sandler (1906–48), a contemporary of Campoli's, who died tragically at the age of 42 from a liver disease. Robert Lewin wrote of him:

> He loved what we call light music and hardly ever in his whole life attempted the serious classics. He was a natural for light popular music and with a violinistic equipment almost the equal of any virtuoso could handle a large repertory of pieces, from Sarasate to the operatic excerpts the public knew and liked. With his limpid tone and happy phrasing he went straight to the hearts of millions.[1]

Although Sandler's family loved music, no professional musicians had existed until Albert's generation, when suddenly there were three: Albert, his elder brother and his sister. Albert's brother gave him his first lessons, which were punctuated by a sharp box on the ears for every mistake. He quickly moved on to lessons with the Viennese Hans Wessely (1862–1926), a pupil of Hellmesberger at the Vienna Academy and private pupil of Grün. Sandler considered that his most important teacher was another of Grün's pupils, Kalman Ronay, a nephew of Auer, who later studied with Joachim at the Hochschule in Berlin.

On leaving school, Sandler worked as a cinema violinist for five shillings a week, but was soon elevated to the post of leader. At 16 he was engaged to lead an orchestra in one of the Lyons' Corner Houses. These were extensions of the Lyons' tea shops, to cater for shoppers and theatre-goers, and were at strategic points in the West End of London: Oxford Street, Tottenham Court Road, Marble Arch and the Strand; the largest was in Coventry Street, off Leicester Square. Each one occupied four storeys, with a variety of restaurants – each with its own orchestra – to suit every taste. The most popular was the first floor, where the musicians wore evening dress and the patrons could listen for a whole enchanted evening to Albert Sandler and his band for the price of a cup of tea and a slice of Dundee cake.

From the Corner House, Sandler was promoted to the Grill Room at the Trocadero, Lyons' star restaurant. But his greatest opportunity came in 1925, when Arthur Beckwith, musical director of the Grand Hotel in Eastbourne, left to tour the USA with the London String Quartet, standing in for the leader who was suddenly taken ill. Beckwith was offered the leadership of the Cleveland State Orchestra and stayed in the USA. Sandler took over his job at Eastbourne just as the BBC were trying out a Sunday evening broadcast from the hotel. It was highly successful, and 'Grand Hotel' became one of the most famous traditions in British broadcasting, lasting nearly half a century.

After the first year, the BBC decided to send the programme out live and Sandler became a household name. In 1928 he took on a further appointment, that of musical director at the Park Lane Hotel, where he led an ensemble of seven first-class musicians. Later he toured the music halls with his Albert Sandler Trio, and became 'Top of the Pops', 1930s style. The millions who knew Sandler from the radio flocked to see him in the flesh and were not disappointed. One critic wrote that his playing was remarkable in its 'marvellous technical dexterity and sensitive feeling', 'sonority, smoothness and excellent style' and that the trio 'held a large audience enthralled'.[2]

Although Sandler was a powerfully built man, with large, fleshy hands somewhat like Ysaÿe's, he was a very light player. He disliked having to tear at a fiddle to produce tone, and played on a 1701 Stradivarius. Despite his acknowledged preference for light music, Sandler never forced his tone or overdid his portamento or vibrato. He phrased beautifully and disliked 'tricks', a view shared by Campoli, who also contended that, 'if you are good enough as a fiddler you play the virtuoso pieces "straight" and they have more effect'.[3] Sandler never used harmonics because he thought them unsuitable in large restaurants and cinemas, but contended that passages played in the higher positions carry better without loss of tone quality. Sandler did not play more loudly when he wanted to be heard; he simply played an octave higher on the E string. His superb playing could usually surmount any amount of extraneous sound.

Sandler had no illusions about his work and admitted that many of the pieces he played were trifling by necessity, but he claimed that whatever a piece lacked in intrinsic merit, he played it with as much care and preparation as if it were a masterpiece. He would say 'there is beauty in the simplest thing well done'.[4] Tokens of gratitude reached him by every post and many of the letters and presents were highly amusing. One lady admirer sent him a gift of some tiny marzipan violins decorated with pink ribbons. Sandler never missed a concert by Heifetz or Kreisler. He was a master interpreter of the latter's pieces and appeared to have reserves of technical

*Left:* Ole Bull, the 'flaxen-haired Paganini'. RCM
*Below left:* Charles-Auguste de Bériot, a Viotti disciple. RCM
*Below right:* Erica Morini, child prodigy and Ševčík's youngest pupil. Margaret Campbell

*Top left:* Carl Flesch, a great teacher and founder
of the masterclass. <small>Carl Flesch Jr</small>
*Top right:* Josef Gingold, the great
Russian-American teacher. <small>Margaret Campbell</small>
*Above:* Eugène Ysaÿe, who played 'as the birds sing'.
*Right:* Shin'ichi Suzuki, the pioneering Japanese teacher.

*Top left:* Henri Temianka, the warm-hearted virtuoso.
*Top right:* Ruggiero Ricci, a child prodigy and born virtuoso.
photo Hanya Chlala
*Left:* Yehudi Menuhin, a supreme musician and humanitarian.
photo Kenneth Kaye
*Above:* Sandor Végh, the colourful Hungarian chamber musician and teacher. photo Angela Heskett

*Top:* Stephane Grappelli, the great jazz violinist. photo Jean-Pierre Leloir

*Above left:* Marie Leonhardt, the veteran baroque violinist. Marie Leonhardt

*Above right:* Eugene Sarbu, Romanian winner of the Carl Flesch competition. Eugene Sarbu

*Top:* Arthur Grumiaux, the musician's musician. photo Heitha Ramme
*Above left:* Max Jaffa, a virtuoso in light music. Max Jaffa
*Above right:* Tom Jenkins, an entertainer with a touch of genius. Michelle Jenkins

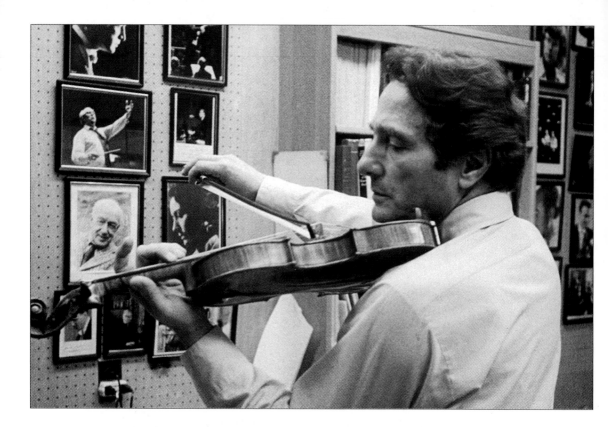

*Top:* Franco Gulli, the Italian-born,
much-loved teacher in the USA. photo Margaret Campbell
*Above:* Maurice Hasson, the French virtuoso and
teacher. Maurice Hasson
*Right:* Felix Andrievsky, the great émigré Russian
teacher. Felix Andrievsky

*Top:* Ralph Holmes, the British phenomenon.

photo Jeremy Grayson

*Left:* Ivan Galamian, the great Armenian-American teacher.

painting by Wayman Adams, 1958

*Above:* Igor Bezrodnyi, the Russian virtuoso and teacher.

Igor Bezrodnyi

*Top:* Max Rostal, a great teacher and Flesch disciple.
Marion Rostal-Busato

*Left:* Josef Suk, Dvořák's great-grandson. Prago Koncert

*Above:* Alfredo Campoli, the *bel canto* virtuoso. Joy Campoli

dexterity that he rarely needed to draw upon.

Tom Jones and Leslie Jefferies followed Sandler as leaders of the orchestra at the Grand Hotel Eastbourne, and in 1937, the 27-year-old Tom Jenkins (1910–57) assumed the post. His name became known throughout the British lsles until he, too, died an untimely death at the age of 47. Born in Leeds of Welsh stock, he took up the fiddle when he was eight. He won first prizes at countless music festivals and appeared in his first concert at the age of 12. At 14, he was already building a reputation as a soloist and had made his first broadcast. Like Sandler, he worked for a short period as a cinema violinist, and found the sight-reading experience invaluable. In 1927 he became leader of the Municipal Orchestra at Harrogate.

At 21, Tom Jenkins was invited by Julius Harrison to join Hastings Municipal Orchestra. During this time he performed as soloist, playing both the Bruch  G minor and Brahms concertos with the orchestra. A critic wrote: 'The technique was uniformly sure, and, best of all, the soloist gave us the spirit as well as the letter of this wonderful music. Never was there a trace of a false sentiment, though he realised to the full the romantic beauty underlying the work.'[5]

A year later Jenkins also appeared as soloist with the London Symphony Orchestra under Sargent at the Queen's Hall, playing the Brahms concerto. In 1936 he studied for a year with Carl Flesch in London and valued the experience very highly. This period of learning caused no break in Jenkins's playing, as so often occurs when a great teacher takes over a mature performer for the first time. In 1950 Jenkins again took some lessons, this time with Sascha Lasserson (1890–1978), for whom he had much admiration. It was during this period that *The Times* reported on 'a dazzling Ravel's Tzigane'.[6]

The appointment at Eastbourne came the following year. Almost all broadcasts of 'Grand Hotel' from the 1950s onwards contained two contrasting violin solos, many of great technical difficulty, such as pieces by Wieniawski and Grigoras Dinicu (Hora Staccato, 1906) or very simple, like MacDowell's To a Wild Rose. Professors at music colleges would tell their students to listen to him on the wireless, records not being as plentiful as they later became. When Jenkins discovered this, it made him pay meticulous attention to every detail in his broadcast performances.

During the Second World War, Jenkins left 'Grand Hotel' and served in the Indian Army until his demobilisation in 1946. Two years later he acquired his 1667 Stradivarius violin  and found it to be everything he could wish for in a fiddle. The 'Grand Hotel' programme had been resumed during the war by Sandler, but was broadcast as a regular programme from the BBC studios. When Sandler died, Tom Jenkins was asked to step in and 'wore the mantle of Sandler with taste and distinction'.[7] He made 'Grand Hotel' very much his own programme until the mid-1950s, when he left to start his own orchestra at Scarborough.

A quiet, modest man, Jenkins was always rather surprised that he should be considered of any importance. Quite simply, he just loved to play the violin, and it made him happy that people wanted to listen. But his press cuttings abound in superlatives. One critic wrote perceptively of his 'vocal' cantilena;[8] Jenkins, like Campoli, listened a great deal to singers and firmly believed that the violin is essentially a singing instrument.

His life's work proved to be the solo pieces in the violin repertory, and he played them with superb musicianship. It was this quality that caused so many people to say that they felt they had met him when they had not, to write him long and touching letters and to compose verses. There were two ladies who, over a period of years, sent him beautifully illustrated poems but who never revealed their identities. Tom Jenkins was yet another virtuoso violinist who proved himself capable of the highest standards of solo playing, but who will be remembered as 'an entertainer'.

In 1995, Tom Jenkins's Stradivarius was sold at Sotheby's for £375,000. His widow, Michelle Jenkins, founded a trust in his memory, which provides an annual award for the best instrument made by a student in the violin-making class of the London Metropolitan University.

For a short spell in the mid-1950s the leadership of 'Grand Hotel' was in the hands of another first-class musician, Max Jaffa (1911–91). His friendship with the pianist Jack Byfield and cellist Reg Kilbey, while playing in the BBC's London Studio Players, led to the formation of the Max Jaffa Trio, which became known throughout Britain. In 1979 Max Jaffa celebrated his 20th year of leading and conducting the orchestra in the Grand Hall, Scarborough. Here, in a non-stop season of 17 weeks, they made it a rule not to repeat any piece of music in their programmes more often than every three weeks in view of the large number of season ticket holders.

London-born Max Jaffa was presented with a fiddle by his father when he was six, with a prophecy: 'You are going to be a violinist!'[9] After training at the Guildhall School of Music, where he was awarded the gold medal, he became leader of the Scottish Symphony Orchestra and played under Weingartner, Barbirolli and many other leading conductors. Jaffa also studied with Sascha Lasserson and later took part in Lasserson's memorial concert at the Wigmore Hall in 1978. By inclination, Max Jaffa was an interpreter of the 'classical' repertory. He appeared in films and on television, toured internationally and provided the music aboard luxury liners on winter world cruises.

Jaffa's attitude to life and music was confirmed by an incident that happened when he was 17. In order to pay for his studies, Jaffa was leading the orchestra in a London hotel. One day Kreisler walked into the lounge and Jaffa was panic-stricken at the thought of playing in front of the great violinist. He did his best and in the interval a waiter came to tell him that Kreisler had invited him to join him for a drink. Jaffa immediately apologised for the kind of music he had been playing. Kreisler rebuked him: 'Now look here, you must never apologise for playing music – whatever sort of music it may be. I, too, have played in cafés. I would like to offer you a little advice for you to remember throughout your professional career. No matter what you play, or where you play it, if you give a good performance – no matter how bad the piece is – your own playing will never suffer and the value of the music itself will be enhanced by your performance.'[10] Jaffa took this advice to heart.

Reginald Leopold (d. 2003) was last in the line of leaders of 'Grand Hotel', and served for over 18 years in the longest-running programme in the history of the BBC. Born in London, Leopold was the youngest of eight children, each of whom played an instrument. At 14 he won a scholarship to Trinity College of Music and was placed under the Hungarian-born Louis Pecskai, who had studied with Hubay in Budapest. However, Leopold considered that the greatest influence on him at this time was the German cellist, Ludwig Lebel (1872–?), head of ensemble playing at Trinity. He was convinced that his thorough grounding in chamber music, especially string quartet playing, laid a foundation that served him well in every kind of music.

In 1934, Leopold met Fred Hartley, 'the man who brought light music right up to date'.[11] Hartley founded the Fred Hartley Sextet with Hugo Rignold as its first leader; Rignold in turn brought Leopold into the group. There were other well-known musicians in the sextet, some of whom were professors from the Academy. The popularity of the sextet often attracted photographers, but as soon as the camera was poised for action, the more eminent members would vanish. It was more than their job was worth to be seen playing light music. The opportunity for Leopold to lead 'Grand Hotel' came in 1956. The programme was broadcast before an invited studio audience at the Concert Hall, Broadcasting House, the musicians attired in formal dress amid a swathe of potted palms. Leading this group for 18 years was a responsibility, and at times a strain, since the programme went out live every Sunday evening.

Another violinist who had reached the top of the orchestral world and turned successfully to the 'virtuoso and gypsy' repertory is John Georgiadis, born in London in 1939 into a Greek family. He started playing the violin at six and, at 12, won a junior scholarship to the Royal Academy of Music where he studied with Joan Rochford-Davies and Frederick Grinke (1911–87). In 1960 he went to Paris for lessons with René Benedetti.

Georgiadis's first professional engagement was with the Hallé Orchestra under John Barbirolli, which he found 'very exciting' and followed this with additional work with various orchestras. When he was appointed leader of the City of Birmingham Symphony Orchestra, he was still only 23; two years later he took up the same position with the London Symphony Orchestra, a post he held until 1979 with a break of three years when he left to explore a solo career. It was then that he turned to performances of light music and, partnered by various pianists, he gave recitals mainly of 'virtuoso and gypsy' music. In Georgiadis's opinion, there is no secret to performing virtuoso music. 'It's a question of achieving a good technical facility and then taking the music seriously. For example, the art of playing Paganini is to make music out of it. I've heard many people *not* making music out of *Brahms*. You only have to listen to Heifetz playing all these virtuoso pieces and they are perfect.'[12]

In the 1930s Carl Flesch accurately forecast that the much-neglected music of Sarasate, especially his Spanish Dances, would one day achieve the popularity it deserved. Sarasate, Georgiadis believes, 'understood the capabilities of the instrument so well and therefore he wrote almost better than anyone else for the violin, and always in good taste'.[13]

### Notes

1. Robert Lewin, *The Strad*, March 1978, p. 1049.
2. *The Strad*, April 1929, p. 706.
3. Quoted from interview, M.C.
4. *The Strad*, March 1934, p. 448.
5. *Hastings and St Leonards Observer*, concert at Brahms Festival, 25 April 1933.
6. *The Times*, 30 May 1951.
7. Jonah Barrington, *Daily Graphic*, 8 July 1949.
8. *Hastings and St Leonards Observer*, 24 June 1950.
9–10. Jaffa (BBC radio broadcast by Gale Pedrick), *A Life on the Fiddle*, pp. 19, 92.
11–13. Quoted from interview, M.C.

# 28   The Violin 'Hot'

Throughout the history of the violin, the Italian influence constantly resurfaces in some aspect of its development. Perhaps the most unexpected is in the field of jazz. While Black America undoubtedly produced several outstanding violinists, including George Morrison, Eddie South and 'Stuff' Smith, it took two Italian violinists to popularise the jazz style throughout the world: Joe Venuti and Stephane Grappelli.

In 1968, Gunther Schuller interviewed the veteran American violinist and band leader, George Morrison.[1] Morrison (1891–1973) came from Fayette, Missouri; his family had produced generations of square dance fiddlers, who played by ear. As a child of five, George made himself a violin from a hollowed-out corn stalk, a piece of wood and some string. He used charcoal for rosin and his bow was a branch of pussy willow. When he grew older he made his fiddles out of cigar boxes. At ten, he bought his first real violin with the money he earned shining shoes at a barber's shop in Boulder, Colorado. He had his first music lessons from a local teacher, and practised his Kreutzer studies in the alley behind the barber's shop, the music propped up against a lump of coal. His progress was so exceptional that he was subsequently accepted as a private pupil of Howard Reynolds, a teacher of considerable reputation.

Morrison studied with Reynolds for 12 years, and in 1911 he competed with Reynolds's 41 other pupils for a place at the New England Conservatory. Morrison, the only black pupil, won it, but he never took up the scholarship. That same year he married and moved to Denver, where he played both violin and guitar in the 'parlor houses' for Mattie Silks, one of the famous madams. About this time Morrison encountered jazz and could later recall having heard violinists improvise, one of the most outstanding being Benny Goodman (not the famous clarinettist, but a violinist who had his own band). It was Goodman who first inspired Morrison to jazz up popular tunes by improvisation.

Jazz was in fact the only field in which a black musician could hope to succeed. Although Morrison studied theory and composition with Horace Tureman, conductor of the Denver Symphony Orchestra, and reached a high standard of musicianship, he could never have been considered for a place in the orchestra. Tureman often told him that he would have hired him as his leader had he been white.

Morrison completed his musical education at the Chicago Conservatory under Carl Becker, and subsequently found his way to New York and modest fame. While leading the band at the Carlton Terrace Hotel in New York in 1920, he had an experience that he would remember vividly for the rest of his life. He was required to play violin solos each evening and on one occasion had just played Kreisler's Tambourin Chinois when a man came up to him and said: 'Young man, you are a very, very talented musician. . . .Would you accept my card?' Morrison was delighted but he nearly dropped his violin when he read the name 'Fritz Kreisler'. There was an unusual sequel to this meeting. Kreisler invited Morrison to his home, and exceptionally, gave him six lessons free of charge. Morrison recalled: 'He gave me some help on my flying staccato in the Mendelssohn and showed me how to get a beautiful clean-cut pizzicato.'[2]

Eddie South was Morrison's fellow student at the Columbia Conservatory of Music. 'He was a trained musician, and one of the best in the popular field . . . . Terrific in jazz.'[3] In Morrison's opinion, Eddie South was outstanding because he had technique and when he went over to jazz and popular music, 'he could just turn it upside down'.[4] Born in Louisiana, Eddie South (1904–62) was brought up in Chicago. He had his first violin lessons at the age of ten and later studied at the Chicago School of Music. He was inspired to turn to jazz by Daniel Howard, the New Orleans jazz clarinettist who also played violin in many of the groups in which South performed. Known as 'the Dark Angel of the Violin', South was soon considered one of the most brilliant of all jazz violinists. More than a technician, he played with great depth of feeling. His phrasing and remarkable beauty of tone were compared to those of the great classical violinists.

During the 1920s, South played in Chicago and New York with many groups including those of Charlie Elgar, Erskine Tate and Jimmy Wade. Be it jazz or exotic music of all kinds – gypsy, samba, rumba, bolero, tango or European – to Eddie South playing them was as natural as breathing. From 1928 up to the 1940s, he led his own group. Although the connoisseurs regard him as one of the major jazz soloists, Eddie South never became particularly famous. If he had not spent time in Europe in the 1930s and made recordings, it is quite likely that his name might have been forgotten altogether. The recordings he made with Stephane Grappelli of Dinah and Fiddle Blues are fine examples of his art, as are two interpretations of a section from the first movement of the Bach Double Concerto, in which the violinists first play the music straight and then improvise. On the same record South is accompanied by Django Reinhardt in Eddie's Blues, a performance that has been described as 'the greatest example of violin playing in jazz'.[5]

Hezekiah Leroy Gordon Smith (1909–65) – better known as 'Stuff' Smith – is the other great black jazz violinist who also never attained the success he deserved. Born in Portsmouth, Ohio, he had his first, somewhat unorthodox, violin lessons from his father. When he was 15, he joined a music hall troupe where he danced and played violin. He subsequently played in various bands and in 1929 formed one of his own. In the years just before the Second World War he led a lively three-piece band at the Onyx Club in New York and, wearing a battered top hat, and sometimes with a monkey on his shoulder, he would deliver comic patter as an accompaniment to his virtuoso improvisation. But his talent as a comedian proved a dubious asset since many critics refused to take him seriously.

Smith was one of the first to electronically amplify his violin and it gave his playing a penetrating, forceful quality. His vibrant, singing tone and swinging rhythm combined to give some of the 'most dazzling violin playing ever heard in jazz'.[6] His improvisations were audacious in the extreme; Milton Mezzrow called him the 'mad genius of the violin'. His recordings highlight his originality, not only in his improvisation on the violin but also as an all-round entertainer. His vocalising is reminiscent of Fats Waller, whose group he took over for some time in 1942. Smith has also recorded with Herb Ellis and Dizzy Gillespie, and he provided the backing for Nat King Cole in *After Midnight*.

Joe Venuti (*c.*1890–1978), born Giuseppe Venuti in Lecco on Lake Como, picked up the violin when he was four and soon began taking regular lessons. When he was still a child, his parents emigrated to the USA and settled in Philadelphia. One of his playmates in this city was another Mediterranean *emigré*, Salvatore Massaro, who played the guitar. He later became world-famous as Eddie Lang.

The two youngsters teamed up together and took lessons on their respective instruments; and so great were their individual talents that they frequently exchanged instruments without difficulty. Both were born improvisers. They moved to New York and found work in the rapidly expanding recording business. By the mid-1920s they were famous. Their 'Blue Grass' series, dating from this time, is a prime example of the richness of their individual skills and the depth of their musical understanding. Both were equally at home in larger ensembles, as they proved in the superb version of Beale Street Blues that they recorded in 1931 with Benny Goodman and the Teagarden brothers. When Venuti died in 1978, Sinclair Traill wrote: 'Together, in terms of jazz, they brought out all the best qualities and powers of violin and guitar. Rhythmically they mated with consummate understanding, attack and tone, the music they made being perfectly balanced and always in the best of taste.'[7]

Venuti and Lang both worked for the two most prominent white band leaders of the 1920s, Jean Goldkette and Paul Whiteman. During his time with the latter, Joe's genius for practical joking caused him trouble. While filming *The King of Jazz* (1930), Whiteman told the band they were behind schedule and asked for their maximum cooperation in the last hurried extra sessions required. Venuti's response was to fill the bell of the sousaphone with five pounds of flour. The flour-storm that ensued lost them a morning's shooting. Joe was sacked and remained out of work for six months.

After leaving Whiteman, Venuti successfully led his own bands for many years. He appeared frequently on radio shows, many of which featured his life-long friend, Bing Crosby. He worked consistently throughout the 1940s and 1950s in an unspectacular way, then in the 1960s there was a revival of interest in his playing and he resumed international touring, visiting Britain in 1969 after an interval of 35 years. He was often to be seen at jazz festivals during the 1970s and his participation in jam sessions was always catalytic.

Venuti retained a pride in his own playing to the end of his days. He maintained that growing old did nothing to diminish his musical imagination, he just had to practise harder to keep his reflexes sharp. Venuti once described his earliest encounters with jazz: 'My people were mountain people, and they loved the pulse of the mountain music. When I first heard jazz, it seemed to have a very similar beat. It came easy to me.'[8] It was this ease that enabled Joe Venuti to be such a remarkable innovator, and since he was the first in the field, his work will always remain important in its influence. His recorded solos testify to his ability to improvise which has seldom been surpassed.

Stephane Grappelli (1908–97) was born in Paris, the son of an Italian teacher of philosophy who loved music. After his French mother died, when he was three, he was placed in a poor Catholic orphanage. At six he was picked to play the part of an angel in one of Isadora Duncan's dance performances at her school at Bellevue near Paris. Grappelli said: 'I was not a good dancer but I looked cherubic. When you are not an angel, it is *difficile*.'[9]

In July 1914, Grappelli heard the Colonne Orchestra play Debussy's Prélude à l'après-midi d'un faune. It was his first encounter with live music and it made a lasting impression on him. But a few weeks later the outbreak of war led to the closure of the school. Grappelli's father was conscripted into the army. For the child who had had such a brief glimpse into another world, it was back to yet another orphanage where conditions were appalling. The children slept on the floor and suffered from malnutrition. In desperation, he absconded, wandering the streets until his father returned from the front.

When father and son were finally reunited, the one room that they could afford was paradise. His father took him to concerts and the boy's musical taste began to develop. Soon he wanted to play an instrument himself and they purchased a cheap three-quarter-size violin. Grappelli always kept that fiddle in his desk in Paris. He once admitted: 'I love it very much: I remember hugging it all the way home: it's a wonder it didn't break.'[10]

The 12-year-old child mastered the instrument by ear in a few weeks. Then his father decided they should learn to read music. He borrowed a book from the library and together they gained a rough knowledge of the elements of solfeggio. The young Grappelli subsequently tested his skill by joining some street musicians and found he could earn some money. He said: 'My father was a wonderful scholar – but a dreamer. You do not get money that way – so I see what I can do myself.'[11]

At 15, he joined a pit band in a cinema, playing accompaniments to silent films. He said: 'It was here that I really learned to read music properly. I was there for a year and we played for three hours twice a day – you have a lot of reading in this time and it can be all kinds of music from Mozart to popular songs.'[12]

A year later Grappelli began playing in clubs. He not only earned more money than in the cinema but found that he could play the music he liked: George Gershwin, Cole Porter and Irving Berlin. 'I also began to hear jazz about this time and it made a great impression on me. I heard Louis Armstrong and that changed my destiny. I decided I would try it on my violin. At first it worked slowly because it was something new, but gradually it developed; like improvisation – it just happened.'[13]

Meanwhile, the Grappellis had acquired a cheap piano and the younger man proceeded to teach himself to play that instrument, as he had most things: 'from books and by watching others'.[14] Soon he was as nimble-fingered on the piano as on the violin. He later added saxophone and accordion to his accomplishments. With the discovery that he preferred the harmonic capabilities of the piano, he put away his violin and for the next four years he made a living from playing at parties and at the Ambassadeurs in Paris, where 'five hundred women covered with diamonds'[15] dined every night with their wealthy escorts.

In 1930, Grappelli was working in a club in Montparnasse when he first met the gypsy guitarist, Django Reinhardt. But not until four years later, when they were both playing in an orchestra for tea dances at the Hotel Claridge in Paris, did they think of a partnership. One day, after replacing a string, Grappelli began to play Dinah. Django joined in. From then on they would improvise in their breaks. At first they played free jazz together. Then, later, they were joined by the bassist Louis Vola and Django's brother, Joseph, on guitar. Finally, Roger Chaput provided the third guitar. Thus was born the first modern all-string jazz ensemble, one of the greatest groups of the 1930s, the Quintet of the Hot Club of France. Their success was phenomenal and everyone flocked to Paris to hear them. Many of the hundreds of 78 rpm records they made are still selling in reissues on CD. During the war Grappelli found himself in Britain, separated from the other members of the quintet. After the war he teamed up again with Reinhardt for a time, but they had lost the closeness of the Hot Club association. The group as such had disintegrated. When in 1953 Reinhardt died of a stroke at the age of 42, Grappelli faded from the limelight.

For the next 20 years, Grappelli played and recorded with some of the most famous jazz instrumentalists in the world, including Duke Ellington, Oscar Peterson and George Shearing. But none of these was a guitarist. In 1973 he formed an all-string ensemble with the Canadian Diz Disley and his Trio (Diz Disley and John Etheridge, guitars, and Brian Torff, string bass). 'We leave the fifth chair empty – for Django.'[16] This latest ensemble brought Grappelli before a new generation of younger listeners, who responded with unexpected enthusiasm to his style. To the older generation he represented a nostalgic visit to an enchanted past. But Grappelli had the rare gift of making that past contemporary. He was great not only because he was a great jazz violinist, but because he was a great musician.

The partnership that best illustrates this point is Grappelli's association with Yehudi Menuhin. Their recording of Tea for Two topped the charts in 1978. Michael Parkinson brought them together to perform on television. The two artists, from such widely differing fields, worked together with a compatibility that is difficult to comprehend. When asked, Grappelli gave a Gallic shrug: 'I tell you frankly, I have no technique at all. Instinctively I think I have a good hold for the bow. But when I play with Yehudi I see how much I can learn. I watch him for the perfect position for his fingers: *alors!* – this I cannot do because I have never studied it. Now it is too late for me to learn. But we *enjoy* to play together.'[17] Grappelli confessed that the only experience that made him nervous was when he appeared with a string backing, 'because I know they play better violin than me'.[18] Nevertheless, there is another side to the coin. Once when he and Menuhin were rehearsing, the latter looked at him in amazement, and said: 'Stephane! What you are doing is impossible on the violin!'[19]

These 'impossibilities' remained inexplicable. Grappelli said: 'My improvisation is always different. When I walk onto a stage, I do not know what will happen until it happens. When I improvise and I'm in good form, I'm like somebody half sleeping. I even forget there are people in front of me.'[20]

In December 1978 Grappelli celebrated his 70th birthday by making his debut at the Royal Albert Hall, with George Shearing, Julian Bream, and the young French rock violinist Didier Lockwood. As always, Grappelli's performance was elegant and stylish. Young and old alike were bewitched by his playing. At almost 90 he was still at the height of his powers on the one instrument that tends to leave its devotees deaf or crippled in their advancing years.

## Notes

1. Gunther Schuller, *Early Jazz: Its Roots and Musical Development*, Appendix.
2. Ibid., p. 368.
3–4. Ibid., p. 372.
5. Fox, Gammond, Morgan, *Jazz on Record: A Critical Guide*, p. 287.
6. Ibid., p. 285.
7–8. *Jazz Journal International*, November 1978.
9–14. Quoted from interview, M.C.
15. Whitney Balliett, *The New Yorker*, 19 January 1976.
16. Quoted from interview, M.C.
17. *The Strad*, November 1979, p. 517.
18–19. Quoted from interview, M.C.
20. *The Strad*, November 1979, pp. 517–8.

# 29  The Ladies' Progress

'We do not think the violin a lady's instrument. Better endeavour to excel on the piano or harp.' So wrote the correspondent in answer to a query in the 12 September 1863 issue of *Choir*. Professional women players were rare at the time, and the few who managed to surmount prevailing prejudice were probably influenced by the example of Lady Hallé (1839–1911), who did much to encourage women to take up the instrument.

Musical institutions were slow to accept women violin students. During its first half century the Royal Academy of Music (founded 1822), London, for example, did not admit a single female to study the instrument. By 1872 it had one. At the turn of the century there were rather more. What happened to the graduates is uncertain. In the orchestras there was fierce opposition to employing women (one reason put forward was that the conductor would not feel free to swear in front of the ladies). One who broke through in the 1880s was the Cheltenham-born Emily Shinner, a pupil of Joachim in Berlin. She maintained a highly successful career as soloist and quartet player, and was widely praised in Britain. In 1887 she founded the first all-female string quartet.

Marie Hall (1884–1956), the first British female violinist to achieve an international reputation, was born in Newcastle-upon-Tyne and, as a child, performed in the streets, accompanied by her father on the harp. At the age of ten she attracted the attention of Elgar, who gave her some preliminary instruction. She subsequently received lessons from August Wilhelmj, Max Mossel (1871–1929) and Johann Kruse (1859–1927), a member of the Joachim Quartet. In 1899 she won an Exhibition to the Royal Academy of Music against 40 competitors, but could not afford to take it up. A year later, Jan Kubelík heard her play and, acting upon his advice, she went to Prague to study under Ševčík, who said that he had seldom, if ever, instructed a pupil with a talent equal to hers. When she played with the Queen's Hall Orchestra under Henry Wood in 1903, the *Musical Times* tells us that 'she was recalled six times after the Tchaikovsky concerto, and at the conclusion of Wieniawski's Faust Fantasia, she had to return no less than nine times to the platform'.[1]

By 1902 Marie Hall was ranked as one of the leading virtuoso performers in Europe. She subsequently undertook worldwide tours and was received like a queen everywhere. She was also not afraid to play either contemporary music or works by lesser-known composers. She introduced Ralph Vaughan Williams's The Lark Ascending (1914) with much success. In 1911 she married her impresario and afterwards was gradually seen less on the concert platform. But her name remains among the great ladies of the bow.

The first American woman to earn an international reputation was Maud Powell (1868–1920). Born in Peru, Illinois, of an American father and German mother, she was given instruction on the piano at the age of four, and at eight took violin lessons from William Lewis (1836–1902) of Chicago. Five years later she was taken to Germany to study with Henry Schradieck (1846–1918) at the Leipzig Conservatory. After receiving her diploma within a year, she was selected from 80 applicants for a place at the Paris Conservatoire. Here she became a pupil of Charles Dancla, and then completed her studies under Joseph Joachim at the Hochschule in Berlin.

Quickly achieving an international reputation, Maud Powell toured Europe and America and was hailed by the critics as one of the most outstanding violinists of her day. She made her British debut in 1882 and two years later appeared in New York for the first time, giving the first performance of Dvořák's Violin Concerto at one of the Philharmonic Society's concerts. She subsequently toured Germany and Austria and in 1892, on her return to New York, she became the first American woman to form a string quartet. In later years she returned many times to Europe and became known for her immense repertory. In her will she bequeathed her beautiful Guadagnini violin to 'the next great woman violinist': it was presented to the 16-year-old Erica Morini after her 1921 Carnegie Hall debut.

Of Italian extraction, Erica Morini (1905–95) was born in Vienna and received her first lessons from her father, who ran a private music school there. At three she had perfect pitch: she would hide behind the large stove in the studio and call out 'wrong' when one of the students played or sang off pitch; her father then sat her at the piano, where she would pick out the right note with one tiny finger.

At a surprise party for the Austrian Emperor Karl Josef, she was placed behind a screen to perform. When she emerged, he was dumb-founded to see that a five-year-old child had been playing like a mature artist. He lifted her onto his lap and asked what she would like as a reward. 'A doll with eyes that move,' she replied.[2] The request was granted.

Morini's development was phenomenal. In 1913, when she was only eight, she was admitted into Ševčík's masterclass in Vienna. She vividly recalled his unique approach to the technique of the left hand: 'When his pupils had a particularly difficult run, he would make them learn it backwards first and it became much easier to play correctly.'[3] That same year she brought off a dual triumph in Vienna by making her first appearance at a public concert and taking part in the Beethoven Festival. This was closely followed by her German debut in Leipzig, with the Gewandhaus Orchestra under Nikisch. 'It was the most important experience in my life. I was the only child allowed to play there.' After the performance Nikisch said, 'She is not a wonder-child: she is a wonder and a child.'[4]

During the First World War Erica's concert activities were limited to central Europe: Germany, Austria, Hungary, Czechoslovakia all welcomed her. When she appeared for the first time in Bucharest, only about 20 seats were occupied, but she was well received and the news travelled fast. A second concert was planned for the following day and this time the hall was full.

In 1917, the effects of the First World War were beginning to change the face of Europe, so Oscar Morini took his wife and six children to the USA. Although Erica toured the country with success, it was not until 1921 that she made her New York debut at Carnegie Hall with the New York Philharmonic Orchestra under Artur Bodanski; she played concertos by Mendelssohn, Vieuxtemps and Mozart, and evoked an enthusiastic response from the press.

Morini subsequently appeared with all the great symphony orchestras the world over. Something of her appeal is captured by a critic writing of her playing at a recital in 1931 at Hunter College, New York: 'The violinist kept the mechanics of violin playing unobtrusive. Her inward, withdrawn style often gave one the feeling that she was performing for herself and letting us listen.'[5] In 1968, on her last visit to Israel, she gave 12 concerts with the Israel Philharmonic Orchestra to capacity audiences. The demand for tickets was so great that two extra concerts were sandwiched in and appropriately dedicated to the late Bronislav Huberman. Only two hours after the announcement was made, the 3,000-seat auditorium in Tel Aviv was sold out.

As a violinist, Morini was always praised for her 'soaring lyricism' as well as her dazzling technique. 'Through my father I was lucky to have the benefit of his knowledge of the Grün and Joachim method for the right hand and Ševčík for the left.'[6] When she played the Mendelssohn concerto under Georg Szell, Louis Biancolli of the *New York Telegram and Sun* wrote: 'This was Mendelssohn, the poet and singer . . . . It is as new as last night's performance.'[7] Morini treasured this experience – 'working with Georg Szell was an unforgettable joy in my life'.[8]

Her repertory contained many of the much neglected classics. She believed that too many violinists rush to play new works and overlook the beauties of the older music. She gave the example of Spohr's *Gesangsscene*, which runs the entire gamut of technique. In fact, Morini played all the Spohr concertos and advised violinists to include them in their repertory as well. She has also played the Viotti Concertos Nos. 22 and 23 and regretted that his works are so little played today.

Erica Morini, like Lady Hallé, was one of the few women who preferred to play without a shoulder rest or pad. She explained: 'I have my own way of supporting the instrument with my neck. Without a shoulder pad you are much more at one with the instrument.'[9] Morini convinced many violinists to follow suit. In 1930, she coached a few members of the Vienna Philharmonic Orchestra, eventually persuading the entire violin section to abandon their shoulder rests.

At her home in New York, Morini was surrounded by treasures she had collected from all over the world. Hanging on the wall in her sitting-room was an embroidered linen handkerchief in a frame. Presented to her by the Music Society of Madrid, it is the handkerchief which Sarasate wore in his breast pocket every time he played. He bequeathed it to 'the finest exponent of my Spanish Dances'.[10] It is no wonder that when Morini was asked when she first became interested in music, she replied: 'I was born with music; it is like breathing.'[11]

In the 1950s, one name among women violinists predominated, that of Gioconda de Vito (1907–94), whose interpretations of the Classical and Romantic repertory earned her an almost unrivalled reputation throughout Europe. She never went to America despite invitations from Arturo Toscanini and Charles Munch. In 1961, at the age of 54, she retired from the concert platform because, in her own estimation, she had 'reached the apogée of her abilities'.[12]

Gioconda de Vito was born into a cultured and musical family in the little town of Martina Franca in southern Italy. As a small child, her first instrument was the mandolin, but at eight she taught herself to play the violin. Within six months she could play Bériot's Concerto No. 9. She had her first violin lessons from her uncle, a professional violinist, and theory lessons from the conductor of the municipal band. At the age of eleven she entered the conservatory at Pesaro under Remy Principe (1889–1977) and within two years she obtained her diploma. She made her orchestral debut at 16 in Rome, where she played the Tchaikovsky concerto.

In the Vienna International Competition of 1932 de Vito took first prize. Two years later she succeeded Teresina Tua (1866–?) as professor of violin at the Accademia di Santa Cecilia in Rome. By the late 1930s she was in constant demand as a soloist. She was allowed only 30 days leave annually for concerts outside the Accademia and these were fully taken up by her tours of Germany. She did not play in Britain until after the Second World War.

De Vito finally came to London in 1948, making her debut at the Royal Albert Hall playing the Brahms concerto. The audience loved the warmth and vibrancy of her playing and critics praised her exquisite phrasing and musicality. She appeared at the Edinburgh Festival with Yehudi Menuhin and Isaac Stern in 'The Festival of the Violin' and was inundated with further offers to play all over the country.

Throughout her career de Vito steadfastly refused to play works by modern composers. She made two concessions – a work by Mario Castelnuovo-Tedesco which had been compulsory in the Vienna International Competition, and the concerto (1944) by Ildebrando Pizzetti. The latter work was written for her in a deliberately archaic and unabrasive style. The mere mention of Schoenberg, Bartók, Berg or Stravinsky had her raising her hands in horror, and even the concertos by Elgar and Sibelius never appealed to her as being suitable for her own style of playing. She stressed the importance of the Italian classical repertory, and considered the Paganini Caprices 'musically beautiful'. But her favourite composer was Bach.

De Vito's favourite concerto was the Brahms – her recording with the Philharmonic Orchestra under Rudolf Schwarz remains one of the most compelling performances in or out of the catalogue. However, despite the success of this and other recordings, de Vito did not feel that she was ever temperamentally suited to this medium. She was an expressive violinist who moved about while playing, and as this affected the microphone, she felt restricted in her performance.

She had a number of individual ideas that were sometimes startling, such as her habit of commencing the solo entry of the Brahms concerto with an up-bow to produce greater sonority. Her superlative readings of the concertos by Bach, Beethoven and Brahms are landmarks in the history of violin playing. In 1954 Eric Blom wrote: 'Her way of holding the balance between the outward appearance of a serene graciousness and a vibrant inner passion that is always felt in her playing without ever breaking through boundlessly is, if not unique, at any rate very difficult to discover in any other violinist of today.'[13]

### Notes

1. *Musical Times*, March 1903.
2–4. Morini, letter to M.C.
5. *New York Post*, 9 February 1976.
6. Morini, letter to M.C.
7. *New York Telegram and Sun*, c.1962–3.
8–9. Morini, letter to M.C.
10. Applebaum, *With the Artists*, p. 88.
11. Quoted from interview, M.C.
12. Collins, *The Strad*, October 1977, p. 481.
13. *Grove*, 5th edn., ix, p. 23.

# 30  The Enkindling Spirit

In one of their many heart-to-heart talks Yehudi Menuhin once asked David Oistrakh if he would ever consider living in the West. The reply was characteristically honest: 'I owe the State everything. They are responsible for my upbringing and have seen to it that I have had the best musical education and training. My family are there. It would be disloyal of me to live elsewhere.'[1] Oistrakh paid a price for that loyalty when, as a sick man, he undertook far too much work in his last years. No one in power ever suggested that he should begin to rest more and play less. His relentless travelling schedule was finally broken when he died in Amsterdam in 1974 at the age of 66.

David Fyodorovich Oistrakh was born in Odessa in 1908, into a musical family. His father, a poor book-keeper, played the violin and trained the chorus of the local operatic society. His mother was a singer and actress. Not surprisingly, from childhood Oistrakh thought of himself as a performer. 'I cannot think of my childhood without music. My father gave me a toy violin when I was about three-and-a-half and I remember trying to join a party of street musicians.' His enthusiasm was rewarded by the presentation of a real eighth-size fiddle at the age of five. He recalled his first audience. 'I can see myself standing in a courtyard surrounded by other children. I had some sort of music in front of me which I pretended to read but did not understand as I eagerly scratched away on that canary-yellow instrument. But the notes I drew from it sounded heavenly to me at the time.'[2]

That same year, David was accepted as a pupil of Pyotr Stolyarsky (1871–1944) at the Music School of Odessa. His lessons were free but irregular. Stolyarsky never turned away a pupil who could not afford to pay. 'From the very beginning he instilled in us the need for perseverance and showed us how to enjoy the pleasures of the creative side of music.' Renowned for his special gift for instructing young children, Stolyarsky worked from seven in the morning until late at night. 'His incredible enthusiasm was contagious and we were all affected by it.'[3]

Even as a child, Oistrakh had an excellent musical memory and a marked perception of form and rhythm. Most remarkable of all was his highly developed musical imagination – rare in one so young. Nevertheless, he was not a child prodigy and Stolyarsky was wise enough to allow his talent to ripen slowly. At the age of 15 he was admitted to Stolyarsky's masterclass at the conservatory in Odessa. His first position in the orchestra was as a rank-and-file viola player but he was soon appointed leader and within a few months appeared as soloist, playing the Bach

Concerto in A minor. A year later, he made his debut at a solo recital in Odessa, and followed this with a tour of the Ukraine.

Oistrakh had no more tuition after the age of 18 and spent the next two years touring the Soviet Union. In that country, news of an outstanding violinist travels fast, and he found himself playing to capacity audiences everywhere. When he made his Leningrad debut in 1928, playing the Tchaikovsky concerto under Nikolai Malko, he was acknowledged as a master and given a standing ovation. A year later, he repeated this success in Moscow.

In 1930 Oistrakh married Tamara Ivanovna Rotaveva, a professional pianist who gave up her own career to devote herself to her husband. In later years, when he spent most of his time travelling abroad, she was always at his side. Their only son, Igor, was born on 27 April 1931. Oistrakh now added teaching to his accomplishments. In 1934 he took on a lectureship at the Tchaikovsky Conservatory in Moscow and he and his family left Odessa for a three-room apartment in the capital.

Two years later he came second in the Wieniawski Competition in Warsaw. The first prize was awarded to the 15-year-old Ginette Neveu. Ida Haendel, then aged seven, took the first Polish Prize at the same competition. She was 'captivated by his beautiful tone and brilliant technique'.[4] In Brussels, in 1937, Oistrakh surmounted the first hurdle in the international field by winning the Queen's Prize in the first Ysaÿe Contest. Ysaÿe had long dreamt of holding a competition, but it was only after his death that Queen Elisabeth, a friend and devoted pupil of Ysaÿe, brought these plans to fulfilment. (The competition was held in Ysaÿe's name for only two years before being renamed the Concours Musical International Reine Elisabeth.)

Lionel Giraud-Mangin, director of the Beaux-Arts in Brussels, recalled the touching scene when this unknown Russian received the jury's unanimous approval and a standing ovation. 'The Queen called the young man into her box and personally presented him to the audience for a round of further applause.'[5] A warm friendship grew between Oistrakh and the Queen. She was an accomplished director violinist and they often played together; she also took lessons with him and, although well into her seventies, would always be open to his suggestions as to how to improve her playing. Elisabeth remained devoted to Oistrakh until her death and bequeathed her Stradivari violin – a family heirloom – to him. (After his death, Tamara and Igor placed it in trust with the Glinko Museum of Musical Culture in Moscow.) When the Ysaÿe Foundation was created in 1961, Oistrakh became its first president.

Oistrakh's success in Brussels prompted many offers to play abroad. Thibaud, one of the most enthusiastic members of the jury, pressed him to come to Paris at the first opportunity. But at this time the Soviet Union was slow to allow artistic freedom, and before any plans could be discussed Europe was plunged into war.

Now elevated to professor of violin at the Moscow Conservatory, Oistrakh continued to teach and to play in his own country. When Hitler's armies invaded the Soviet Union in 1941, he travelled to the front, giving concerts to the troops and to workers in the factories. The conditions were sometimes unbearable. During the occupation of Leningrad he gave a memorable performance of the Tchaikovsky concerto in an unheated hall, with the temperature well below zero. Against a background accompaniment of intermittent gunfire and fire alarms, Oistrakh remained unshaken throughout.

When the war ended, Oistrakh was at the height of his career, but without provision for concerts outside the Soviet Union. It was almost as difficult to organise appearances of visiting foreign artists. Ernest Krause in his biography *David Oistrakh*, states incorrectly that Oistrakh played the Bach Double Concerto in Moscow with Menuhin in 1945. The two men certainly met for the first time that year in Moscow – Menuhin records the occasion in touching detail in his autobiography. Excited at the thought of meeting this great violinist, of whom he had heard so much, Menuhin arrived at the airport to find Oistrakh waiting on the tarmac, 'in the wind and wet of the November afternoon', to welcome a fellow artist to his country. An immediate affinity sprang up between the two and resulted in a friendship which endured for almost 30 years. Menuhin recalls the visit as being fraught with rebuffs and bureaucratic obstacles. He had to leave Moscow without even hearing Oistrakh play, let alone taking part in a joint performance.

Oistrakh's earliest appearance outside the Soviet Union after the war was at the first Prague Spring Festival in 1946. A year later at the same festival, Menuhin and Oistrakh were finally brought together professionally to play the Bach Double Concerto. For Menuhin the experience was significant:

> We were to play the same work together in Paris and Brussels and many other places. Playing this was interesting, not only because of the personal rapport that existed between us but because it gave me an insight of what was still Russian to me. My parents had come from Russia and we shared the same Russian-Jewish background. It was curious how our styles seemed to be almost identical when we played together. We both gained so much from this contact: I for the reasons already stated and he, perhaps something that was useful to him right after the war, when he had been immured in Russia all his life and knew little of what was going on in the Western world.[6]

When restrictions were finally lifted and opportunities to travel abroad became a reality, it was not to satisfy the egocentric ambitions of a star performer that Oistrakh set forth on his journeys. He was convinced that he had a mission to use his influence in representing the traditions of the Russian school of violin playing, and was particularly keen to pass on his ideas to the younger generation.

*The Strad* critic wrote of a performance in Paris in the early 1950s that 'he fully justified his reputation'. The qualities of his playing:

> ... lift it into a class by itself .... His playing of the Mozart Fifth Concerto in A (K219) with Jacques Thibaud conducting was 'spacious, gracious and virile', with no signs of affected prettiness in the beautiful phrasing. Though always alive with a compelling

interior warmth and strength, his feelings never ill-treat either the music or the violin. He never seemed to be in a hurry, a feature we have now come to accept as almost inevitable in anyone under sixty! The keynotes of his playing are nobility, sincerity and the simplicity which goes with profound and balanced musicianship.

England did not see Oistrakh officially until 1954, although he had been sent on a delegation to London some years previously and had played at a private party at the Soviet Embassy. The impresario Victor Hochhauser was responsible for bringing Oistrakh to Britain. He had heard him play at the Prague Spring Festival in 1949 and recognised an extraordinary talent. After a long campaign of bombarding the Soviet Embassy, Hochhauser managed in 1953 to organise a London concert by Oistrakh's son, Igor, who was by then a fully-fledged performer. A year later Hochhauser brought David Oistrakh to London.

Accompanied on the piano by Yampol'sky, Oistrakh gave his long-awaited recital to a packed Royal Albert Hall on 10 November 1954. He played Beethoven's First Sonata and Prokofiev's F minor Sonata, which the composer had dedicated to him. An unusual choice was Schumann's rarely played Fantasia in C, 'composed for Joachim and touched up by Kreisler', and unpopular on account of its fiendishly unviolinistic passage-work. In this work and Ysaÿe's Ballade No. 3, 'the multiple stopping was carried with such truth of intonation and such smoothness of bow that one almost overlooked its difficulty'.[7]

Oistrakh's British orchestral debut took place two weeks later, again at the Royal Albert Hall with the Philharmonia Orchestra under Norman del Mar. He played concertos by Brahms and Aram Khachaturian, the latter conducted by the composer himself. In the Brahms, Oistrakh was inevitably compared with Heifetz who had played it in London the previous week. *The Times* critic appears to prefer Oistrakh. Whereas Heifetz '. . . was all objectivity, Oistrakh's performance . . . had a more classical feeling, more identification of himself with the composer, than Heifetz'.[8] Since the end of the Second World War, Oistrakh's recordings had appeared in Europe and America on a variety of labels, and he had made a reputation as a violinist who possessed a large, luscious tone with tremendous intensity and power. When he finally played to Western audiences in the flesh, however, they responded to his simple unaffected manner. In person his tone was not overwhelming as his over-amplified recordings implied: it had refinement and delicacy.

Oistrakh made his debut in New York in a Carnegie Hall recital on 20 November 1955. The audience filled every seat and overflowed onto the stage. Several times they broke into cheers and would not let him go before he had played several encores. The next morning, Howard Taubman wrote in the *New York Times*: 'In Tartini's "Devil's Trill" sonata he had a masterful command of all the bravura requirements [but] . . . the most impressive thing about Mr Oistrakh was the thoughtfulness and sensitivity of his musicianship. He is unmistakably a violinist who does not begin by thinking how to subdue an audience through sheer brilliance.' Taubman illustrates his point by describing Oistrakh's playing of Beethoven's Sonata No. 1 in D, Op. 12. In the slow movement 'the framework of the conception was classic, but the feeling had a romantic glow'.[9]

This particular November day is probably unique in the history of this famous hall. At 2.30 p.m., Mischa Elman gave a recital. Oistrakh's was at 5.30 p.m. Three hours later, Milstein took the stage. In Oistrakh's audience was a galaxy of famous musicians. 'But the presence of Kreisler excited me more than anything else. When I saw him deep in thought listening to my playing, and then rising to applaud, I was so overcome I thought I was dreaming.'[10]

By this time, Oistrakh was giving some 90 concerts a year in the Soviet Union in addition to his foreign tours and international recordings. At the Moscow Conservatory he had about 15 master pupils, who came from all over the world. He loved his students and they adored him. He would travel any distance to be with them when they were entering international competitions and the high rate of success of his pupils is proof of the excellence of his teaching: Viktor Tret'yakov, Valery Klimov, Viktor Pikayzen and Oleg Kagan are some of the most outstanding.

The Russians claim that the superb technical equipment with which their soloists are blessed is largely due to the fact that all their great players are teachers. They acknowledge their debt to Auer and his school. Although modified by intervening generations, modern Russian traditions are firmly based on his principles which, through his predecessors Vieuxtemps and Wieniawski, are linked to the Italians through Viotti and his pupils.

Howard Taubman described Oistrakh as a player 'with head and heart inextricably linked'. Time and time again, critics and colleagues alike were to remark upon this quality. In the Tchaikovsky concerto, Oistrakh '. . . took its lush tones and gave them dignity without robbing them of their essential character. It was lyrical without being maudlin.'[11] And yet, when it came to Mozart, Oistrakh's individual approach seemed to embrace the eighteenth-century style with virility as well as refinement. In his performances of contemporary works by Soviet composers, Oistrakh was regarded as an important propagandist by the Russian government. Shostakovitch dedicated both his concertos to him.

On the platform his playing seemed effortless. One London critic expressed something approaching regret at his making the difficulties imperceptible, on the grounds that half the enjoyment of listening to a virtuoso is to witness the phenomenon. Behind this apparent ease was a fine analytical musical mind. Oistrakh would spend hours studying scores and listening intently to tape-recordings. When he mounted the platform, he played the way he was, honestly and without vanity. He never took liberties with the music.

Technically, he was a master by any standards. Despite his heavy build his bowing was elegant and consistent for the whole length of the bow. After his first appearance in Paris, in 1953, *The Strad* critic wrote that 'with only about two inches left at the heel on an up bow, he is able to add another note which is perfectly phrased and clear, only then going to a down bow at the extreme limit and with complete smoothness'.[12] Frederick Riddle, principal violist of the Royal Philharmonic Orchestra for many years, was able to study Oistrakh's playing at close quarters; he said: 'His bowing was a lovely example of the Auer School – the little finger comes off at the point of the bow and the first finger comes out so that the wrist is kept well down as the bow is drawn up. A beautiful motion to watch. And a great influence on violin playing the world over.'[13]

Ricci tells a revealing story about Oistrakh's approach to music. It seems that someone once asked him: 'What is the most difficult piece you play?' Oistrakh replied: 'I don't play the most difficult pieces.'[14] Oistrakh, like Adolf Busch and Szigeti, belonged in the very good company of those who place music above pyrotechnics.

In private life, Oistrakh was an inveterate collector. His Moscow flat was crowded with instruments, music, books and mementoes of all kinds. Cameras and small mechanical toys always held a fascination for him, and his colleagues would smile at his boyish enthusiasm as he proudly demonstrated his newest acquisition. A fine chess player, he followed the international competitions with interest. But best of all, he liked to play chess with his son.

Oistrakh's continuing close relationship with his orchestral colleagues long after he had become an internationally famous soloist is reminiscent of Kreisler – a man who never became proud. His friend Victor Hochhauser considered him to be:

> . . . quite the most outstanding man I have ever known – and I don't exclude all the great names. He was a character who combined the sense of tragedy of the Russian and the Jewish people. He just wanted to be left alone to play the violin, to teach and give pleasure to the masses. He was great fun to be with. His sense of humour was delightful – never cruel or cynical at someone else's expense. Mostly he laughed at himself.[15]

Menuhin drew attention to the wider significance of Oistrakh's achievement:

> The Revolution and World War I having interrupted the regenerating contribution of the great Russian School to our violin world, Oistrakh was the first to rekindle it. For decades Jascha Heifetz and Mischa Elman had carried the torch and I am modestly proud to have been instrumental in persuading Oistrakh at a time when relations between Russia and America were strained that he would be welcomed by the great American public. Indeed he evoked unbounded affection, admiration and gratitude and picked up and renewed the current of great Russian violinists that had crossed the Atlantic thirty years previously.[16]

When David and Igor Oistrakh played the double concertos by Bach and Vivaldi in London in 1961, *The Times* described them as being 'in perfect sympathy, in both thought and expression, their two personalities fused into a single overall conception'.[17] Nonetheless, being the son of a famous father can be a dubious advantage. In the history of the violin there are no previous examples of father and son both achieving fame on the same instrument. Igor Oistrakh has not only accepted that challenge but has also made his own individual mark as a musician, and furthermore encouraged his son, Valery (b. 1961) to carry on the tradition.

Igor Oistrakh was born in Odessa in 1931 and had his first lessons on the violin at the age of six, but soon lost interest, rekindled when he was 12. This came about when the family moved to Sverdlovsk and he met Pyotr Stolyarsky, his father's teacher. Oistrakh explains: 'He had an intuition about a youngster's musical gifts, and he felt strongly that, although I was quite a lazy boy, I was destined to be a violinist.'[18] Stolyarsky obviously succeeded where the young Oistrakh was concerned because, although he worked with the great man for only a few months before the family moved on to Moscow, he is convinced that he would never have taken up the violin seriously had it not been for that short encounter.

In Moscow Oistrakh entered the Central Music School where he studied with Valeria Merenblum for six years, and admits that he became more and more enthusiastic about the violin every day. He was particularly inspired by the postwar cultural exchanges between the West and the East: 'I was used to hearing my father play the violin: I took it for granted, like seeing the sun or having fresh air. But it was a new impression to hear Enescu and Menuhin when they played in Moscow in 1945. I was overwhelmed with Menuhin's performance of the Beethoven concerto.'[19] These experiences set Oistrakh on a period of intensive practice, working seven or eight hours a day; he was even reprimanded by his father for practising too much in a technical direction. Eventually he was able to turn his attention to interpretation and experimentation with tone and colour. He admits that even today he is still trying to grow in these directions.

When he was 18, Igor entered his father's class at the Moscow Conservatory and encountered all the obvious difficulties of being the teacher's son. David Oistrakh was known for not compromising where perfection was concerned and his own son was not spared on this score. Igor admits to feeling uncomfortable sometimes but accepts that his father's remarks were seldom without foundation and that he learnt much from the man he regarded as ' not only a great musician but a great teacher'.[20]

In 1952 Igor won the Wieniawski Competition in Warsaw and began undertaking his own concert tours, playing in London, Paris, Vienna and Berlin, and gradually he gained his independence. While obviously still under the influence of his father, he was gradually finding his way to his individual artistic personality. For him a remark from the critic Bernard Gavoty signalled a turning point. After a concert in Paris, Gavoty wrote: 'Igor Oistrakh is no longer the son of David.'[21]

In 1958 Igor became his father's assistant at the conservatory and later held his own class. By this time his father was playing regularly in the West and soon both father and son were appearing together everywhere to rave reviews.

There were also occasions when David Oistrakh conducted his son playing some of the romantic concertos; sometimes there were disagreements. Igor explains: 'I allowed myself more rubato and more contrasts in dynamics and tempos than he would have liked. I think that in general – without entering into the contrasting styles that exist in music – my father was very perfect, very Olympian, very balanced not only as a musician but as a person. Maybe I am more emotional and not so well balanced.' He would tell his father: 'I have a right to disagree with you because you belong to the older, more conservative school of Professor Stolyarsky, but I belong to the more modern school of David Oistrakh.'[22]

Today Oistrakh is active in many musical fields: in addition to his solo career, conducting and teaching, he gives recitals with his wife, the pianist Natalya Zertsalova, whom he met when they were both students at the Moscow Conservatory. He has also served on the juries of many international competitions and in 1978 he chaired the Tchaikovsky Competition in Moscow. Of his many recordings, those made with his wife – a superb musical partnership – of the complete sonatas of Mozart and Beethoven are particularly outstanding.

**Notes**

1. Quoted from interview, M.C.
2–3. Krause, *David Oistrakh*, p. 13.
4. Haendel, *Woman with Violin*, p. 51.
5. Ysaÿe, extract in *Journal des Beaux-Arts*, 1955, p. 175.
6. Quoted from interview, M.C.
7–8. *The Times*, 11 November 1954.
9. *New York Times*, 21 November 1955.
10. Krause, op. cit., p. 19
11. *New York Times*, 21 November 1955.
12. *The Strad*, August 1953, p. 124.
13–15. Quoted from interview, M.C.
16. Menuhin, letter to M.C., 30 October 1978.
17. *The Times*, 6 March 1961.
18–22. *The Strad*, March 1989, pp. 210–12.

# 31   A Man for All Music

There can be few violinists who have made a greater impact on the musical world than the young Yehudi Menuhin. His name became known internationally before he had the strength to tune his own fiddle. When he played at a concert in Philadelphia on 26 June 1978 in a series to celebrate his 50th year on the concert platform, James Felton of the *Evening Bulletin* wrote:

> The man seems truly ageless, ever modest, still the elegant violinist who avoids virtuoso tricks, ever in search of melody in all its sweetness. He doesn't tune slightly sharp, as some others do, to get a deliberately sharp, commanding tone. He doesn't grind the threads of his bow to tatters in passionate frenzy. Mendelssohn's Violin Concerto was a perfect choice for him .... Menuhin handled it with gentle, loving care, and a slight private smile as if he and his instrument were revealing themselves as partners. . . . His solo cadenzas didn't capitalise on showiness but rather moved deliberately and thoughtfully, remaining faithful to this overwhelmingly lyrical work. A performance of taste. Menuhin typically insisted on sharing the applause with everyone on stage, as if they had all been playing chamber music together.

Yehudi Menuhin (1916–99) was born in New York, the son of a poor Jewish schoolmaster who shared with his wife a great love of music. They took their child to concerts from the age of 14 months. He responded so well to musical sound that when he was four they gave him a small violin.

His first teacher was a 'drill-sergeant'[1] who knew little of the classics and less of the subtleties of violin playing, but in 1921, when Yehudi was five, he began lessons with Louis Persinger. On 29 February 1924, accompanied by Persinger on the piano, the seven-year-old Yehudi played Bériot's Scène de Ballet as an item inserted into an orchestral programme at the Oakland Auditorium in California. The following year he made his first appearance with the San Francisco Symphony Orchestra, playing the Lalo Symphonie Espagnole to an excited and appreciative audience. Menuhin's most vivid memory of the occasion was of being picked up and embraced by the conductor, whose beard '. . . felt like a moist whisk broom'.[2] A month before his ninth birthday, he gave his first full-length recital, in the Scottish Rite Hall in San Francisco.

In the autumn of 1925, Persinger moved to New York. The Menuhins followed. Menuhin's New York debut was not the Carnegie Hall concert that was to bring him fame overnight a year later, but a recital with Persinger at the Manhattan Opera House on 17 January 1926. With the exception of the impresario, Walter Damrosch, the audience lacked any distinguished musicians. But there were three elderly gentlemen sitting in the front row who had good reason to attend. They were Papa Heifetz, Papa Elman and Papa Max Rosen.

In the autumn of 1926 the entire Menuhin family – father, mother, Yehudi and his two sisters, Hephzibah and Yaltah – sailed for Europe, an undertaking sponsored by Sidney Ehrman, a wealthy lawyer and one of the best-known Jewish philanthropists in New York at the time. Yehudi made his European orchestral debut by appearing in two highly successful concerts in Paris with the Lamoureux Orchestra under Paul Paray, playing the Lalo Symphonie Espagnole and the Tchaikovsky concerto.

It was also at this time that he was taken to audition with Ysaÿe in Brussels. As a former student of Ysaÿe, Persinger had created an image that had filled his young pupil with awe. When the boy and the legend came face to face, Yehudi was disappointed: 'In place of the giant of my childish vision, I found a too human man in too human surroundings.'[3] Menuhin played the first movement of the Symphonie Espagnole while Ysaÿe strummed chords to create the illusion of an orchestral accompaniment. When Menuhin had finished, Ysaÿe told him: 'You have made me happy, little boy, very happy indeed.' Then he asked him to play an A major arpeggio in four octaves. The astonished boy 'groped all over the fingerboard like a blind mouse'. Ysaÿe not only offered to teach him but gave him some obvious advice: 'You would do well, Yehudi, to practise scales and arpeggios.'[4] In retrospect, Menuhin realised that he might well have shortened his long search for musical understanding had he accepted Ysaÿe's offer. But even as a ten-year-old he instinctively resisted learning an imposed method and was unable to accept anything ready-made. 'Music was something very alive to me, an essential means of expression, and I suspect that unending hours of work on dull material might well have blunted rather than polished my interpretation of it.'[5]

One of the most important later influences on Yehudi's playing was George Enescu. The association had begun in a legendary encounter at a concert in San Francisco when he was about eight years old. 'Before a note was sounded he had me in thrall. His countenance, his stance, his wonderful mane of black hair – everything about him proclaimed the free . . . man who is strong with the freedom of gypsies, of spontaneity, of creative genius, of fire.'[6]

Much later Yehudi was taken to an Enescu concert in Paris. He went alone to the artists' room after the concert and persuaded Enescu to hear him at six o'clock the following morning, while he was packing his bags to leave Paris. As soon as Enescu heard the boy play, he agreed to give him some lessons, each of which was:

> . . . an inspiration, not a stage reached in a course of instruction. It was the making of music . . . While he accompanied me at the piano he also sang the different voices of the score . . . . What I received from him – by compelling example, not by word – was

the note transformed into vital message, the phrase given shape and meaning, the structure of music made vivid.[7]

When he looked back on those early studies with Enescu, Menuhin found that his direct influence was submerged in the very conception of a work, a conception which was unified, its elements no longer traceable to direct sources. 'I must make an effort now to recall any specific things he said, but I know that everything I do carries his imprint yet.'[8]

The autumn of 1927 saw the Menuhins back in New York so that Yehudi could fulfil two concert engagements, including one on 26 November at Carnegie Hall with the New York Philharmonic Orchestra. When Fritz Busch learnt that he was to conduct an eleven-year-old boy playing the Beethoven concerto, he said: 'One doesn't hire Jackie Coogan to play Hamlet.' But after the audition he revised his opinion: 'My dear child, you can play anything with me, anytime, anywhere.' However, the orchestra remained unconvinced, especially when the small boy handed his violin to the leader to be tuned. Menuhin recalled: 'By the end of the first movement, however, I knew they were on my side.'[9] It was not only the triumph over scepticism that had so pleased the young performer, it was being accepted by the hardened rank-and-file members of the orchestra, who knew what they were about.

The concert was an unqualified success. There were 3,000 in the audience and tears streamed unashamedly from their eyes as Fritz Busch came down from the rostrum and embraced the small boy who had played like a virtuoso with a lifetime of experience behind him. The next morning, Olin Downes wrote in the *New York Times*:

> Menuhin has a technique that is not only brilliant but finely tempered. It is not a technique of tricks, but one much more solidly established, and governed by innate sensitivity and taste. It seems ridiculous to say he showed a mature conception of Beethoven's Concerto, but that is the fact. Few violinists of years of experience, known to the public, have played Beethoven with as true a feeling for his form and content.[10]

Early in 1929, the Menuhins departed once more for Europe. A few days before Yehudi's 13th birthday came the concert that marked the start of his adult career. On 12 April 1929, he played the Bach, Beethoven and Brahms concertos with the Berlin Philharmonic Orchestra under Bruno Walter. Berlin was then the musical centre of the western world. Adolf Busch and many like him were able, at this time, to make a good living out of music without ever crossing the German frontier. This was not possible in any other country. In the USA, where the musical scene was still largely German, it was essential that any artist seeking international status should first succeed in the German arena.

The original idea of returning to Europe was hastened by Enescu's advice that Yehudi should study with Adolf Busch in Basle. Enescu had occasionally to check Yehudi's over-passionate rendering and it was probably this inclination that spurred him to suggest a different type of teacher. Yehudi spent two summers with Busch. 'If he didn't have Enescu's flair or glamour, as a musician he was extremely serious and deep, a passionate fundamentalist who ate, breathed and slept Bach and Beethoven. I think that musicians, more particularly chamber musicians, are to this day, whether knowingly or not, in debt to his combined passion and profundity.'[11]

In November 1929 the Menuhin family made their first trip to England. Yehudi's debut at the Queen's Hall on 4 November and a recital at the Royal Albert Hall a few days later were both sell-outs. The London critics were, as always, reserved in their judgement on child prodigies. Of his concert at the Queen's Hall with the London Symphony Orchestra under Fritz Busch, *The Times* of 5 November 1929 made the following points:

> Judged by the absolute standards, Menuhin's performance was very good. His command of technique is remarkable . . . and the tone was always musical if not very full. But whilst there was something more than a mere cold perfection in his playing there was little real feeling. All the obvious points were duly made but the subtleties escaped him . . . . Yet it is the measure of the boy's ability that his performance of a work so exacting both technically and emotionally, can be judged by the same standards as that of his elders.[12]

It was Yehudi's second visit to Britain, in 1932, that has now slipped into musical history and, indeed, remained clearly in the violinist's memory to the end of his life. It came about through Frederick Gaisberg, recording manager of HMV, who felt that the Elgar concerto had been neglected. The magnificent recording by Albert Sammons made in 1929 would in his opinion never be bettered, but he nevertheless dreamed of making a recording with Elgar conducting the work. He thought that 'a youthful and pliant performer without prejudice'[13] like Yehudi would respond best to Sir Edward's wishes. The septuagenarian composer and the 16-year-old boy met for the first time in the spring of 1932 at the recording studios in Abbey Road. Gaisberg wrote: 'Yehudi's fresh, agile mind, so quick to grasp the instructions, drew from Sir Edward high praise and encouragement.'[14] Menuhin recalled that Sir Edward arrived looking not in the least like a composer but more like a 'country gentleman', who should have had hounds at his heels. With Ivor Newton as his accompanist, they started to play, but a few bars after the soloist's entry, Elgar stopped them saying he was sure that everything would go beautifully and if they would excuse him, he was off to the races. The feeling of trust he inspired was well-founded. 'At the recording studio, Elgar was a figure of great dignity but without a shred of self-importance. I had never seen anyone conduct less, or show less determination to impose himself. All was ease and equanimity.'[15]

Some months later, following the success of the recording, Menuhin performed the concerto again in the Royal Albert Hall. This was a concert to make the young performer both proud and humble. In the first half Sir Thomas Beecham conducted him in concertos by Bach and Mozart and in the second, Elgar, 'propped on a red velvet stool', conducted his own. 'To appear with England's most beloved composer as well as with her most distinguished conductor was like being given the freedom of the city or made a member of the family.'[16] Gaisberg, too, recalled the occasion:

> The Albert Hall was filled to the last seat. A brilliant and expectant audience such as only London could produce had come to hear the 15[sic]-year-old boy and 75-year-old composer collaborate in what proved to be a thrilling and moving performance. I have never seen such spontaneous enthusiasm as that which recalled to the platform again and again the old man and the young boy hand in hand.[17]

The next morning *The Times* critic wrote without reservation, 'Menuhin's playing has a singularly musical quality, and if he does not produce a tone of exceptional power, it is always beautifully smooth and his execution is of masterly ease. Throughout one was impressed by the sympathy of the phrasing and the general vitality of the playing.'[18] Elgar, too, was pleased. Afterwards he wrote to Gaisberg, thanking him. 'Yehudi was marvellous and I am sure would never have heard of the concerto if you had not set the thing in motion.'[19]

In the years that followed, Menuhin became known the world over and earned a vast income from concert appearances and recordings. But in 1936, twelve months before his 21st birthday, he took a year off from concert-giving in order to study and to live a little of the private life denied him through the relentless demands of being a travelling virtuoso. Until then he had always played the violin instinctively. It was at this time that he first began to analyse his own approach. He later wrote:

> Considering that I played without thinking, without analysis, without as it were, taking the machine apart for overhaul, just keeping it running at any cost, my performance stood up remarkably well; but there were times when I knew I wouldn't be able to go on until I understood technique and could recapture that ease I had once possessed without thinking and which was now deserting me. I also knew I had fallen into bad habits. This double warning drove me to a search for first principles which was to last for years (indeed it has not ended: every day brings new discoveries).[20]

He studied the manuals of Carl Flesch and D.C. Dounis from cover to cover, he discussed the situation with his friends and took more lessons. But still he felt he was not making any progress. Finally, through Antal Dorati, he was introduced to Bartók in New York. He played the composer's first violin sonata and at the end of the first movement Bartók stood up and said: 'I did not think music could be played like that until long after the composer was dead.'[21] Menuhin's period of self-doubt receded.

At that first meeting Menuhin asked if he might commission Bartók to compose a work for him. 'I was not hoping for a third concerto, just a work for violin alone.'[22] Menuhin was rewarded with a masterpiece. When the score arrived in March 1944 he was shaken. It seemed to him almost unplayable. Later he realised that this first hasty impression was ill-judged:

> The Solo Sonata is eminently playable, beautifully composed for the violin, one of the most dramatic and fulfilling works that I know of, the most important composition for violin alone since Bach. It is a work of wild contrasts. The Tempo di Ciaconna, the first movement, translates the greatest of Bach's own works for solo violin . . . . That I should have evoked this magnificent music is a source of infinite satisfaction to me; that I should have played it to Bartók before he died remains one of the great milestones of my life.[23]

The collaboration between composer and performer is interesting. In Bartók's original conception of the work, the recurring passages in semiquavers in the last movement were to be played in quarter-tones – the notes between the semitones of the tempered chromatic scale, which are still common to oriental and gypsy music. Bartók gave Menuhin the option of playing these passages in quarter-tones or semitones; since he had only a few weeks to prepare the work for performances, he chose the latter. He found the playing of accurate quarter-tones too demanding.

Sadly Bartók was dying of leukaemia when he wrote to Menuhin from Asheville, North Carolina:

> I am rather worried about the 'playability' of some of the double stops, etc. On the last page I give you some of the alternatives. In any case, I should like to have your advice. I sent you two copies. Would you be so kind as to introduce in one of them the necessary changes in bowing, and perhaps the absolutely necessary fingering and other suggestions, and return it to me? And also indicate the impracticable difficulties? I would try to change them.[24]

Menuhin suggested few changes and their subsequent correspondence is mainly concerned with working out technical points. He gave its first performance on 26 November 1944 at Carnegie Hall, packed to the rafters, with hundreds of men and women from the armed forces seated on the stage. Olin Downes declared the sonata to be in Bartók's 'latest and most boldly dissonant style . . . a test for the ears, the intelligence, the receptiveness of the most learned listener'.[25]

The war years and an unsuccessful youthful marriage had left him in a state of unrest and indecision and Menuhin's next step was to re-establish himself with audiences at home and abroad. He encountered little difficulty in this quarter. His private life also began to take on a more optimistic pattern. His first marriage ended in an amicable divorce and in 1947 he married Diana Gould; their two sons, Gerard and Jeremy, are both musicians.

Menuhin's interest in humanitarian causes was always as important as his own performances. Shortly after the Second World War, he toured Europe with Benjamin

Britten. One of their saddest appearances was playing to the recently liberated inmates of the concentration camps. Over the years he gave innumerable concerts in support of refugees from war, poverty, famine and flood in every corner of the world: there is scarcely a country in which he did not appear. He was invited to India in 1952, at the invitation of the prime minister, and later promoted many visits of Indian artists to the West. He founded the Gstaad Music Festival in 1957 and, at the invitation of Ian Hunter, took on the artistic direction of the Bath Festival between 1959 and 1968. At Bath he founded a new orchestra and was responsible for bringing many internationally famous artists to perform there. He devised programmes that blended classic favourites with an infusion of new works, and he was innovative: for example, Margot Fonteyn and Rudolf Nureyev danced to his playing of a movement from Bartók's Solo Sonata.

Perhaps the achievement closest to Menuhin's heart is the Surrey school that bears his name in Stoke d'Abernon, which he founded in 1963 to provide talented youngsters with a full-time musical education. The tutors are drawn from some of the finest musicians in the world. Menuhin liked to claim that the chamber music playing in his school is in advance of anything in Russia or the USA:

> The important thing is to train young people so that they can take their place according to their talents. Opportunities dictate the need for soloists, orchestral players, quartet players or teachers. One boy has decided he wants to be a composer. It is also possible that some will go on to university and become ethno-musicologists. That kind of musical background cannot be found everywhere. In Russia and elsewhere they are trained as soloists and if they end up in an orchestra, they are disappointed.'[26]

Menuhin applauded the fact that in Britain the democratisation of life has had its effect on musical values. The discrepancy between the soloist and the orchestral player or tutor is no longer as great as it used to be. The idea of stratification is now becoming a thing of the past. 'There is [still] specialisation of a sort but each one of us is as important as the other and that is what my school is achieving. It is also true that with this broader preparation the young musician can achieve a higher degree of expression and response: a sensitivity in hearing other voices and lending an ear to what happens in the orchestra.'[27]

The classic style of Menuhin's own playing was in a direct line from the old Italian masters through Enescu, Marsick, Habeneck and Baillot to Viotti on one side, and through Busch, Hess, Joachim, Böhm and Rode back to Viotti on the other. This was playing in which virtuosity took second place to musicianship, and it is nowhere better displayed than in his duo performances with his sister Hephzibah, especially of sonatas by Beethoven. Menuhin enriched the art of violin playing in many ways. Perhaps the most compelling example of his art was his playing of the slow movement of the Beethoven concerto. His recordings of the complete set of J.S. Bach's partitas and solo sonatas show not only sensitivity towards the composer, but humility towards the music itself. Furthermore, Menuhin played Indian music with Ravi Shankar, the celebrated sitar player, and joined Stephane Grappelli in jazz. He was indeed a man for all music.

**Notes**

1. Menuhin, *Unfinished Journey*, p. 27.
2. Ibid., p. 50.
3–4. Ibid., p. 66.
5. Ibid., p. 67.
6. Ibid., p. 57.
7. Ibid., p. 71.
8. Ibid., p. 72.
9. Ibid., pp. 85–6.
10. *New York Times*, 27 November 1927.
11. Menuhin, op. cit., p. 102.
12. *The Times*, 5 November 1929.
13–14. Gaisberg, *Music on Record*, p. 237.
15–16. Menuhin, op. cit., pp. 122–3.
17. Gaisberg, op. cit., p. 238
18. *The Times*, 22 November 1932.
19. Letter from Elgar to Gaisberg, 22 November 1932.
20. Menuhin, op. cit., p. 162.
21. Ibid., p. 164.
22–23. Ibid., p. 166.
24. Ibid., p. 167.
25. *New York Times*, 27 November 1944.
26. Quoted from interview, M.C.
27. Ibid.

# 32  The Born Virtuoso

Two years after launching the young Menuhin, Persinger brought another Wunderkind before the public of San Francisco: Ruggiero Ricci. Not only has he survived the hazardous transition from prodigy to adult virtuoso without artistic mishap, but he is still acknowledged as one of the world's great violinists of his day.

Ruggiero Ricci was born in 1918 in San Francisco, California, the third of seven children of a poor Italian immigrant trombonist. The family had anglicised their name to Rich and, in a burst of enthusiasm, had called their son 'Woodrow Wilson' after the current president of their adopted country. It was only when Ruggiero showed marked musical talent that they reverted to the more mellifluous Italian. But 'Woodrow Wilson Rich' is still the name on Ricci's passport. Ruggiero received his first musical instruction from his father and cannot remember a time when he did not have a violin in his hands. Not only was there the possibility of his becoming a second Menuhin, but a poor family could use the money earned by a child prodigy. To make an even more convincing display, they lopped two years off the child's age.

When Ruggiero was seven, he was auditioned by Persinger and passed over to his assistant, Elizabeth Lackey. So convinced was Persinger of his talent that he arranged for Miss Lackey to take him into her home, thus fulfilling the roles of both foster-mother and teacher. In addition to his daily lessons the young child also received regular instruction from Persinger and was rewarded by winning a gold medal in a local contest at the age of eight. A year later in 1927, he was awarded the Oscar Weil Scholarship, the youngest contestant in a field of 23 aspirants of all ages.

Wearing a black velvet suit and playing a $30 three-quarter-size fiddle, he gave his first public recital on 15 November 1928 at the Scottish Rite Hall in San Francisco. Accompanied by Persinger on the piano, he played music by Vieuxtemps, Saint-Saëns and Wieniawski, rounding off his programme with an electrifying performance of the Mendelssohn concerto. By both audience and critics he was hailed as 'nothing short of genius'.

A year later, Ruggiero made his orchestral debut playing the Mendelssohn concerto with the Manhattan Symphony Orchestra under Henry Hadley, at the Mecca Temple in New York. Olin Downes wrote: 'It was immediately apparent that the boy had something to say, that he was playing with a native fire, musical sensitiveness and taste which are much more phenomenal than the mere physical dexterity . . . . It was the playing of one born to play his instrument.'[1]

A capacity audience who had paid a then record $6,000 greeted the ten-year-old Ruggiero for his recital debut at Carnegie Hall the following year. They cheered and cheered and would not let him go. Instead of the usual floral tributes, the young performer was handed a model aeroplane while his dressing room was heaped with toys and boxes of sweets.

A series of concert tours throughout the USA brought him countless admirers, but the pressures and loneliness of the travelling prodigy gave him scars in his formative years. He was once the central figure in a legal battle that obliged New York's Mayor 'Jimmy' Walker to cancel a sold-out Carnegie Hall concert, while charges of 'juvenile exploitation' were brought against his guardian. 'At nine, some uninhibited critic called me the greatest violinist playing. I have had to fight that kind of competition ever since.' But Ricci has a remedy for precocity: 'First shoot the parents of all prodigies and then put the kid up against the wall and finish the job.'[2]

The London public first heard Ruggiero at the age of 14, with the London Symphony Orchestra under Sir Hamilton Harty. Critics were loath to believe the extravagant claims made by the American press. But he played Mendelssohn's concerto 'with complete assurance . . . even as though he were already a little tired of playing it', wrote *The Times* critic. He further praised the child's technical equipment in a series of virtuoso short pieces that concluded with an unaccompanied prelude by Bach. 'Here was something more than the faithful copy of a mature performance. It had spontaneous impulse and rhythmic vitality. It showed the artist in the child.'[3]

Ricci repeated this success in every capital city in Europe. In Berlin, Germany's Chancellor, Count Franz von Papen, cheered from one box, the playwright Gerhard Hauptmann from another, and Professor Albert Einstein from another. When he played in Budapest, Kreisler called him the greatest musical genius since Mozart. A more analytical approach to the young Ricci comes from the critic and musicologist Henry Roth, who first heard him at the Hollywood Bowl when he was about 14:

> After breezing through the difficult Vieuxtemps Concerto No. 5 [with the Hollywood Bowl Orchestra] he returned to play several solos with piano accompaniment, among them the Tchaikovsky–Auer 'Waltz No. 2 from Serenade in C', and Sarasate's Introduction and Tarantella. No doubt about this – it was a blazing violin talent. His tone was large and penetrating, with the intense vibrance necessary for a modern soloist career, and his technique was already of virtuoso proportions. Purity of line, clarity of phrasing and neatness of detail characterised his musical approach, and all was infused with an audacious flair. There was not the imaginative expressiveness and inner spirit of the boy Menuhin, but the Ricci muse had a distinctive aura of its own, rich in the promise blossoming into artistry of extraordinary stature. At that time, the boy Ricci already projected, in adolescent form, the best elements of the adult Ricci.[4]

After some 14 years of concert-giving, with an annual income higher than that of the president of the United States, Ricci, at the age of 24, was called up during the

Second World War to serve in the US Army Air Force for three years. He performed frequently in entertainments at army camps and hospitals, even where no suitable piano was available. This exigency prompted Ricci to explore the unaccompanied literature for his instrument. Impressed with the variety of opportunities for projecting a single interpretative point of view unaffected by the inevitable differences between soloist and accompanist, he made a feature of this form of recital. In November 1946, immediately after his discharge, he gave a recital at the Town Hall, New York, which included the Bach Solo Sonata in A minor, Ysaÿe's Sonata, Op. 27 No. 4, the Hindemith Sonata, Op. 31 No. 2, two Paganini Caprices, and other unaccompanied pieces by Wieniawski and Kreisler. Since that time Ricci has given unaccompanied recitals in New York, London, Paris and Berlin. However, it was through an intense period of study of Paganini that Ricci overcame many of the technical difficulties inherent in the solo repertory. Consequently he is sometimes branded a Paganini 'expert' by those who cannot, despite the ample proof of history, equate a flawless technique with musicianship. Yet Ricci not only possesses a fine musical mind but is also something of a purist. He is aware that this may stem from an early reaction to Persinger, a very stylish player who loved the portamento. Ricci has an aversion to slides and glissandos. In his opinion too much 'feeling' can lead to over-interpretation.

Ricci has carefully analysed all 24 Paganini Caprices, breaking them down into a system so that he could see Paganini's manner of fingering, shifting and bowing. 'I learnt more about technique from Paganini than I did from any of my teachers.'[5] Ricci is one of the few violinists who has played all the Caprices at a single recital. He was also the first to record them.

Ricci's tone is round and intense and his vibrato can vary at will. His bow arm is extremely powerful. Although his fingers are not long, his left hand is broad and his stretch from the lower positions can reach notes high up on the strings. This he achieves by shifting very little and using the thumb as a pivot. As a brilliant technician Ricci has few rivals. His left-hand pizzicato has been described as 'hair-raising', his trills 'electric' and his harmonics 'airily transparent'.[6] His staccato and spiccato bow strokes evoke similar superlatives. This technical prowess and perfect intonation has been accomplished by the concentrated practice of scales in thirds, sixths and octaves, and the playing of piano music on the violin. He maintains: 'Keyboard studies are invaluable for developing technique on the fiddle, especially extensions',[7] an opinion shared by Milstein. These two violinists once took the same train together on a long journey and entertained each other by playing all the Chopin piano Etudes, which they both knew from memory on the violin.

The effect of Ricci's brilliant technical gifts tends to obscure other facets of his career. It is not always recognised that he has another image in which he stands on common ground with Joachim and Szigeti, that of a programme innovator. His is probably the largest and most original repertory of any living violinist. A recital he gave in 1969 included the Prokofiev Sonata for two violins, a set of songs for soprano and violin by Hector Villa-Lobos, and the Saint-Saëns Fantasie for violin and harp. His unusual programme building struck Ronald Crichton of the *Financial Times* as 'a taste eclectic and enquiring to a degree rarely found in star violinists or indeed in star performers of any kind'.[8] Ricci was the first to perform in New York the unaccompanied Prokofiev Sonata in D. In 1964 he played 15 great violin concertos in a series of four concerts in New York, tracing the influences from the Baroque to the avant-garde, and in 1977 he partnered Ernest Bitetti in a programme of duos for violin and guitar. With the New York Philharmonic under Leonard Bernstein he gave the world première of the Ginastera concerto. Ricci has premièred works by Gottfried von Einem, Alexander Goehr and Joseph White.

On the platform the diminutive Ricci – he is only 1.6 metres – is an undemonstrative performer. Everything appears to fall into place with the utmost ease. And yet he does not over-practise any work before a concert, especially Romantic music. 'I can *play* it but I can't practise it. If my performance has to be emotionally spontaneous then I must walk onto the platform ready to be spontaneous. It is the only time that I really surprise myself.'[9]

Surprise is an element never far from Ricci's daily life. More than once he has tucked his fiddle under his chin at a rehearsal about to play a Mozart concerto, only to find the orchestra striking up another by the same composer but in a different key. Fortunately he has always managed to switch over in time.

But there was another occasion when Ricci was due to play in Boston and had arranged with the management to leave without playing an encore. He had a plane to catch for Lisbon within an hour of the finishing time. The recital went well until he had played the final movement of the last item. He was greeted with a chilling silence. He stood for a minute thinking his audience might be too emotionally affected to applaud, but no-one moved a muscle. He laughed nervously and retreated from the stage. During the drive to the airport the manager asked: 'Why didn't you play the last two movements of the Hindemith sonata?' Ricci gasped. 'Hindemith! I was playing the Prokofiev!'[10]

Ricci is not only a prodigy who has survived: he is one of the few great violinists who concentrates all his energies on performing. So many top-ranking artists of today have commitments outside their platform appearances; but teaching apart, Ricci lays no claims to anything but 'fiddling'.

Exhaustive researches into the art of technique have equipped Ricci with a knowledge and execution that have few equals. Although his exciting but always *musical* performances of some of the most difficult pieces in the repertory remain among the best of modern recordings, Ricci is concerned about some of the attitudes of today:

> Somehow there has been for some time a stigma on virtuosity as though it were socially unacceptable. But this is nonsense. It should signify that one is master of one's instrument. The fiddle is a virtuoso instrument. When you start going in the opposite

direction you eradicate the fiddle. In the years since World War II when soloists stopped playing short pieces, we began to lose our audiences. We started to play sonatas at every recital, and the people who wanted to hear virtuoso pieces stayed away. Fortunately I think they are beginning to change this rigid attitude to programme building. I remember hearing Kremer, the great Russian violinist, play The Last Rose of Summer and it was beautiful.[11]

'I love the violin as Kreisler played it,' says Ricci, 'and I would rather hear *Liebesleid* played well than Beethoven played badly.'[12] Like his eminent predecessor, Ricci can do justice to both composers. At his 80th birthday recital at the Wigmore Hall in London in March 1998, Ricci's programme included music by Bach, Kreisler, Ysaÿe, Wieniawski and Paganini – performed with faultless intonation and innate musicianship that would have done credit to someone half his age.

## Notes

1. *New York Times*, 20 Octrober 1929.
2. Alix B. Williamson, publicity brochure.
3. *The Times*, 8 November 1932.
4. Roth, *The Strad*, August 1976, p. 303.
5. Quoted from interview, M.C.
6. Roth, *The Strad*, August 1976, p. 303.
7. Quoted from interview, M.C.
8. *Financial Times*, 1969.
9–12. Quoted from interview, M.C.

# 33  The Elder Statesman

For 'a life's work dedicated to music and devoted to humanity',[1] Isaac Stern (1920–2001) received the first Albert Schweitzer Award in 1975. As the elder statesman of violin playing, there is probably no other figure on the American violin scene today who was more respected by his colleagues. His ability as a performer was taken for granted. But he was also a tireless organiser in musical affairs, from saving Carnegie Hall to finding a dentist for an immigrant prodigy.

Isaac Stern was born in Kriminiesz, a small town on the Polish–Russian border, and brought to San Francisco when he was a few months old. His musical studies began with the piano when he was six, but two years later, when he heard a neighbour practising the violin, he decided that he preferred that instrument. He entered the San Francisco Conservatory of Music and studied with Naoum Blinder, leader of the San Francisco Symphony Orchestra. Blinder (1889–?) was a pupil of Brodsky, who had studied with Hellmesberger in Vienna, thus forming a direct link with Viotti through his teacher, Robberechts. When he was 15, Isaac made his debut, playing the Bach Double Concerto with his teacher and the San Francisco Symphony Orchestra.

The young Stern subsequently gave a number of recitals in Pacific coast cities and appeared with the Los Angeles Symphony Orchestra. His New York recital debut came in October 1937, when he was 17. At New York Town Hall he played an ambitious programme with Arpad Sandor that included Tartini's 'Devil's Trill' Sonata and the Glazunov Concerto, attracting a large audience. The *New York Times* praised the 'extent of his technique' and his 'spirited straight forward playing', but was critical of the fact that 'his bow presses too hard and vibrates the string too little', noting that it gave 'a fine sonority on the lower strings but frequent stridency in upper registers'.[2] However, Stern's New York recital the following year was declared an unqualified success by public and critics alike. When asked exactly where or when these early concerts took place, Stern himself was unable to say with accuracy. He never collected press cuttings, nor requested an agent to do so, because he modestly felt they would never be of any interest to anyone.

After the age of 17, Stern had no further formal lessons. 'I was responsible for my own mistakes. It is a process of intellectual and personal involvement with music as an idea and a way of life, not as a profession or career, but a rapport with people who think and feel and care about something – you have to find your own way of thinking, feeling and caring.'[3] That this philosophy had borne fruit was evident at his Carnegie Hall recital debut in 1943. The *New York Times* was in no doubt this time. 'He produced a voluminous, round, singing tone from the strings capable of a wide range of dynamic effects and most sensitive gradations. The bow was under admirable control, the left hand unswervingly accurate. It seems the youthful artist made known every asset needed for the negotiation of the exacting compositions he had chosen to expound.'[4] The programme included the Bach Sonata in G minor for unaccompanied violin, the Mozart duo Sonata in E minor and the Brahms D minor Sonata.

In the intervening years Isaac Stern played with almost every major orchestra in the world and under most of the great conductors. This versatile artist recorded virtually all the significant classical and contemporary violin literature and appeared on TV and in films (once impersonating Ysaÿe in *Tonight We Sing*).

Stern was not only a great violinist, but an accomplished musician. For him, the two were as inextricably linked as a man with his own shadow. Stern was familiar with the orchestral score of any music he undertook. He could relate his own phrasing and style to the orchestral requirements, and had the patience to work with the players until everyone was satisfied. He was aware of the structure of the music and instinctively felt the harmonies underlying every phrase. For him 'the inevitability of the harmonic structure was automatically part and parcel of the ear'.[5] He applied the same principle to the hand. It is for this reason that Stern's phrasing had such meaning. There was a deep logic underlying each phrase. If asked, he could give a reason for every note he played.

As a musician he was totally committed to the composer's intentions as he understood them. If we first observed Stern playing Mozart, and he then turned to Tchaikovsky, we saw that not only did his style change, his face and body also were transformed. This total commitment to the music was the hallmark of his interpretations. Stern believed that his earliest and most important musical influences were playing chamber music with members of the San Francisco Symphony Orchestra. 'I was the young kid around town who played the fiddle not too badly, who was interested, and the older men took me through the entire chamber music repertoire.'[6] Stern retained a lifelong passion for chamber music. He could always find three friends to play quartets, even at the end of the longest day. The public side of this was the famous trio with pianist Eugène Istomin and cellist Leonard Rose (1918–84), in its day one of the most admired ensembles in the USA. They recorded the complete piano trios of Beethoven, Brahms and Schubert, and made television films of the complete Beethoven and Brahms.

For most of his performing life, Stern had been in constant contact with two of the most important influences in the world of string playing: Pablo Casals and Ivan Galamian. His close personal and professional relationship with Galamian must have coloured his ideas on violin playing, especially from the analytical aspect. Stern was playing chamber music with Casals at Prades when the latter was in his prime. The cellist Christopher Bunting once remarked that you could not sit in the same room with Casals and emerge unchanged. Many of Stern's approaches to music resemble those of Casals. A story told about him could as easily apply to Stern. A conductor once asked: 'Maître, what tempo would you like?' Casals chewed his pipe and replied quietly, 'The *right* one.'[7] This was the essence of Stern. Whatever he played was right for him. And at the time, for the listener, there was no other way.

This single-mindedness was another of the ingrained qualities in Stern. It is epitomised in his efforts to save Carnegie Hall. In 1959 civilised America was shocked by the announcement that the owners of Carnegie Hall had contracted to have it demolished in order to erect a new building on the site. A deadline was set for May 1960 to complete negotiations. Isaac Stern immediately approached the mayor of New York. On discovering that Federal aid was not possible, he swiftly gathered together a group of people interested in a campaign to save the hall. On the eve of his departure for an extended European tour, Stern held a meeting at his home, where the Citizens Committee for Carnegie Hall became a reality.

As a result of the Committee's prompt action, two bills were passed by the State Legislature and, as a measure of support for the approval of the City's Board of Estimate, the Committee sent a telegram to Mayor Wagner: 'To destroy Carnegie Hall now for "practical reasons" is an act of irresponsibility damaging to the United States and our prestige in the entire civilized world.'[8] Among the signatories were Casals, Bernstein, Piatigorsky, Heifetz, Horowitz, Ormandy, Szell, Kreisler, Elman, Munch and Stern.

Authorisation for the hall's acquisition was obtained in April 1960. In May, the Board of the Carnegie Hall Corporation was formed, with Isaac Stern as president. At the historic re-opening concert on 25 September, with the New York Philharmonic Orchestra under Bernstein, Stern flew to New York (in between performances in Geneva and London) to take part. This was the culmination of countless events to raise millions of dollars, organised in every detail by Stern.

Stern had another important role – that of fairy godfather to promising youngsters: 'It gives me particular pleasure to hear the magnificent work, the power, the brilliance, the authority, the joy of young colleagues like Pinchas Zukerman, Itzhak Perlman, Miriam Fried, Sergiu Luca and others . . . all these young people we heard when they were little children . . . . To be on the stage next to them from time to time, to see these healthy, vital, gifted young people carrying on traditional violin playing as brilliantly as they do, and to know you have been a part of it . . . to me is the greatest of all satisfactions.'[9]

Stern was aware that standards of performance are continually rising, and that competition for places at the top is fiercer than it has ever been. But he thought that we sometimes underestimate the giants of the past, such as Huberman, Kreisler, Joachim and Sarasate:

These men not only had the agility and grace but they had a mastery and a kind of majestic authority over their playing that stamped them as very special people. It's this individuality I think that we see less of today except in a very few cases. I think that one of the things that pleases me most about the young people that I've mentioned is that each of them plays well but entirely different. Each has an individual view, an individual approach. But one thing they have in common – they don't *ask* you to listen ... they demand your ears.[10]

Stern's playing reflected this approach; feet firmly planted on the earth, but with a spirit that soared in a common emotion that all can share. 'If you do not speak with the violin, and just play it, you might as well get a machine to do it better.'[11]

## Notes

1. *The Strad*, August 1977, p. 293.
2. Olin Downes, *New York Times*, 12 October 1937.
3. *The Strad*, August 1977, p. 293.
4. *New York Times*, 9 January 1943.
5. Quoted from interview, M.C.
6. *The Strad*, August 1977, p. 291.
7. Quoted from interview, M.C.
8. Carnegie Hall, *Looking Ahead*.
9–10. Philadelphia Guide, *Master Fiddler*, June 1978.
11. *The Strad*, August 1977, p. 295.

# 34 The Musician's Musician

For Arthur Grumiaux, virtuosity was merely a means to an end. As the natural successor to Vieuxtemps, Ysaÿe and César Thomson in the great Belgian school, Grumiaux was one of the most important violinists of our time. His faithful interpretations of the classics and his musicianly readings of modern works have exerted considerable influence not only upon his contemporaries but on the younger generation as well. In an age when everyone aspired to play like Heifetz, it was refreshing to find a violinist who struck a harmonious balance between virtuosity and the musical demands of the composer.

Arthur Grumiaux (1921–86) was born in the little village of Villers-Perwin in the Walloon province of Brabant and brought up in the home of his maternal grandparents. It was his grandfather, a self-taught musician, who first aroused his interest in music. At the age of three, he was discovered trying to imitate violin playing by using two pieces of wood. Even with these primitive substitutes, his grandfather noticed the child's keen sense of rhythm in manipulating the 'bow' with exactitude. He bought him a quarter-size fiddle and bow, and gave him some lessons on the instrument together with some elementary instruction in the rudiments of music. Arthur quickly mastered the notes of the scale and within a few days astonished his grandfather by revealing his gift of perfect pitch by naming the notes of the church bells.

Arthur's first concert took place when he was five, in a cinema that held 800 people. The audience responded warmly and he was asked to play the national anthem, the 'Brabançonne', to end the programme. After a few bars he stopped, complaining that everyone was sitting down. He refused to continue until they were all standing. They not only obeyed his command but remained on their feet to cheer. His reward was a large rocking-horse which he 'rode home triumphantly',[1] entrusting his precious violin to his grandfather. It was the first time it had been out of his hands.

A year later Arthur began lessons on the piano and made such good progress with his combined musical studies that, at the age of six, he was admitted to the conservatoire at Charleroi, the normal age of entry being eleven. Five years later, he graduated with the highest honours on both instruments and was then given a place at the Brussels Conservatoire. At this point, a heartbreaking choice had to be made between piano and violin since it was impossible to pursue the study of both instruments in addition to the general curriculum. Arthur refused to decide. Finally his grandfather took the matter in hand and chose the violin.

Under the 'admirable teaching and kindness'[2] of Alfred Dubois, a former pupil of Ysaÿe, the boy progressed so well that at 14 he made his debut at the Palais des Beaux Arts in Brussels, playing concertos by Vieuxtemps and Paganini. In 1939, after winning the Prix Vieuxtemps, the 18-year-old Grumiaux took Dubois' advice and went to Paris to attend the Enescu masterclasses in June and July. Grumiaux said: 'The contact with this great master and the privilege of playing before him, and the atmosphere he created in the class, revealed to me that indispensable serenity which is an integral part of the works of the great composers.'[3]

Now ready to embark upon an international career, he returned to Brussels to receive the Special Prize for Virtuosity created by the Belgian Government. He remains today the sole recipient of the honour. The outbreak of the Second World War disrupted all plans. The occupation forces decreed that all students and performing artists must apply every three months for exemption from enforced factory work. Grumiaux was appointed assistant to Dubois and managed to obtain some respite. The Germans were not slow to recognise his worth and put pressure on him to become leader of the Dresden State Orchestra. He chose instead to go into hiding. From this time he lived the life of a fugitive, flitting from house to house to escape capture, until the arrival of the British Army of Liberation.

Following closely behind the British Army came the Entertainment National Service Association (ENSA), the unit responsible for organising entertainment for the troops. Their musical director, Walter Legge, promptly arranged auditions for Belgian artists. As soon as Legge heard Grumiaux, he offered him engagements in Europe and in Britain. The artists who travelled under the auspices of ENSA were a devoted group of international performers who gave concerts wherever it was possible to set up a stage or platform, however primitive. The 'theatre' could be anything from a tent or a factory canteen to a hospital ward. Conditions were sometimes appalling, with freezing halls and cramped, makeshift dressing rooms. At other times the surroundings were almost luxurious, such as Grumiaux's own first concert for ENSA at the Ghent Opera House, when he played the Mendelssohn Concerto under Barbirolli. But rehearsals were almost unknown. 'There was no time for niceties in these troubled times. Sometimes we played under gunfire and with bombs dropping at the same time. In Holland it was particularly bad.'[4]

So impressed was Legge with Grumiaux's playing that he signed him up for his first recording contract with HMV, and made him a present of the score of William Walton's Violin Concerto, a romantic work with a solo part of phenomenal difficulty. Grumiaux mastered the work in three weeks, in time for its first European performance on 14 February 1945. The programme survives in a faded sheet of pale green duplicating paper with the information that the concert is organised by NAAFI (Navy, Army, Air Force Institutes), and that they present the Belgian National Orchestra conducted by Constant Lambert. The Walton concerto had been written for Heifetz, who gave the first performance in Cleveland, Ohio, in December 1937. But he had also reserved the performing rights for two years, so it was not heard in

Britain until 1941, when Henry Holst played it in London with the composer conducting. Grumiaux subsequently made the Walton his own, and played it under many great conductors, including the composer.

When the war ended, Grumiaux's reputation quickly spread throughout Europe. Of a performance of the Brahms concerto conducted by Sir Adrian Boult at the Albert Hall on 6 March 1946, *The Times* critic wrote: 'His classical purity, alike in style, tone and intonation, was balanced by a romantic warmth, while on the rhythmic side of the account his phrasing was supple, and withal beautifully moulded, without liberties being taken with the time. Could any combination of qualities better suit Brahms?'[5]

Grumiaux first crossed the Atlantic in 1951 and made his debut in Boston playing the Mozart Concerto in G, K216 and Ravel's Tzigane with the Boston Symphony Orchestra conducted by Ernest Ansermet. It was a triumph. At his next appearance, with the Chicago Symphony Orchestra conducted by Rafael Kubelík, the 'no encores' rule for soloists had to be relaxed because the audience refused to stop applauding until Grumiaux put his violin back under his chin.

The following season Grumiaux was invited back as guest soloist with six of America's leading orchestras, whose conductors had heard him in Europe. He had now become identified with the Mozart concerto and was always asked to play it at every concert. The *Minneapolis Morning Tribune* critic commented: 'He has that subtle knack of within-the-phrase varying of tone colour and weight that creates a cogent and significant musical sentence. . . . The whispered cadenza of the second movement had all the customers breathless.'[6] Another critic wrote: 'Everything was played with a silken tone which seemed to come from the instrument without any effort on the part of the performer.'[7]

In the mid-1950s Grumiaux gave the first modern performance of the rediscovered Paganini Concerto No. 4, in D minor. After Paganini performed it in Paris, it was lost. Obsessed by his constant fear of theft, Paganini had separated the solo and orchestral parts, depositing them in different places. An Italian collector named Gallini subsequently came into possession of the solo part. Many years later the orchestral score was found among a bunch of papers offered for sale by a beggar, and eventually acquired by Gallini. Grumiaux performed the concerto at the Salle Pleyel in Paris on 7 November 1954, with the Lamoureux Orchestra directed by Gallini, son of the collector. A recording was made the following day, and so great was the demand for the disc that it was issued within three days of the performance.

In his last years, Grumiaux was still in constant demand all over the world. His recordings include a number of classic performances, for example the Bach sonatas and partitas for solo violin. But it was his sensitive playing of Mozart that won him the respect and admiration of his colleagues. His line, his attention to detail and immaculate phrasing, allied to the emotional expression that is an integral part of Mozart's music, seem to be inborn. His recording of the Mozart concertos made in Vienna for the Mozart Jubilee in 1956 is a masterpiece. The slow movement of the

Divertimento for string trio (K563) must surely be one of the great moments of recorded sound. François Poulenc wrote, after hearing Grumiaux play Mozart, 'I have for a few seconds tasted the great and exceptional delight of shedding tears of joy.'[8]

Shortly before he died, Dinu Lipatti wrote to Grumiaux asking him to form a duo to record the sonatas of Bach, Beethoven and Brahms. But the untimely death of Lipatti occurred before they were able to work together. Shortly afterwards, Grumiaux met Clara Haskil at the Casals Festival in Prades. Here they played together in the first of innumerable concerts. The recordings they made of the sonatas by Mozart and Beethoven are examples not only of superb musicianship, but of the rapport that must exist between artists in such an undertaking. Grumiaux set great store by his friendship with Haskil. For him, it was one of those professional associations that happen only once in a lifetime: 'At our first session we rehearsed for less than an hour and were then ready to record. In our approach to the works we had a complete unity of views and feeling.'[9]

In this respect, Grumiaux had a distinct advantage over most of his colleagues. He always played the piano and was equally familiar with both parts of a duo. Ample proof of his dual ability exists in what must be a unique recording made in 1957, of Grumiaux playing both violin and piano in the Brahms Sonata No. 2 in A major, coupled with Mozart's Sonata in E flat major, K481.

Grumiaux also played Bartók, Stravinsky and Berg. His recording of the Berg concerto has been described as one of his finest accomplishments. A reviewer said that although he has the technique to 'sail through its difficulties with no sense of strain', unlike so many exponents who do have the technique 'he does not play it so as to show you what a big violinist he is'.[10]

Avant-garde music had no appeal for Grumiaux. He was yet another who said that 'the violin is a "singing" instrument and not built for peculiar effects or sounds'.[11] He was always proud of the Belgian school's rich heritage of violin playing, established as a primary world influence by Viotti, Bériot and Vieuxtemps and continued by Massart and Marsick in Paris, Ovide Musin in New York, and more recently Thomson and Ysaÿe – and numbering among its international heirs Kreisler, Thibaud, Wieniawski and Sarasate. It is the wealth of this tradition that Grumiaux brought to his own students at the Brussels Conservatoire.

With a platform manner that was reserved and totally lacking in showmanship, Grumiaux spoke to his audience through the sonority of his violin. His approach was the opposite of the head tossing and agonised gestures of the exhibitionist player. His inborn sense of style permeated every movement right down to his bow grip with the second phalanx of his index finger on the stick – the classic Franco-Belgian hold. He never had an exalted opinion of himself as a great virtuoso. His greatest pleasure was when he gathered fellow artists around him to perform chamber music for a festival in a small mountain town in Belgium every summer. His colleagues rightly still speak of him as 'the musician's musician'.[12]

**Notes**

1–4. Letter from Grumiaux to M.C.

5. *The Times,* 7 March 1946.

6. *Minneapolis Morning Tribune,* 1952.

7. *Brooklyn Eagle,* 16 January 1953.

8. Philips publicity brochure.

9. Interview, Bernadette Morand (Grumiaux).

10. *Stereo Review,* November 1968, p. 87.

11. Interview, Bernadette Morand (Grumiaux).

12. Philips publicity brochure.

# 35   The Flesch Heritage

The Flesch pupil who had the most profound influence on violin playing in Europe in the first half of the twentieth century was the Austrian Max Rostal (1905–85). Born in Teschen, he studied with Arnold Rosé in Vienna and Carl Flesch in Berlin. In 1928 he became Flesch's assistant and two years later was the youngest professor to be appointed at the Hochschule. When the Nazis rose to power in 1934, he was dismissed from office and left for London where he was reunited with Flesch who had left Germany at the same time.

In 1939 Flesch made the decision to go to Holland, which was then neutral, and recommended his students to go to Rostal, whose teaching skills had been recognised soon after his arrival in the UK. In 1944 Rostal was appointed a professor at the Guildhall School of Music, and among his many students was Yfrah Neaman (1923–2003), later head of the Violin Department there. Rostal has been described as 'a thinking violinist' because he expected his students to look into the life and background of a composer before attempting an interpretation and he would insist they study the full score of a concerto and not make do with a piano reduction, nor just their own part. He would also insist upon his pupils using his fingerings and bowings and would allow no leeway, and as such was accused of cloning – which he strongly denied.

In his youth Rostal was a fine soloist and critics remarked upon his ' sweet and transparent tone' and 'rhythmic drive.' In 1935 he gave a Wigmore Hall recital that included Sarasate's Carmen Fantasy. During the Second World War, he regularly took part in the lunchtime concerts run by Myra Hess at the National Gallery in London, appearing quite often with the pianist Franz Osborn, with whom he gave sonata recitals for many years. He premiered many works of which he was the dedicatee and gave the first British performances of both the Khachaturian Violin Concerto (1940) and Bartók's Violin Concerto No. 2 (1937–8).

Rostal used to tell a story about when he was crossing the border from the USA into Canada at a remote part of the frontier. When the official saw his double violin case, he asked him how much the contents were worth. Rostal quoted a figure which made the man gasp. 'Where were they manufactured and who by?' Rostal told him that they were made in Cremona in Italy by two makers, Antonio Stradivari and Guarneri del Gesù. 'When were they made?' insisted the man. When he was told they were made in the eighteenth century, he was nonplussed and said he would have to call his boss. The 'boss' went through the same questioning but suddenly looked closely into Rostal's face and asked: 'Why do you need *two* violins?' Without moving a muscle, Rostal replied: 'I have just come from New York where I have been playing Bach's Concerto for two violins.' The man threw up his hands in despair: 'OK, go through!' [1]

In 1973, together with Menuhin, Yfrah Neaman, Nannie Jamieson and others, Rostal formed the European String Teachers' Association (ESTA) for the exchange of information on the technique and teaching of string playing. Rostal had left Britain in 1958 to take up a professorship at the conservatory in Berne, Switzerland but he maintained an active interest in ESTA right up until his death in 1985.

A near contemporary of Rostal, the Australian-born Alma Moodie (1900–43) had studied with Oskar Back (1879–1963) and César Thomson in Brussels before coming to Flesch in 1918. He considered her to be the most outstanding female violinist of her time and a worthy successor to Wilma Norman-Neruda. After two years with Flesch she made a sensational debut and from this time followed a solo career. It was in contemporary music that she excelled, and her performance of Busoni's Violin Concerto at a Philharmonic concert in 1934 made a deep impression on the British critics. Flesch remarked that, between 1920 and 1930, she 'stimulated modern compositions for the violin in a similar way as Joachim, Sarasate and Ysaÿe had done before her.'[2]

In his *Memoirs*, Carl Flesch particularly praised one of his young pupils at the Curtis Institute and predicted that '. . . he may well come to play an important part in America's musical life'.[3] He was referring to Henri Temianka (1906–92) who was to become a close friend and was indeed instrumental in getting Flesch to England in the early 1930s.

Temianka was born in Greenock in Scotland into a wealthy family of Polish–Jewish immigrants and had his first lessons on the violin when he was six. The following year the family moved to Holland where Henri had some lessons from Carel Blitz; it was from him that the young child learnt the self-discipline and perseverance which was to stand him in good stead for the rest of his life.

At 15, on the advice of Bronislav Huberman, Temianka entered the Berlin Hochschule to study with Willy Hess (1859–1939) who, it seems, had a sadistic streak. 'He was a remarkable man who knew all about technique but nothing about humanity.'[4] Then came a further two years at the Paris Conservatoire with Jules Boucherit. 'This was the French School par excellence. He was a relentless slave-driver – for which I am deeply grateful. From him I acquired finesse of bowing technique which I would never have had otherwise.'[5]

The turning-point in Temianka's life came when he returned to Scheveningen in Holland to audition for Flesch. After playing only a short while, he was stopped by Flesch: 'Can you come with me to America on Saturday?' Two days later he boarded an ocean liner bound for Philadelphia, where he studied with Flesch for four years.

On graduating from the Curtis Institute in 1930, Temianka decided to try his luck in England and called on the impresario Harold Holt. It so happened Holt had a last minute cancellation from an indisposed Huberman, who was to appear the following day in Leicester with the legendary soprano Luisa Tetrazzini, who was making one of her habitual farewell tours. Temianka arrived too late to rehearse with the pianist, Ivor Newton, and had to go straight on stage to play the virtuoso La Folia. The audience were wildly enthusiastic, rewarding him with four curtain calls. The astute Holt recognised that not only did he have a brand new talent on his hands, but that he could engage him for the remainder of the tour for a fraction of Huberman's fees. Temianka once said: 'Young soloists should always make their debuts as a last-minute replacement for someone else.'[6]

In 1946, Temianka formed the Paganini Quartet, so called because all four instruments had once belonged to Paganini. For over 20 years the quartet achieved an international reputation and made many recordings of both the classical and contemporary repertory. He also founded his own chamber orchestra, which he conducted from 1960 until his death in 1992. In the meantime he maintained a busy teaching career and gave masterclasses worldwide. At his 80th birthday gala celebration concert in Los Angeles, Efrem Zimbalist Jr quoted the Talmudic sage, Rabbi Abraham Henschel: '"Life is an art, a celebration and a discipline." Henri appears to have made that statement his own.'[7]

In Flesch's Paris studio Ida Haendel recalls her first meeting with another of his pupils, a young woman of about 16. Only seven years old, Ida was overawed by the girl's great height and strong build. Her deep, husky voice, close-cropped hair and wide neck made her look very masculine. When she attacked the Wieniawski F sharp minor Concerto, Ida was dumbfounded. 'I stared at her fascinated, and, child though I was, I realised that I was listening to an extraordinary artist, totally dedicated to music and absorbed in it to the exclusion of all else. Even then her playing was intense and passionate, her tone large and vibrato wide. Her dramatic approach had the impact of a volcano.'[8] The girl was Ginette Neveu (1919–49).

Ginette was born in Paris into a musical family of several generations. Her father was an amateur string player and her mother a teacher of the violin. Her brother Jean was a fine pianist who later became her accompanist. While a baby in her pram, Ginette could sing tunes after a single hearing. As a small child she was taken to a concert and, on hearing the music of Chopin, was moved to tears. She was given a quarter-size violin, and lessons from her mother. Her swift progress merited further study with Madame Talluel at the Ecole Supérieur de Musique, with a view to continuing at the conservatoire. Madame Talluel recalled that, at the age of five, Ginette displayed sensational gifts, notably a capacity for work unique in so young a child. She would practise quite easy phrases as many as 50 times, and if Madame said 'enough', Ginette would argue, 'but it has got to be beautiful'.[9]

When she was seven, Ginette made her concert debut at the Salle Gaveau, playing the Bruch G minor Concerto. Two years later she won both the Premier Prix at the Ecole Superieure de Musique and the Prix d'Honneur awarded by the City of Paris for her performance of the Mendelssohn concerto. As a result, she was invited to

Switzerland to play the Nardini and Mendelssohn concertos under Ernst Walter at Winterthur. She was described as 'Mozart in petticoats, who already possesses a very extensive technique, a full, even tone of great beauty, masterly bowing, clear-cut articulation'.[10]

On her return to Paris she studied with Enescu, who was greatly impressed by her fire. One day, when working on the Bach Chaconne, Enescu stopped her. 'I don't play that passage like that.' Without batting an eyelid, Ginette replied: 'I play this music as I understand it; not in a way which escapes my comprehension.'[11] Enescu would not have taken such a retort from anyone but Ginette. He simply smiled and motioned to her to continue.

In November 1930, Ginette was accepted at the Conservatoire under Jules Boucherit; she also studied composition with Nadia Boulanger. In June of the following year she won the Premier Prix. Such a triumph had not occurred since Wieniawski carried off the prize almost a hundred years before. In 1922, she competed in the Vienna International Competition and came fourth. The disappointment was to have an interesting sequel. One of the adjudicators on the panel was so impressed by her playing that he sent a message scribbled on the back of a visiting card to her hotel. 'If you can come to Berlin, I undertake, without any thought of personal gain, to make myself responsible for the young violinist's musical education.'[12] It was from Carl Flesch.

But all the family resources had been used up for the trip to Vienna, so two years elapsed before Ginette and her mother were able to make the trip to Berlin. When Flesch heard her play for the second time he said: 'My child, you have received a gift from heaven, and I have no wish to touch it. All I can do for you is to give you some purely technical advice.'[13] Ginette studied for four years with Flesch in Germany and Belgium, and regarded it as the most important period in her life.

At 16, she entered the Wieniawski Competition and won first prize, with the 26-year-old David Oistrakh in second place. She took the Germans by storm when she made her début in Hamburg, playing the Brahms concerto under Eugen Jochum. Neveu was now acclaimed all over Europe as a virtuoso of the first rank. From Germany, she went to Russia, where she toured from Moscow to Baku. In the latter town she played to an audience of 10,000 in an outdoor amphitheatre, with the temperature well up into the 90s (F). At every stop on the 15,000-mile train journey she was presented with a bouquet of flowers, so that by the end of the journey there was no room in her compartment even to sit, let alone practise her violin.

Berlin, Paris and Amsterdam audiences clamoured to hear this brilliant girl, and life was a constant round of packing and travelling. When, in 1936, she crossed the Atlantic, the Americans could not find words to express their delight in her playing.

When war broke out in 1939, Neveu continued to tour in France until the German occupation of 1940 put a stop to it. During the Second World War she led a secluded life in her studio, practising and writing; she was a composer of some substance. The Germans offered her enormous fees to undertake a concert tour from Berlin to

Stuttgart, but she firmly refused. In the four years of occupation, she kept out of the public eye.

For her London orchestral debut at the Royal Albert Hall on 24 March 1945, she chose the Beethoven Concerto. *The Strad* critic commented on her 'masterly technique, with a phenomenal range of tone values and a bow-arm which is a joy to watch'.[14] In July, in the same hall, she played the Brahms Concerto with the Ravel Tzigane as an encore. The *Daily Mail* critic wrote: 'Her performance is the best we have heard since Kreisler. I know no woman violinist, and very few men, to equal her.'[15]

For the next three years, Neveu had the world at her feet. Of her New York debut at Carnegie Hall on 13 November 1947, Virgil Thomson wrote:

Ginette Neveu . . . is the finest, from every point of view, of the younger European artists whom we have had the pleasure of hearing since the war. . . . She is a great artist because she has tone, technique and temperament. And she is an interesting artist because she has rhythm and a special intensity of communication all her own. It is not often that we hear the Brahms Violin Concerto read with such breadth and nobility and withal so graciously.[16]

Despite having been trained by Flesch and Enescu, Neveu represented no one particular school. She borrowed from the French, Belgian or Russian schools whatever seemed to suit the best way of solving technical problems. The only difficulty she ever encountered was that of the staccato bow stroke and she experimented for many years to attain the absolute mastery that became her hallmark.

Her manner of holding the bow baffled all authorities on violin playing. One day she would hold it like Heifetz, another like Zino Francescatti: sometimes she appeared to bow like Thibaud. A Viennese critic who had observed this enigma wrote:

What one finds so fascinating about her is the perfect harmony which exists between her actual playing and her very remarkable personality. Without showing the slightest bias towards any particular school, her right hand with incomparable concentration and guided by a noble sensitive mind, governs all the technical variations of tone. But the tone which, in all its splendour, forms the melody, and that incredible assurance with which she handles her bow in a diabolical pizzicato are not the only outstanding characteristics of the personality of Ginette Neveu. To create and recreate; there lies her talent.[17]

As a person, Neveu was a curious mixture. From an early age she had possessed the gift of being able to withdraw into isolation, showing a mask of seeming indifference to the outside world. Her spiritual strength came from within. Before going onto the concert platform she would make a point of spending the last moments alone in the artists' room. In complete contrast was the vigorous, vivacious, fearless young woman with seemingly boundless energy who walked for miles, swam, rode and played ping-pong and was a superb chess player. On holiday she was gregarious and game for anything. Everything she did was intensive and on a large scale. Her maxim for life and for music – which were for her inseparable – was 'Aim high aim – at beauty'.[18]

At the height of her brilliant career, at the age of 30, Neveu met her death in a plane crash in the Azores, on the way to America. Clutching her precious Stradivarius to her chest, she 'died as she lived, with the wheels of her life in full motion'.[19] Her brother Jean died with her. She had just written in her notebook:

> Nothing great is achieved without the solitude of vocation, and true greatness is, perhaps, radiant solitude. . . . Men are sometimes fainthearted because they fear death. But death is something sublime which one must deserve according to the life and the ideals one has within oneself. This sad sojourn which we make on this earth is but a time of great suffering which men have no wish to accept.[20]

Ivry Gitlis would seem to have come under the influence of many of the best-known European teachers, and since he is a 'free spirit' in every sense of the word, it is impossible to pin him down to any one 'school'. The result is a remarkable musical personality who was able to electrify his audience at a Wigmore Hall recital in 1996, 50 years after his debut in that same hall.

Gitlis was born in 1922 in Haifa (Palestine, as it then was) of Jewish immigrant parents from the Ukraine. His first instrument was the harmonica, which he could play before he could walk or talk, and at five he had his first violin lessons from Mira Ben-Ami, a pupil of Szigeti. He gave his first public concert at the age of nine-and-a-half in Tel Aviv, when he played music by Handel, Bach and Vieuxtemps. He attracted the attention of Huberman who insisted that he should go to Paris and provided the necessary financial support. On arrival in Paris accompanied by his mother, Ivry had some private lessons with Jules Boucherit, and the following year gained entry to the Ecole Normale de Musique, where he continued with Boucherit and also with Marcel Chailley, whom he regarded at the time as being the more important teacher.

After graduating at 13 with the Premier Prix, Gitlis studied briefly with various teachers. He spent a year with Flesch at Spa (Belgium), developing the technical side of his playing. Next he went for several months to Enescu. Gitlis describes this period as 'sheer Heaven': 'For me, he was a musical god. So unassuming, so courteous and so talented. I shall never forget that incredible man who sat at the piano playing every accompaniment without music – to perfection.'[21] On his return to France in 1939, Gitlis had some lessons with Thibaud; when war threatened, Thibaud suggested Gitlis accompany him to St-Jean-de-Luz, where they spent the summer and early autumn. At morning lessons, Thibaud taught in his dressing-gown, a cigarette between his lips.

> He would tuck his violin between his chin and shoulder a little to one side so that the ash from his cigarette would not fall on it and he would play. It was more beautiful than

anything you can imagine. I was not in the presence of a violinist, but a man who *played* the violin. Lovely phrases poured out and I learned more about style from that experience than I ever learned with anyone else.[22]

In 1940, Gitlis arrived in London, having sailed on the last boat to leave Bayonne in the South of France. During the Second World War he worked in a munitions factory and also gave concerts for troops and factory workers. In 1945 he made his orchestral debut with the London Philharmonic Orchestra at the Royal Albert Hall and followed it with a highly successful Wigmore Hall debut recital in 1946.

Gitlis went to New York in 1951 to continue his studies with Theodore Pashkus and his wife Alice. Pashkus approached teaching from the psychoanalytical angle, and for Gitlis this was yet another dimension to his learning and development process.

Through a chance encounter in 1955 with a European scout from Sol Hurok, Gitlis was signed up for a tour of the USA which included concerts with the New York Philharmonic under Szell, and the Philadelphia Orchestra under Ormandy. From this time, his career as an international soloist was assured. Widely in demand for masterclasses, Gitlis has recorded everything from Paganini, Wieniawski and Sarasate to twentieth-century music of which he has been a superb exponent. Many people consider his performance of the Bartók Solo Sonata unsurpassed He has also acted with success in films, and in the 1960s, he created his own festival at St Paul de Vence in which both artists and audience participate.

Yfrah Neaman (1923–2003) was probably one of the most widely travelled teachers of his time. There was scarcely a country in Asia or Europe where he was not invited regularly to give masterclasses or sit on juries. He became a legend at the Guildhall School of Music and Drama in London, where he was appointed professor in 1958 and was later head of the String Department. He was also for many years artistic director of the Carl Flesch International Violin Competition.

Neaman was born in Sidon (Lebanon) and began learning the violin at the age of six; three years later, he went with his family to Paris where he studied for five years without making much progress. 'When I started playing Mozart violin concertos at the age of ten, all I was told was "play gracefully; imagine frilly cuffs." '[23] Although Neaman won the Premier Prix in 1937, he still felt that something was missing in his playing. He went to study with Carl Flesch where 'a curtain was torn away'. 'I remain completely faithful to the philosophy that a musical work is brought to life by taking the text and absorbing it, and then giving it back through your own sensibility and understanding. Flesch did not put it into these words but that is what he meant.'[24] Neaman then returned to Paris for further studies with Thibaud.

Neaman, like Rostal, was better known as a teacher than a performer, but he, too, began his career as a soloist and considered that it would have been difficult to guide his students towards performance had he not been. He made an unexpected debut in 1944 when he stepped in at the last moment for an indisposed Rostal, playing the Beethoven concerto with the LPO under Anatole Fistoulari. The favourable reviews led to recitals and concert appearances, and he also formed a trio with the pianist Lamar Crowson and cellist Eleanor Warren. Some of his earliest concerts were at the National Gallery in wartime London: 'If I hadn't had to communicate with large raincoated audiences sitting in the cold munching sandwiches, I might not have progressed as well as I did.'[25]

Neaman gave dozens of first performances of works by contemporary composers and was the dedicatee for a number of these, which include Roberto Gerhard's *Chaconne* (1959), Michael Blake Watkins' Violin Concerto and Michael Berkeley's Sonata (1979). He also made many recordings of contemporary chamber music.

Igor Ozim is one of those rare musicians who manage to combine solo appearances, recording and teaching; however, if he were asked to choose one field as a priority, it would almost certainly be teaching. Ozim was born in Ljubljana (Slovenia) in 1931; both his parents played the piano and his brother the violin, so he cannot recall a time when he was unable to read music. His first lessons (at the age of five) were with Leon Pfeifer, a professor at the Ljubljana Academy of Music who had himself studied with Ševčík in Prague. Ozim entered Pfeifer's class at the Academy at eight. Ozim attributes his progress to Pfeifer's teaching skills. 'I never had any books of exercises; Pfeifer wrote them out especially for me. He also taught me two things that I have found invaluable throughout my career. One, play in tune. Two, play rhythmically. He was a stickler for those two things and would never pass anything that was not first class.'[26]

When he was 18, Ozim was awarded a British Council Scholarship to study in the UK. While most of his fellow students went to Moscow to finish their training, he was the first to go to the West. When he first arrived in London, he spent three months at the Royal College of Music with the legendary Albert Sammons. 'He was a wonderful man and gave me exactly what I needed at the time. I studied the Elgar concerto with him and he used to play a second violin accompaniment which was customary in those days. I still have that sound in my ears.'[27] From Sammons he went to study privately with Rostal. Of those two years Ozim says: 'I owe Rostal an enormous amount because I came to him with a very bad bow arm and he put that right so it never recurred. He also taught me to think for myself. And if we did not always see eye-to-eye, that in a way was a product of his school – though I don't think he saw it like that at the time!'[28]

In 1951 Ozim won first prize in the Carl Flesch Competition and made his Wigmore Hall recital debut two weeks later. The critics were charmed and were equally enthusiastic when he followed this with his orchestral debut, playing the Mendelssohn concerto with the Liverpool Philharmonic Orchestra under Hugo Rignold.

On his return to what was then Yugoslavia, Ozim could do no wrong. The first fully professional solo violinist the nation had produced, he was invited to play all over the country. This was soon extended to the USSR and Western Europe, followed by concerts in the USA, the Antipodes and the Far East. He was only 30 when he was appointed professor at the Ljubljana Academy of Music, and discovered his real vocation.

Ozim agrees with Neaman that being a performer is a prerequisite for teaching. He says: 'I can deal with certain problems that the teacher who only teaches cannot visualise, or has forgotten. An important situation is when a student has a bad day. We all have bad days and, if I sense this is so, I am not harsh on them.'[29]

Ozim gives masterclasses worldwide and teaches in both Cologne and Bern, but says he is still on the road to discovery himself. 'All I ask of the young people I teach is that they should have open, inquisitive minds. Curiosity is what matters.'[30]

The Polish-born Krzyzstof Smietana is another Neaman pupil who performs and teaches. In 1982, he won both Second and Audience prizes in the Carl Flesch Competition. He treasures the latter in particular: 'In a normal situation, you play only for the public. Gaining the prize gave me a lot of confidence and really made me believe in myself. I think the audience involvement in the judging is a very good idea.'[31]

Born in Krakow in 1956, Smietana began lessons on the violin at the age of five at the local music school. When he was 12, he entered the Krakow Academy of Music as a pupil of Zbigniew Szlezer, a student of David Oistrakh, and considers himself fortunate to have had a good grounding in the Russian School. However, in retrospect, Smietana thinks that the 13 years he spent with Szlezer were too long, because he was not encouraged to think for himself. Too much of a Soviet-bloc musician's time was spent reaching the exacting technical standards demanded by competition judges.

Smietana's first entry to the Flesch Competition brought him only a fifth prize, but he was spotted by Yfrah Neaman, who in 1980 invited him to come to London to take up a scholarship as his student at the Guildhall School of Music and Drama; two years later came his Flesch Competition successes. It was only when he began his studies with Neaman that Smietana realised the restrictions inherent in the teaching in Poland, where violinists tend to select either the French or Russian School, never a fusion of the two. In the UK the violin teachers combine the best of every system, offering students the opportunity to draw from a wide variety of 'schools' and shape their own playing accordingly. Smietana himself has taught at the Guildhall since 1982.

Ernst Kovacic would seem to have inhabited the best of all worlds; his main teacher, Franz Samokyl, was brought up in the Ševčík tradition, but was greatly influenced by his contact with the Eastern European branches of the Auer School, while his two other teachers, the Austrians Eduard Stöckl and Gottfried Rexeis, were brought up in the Flesch tradition. Kovacic was born in 1943 in Kapfenburg, and received his first lessons on the violin at the age of four from his father. He went on to attend the local music school under Eduard Stöckl and, when he was 16, he spent a year in Graz with Rexeis, who was a Flesch pupil. At 18, he attended the Vienna Academy of Music under Samokyl, who was leader of both the Vienna Philharmonic Orchestra and his own string quartet. After his graduation, Kovacic won prizes in several major international competitions and embarked upon a solo career which now takes him all over the world.

Kovacic's musical training did not follow the normal pattern for a violinist.

Besides attending masterclasses given by Milstein, Szeryng and Rostal (who gave him valuable advice) he studied and played the organ, which made him aware of the counterpointal structures that are an essential part of keyboard mastery. He also studied composition, from the age of 13, and this, too, broadened his horizons and had a profound effect upon his all-round musical development. It is therefore not surprising that Kovacic's playing is described as musically prodigious, imbued with intellectual grasp, and possessing a big, silvery tone. Reflecting on the main influences on his musical development, Kovacic says: 'Although I appreciate what I learned through Flesch and Rostal, today my playing has not so much to do with Flesch traditions. The more my adult personality emerged from my roots, the more I grew into new imagination of how to use the body and the mind.'[32]

Kovacic's repertory is vast, containing all the standard works for violin as well as contemporary music. Many composers have written works especially for him, including Ernst Krenek, Ivan Erod, Robin Holloway, Nigel Osborne and Helmut Eder. He particularly enjoys the experience of communicating with a living composer.

A second-generation student of Flesch through both her teachers, Anne-Sophie Mutter is one of the brightest stars in the international firmament today. Born in Rheinfelden in 1963, she showed early talent for music and had her first lessons from Erna Königsberger when she was five years old. At 13 she entered the Winterthur Music College, where she studied for eight years with Aida Stucki.

When Anne-Sophie was only seven, she won the first prize 'with special distinction' in the West German Youth Competition. In 1976 she made her debut in a recital with her pianist brother, Christoph, at the Lucerne Festival, attracting the attention of Herbert von Karajan. After she had auditioned for him, he pronounced her 'the greatest musical talent since Menuhin' and engaged her to play in the 1977 Whitsun Festival at Salzburg. That same year she made her UK debut with the English Chamber Orchestra under Daniel Barenboim, and her debut with the Berlin Philharmonic under Karajan took place the following year. With Karajan as her mentor, Mutter swiftly built an international career. She was only 15 when she made the first of many recordings with Karajan and the Berlin Philharmonic.

Mutter is rare among artists in that she confesses never to feeling nervous, and for her, technical problems do not exist. She has a beautifully even and focused tone which seems to flow naturally from her instrument; her interpretation of Mozart is particularly captivating and he is obviously a composer with whom she has an affinity. For many years Mutter was uncompromising in her preference for the classic repertory on which she had been reared; that was until she was asked to perform Witold Lutoslawski's Chain 2, commissioned by Paul Sacher, who suggested her as soloist. She admits she was amazed at his choice and, since it was the first contemporary work she had tackled, she had her doubts. 'It put me into a real panic. It took me a very long time to find my way in – I had to dig for a key. But eventually I found it.'[33] Mutter was amazed to find that once she had mastered the Lutoslawski work she began to understand the music of Berg, Stravinsky and Bartók. When the première of

Chain 2 took place in Zürich in 1986, she received enthusiastic response from the critics, who praised the way she tackled 'the technically and unmusically demanding violin part with fascinating sensitivity, agility and tonal projection'.[34] She recorded the work in 1988. Mutter has since had several works dedicated to her including Norbert Moret's *En rêve* and Penderecki's Second Violin Concerto (1972) and has made recordings of both.

## Notes

1. Quoted from interview, M.C.
2. Flesch, *Memoirs*, p. 317.
3. Ibid., p. 356.
4–6. *The Strad*, January 1993, pp. 32–3.
7. *The Strad*, July 1986, p. 34.
8. Haendel, *Woman with Violin*, p. 45.
9. Ronze-Neveu, *Ginette Neveu*, p. 31.
10. Ibid., p. 36.
11. Ibid., pp. 36–7.
12. Ibid., p. 41.
13. Ibid., 41–2.
14. *The Strad*, April 1945, p. 268.
15. *Daily Mail*, 4 July 1945.
16. Virgil Thomson, *New York Herald Tribune*, 24 November 1947.
17. Ronze-Neveu, op. cit., pp. 49–50.
18. Ibid., p. 79.
19. Haendel, op. cit., p. 201.
20. Ronze-Neveu, op. cit., p. 81.
21–22. Quoted from interview, M.C.
23. *The Strad*, February 1998, p. 131.
24. *The Strad*, December 1994, p. 1225.
25. *The Strad*, February 1998, p. 130.
26–30. *The Strad*, July 1995, pp. 696–9.
31. *The Strad*, July 1984, p. 177.
32. Letter from Kovacic to M.C.
33. *Gramophone*, February 1989, p. 1262.
34. *Neue Zürcher Zeitung*, February 1986.

# 36   Flesch and the Poles

The Polish-born Josef Wolfstahl (1899–1931) was ten when he went to study with Carl Flesch in Berlin. Although at 16 he played in a few concerts, Flesch thought it wise to 'widen his horizons' by placing him in an orchestra. In Flesch's opinion, Wolfstahl was one of the finest violinists in Germany, his bowing 'near absolute perfection'.[1] Wolfstahl subsequently sat on the first desk of orchestras in Bremen, Stockholm and Berlin and, as leader of the Kroll Opera in Berlin under Otto Klemperer, he was often called upon to perform as soloist, particularly in premieres of new works such as Hindemith's Kammermusik No. 4. He was also in a trio with Hindemith on viola and the cellist, Emanuel Feuermann, that specialised in contemporary music. He was only 26 when he took up a teaching post at the Berlin Hochschule, but died at the age of 31 from a virulent attack of influenza.

The son of an architect, Roman Totenberg was born in Lodz in 1911. With the outbreak of the First World War, the family moved to Moscow, and Roman had his first lessons from a neighbour who was the leader of the Bolshoi Orchestra. When the family moved back to Poland in 1921, he entered the Chopin Academy of Music, graduating with the Gold Medal in 1928, along the way having played a solo in a concert with the Warsaw Philharmonic Orchestra. The following year, he went to Berlin for a period of study with Carl Flesch.

His first important engagement came in the winter of 1931 when he was invited to tour the Soviet Union, where he appeared in Moscow and Kiev. It was also his introduction to chamber music recitals: 'The most frequently requested piece was the César Franck Piano Quintet. We played it everywhere . . . . To me it has an elevated, spiritual quality.'[2] Totenberg's next achievement was winning the Mendelssohn Prize in Berlin; shortly afterwards, he made his recital debut in that city with the pianist Artur Balsam. He had already developed a taste for contemporary music and, since Paris was the centre for new music in the 1930s, he moved there in 1932 and undertook further periods of study with Enescu and Pierre Monteux. In 1935 he premièred the Hindemith Sonata in E and made his New York debut the following year with the first American performance of the work.

As the political situation in Europe became more threatening, Totenberg decided to emigrate to the USA and was greeted with open arms in New York. He was engaged as concertmaster of the New Friends of Music Orchestra, with whom he also played solos. When the USA entered the Second World War, Totenberg became Director of Chamber Music at WQXR Radio and founded the WQXR String Quartet.

When the war ended Totenberg left WQXR and, with the pianist Adolf Balter and cellist Gabor Rejto, formed the Alma Trio. In 1946 he became the founder director of the Music Academy of the West in Santa Barbara, which immediately attracted the attention of a number of eminent musicians; Darius Milhaud, Soulima Stravinsky, the Griller Quartet, Ernest Bloch and Schoenberg all participated in the early years. In the 1950s he gave up the Alma Trio in order to devote more time to teaching and, in 1961, he was appointed as a professor at Boston University and Chairman of the String Department. 'I sometimes feel I have been teaching all my life. In fact, my first student was a boy of eight. I was 11.'[3]

Frederick Grinke (1911–87) was born in Winnipeg into a poor Polish–Lutheran immigrant family. At nine he had his first instruction on the violin from John Waterhouse; as his family could not afford to pay for the lessons, young Fred had to rise at 6 a.m. every day to earn the money delivering newspapers. His progress was so rapid that he appeared regularly in public and made his first broadcast at 11, forming his own trio when he was 15. He won the Canadian Associated Board Scholarship, which enabled him to travel to study with Rowsby Woof at the Royal Academy of Music in London. Grinke was an extremely popular student: two of his contemporaries, the viola players Watson Forbes and Max Gilbert, described him as being so generous and kind that his musicianship, glorious tone and virtuosity never caused envy among his fellow students. Meanwhile, he took every possible prize available at the Academy and was soon tipped by Sir Henry Wood to lead the Royal Academy Orchestra. While still a student, he became the second violinist in the Kutcher String Quartet. He also formed the Grinke Piano Trio with two fellow students, the cellist Florence Hooton and pianist Dorothy Manley. They were a great success and gave numerous concerts and broadcasts, including a Promenade concert under Sir Henry. Kendall Taylor, who later replaced Manley, remembered Grinke's 'impeccable intonation and a splendid range of tone'.[4]

When he was 21, Grinke studied for one summer with Adolf Busch at his home near Basle. He benefited enormously from Busch's influence, recalling in particular how they took long walks and swam regularly in Busch's private open-air pool. (When he became a teacher himself, Grinke stressed the importance of taking plenty of exercise in order to build up the stamina needed for a career in music.) That same year he was approached by Sir Hamilton Harty about taking on the leadership of the London Symphony Orchestra, only to be disappointed when the directors decided he was too young for the post.

Some years later, Grinke took the opportunity to study with Carl Flesch, at first in London and then at Spa. Although Flesch was quite different from Busch in his approach, Grinke felt that to study with two such great teachers would provide a balance that would stand him in good stead for the rest of his career.

In 1937, he became the leader of the Boyd Neel Orchestra, a small but highly accomplished string orchestra which had achieved a worldwide reputation. Grinke first appeared with them at the 1937 Salzburg Festival where they gave the first performance of Britten's *Variations on a Theme of Frank Bridge*, and was associated with them for many years.

Shortly after the outbreak of the Second World War, Grinke volunteered for the Royal Air Force and became co-leader of the RAF Symphony Orchestra. They travelled many thousands of miles and Grinke frequently appeared as a soloist. During one of these tours he was abruptly ordered to return to Britain in order to play the Bax Violin Concerto at the Royal Albert Hall. He recalled later what a thrilling experience it was to be flown back to London – during the war – for a single appearance.

When Grinke was demobilised in 1945, ironically, he was offered the leadership of several famous British orchestras. He declined them all, preferring to follow a solo career, which included a number of recordings with leading British orchestras.

Teaching remained an integral part of his musical life. He had originally been engaged at the Royal Academy of Music to assist Herbert Withers in coaching chamber music and in 1939, had been appointed violin professor. The violinist Jean Harvey (b. 1932) was his pupil for five years: 'His advice was invaluable. He had a happy knack of taking the student's own musical ingredients and putting them together so they could express individualism, even in well-known pieces. Nothing was automatic or had Fred's hallmark.'[5]

Grinke was genuinely loved by his students for his human approach to everything. When Menuhin was setting up his school, he suddenly realised he had overlooked the fact that he had no pupils. He rang Grinke, a close friend and colleague of many years standing, and confided to him his problem. Grinke replied immediately with his usual generosity: 'Yehudi, you can have all of mine!' Grinke was to become one of the pillars of the school until illness forced him to retire. In Menuhin's estimation, 'He was a wonderful violinist, the most generous and honest of men and one who contributed enormously to the musical life of Great Britain.'[6]

When Flesch was asked which of his pupils had come closest to achieving the perfect balance between technique and interpretation, he was unequivocal in selecting Szymon Goldberg (1909–93). Born in Wloclawck, in central Poland, Goldberg first studied in Warsaw with Mieczyslaw Michalowicz, who also taught Josef Hassid and Ida Haendel. When he was ten, the family moved to Berlin, where he began seven years of study with Carl Flesch. He made his debut in Warsaw when he was only 12, playing the Paganini Concerto in D major. Acting on Flesch's advice, he waited until he was 15 before appearing with the Berlin Philharmonic Orchestra, with whom he played three of the most demanding concertos in the repertory: the Bach E major, Joachim's *Hungarian* and the Paganini No 1. Afterwards he was inundated with offers of engagements throughout Germany.

After two years as a travelling virtuoso, he accepted the leadership of the Dresden Philharmonic Orchestra and four years later, when he was only 20, he was appointed leader of the Berlin Phiharmonic Orchestra. When the Nazis came to power and orchestras were obliged to dismiss all their Jewish members, Furtwängler tried in vain to intervene on his behalf, but Goldberg had to leave Germany. He developed a solo career abroad, and, with the pianist Lili Kraus as his partner, he gave recitals all over Europe, Japan, China and the Dutch East Indies; in 1938 he made his American debut at Carnegie Hall.

In 1942 while appearing in Java, he was taken prisoner and interned by the Japanese for almost three years. His captors came for him and his wife one night, scarcely giving them time to dress, and sealed up the house in which they were living. A neighbour happened to note that one small window had been left unlocked and was concerned for the safety of Goldberg's violin, the 'Legnitz' Stradivarius, dated 1711. At great personal risk he climbed in, rescued the instrument and threw it into the garden of the doctor who lived next door; an amateur violinist himself, the doctor put it in a place of safety until its owner was a free man. Unfortunately, Goldberg's collection of valuable bows and fine music library was never recovered.

After his release, Goldberg resumed his solo career, which by now had reached international status. He spent some years in the USA and, for 15 years, was a member of the faculty at the Aspen Festival, where he also formed the Festival Quartet with the pianist Victor Babin, viola player William Primrose and cellist Nikolai Graudan; as such, they made many concert appearances and recordings. In his latter years, Goldberg became equally distinguished as a conductor.

His playing is best described by Boris Schwarz: 'Goldberg is a masterful violinist whose sole concern is the interpretation of great music, to the exclusion of all virtuoso frills. His technique is flawless, his tone warm and pure, his sense of style and his musical taste exquisite.'[7] Goldberg also enjoyed the respect of his fellow musicians. Yfrah Neaman said of him: 'He was never a man for small talk. If he gave an opinion it was only after he had given considerable thought to the matter, and as a result his judgement was never questioned.'[8]

Henryk Szeryng (1918–88) travelled the world in luxury on a diplomatic passport in pursuit of a highly successful solo career. He was born in Warsaw into a rich industrialist Jewish family and, at the age of five, had his first piano lessons from his mother; two years later, he had some tuition on the violin from his brother, a good amateur fiddler. Henryk was intrigued by the violin because it was such a small instrument in comparison with the piano. He wondered how it was possible to fill a large theatre with sound from such a small instrument. His progress prompted his parents to take him to study with Maurice Frenkel, former pupil and assistant of Auer in St Petersburg. Only much later did the debt he owed to Frenkel dawn on Szeryng, and how the different violin schools are in reality 'interdependent, intertwined and closely related'.[9]

When Huberman heard the ten-year-old play the Mendelssohn concerto, he was so impressed that he suggested Szeryng should go to study with Flesch in Berlin. Henryk took his advice and stayed with Flesch for three years. 'Everything I know, violinistically speaking, I learned from him. . . . he was a disciplinarian, a technician, but he had one overriding tenet – not to impress his own personality on pupils who had a personality of their own.'[10] In 1932 the Szeryng family moved to Paris where

Henryk met many of the notable poets, painters and composers, and studied composition with Nadia Boulanger. When he first heard Thibaud and Kreisler, he was captivated by the French style of playing. Kreisler's elegance, finesse and general approach to the violin were unlike anything that he had so far learned from any of his teachers. As for Thibaud: 'He never had the technique of Heifetz or the power of Elman, yet his playing, especially when he was in a good mood . . . was second to none.'[11] This dual influence stirred Szeryng to enter the Paris Conservatoire for further studies and he graduated in 1937, having been awarded the coveted Premier Prix for violin.

When Hitler invaded Poland, Szeryng was 21, and he immediately joined up in the Polish Army. Since he already spoke six languages with fluency he was appointed to the staff of General Sikorski as liaison officer and interpreter. He was allowed to take his violin with him on his travels and he took part in over 300 concerts for the sick and wounded and their families. He also played in prisoner-of-war camps. This experience impressed upon him the power of music as a unifying force linking generals and privates, Anzacs, Czechs, Poles and Mexicans.

In 1942, Szeryng accompanied the exiled Polish premier to Latin America in search of a home for 4,000 Polish refugees who had been displaced by the war. Moved by the warmth with which Mexico accepted the homeless, he returned to Mexico to teach after the war, and in 1946 he became a Mexican citizen. For the rest of his life he served as a cultural ambassador. Acting on his belief that music should be above politics, his chief concern was with fostering cultural exchange between countries that have no diplomatic relations.

In the autumn of 1954, Artur Rubinstein went to Mexico to give a series of piano recitals. Szeryng was in the audience and, overcome with the beauty of Rubinstein's playing, went backstage to congratulate him, speaking in Polish. The maestro, intrigued to find a Polish-speaking 'Mexican', suggested a meeting the following day. When Szeryng played for Rubinstein, the latter was in turn so struck by the violinist's artistry that he encouraged him to return to the concert platform after an absence of some 12 years. An introduction to the impresario Sol Hurok brought about an immediate concert tour of the USA; Szeryng undertook his first post-war European tour in 1956.

Szeryng was 36 when he made his reappearance on the concert stage. From this time until his death, he played all over the world, making recordings and leading an extremely active teaching life. In 1946 he founded and headed the String Department of the faculty of Music at Mexico University. Szeryng's repertory comprised all the classical concertos and many modern works, which included compositions by Mexican composers. At the 1966 Edinburgh Festival, he gave the European première of a concerto by his friend Carlos Chavez.

He caused considerable excitement when he gave the first modern performance of Paganini's 'lost' Violin Concerto No. 3 with the London Symphony Orchestra under Alexander Gibson at the Royal Festival Hall on 10 October 1971. The manuscript was believed to have been destroyed in the Napoleonic Wars. It came to light as a result of some lively detective work on Szeryng's part. After having searched for the concerto for many years, he was delighted to make the acquaintance of Paganini's two octogenarian great-granddaughters. The ladies suggested to Szeryng that he should play more of the maestro's compositions and showed him a stack of music that had lain untouched for well over a century. With Szeryng they set to reassembling the separate sheets. 'It took us five days to put the first movement together! Eventually we discovered a complete concerto.'[12] It was later identified and authenticated as the missing third concerto. Szeryng recorded it and the disc was released the day after the London premiere. Stanley Sadie wrote in *The Times*:

> There were *spiccatos* at a breathtaking pace, the notes as even as a row of pearls; there were handfuls of double-stops in octaves, thirds, sixths and tenths, sometimes with trills thrown in; there were lightning left-hand pizzicatos; there were long passages in harmonics, sometimes double stopped – how many fingers, I begin to wonder, does Mr Szeryng have?[13]

Szeryng believed that it is important to have a complete knowledge of a composer's life and character in the wider context. In his concert and ambassadorial rovings, Szeryng had ample opportunity to investigate the musical conditions in many countries. He was dismayed to discover that Israel, despite its outstanding contribution to the art of violin playing, possessed no Stradivarius violin. In December 1972, at a concert to celebrate the 25th anniversary of the State of Israel, Szeryng presented the country with a superb example of the master's work, the 'Hercules', dated 1734. This violin once belonged to Ysaÿe, but was stolen in St Petersburg after a concert, then reappeared at a shop in Paris in 1925, when it was bought by Mrs Charles Munch for her husband. Szeryng renamed it 'Kinor David', the Lyre of David.

When Kreisler heard Josef Hassid as a young boy at Flesch's house, he said: 'A fiddler such as x [mentioning a very famous name] is born every hundred years – one like Hassid, every two hundred.'[14] Josef Hassid was born in 1923, of poor Jewish parentage, in Suwalki, a remote Polish town not far from the Russian border. His mother had died when he was a baby, so the responsibility for his upbringing rested entirely on his father, an accountant by profession, who loved music. As a small child, Josef taught himself to play the violin and, when he was six, he was given his first lessons by the local violin teacher. He quickly exhausted his teacher's knowledge and was taken to Warsaw where he studied for some time with a violinist named Krystal.

At ten he was accepted into Michalowicz's class at the Chopin Academy of Music. Here he met his first serious rival: Ida Haendel. In her autobiography, *Woman With Violin*, she writes: 'When I heard him I was too young to appreciate his talent and I was not at all impressed by his slow vibrato.' Ida already had a fast vibrato, which she had picked up naturally soon after she began to play. 'At that time vibrato seemed to me of prime importance, and since Josef Hassid was also technically less advanced than [me], I soon dismissed him entirely. But father did recognise in this boy with his round face, black curly hair and ready smile, a talent of enormous range. And soon we became rivals – at any rate in the eyes of our parents and the public.'[15] Josef subsequently appeared with success at a number of concerts in Warsaw, and at the age of twelve, he entered the Wieniawski Competition – unsuccessfully, owing to a lapse of memory. Instead Ginette Neveu won first prize and Oistrakh took second.

It was also at this time that Huberman first heard Josef play and recommended him to have some lessons with Flesch, with whom Haendel was already studying. Her father also made approaches to Flesch on his behalf and he was the first to send the news to Hassid's father that his son had been accepted without fees. The elder Hassid wrote by return to Mr Haendel: 'My Josef, upon hearing the news, danced one solid hour for joy.'[16] In 1937, Josef went to study with Flesch on his summer course at Spa. Not only was Flesch impressed with his talent, but also thought that he possessed extraordinary musical perception and understanding for his age. Flesch once said that he considered him the most gifted pupil he ever had. With nothing to teach him technically, he had only to ripen his style.

But something else happened at that summer course. Josef Hassid fell deeply in love with one of his fellow students. The feelings were reciprocal but the girl was not Jewish. Unfortunately the two families were totally opposed to the match on religious grounds and thwarted every meeting. Eventually they succeeded in destroying the romance and the couple were finally parted. Even today the name of the girl remains a secret. Deprived of female affection from infancy, Josef was emotionally shattered by this treatment.

Meanwhile, his career began to take shape. In 1938 he made his first London appearance at a recital in aid of Ben Shemen, the Palestine training home for refugee children from Central and Eastern Europe, held at the house of Sir Philip Sassoon in fashionable Park Lane. Critics were enthusiastic and spoke of him as a natural violinist. When war broke out in 1939, the Hassids decided to stay in London. Harold Holt took Josef under his wing and arranged a recital and several concerts. But what must be an almost unprecedented occurrence – and extraordinary insight on the part of the recording manager, Walter Legge – was that HMV engaged him for a recording of some 'genre' pieces several weeks *before* his first recital. Gerald Moore, who was Hassid's accompanist in these recordings, gives a vivid account of the experience:

> I . . . was at once struck by his genius. He was a very reserved – not to say shy – boy and had no self-confidence except when he had his violin under his chin. . . . When rehearsing, his concentration was as fierce and well-focused as that of a virtuoso of maturity. I say this advisedly for we rehearsed several times for one London recital when I was moving house and my goods and chattels were 'housed' temporarily in the large house of a friend – tables, tall-boys, chests, desks, pianoforte, crates of china – all in a medley. Nothing disturbed him.[17]

Gerald Moore also accompanied Hassid at his debut recital at the Wigmore Hall, on 3 April 1940. He was billed as 'The Polish Boy Violinist', but his programme would have taxed the skills of a veteran. It included Corelli's La Folia variations, works by Debussy and Schubert, and Paganini's I Palpiti. *The Times* found him a 'mature artist', and admired the 'smooth and full tone' in the Corelli and the 'depth of his musicianship' in unaccompanied Bach.[18]

Three weeks later, Hassid made his orchestral debut, playing the Tchaikovsky concerto with the London Philharmonic Orchestra under Gregory Fitelberg, at the Queen's Hall. It was a benefit concert for the Polish Relief Fund and Fitelberg was himself a refugee and former conductor of the Warsaw Radio Orchestra. *The Times* considered that the strong impression Hassid had made in his recital 'was more than confirmed . . . when after a rather tentative beginning he grasped Tchaikovsky's bravura style boldly'.[19] Ida Haendel, who was at the performance, recalled that 'when we saw him step on to the stage, a charming figure with his unruly black hair and modest manner, we knew he would win all hearts'.[20]

Hassid played in three more concerts, prompting HMV to offer him a contract to make more recordings which would have included the first recording of the Walton Violin Concerto, but the plans never came to fruition. Hassid became moody, depressed and suffered memory lapses; he would not touch his violin for weeks on end. He once attacked his father with a knife. He underwent sporadic sessions of treatment, but with only partial success; finally, he was admitted into a mental hospital in Epsom, an incurable schizophrenic.

In the tragic years that followed, Hassid became withdrawn and totally alienated from anything concerned with music. He rejected any idea that he had ever even played the violin. A letter from Carl Flesch, dating from this period, is a poignant reminder of the hopes he cherished for his pupil's future. 'I hope you will do everything within your will-power to get well again as soon as possible,' he wrote. 'A great artist like you owes it to the world to become active again.'[21] But in November 1950, Hassid underwent a brain operation from which he never recovered. Eight short pieces recorded on four 78 rpm discs, since issued on CD, are all that remain to remind us of his genius, but they are enough to prove that he was one of the great violinists, and justify Kreisler's recognition of that greatness.

After 14-year-old Ida Haendel's orchestral debut at the Queen's Hall, playing the Brahms Concerto under Sir Henry Wood, Ferruccio Bonavia reported in the *Daily Telegraph*, on 1 February 1937:

> Her skill is remarkable even in the days when violinists seem to be born with a command of the fingerboard that their forebears achieved only after long and industrious study. There was no sense of strain or lack of polish in her playing of the most florid passages of the concerto and the cadenza. More striking still in one so young was the justness of an interpretation which suggested not only a ripe lesson and young energy, but temperamental force.

Now, over 60 years later, she is still playing in a ceaseless round of concerts, recitals and recordings all over the world. She is one of the few child prodigies who has fulfilled her early promise as an adult performer, and is today recognised as one of the world's great violinists.

She was born in 1923 into a poor Jewish family in the little Polish town of Chelm. Her father had himself wanted to play the violin, but was forbidden to do so by an over-zealous and strict orthodox parent who was convinced that fiddlers only played at weddings. Nathan Haendel ran away from home and eventually became a painter, but his own frustrated ambition prompted him to vow that if ever he had a child with musical talent, he would do everything within his power to guide and develop it. At the age of three-and-a-half Ida picked up her sister's violin and taught herself to play perfectly by ear.

Her father then knew his pledge had to be kept. Over the years, Nathan Haendel has had many accusations levelled at him, for over-protectiveness and for his prodigious shaping of his daughter's career, but ambition and talent are tempting partners, and when a father is faced with an abundance of the latter in his own child, it is difficult to isolate his motives. In the first few years of her life, Ida's accomplishments were phenomenal. At the age of four, she was accepted without fees at the Chopin Academy of Music in Warsaw under Michalowicz, an ex-pupil of Auer at St Petersburg. A year later, she won the first prize in the Huberman Competition, playing the Beethoven Concerto.

The Haendels went to Paris in 1935 with the intention that Ida should study with Szigeti, who had heard her in Warsaw. But his plans suddenly changed. Fortunately, through a chance meeting with Ignace Rubinstein, brother of the pianist, Artur, contact was made with Carl Flesch. The latter was so impressed he agreed to teach her for nothing. After only a short period of tuition Ida returned to Warsaw to enter the National Competition, and carried off the first Polish prize for her playing of the Wieniawski Concerto in D minor.

Flesch never considered it necessary to give Ida technical exercises: he put her straight away on the Paganini Caprices. The first piece she ever studied with him was Sarasate's Carmen Fantasie, and she played it entirely to Flesch's satisfaction before one of his terrifying little audiences. When Flesch gave her a virtuoso vehicle such as the Kreutzer Sonata, she learned it in a matter of hours. But when confronted with a pianist as partner instead of accompanist, she was hopelessly out of step. Flesch was exasperated and disbelieving. Later that evening Ida asked her father if all those dashes and numbers could possibly mean something. He gasped: 'Do you mean to say you didn't know?' 'Of course not!' retorted Ida. 'Nobody told me!'[22] The poor little wonder child could not read music properly; so perfect was her memory that no one ever doubted that she was acquainted with the theory of music. 'As soon as I had mastered a work technically, no other problems existed. I played musically by instinct. . . . It took me years to understand that it was necessary to analyse and study the thoughts, structure and style which make up a great composition by a great composer.'[23]

Ida's Paris debut took place in 1935, when she was only 12 years old, at a recital at the Salle Gaveau; her first professional concert appearance was at the Casino in Monte Carlo. Following these successes, Flesch, then resident in London, considered that Ida was ready for her concert debut in that city. The Haendels duly arrived, but were painfully short of money. Nathan Haendel painted portraits and Ida made some pocket money by playing at fashionable houses. Flesch eventually introduced the Haendels to the impresario Harold Holt, who obtained an engagement for Ida to play at a Beecham Sunday Concert. But a serious problem arose. At this time in England, no child under 14 was allowed on the concert platform. To wait another two years would have been disastrous, so Harold Holt falsified her age and told the papers that a mistake had been made. It worked. Even as a child, Ida Haendel was aware of the isolation of the prodigy:

> The more I was left to myself, the more I withdrew, as I grew older, I built a wall round me ever more difficult for others to penetrate. I have now come to the conclusion that the upbringing of an artist, particularly one who begins as a prodigy, leads to a life of loneliness and introspection. The fact that one doesn't go to school, where a child first learns to mix and integrate, must also have a bearing on the problem.[24]

In the summer of 1937, the Haendels felt the need for a family reunion and decided to take a trip to Poland. Flesch protested that Ida needed his guidance now more than ever, and told them that if they persisted in their plan, he would wash his hands of them. Undaunted, they ignored his threats. In Paris en route, Ida took the opportunity to have some lessons with Enescu:

> The difference between Flesch and Enescu is difficult to assess. Flesch was a fabulous teacher and knew exactly how to correct your faults. He was like a surgeon in that he could pin-point exactly what you needed to do, and he made sure that you understood. Enescu would not waste time telling you that it should be this way or that; he would show you, get you to try to see what he was driving at, and then he would say 'Go home and get it right'. And somehow you did.[25]

When Flesch heard about the lessons with Enescu, he took umbrage, and protested, but lessons with him were soon resumed and the incident was forgotten.

Although she has been on the concert platform for over 60 years, Haendel's playing has never become stale or even predictable. Each performance is a new experience and her total commitment to the music itself is liable to send the toughest critic home in a state of euphoria. The Brahms concerto is considered by many to be one of Haendel's prime achievements. Although she has played it since childhood, much of the maturity in her interpretation was brought about by her association with the Romanian conductor Sergiu Celibidache. Her recording of this concerto in London with Celibidache was 'undoubtedly . . . a landmark in my life as a musician'.[26]

At the time it was a bestseller and in her opinion it still is the most outstanding performance of her life.

**Notes**

1. Flesch, *Memoirs*, p. 274.
2–3. *The Strad*, July 1987, pp. 543–5.
4. Letter from Kendall Taylor to M.C.
5–6. *The Strad*, April 1991, pp. 346–7.
7. Schwarz, *Great Masters of the Violin*, p. 345.
8. M.C., *Independent*, 23 December 1993.
9. *The Strad*, May 1978, p. 11.
10. Schwarz, op. cit., p. 348.
11. *The Strad*, May 1978, p. 11.
12. *International Herald Tribune*, 29 January 1973.
13. *The Times*, 11 October 1971.
14. Flesch, op. cit., p. 360.
15–16. Haendel, *Woman with Violin*, p. 65.
17. Letter from Gerald Moore to M.C., 2 December 1978.
18. *The Times*, 4 April 1940.
19. *The Times*, 26 April 1940.
20. Haendel, op. cit., p. 115.
21. Letter from Carl Flesch to Josef Hassid, 6 June 1943.
22–24. Haendel, op. cit., pp. 54–6.
25. Quoted from interview, M.C.
26. Haendel, op. cit., p. 224.

# 37  Great Teachers of America

With the passing of Auer, Flesch and Enescu, the twentieth century gratefully inherited their pupils. Sascha Lasserson carried on the Auer tradition in the UK, Max Rostal became the best-known disciple of Flesch and taught in Switzerland, while Menuhin and Helen Dowling both passed on to their students something of the subtle but powerful influence exerted upon them by Enescu.

In the USA, two of the early influences were Franz Kneisel and David Mannes, who founded the Mannes School (now College) in New York. Tossy Spivakovsky, a pupil of Willy Hess, and Louis Persinger and Josef Gingold, two ex-pupils of Ysaÿe, made a significant contribution to the development of violin playing in that country, as did Ivan Galamian, who studied with Lucien Capet in Paris and is not affiliated to any of the mainstream 'schools'. Dorothy DeLay, a Persinger student, was for many years Galamian's assistant at the Juilliard. In the next generation there are two emigré Russians who have made a considerable impact on American violin teaching: they are Victor Danchenko and Eduard Schmieder.

Franz Kneisel (1865–1926) was born in Bucharest of German parents and studied with Jakob Grün and Joseph Hellmesberger at the Vienna Conservatory. He made his debut in 1882 performing Joachim's Hungarian Concerto, and when he was only 19, became leader of the Bilse Orchestra in Berlin. In 1885, Kneisel emigrated to the USA to become concertmaster of the Boston Symphony Orchestra. That same year he made a highly successful solo debut, playing the Beethoven concerto, and also formed the Kneisel String Quartet which was to become one of the great American quartets.

In 1903, Kneisel left the Boston Symphony Orchestra and later joined the faculty of the newly founded Institute of Musical Art in New York, where he gained a reputation as a gifted teacher. He received honorary doctorates from both Yale and Princeton universities where he taught for many years.

David Mannes (1866–1959) was born in New York to poor German–Polish immigrants; he learnt to play the violin as a child, with only occasional lessons from a local teacher. In his teens, he would play anywhere – including honky-tonks and dance halls – to earn a few cents. In 1891 he met Walter Damrosch, who was forming a symphony orchestra for the new Carnegie Hall, and was engaged for the first violin section. In the meantime, Mannes went to Berlin for further studies with Heinrich de Ahna and Karel Halíř (1859–1909) – both pupils of Joachim – and spent a further six months with Ysaÿe in Brussels. He then took up his post in Damrosch's New York Symphony Orchestra, eventually becoming leader; he stayed until 1912. As a performer, he was successful in many different fields; with his pianist wife, Clara, he toured the country giving sonata recitals and also had his own string quartet; later he was equally in demand as a conductor.

Mannes had always been interested in teaching and gained his first experience at the Music School Settlement, for deprived children. He also helped black musicians to gain employment and organised concerts for prisoners. In 1916, Mannes and his wife founded their own music school, Mannes College, in New York. They were determined that it should be a school where high standards were maintained, but without undue pressure.

David Mannes was, without doubt, one of the greatest American musical philanthropists. 'He contributed his art and his initiative for the sake of music, for the good of people. He never forgot his own humble beginnings, his own thirst for great music and encouragement.'[1]

Born in Rochester, Illinois, Louis Persinger (1887–1966) was trained at the Leipzig Conservatory before finishing with Ysaÿe in Brussels. He held leaderships in both the Berlin Philharmonic Orchestra and the Royal Opera Orchestra in Brussels, and in 1915 he was appointed leader and assistant conductor to the San Francisco Symphony Orchestra. After the death of Auer in 1930, he succeeded him at the Juilliard School in New York.

Persinger became best known for his ability to teach gifted children and it was he, as we have seen, who trained and launched Menuhin and Ricci on their careers. Helen Dowling, who also studied with Persinger as a child, praised his faculty for making the music come alive:

> He paid great attention to learning the music as a whole. When a new composition was to be tackled he would begin the lesson by playing the accompaniment or orchestral part on the piano. You followed the violin part with your eyes so that you already knew the composition before you started to play your part. Anything you would eventually play with orchestra was explained in detail, including where most orchestras might go wrong, and how you could hold your own part together regardless. We were only *children*, but it made all the difference in the world to our performance. You didn't just learn a violin part.[2]

Persinger had infinite patience. Menuhin says of him: 'The milk of human kindness may not lubricate a soloist's career; it made Persinger an ideal teacher, at least for someone thirsty for instruction.'[3] When Menuhin was eight years old, Persinger agreed to allow him to tackle the Beethoven concerto, provided he first mastered the one in A major by Mozart. In eight hours of concentrated practice the child memorised the Mozart and played it to his teacher.

> A crueller man than he would have thrown me a coin, complimented the monkey and suggested tunes more appropriate to the hurdy-gurdy, but Persinger mercifully lost his

temper for once – in the middle of the Andante. 'Go home!' he said angrily. 'Use your good mathematical head and figure out for yourself the exact rhythms. I don't want to see you again until you have given thought to every note in each movement.'[4]

Joseph Fuchs (1990–97) was born in New York into a Polish–Jewish immigrant family who loved music; his father – a frustrated violinist – was quick to recognise his son's talent when as a small child he could with accuracy sing the tunes he heard in the synagogue. However, the choice of instrument came about by necessity. When Joseph was three years old, he had a bad fall which resulted in a compound fracture of his left elbow; after having the arm in a plaster cast for three months, the doctor suggested he should have some violin lessons as therapy. After initial instruction from his father, the boy's progress was so swift that he had some lessons with Max Fonaroff, who, in turn, was so impressed that he took him to the School of Musical Art (now the Juilliard) in New York where the six-year-old was accepted into the violin class. At 11 he became a student of the great Franz Kneisel and graduated at 18 with some $2,500 in prizes.

In 1926 he became leader of the Cleveland Orchestra, but left in 1940 to pursue a solo career. From 1941 to 1943 he led the Primrose String Quartet, with Josef Gingold as second violin, William Primrose on viola and Harvey Shapiro on cello. He made a highly successful Carnegie Hall debut in 1943 and, during the Second World War, was a tireless performer in military hospitals. He was also co-founder of the Musicians' Guild, a chamber music ensemble that he directed for over ten years.

From this time Fuchs was in demand as a soloist the world over and appeared many times at the Prades Festival under Casals. Although his repertory encompassed the classic works he was also a strong advocate of new music. He obtained a Ford Foundation grant in 1960, enabling him to commission a violin concerto from Walter Piston and he gave the first performance in Pittsburgh that same year. In 1947, he and his sister Lillian gave the posthumous première of Bohuslav Martinů's Madrigaly for violin and viola, which was dedicated to them.

Fuchs was also a dedicated teacher, having been at Juilliard since 1946. In 1971 he received the Artist Teacher's Award from the American String Teachers' Association. After he retired in 1995, his students came to his apartment for lessons. He was convinced that players make the best teachers and said: 'You must have experience in order to put yourself in a student's shoes.'[5]

Tossy Spivakovsky (1907–98) was that rarity, the child prodigy who went on to become not only an adult virtuoso but a highly respected teacher. He was born in Odessa and as a young boy was taken to Berlin to study with Willy Hess and Arrigo Serato (1877–1948). He made his solo debut at ten and undertook his first European tour when he was 13, becoming leader of the Berlin Philharmonic Orchestra under Furtwängler when he was only 19, the youngest ever to be appointed. It soon became evident that he was destined for a solo career and in 1927 he resigned to follow that path. From this time onwards he was in constant demand for recitals and concerto performances throughout the world. In the USA, he played with every major orchestra; critics wrote of his 'brilliant execution' and 'peerless artistry'. He formed a trio with his pianist brother Jascha and the cellist Edmund Kurtz, and they toured the international circuit with equal success.

Spivakovsky premiered a number of works by Bernstein, Frank Martin, Carl Nielsen and others, and in 1943 he gave the first American performance of Bartók's Second Violin Concerto with the Cleveland Orchestra under Artur Rodzinski; it was the only performance the composer heard.

Spivakovsky made a lifelong study of bowing techniques pertaining to the works of J.S. Bach. He could sustain three- or four-note chords for longer than is customary. Spivakovsky contributed many writings to musical periodicals and also composed cadenzas for a number of concertos including those of Mozart and Beethoven.

Spivakovsky was an excellent teacher, who could not only demonstrate his ideas, but also encouraged even the most timid students to experiment for themselves. His first teaching post was in Australia, at Melbourne University Conservatorium, from 1933 until 1939; after settling in the USA in 1940 he took up a post at Fairfield University in Connecticut and in 1974, he joined the faculty of the Juilliard School of Music in New York, remaining until his death at the age of 91.

Josef Gingold (1909–95) was born in Russia and emigrated to the USA in 1920. At first a pupil of Vladimir Graffman in New York, he later spent two years with Ysaÿe in Brussels.

Gingold was a member of the NBC Symphony Orchestra under Toscanini and later leader of both the Detroit and Cleveland Symphony Orchestras. He remained in Cleveland for 13 years, serving as the soloist in 15 concertos. In 1960 he joined the faculty of the Indiana University School of Music at Bloomington, where he was named 'Distinguished Professor of Music'. For many years, he was head of the Chamber Music Department of Meadowmount School of Music, and, in addition to his teaching, recording and concert appearances in the USA, he gave masterclasses at the Paris Conservatoire and at the Toho School of Music in Tokyo.

Gingold also represented his adopted country on the juries of a number of international violin competitions, including the Queen Elisabeth, Paganini, Wieniawski, Leventritt, Sibelius and Tchaikovsky. He served as the first honorary chairman and president of the Indianapolis Violin Competition, from its foundation in 1982 until 1994 when Jaime Laredo was appointed as his successor. He edited over 30 works in the classical and modern violin repertory and his recording of Kreisler pieces is a masterpiece of style.

Gingold's teaching gifts were remarkable and his warm, friendly personality endeared him to all who came within his ken. Miriam Fried studied with him before going to the Juilliard School under Galamian. 'Gingold directed in a way I had never thought about before. He made me aware of sounds. He showed me how the violin differs from the piano and where its possibilities lie. I had neglected this aspect before and have been grateful ever since for his opening up this new dimension for me.'[6]

Ivan Galamian (1903–81) was born in Tabriz, Iran, of Armenian parents, who brought him to Russia when he was two months old. His father was a businessman who loved music. When, at the age of eight, Ivan showed interest in the violin, he was sent to the School of the Philharmonic Society in Moscow, where he had lessons with Konstantin Mostras, a pupil of Boris Sibor (1880–1961). Ivan's graduation coincided with the Revolution of 1917; he fled first to Germany and then on to Paris, where he became a pupil of Lucien Capet (1873–1928), who became 'a strong influence, both musically and pedagogically'.[7]

In his youth Galamian achieved a reputation as a virtuoso performer and, in the 1920s, made many successful European tours. But, from an early age, he was interested in teaching; he kept a special diary in which he recorded the progress of his pupils and sometimes the notes ran into several pages. In 1923, when Capet began to pass on his surplus students, Galamian began to take his teaching seriously.

In 1930 he was appointed vice president of the Russian Conservatoire in Paris and, from 1936 to 1939, he was a member of the faculty at the Paris Conservatoire. In 1939 he emigrated to the USA, taking citizenship in 1944.

That same year, Galamian was invited by Efrem Zimbalist, who was then director of the Curtis Institute, to become a member of the faculty. Two years later he was appointed to the staff of Juilliard, where he built himself a reputation that can only be compared with that of Auer at St Petersburg.

In addition to his teaching in New York City, during the summer months he taught at the Meadowmount School in the Adirondack Mountains at Westport (NY), which he founded in 1944. Galamian worked from 8 a.m. until 6 p.m. until his 75th birthday, after which he delayed his start until 9 a.m. However, he was not above telephoning a sleeping student before that hour, to ask 'Why aren't you practising?' Galamian had firm views on practising. 'If we analyse the development of the well-known artists, we see that in almost every case the success of their entire career was dependent upon the quality of their practising. . . . The lesson is not all. Children do not know how to work alone. The teacher must constantly teach the child how to practise.'[8]

Galamian's main principle was that the player must develop a sense of responsibility for his own technique, beginning with the development of a practising routine. At Meadowmount, Galamian and his coaching staff would spend considerable time touring the practice cabins and listening in. They would then advise pupils on what to practise and for how long. Sidney Mann, who helped Frances Kitching to run a Galamian-inspired course in Britain in 1969, said: 'When you hear someone in the next cabin practising two Kreutzer studies, a movement from a concerto and some unaccompanied Bach – most of it from memory – it really makes you improve.'[9] The underlying strength of the Galamian method is, then, the constructive and economic use of available time. 'From an early stage in the pupil's development the teacher should try to encourage a personal initiative while at the same time constantly striving to better the student's understanding and to improve his taste and sense of style.'[10]

Another important aspect of Galamian's teaching is the necessity to keep a balance: evenness and consistency were his bywords. He recalled one of his teachers in Russia as moody, so that everything depended upon the way he felt. 'I promised myself I would never react to pupils that way . . . . I have patience and I teach my students to have patience. Especially I try to be patient in letting them find their own way. The teacher must always bear in mind that the highest goal should be for him to make the student self-sufficient.'[11]

Some of his students found him too strict, but the most successful ones had no complaints. Miriam Fried found Galamian to be one of the most organised people she had ever met. 'His head probably has little drawers in it, and his brain pulls out little bits of information one at a time.' She found him particularly expert at diagnosing problems:

> Students will practise at home and become depressed because they are not achieving the right results. A talk with Galamian will evoke an immediate response. He will demonstrate and say: 'Why don't you do it this way?' Miraculously the student finds that it works. But you couldn't get away with anything less than what he wanted. He would make you play the same piece for a week if he didn't think you had reached your individual maximum. A classic remark of his was: 'You do things very well up to ninety-five per cent – now let's do the last five.'[12]

Kyung-Wha Chung recalls the way in which Galamian prepared his students for the concert platform: 'It is like an actor wearing strong make-up. If you are near it is too strong, but on stage it looks perfect. Galamian based his teaching on this kind of projection. In a room it can be too strong but on stage it's fantastic.'[13]

Galamian acknowledged that the standards were higher than they had been 20 years earlier. 'Violinists these days are technically more developed, and from the musical aspect more faithful to the text of the composer's writing. Repertoire is also much more extensive than before. When I studied in Paris with Capet, I had to learn about a dozen concertos: now it is more like fifty.'[14]

There is no doubt that Galamian made a unique contribution to the development of violin playing. He devoted a lifetime to the study and practice of every aspect of playing. His book *Principles of Violin Playing and Teaching* contains precise directions and explanations for every mental or physical action. But he also treated each pupil as an individual according to his needs. He believed that the differences between great players is much bigger than between good players. The list of great violinists who have been trained by Galamian would occupy several pages of a fiddlers' *Who's Who*.

Galamian once summed up his philosophy:

> Interpretation is the final goal of all instrumental study, its only *raison d'être*. Technique is merely the means to this end, the tool to be used in the service of artistic

interpretation. For successful performance, therefore, the possession of the technical tools alone is not sufficient. In addition, the player must understand the meaning of the music thoroughly, must have creative imagination and a personal approach to the work if his rendition is to be lifted above the dry and the pedantic. His personality must be neither self-effacing nor aggressively obtruding.[15]

When a reporter once asked Galamian who was the most outstandingly gifted violinist he had ever taught, he replied without hesitation. 'Michael Rabin. There was an extraordinary talent – no weaknesses, never!'[16] Born in 1937, Michael Rabin made an extraordinary impact on the violin world as a prodigy. He died in 1972, at the age of 35, at the height of a brilliant but troubled career, which was undermined by drug problems and mental instability. It would have been interesting to have followed the development of a talent so reminiscent of Flesch's most promising pupil, Josef Hassid.

Felix Galimir (1910–99) was still teaching at Juilliard, Mannes College, the Curtis Institute and the Marlboro Festival right up until his death. Born in Vienna, he began playing the violin at five and entered the New Vienna Conservatory when he was 14, studying violin with Adolf Bak and chamber music with Simon Pullman. Galimir remained eternally grateful to Pullman, who undoubtedly had the greatest influence upon his early development. 'He was never direct and rough in his teaching; he went to his goal in a round-about way. He would often say: "You have to play so that a blind man can see the score."'[17] Galimir's love of chamber music began at this time and, as a teenager, he played in a string quartet with his three sisters.

Pullman was also an authority on contemporary music and encouraged the young Galimir Quartet to explore the quartet literature of the time. One of the works in which they specialised was Alban Berg's 'fantastic but unplayable' Lyric Suite. After working on it for several months, Pullman invited the composer to listen to them and he was amazed. When they first performed the work in public, Berg inscribed Galimir's score with the words: 'To Felix Galimir, the outstanding quartet leader – famous violinist, wonderful musician, in remembrance 9 April 1931.' Galimir was just 21.

When he was 22, he spent a year studying with Flesch in Berlin and at Baden-Baden. He once recalled: 'Flesch was highly methodical in his approach to the violin. He seemed to focus more on security and precision than the artistic side, but he might have been attending to my specific needs. . . . He had a true vocation for teaching.'[18] On his return to Vienna, Galimir continued to give concerts with his sisters and on one occasion when they played the Ravel Quartet, the composer was present. He was so pleased with their performance that he arranged for them to record the work in Paris where it was awarded the Grand Prix du Disque. The quartet went on to give concerts throughout Europe and became known particularly for their performances of contemporary music.

In 1935, Galimir auditioned successfully for a vacancy in the Vienna Philharmonic Orchestra, only to learn that Jewish musicians were being weeded out and that he would not be allowed to play. He was then invited by Huberman to go with him to Palestine. The family quartet was disbanded and Galimir became assistant leader and soloist of the Palestine Symphony Orchestra (now the Israel Philharmonic). At the opening concert, Galimir first came under the baton of Toscanini. In 1938 he emigrated to the USA. He became leader of the NBC Symphony Orchestra in New York under Toscanini and except for two years in the US Army during the Second World War, remained there until the maestro's retirement in 1954.

Dorothy DeLay (1917–2002) probably held the record for having taught the largest number of violinists to achieve international fame. She was born in the small town of Medicine Lodge in Kansas, into a musical family of several generations of teachers.

As a young girl she became interested in the violin, took it up and made good progress. In 1933 she embarked on studies at Oberlin College, but the following year transferred to Michigan State University, where she studied with Mikhail Press (1871–1938), a pupil of Auer. She also studied psychology, a subject that was to become of vital importance in her teaching. In 1937 she entered the Juilliard Graduate Division under Persinger and Raphael Bronstein. She founded the Stuyvesant String Quartet and began her professional career as both a soloist and chamber music player.

However, DeLay discovered quite early on that performing was not her *forte*. She found that she did not enjoy the constant travelling and she suffered from nerves when performing. She began teaching by taking on a few young children and enjoyed the experience so much that she decided to make it her career. In 1946, when Galamian joined the staff of the Juilliard School, DeLay became interested in his teaching methods and, in 1948, was appointed his assistant, a post she held for the next 23 years.

There has been much speculation as to why this partnership was finally dissolved. Some say Galamian was too authoritarian, while others claim that DeLay wanted to develop hed own ideas, which differed considerably from his. Whatever the reason, DeLay had a way of communicating with her students that went far beyond the technical side of teaching. Her training in psychology proved invaluable when dealing with a student with personal problems. She also paid attention as to how a student should approach the concert platform and how to project to an audience. Her pupils all say that she was a good listener and did not impose her will. On the contrary, she had a way of making the student feel that the decision to carry out a particular approach or technique was his or hers, not DeLay's.

Victor Danchenko was born in Moscow in 1937, the son of a violinist in the State Orchestra of the USSR. He entered the Central Music School at the age of five in the class of Anna Zilberstein, who was particularly good with small children. He went on to study with Mikhail Garlitsky and made his solo debut in 1954 playing the Kabalevsky Violin Concerto, a year before he graduated with a gold medal. The opportunity came about because the violinist who had been originally engaged had been double-booked; Danchenko had four days in which to put it in shape. His performance elicited a glowing review in the *Soviet Music Magazine*, which was spotted by David Oistrakh, who offered there and then to teach him.

As a result, Danchenko studied with Oistrakh at the Moscow Conservatory and stresses the importance of being Oistrakh's pupil. 'He was at the height of his powers; he was concertising intensively so the individual attention his students received was limited, but it was common practice that after our lessons we would sit in his studio for three to four hours and listen to our friends having their lessons.'[19] He confirms what all students of Oistrakh say, that rhythmical stability and discipline were of prime importance and that he could be very encouraging if a student played well, but very harsh if he thought he were not trying his best.

Following his debut recital in the Hall of the Moscow Conservatory, Danchenko's career gained momentum; he played all over the USSR and Eastern Europe, then emigrated to Canada in 1977, via Vienna and Rome, finally settling in Toronto where he had relatives. Danchenko's reputation as a teacher quickly became known and in a short while he found himself a member of the Faculty of Music at Toronto University as well as teaching at the Royal Conservatory of Music. He later taught at the Meadowmount School of Music, and today divides his time between the Peabody Institute in Baltimore and the Curtis Institute in Philadelphia.

Danchenko is explicit when talking about his teaching methods:

> The violin is one of the most unnatural and awkward instruments ever invented. If you ask anyone who does not play to take a fiddle and hold it in a playing position for ten to fifteen minutes, he or she will cry out in pain. So how do we teach people to play this awkward instrument in an easy and relaxed manner? . . . We are all different, so I tell my students they must learn to adjust the instrument to their own body.[20]

Danchenko believes that as long as the student has the musical talent, if he finds the perfect angle to suit his anatomy, he can become a good violinist. 'I like to think that my students leave me having learnt as much as possible but at the same time having found their own musical voice and path.'[21]

Eduard Schmieder was born in L'viv, Ukraine, in 1948, the son of a surgeon. He had his first lessons on the violin when he was five and two years later, he played the Bach A minor Concerto at a public concert. He went on to study with Mikhail Vaiman at the Mussorgsky Conservatory in Leningrad. When he was only 16, he was chosen to represent the USSR at the Paganini Competition in Genoa, but a heart attack – rare in one so young – prevented him from taking part. He was sent to recuperate at Piarnu, on the Baltic coast, where all the famous Soviet musicians had their dachas. He was given permission to practise in the local concert hall, and one day, having just played to the end of the first movement of the Tchaikovsky concerto, he heard loud applause and was astonished to see David Oistrakh sitting in the stalls. Schmieder was overwhelmed when the great man said he would like to give him some lessons. So for the next seven summers at Piarnu, Schmieder studied privately with Oistrakh.

In 1970, Schmieder went on to the Gnessin Institute where his main teacher was Felix Andrievsky (b. 1936), who two years later emigrated to Israel. Schmieder then continued his studies with Mikhail Garlitsky and was subsequently appointed as a lecturer in methodology at Gnessin, where he combined playing, teaching and studying for a doctorate. In 1980, Schmieder decided to emigrate with his family to the USA. He arrived without a word of English. When he applied for his first post at Lamar University at Beaumont, Texas and signed his contract, he had no idea of the wording. However, when Schmieder joined them they had just one violin student; two and a half years later, he had 12, several of whom had won prizes in competitions. 'I think if you teach, then you know the terminology – I had some foreign students when I was still in the USSR – if your face is expressive enough you can normally put over your ideas.'[22] When approached by the dean of the Meadows School of Music at Houston's Rice University to take on the violin department there, he accepted; but in order not to abandon his students at Lamar, he commuted between the two institutions for the first year of his new appointment. The number of students tripled.

Schmieder moved west, from Houston to Los Angeles, to become professor of violin at the University of Southern California, the position formerly occupied by Heifetz, and in 1990 he was appointed professor of violin at the Meadows School of the Arts at the Southern Methodist University in Dallas, Texas, where he now holds the Algur H. Meadows Distinguished Chair of Violin and Chamber Music Studies. Schmieder is visiting professor at the Paris Conservatoire and many other institutions throughout Europe, he gives masterclasses and has sat on many juries of international competitions, including the Paganini, the Sibelius and the Queen Elisabeth Concours. He has also been warmly welcomed on many occasions when returning to his native Russia. In 1996 he accepted an honourary distinguished professorship at Almaty Conservatory in the Republic of Kazakhstan.

## Notes

1. Schwarz, *Great Masters of the Violin*, p. 503.
2. Quoted from interview, M.C.
3. Menuhin, *Unfinished Journey*, p. 34.
4. Ibid., p. 36.
5. M.C., *Independent*, 18 March 1997.
6. Quoted from interview, MC.
7–8. Applebaum, *With the Artists*, p. 282.
9. Quoted from interview, M.C.
10–11. Galamian, *Principles of Violin Playing and Teaching*, p. 8.
12. Quoted from interview, M.C.
13. Quoted from interview, M.C.
14. Letter from Galamian to M.C., 12 May 1977.
15. Galamian, op. cit., p. 6.
16. *New York Times*, 23 November 1977.

17–18. *The Strad,* May 1993, pp. 456–8.
19–21. *The Strad,* March 1997, pp. 281–5.
22. Quoted from interview, M.C.

# 38   Great Teachers of Europe

It has been said that the best teachers are those who have plenty of experience of the concert platform, whereas great performers *per se* are not necessarily good teachers. In Europe, a few have fulfilled both roles successfully. While coming from countries as far removed as Russia and Argentina, they have similar aims, to which their many pupils can testify.

Adolf Brodsky (1851–1929) was born in Taganrog, in Russia, and showed early talent for the violin. He studied with Joseph Hellmesberger at the Vienna Conservatory and later became a member of the celebrated Hellmesberger String Quartet. He also followed a successful solo career, which he combined with chamber music and teaching. He took the violin class at the Moscow Conservatory from 1874 until 1878 and, in 1880, was appointed senior professor at the Hochschule in Leipzig.

Thanks to Brodsky, Tchaikovsky's Violin Concerto reached the concert hall. It had originally been written for Auer, who rejected it as unplayable. In 1881, three years after Tchaikovsky completed the manuscript, Brodsky persuaded Hans Richter and the Vienna Philharmonic to give the first performance with him as soloist. Hanslick wrote an acid review; undeterred, Brodsky played it in London and Moscow the following year, but the critics remained lukewarm.

In 1890, Brodsky went to the USA to lead the New York Symphony Orchestra under Walter, but in 1894, when he was invited to lead the Hallé Orchestra under Sir Charles Hallé, he was happy to return to Europe; at the same time he was appointed senior violin professor at the newly opened Royal Manchester College of Music. Brodsky played only one concert under Sir Charles, who died in the autumn of 1895; he then succeeded Hallé as principal of the college and resigned his leadership.

Brodsky was not only a fine teacher but a first-class performer, who contributed greatly to the musical life of Manchester for almost 30 years with the Brodsky Quartet, which he formed soon after his arrival in the UK. He gave up solo playing in 1921 but came out of retirement for a performance of the Elgar concerto in 1927 to celebrate the composer's 70th birthday.

Willy Hess (1859–1939) was probably the most ubiquitous violinist of all time: he seems to have lived, played and taught in at least a dozen cities in Europe and the USA which, like his eminent predecessor, Brodsky, included Manchester. Hess was born in Mannheim and had his first lessons at the age of six from his father, Julian Hess, a professional violinist who had studied with Spohr. That same year his family moved to the USA, where they stayed for seven years; Willy had made his debut, at the age of ten, as a soloist with the Theodore Thomas Orchestra who were on an American tour. The Hess family returned to Europe in 1872, finally settling in Heidelberg. Hess's solo career gained momentum and he appeared in most of the capital cities of Europe, making his London debut in 1874. He gave many of the recitals with his pianist sister, Johanna.

In 1876, Hess went to Berlin for two years' further study with Joachim. It was a turning point in his musical development. He had the greatest respect for Joachim's teaching and the master would seem to have looked favourably upon him as a pupil. Much later, Flesch described Hess in his memoirs as a 'passionate and inexhaustible teacher', but criticised his 1911 performance of Joachim's Concerto in Hungarian Style, when Hess was 52 and making his last appearance as a soloist: 'He was one of the great talents who had been ruined by the unprecise finger technique and the wrong bowing technique of the Joachim school.'[1]

After leaving Joachim, Hess was appointed leader of the Opera and Museum Concert Orchestra in Frankfurt, where he stayed for eight years; in addition to his orchestral playing and solo work, he also taught and founded a string quartet and a trio. Rotterdam was Hess's next port of call, where he was a professor at the Conservatory for two years, after which in 1888 he accepted Sir Charles Hallé's invitation to lead the Hallé Orchestra in Manchester, remaining there until 1895. He returned to Germany to become principal professor of violin at the Cologne Hochschule. In 1903 he accepted an invitation to become a professor at the Royal Academy of Music in London, but resigned after a year to succeed Franz Kneisel as leader of the Boston Symphony Orchestra. In 1910 he returned to Europe to settle finally in Berlin, where he was professor at the Hochschule and also led the Halir Quartet.

The Danish Henry Holst (1899–1991) was another emigré violinist who made a significant contribution to British musical life both in Manchester and London. He was born in Saeby, a small fishing village near Copenhagen, the son of a schoolmaster whose family had for many generations been interested in the arts. One of his most vivid childhood memories was of being allowed to listen late into the night to his father's string quartet, and how the viola player would come straight from his fishing boat with scales still stuck to his fingers.

Holst received his first instruction from his father and, in 1913, entered the Royal Danish Conservatory in Copenhagen to study the violin with Axel Gade, and piano and harmony with Carl Nielsen. When, at 20, he made his debut as a soloist in Copenhagen, the critics predicted a bright future for him. A chance meeting with Emil Telmányi brought about a further year's tuition with him after which Holst went on to Germany to study with Hess. He was only 24 when he was appointed leader of the Berlin Philharmonic Orchestra under Furtwängler; he stayed for eight years.

In 1931 Holst accepted an invitation for a professorship at the Royal Manchester College of Music, a position held by his teacher Willy Hess some 30 years before. He spent the next 14 years teaching and playing in concerts throughout the British Isles. His performance of the Sibelius concerto under Sir Thomas Beecham was regarded as one of the finest at the time and he also gave the first performance of the Walton Violin Concerto – originally written for Heifetz – with the Royal Philharmonic Orchestra conducted by the composer.

In 1945, Holst came south to take up a professorship at the Royal College of Music in London, where he stayed until 1954. During this time he figured prominently in the musical life of the capital, not only as a respected teacher but as a soloist and leader of the Philharmonia String Quartet, which he had formed in 1941 at Walter Legge's instigation to record for Columbia; his associates were Ernest Element (second violin), Herbert Downes (viola) and Anthony Pini (cello). The recordings he made of the Beethoven 'Archduke' Trio with Solomon as pianist and Pini on cello remained a bestseller for some time.

Holst returned to Denmark in 1954 to teach at the Royal Danish Conservatory in Copenhagen; he also spent three years in Japan giving masterclasses at the Tokyo University of the Arts. The outstanding feature of Holst's playing was his full tone which he achieved through a strong and steady bow arm, often described as 'vigorous'. He retained his physical and mental powers well into old age and played the Sibelius concerto without difficulty at his 80th birthday concert. Even more remarkable was that, as an octogenarian he had no intention of retiring and in 1988 he asked Herbert Downes to join him in the Mozart Sinfonia Concertante (K.364/320d) at a concert in Copenhagen to celebrate his 90th birthday; Downes, who was then 82, retired and living quietly in the country, declined the invitation.

Yet another violinist associated with Manchester was Leonard Hirsch (1902–95). He was born in Dublin and had his first lessons from a local teacher; at 17 he entered the Royal Manchester College of Music under Brodsky, with whom he studied for eight years. He joined the Hallé Orchestra under Hamilton Harty when he was 19 and graduated to become both leader and soloist. Harty, himself an excellent pianist, often joined members of the Hirsch String Quartet that Hirsch had founded in 1925.

Hirsch came south in 1936 to lead the BBC Empire Orchestra until it was disbanded at the outbreak of the Second World War. During the war, Hirsch pioneered the idea of giving concerts in air-raid shelters, often giving as many as three in one evening. He also became leader of the RAF Symphony Orchestra and succeeded in raising the standards by enlisting a number of famous musicians. They made tours throughout the UK and the USA; in 1945 they played for Winston Churchill, Joseph Stalin and Harry Truman at the Potsdam Conference. After the war, Hirsch led the Philharmonia for a further four years, but left to devote more time to his increasingly active solo career. In addition to leading the Hirsch Quartet, he also directed his own Hirsch Chamber Players. His playing was stylish and unmannered. He made a number of recordings, mainly with the quartet.

In demand as a teacher, Hirsch coached the string section of the National Youth Orchestra from 1948 to 1966, and, in 1961, he became the first musical director of the newly formed BBC Training Orchestra in Bristol. He shared the view of many of his colleagues that too much emphasis was placed on London, and for a time he settled in the west country with the aim of founding a centre of musical excellence that would attract students away from the metropolis, where everything was more competitive and expensive. Few would have risked such a venture, but Hirsch was a man of wisdom and vision and his risk paid off handsomely.

As a professor at the Royal College of Music from 1964 until 1979, Hirsch was clearly in his element. His ability to teach and work with young people was legendary. He was exceptionally astute in spotting young talent and had a genius for nurturing it. Korched Gruenberg, a pupil for some years, recalls that she and her fellow students enjoyed their lessons immensely: 'He was always so cheerful and understanding. He knew that youngsters can't always be on top of their problems and made allowances for this. He was the most supportive and communicative teacher I have ever known.'[2] Hirsch's colleague, Yfrah Neaman, confirmed this view: 'His enduring creativity, which he could exercise in a remarkable way, enabled him to bring out the very best in his students. I have never known anyone who could instil musicianship in the way that Leonard did.'[3]

Herman Krebbers was born in Hengelo (The Netherlands) in 1923, the son of an amateur violinist who played for the silent films. He had his first lessons when he was five from a good local teacher who, he says, 'had the wisdom to know when to send me off to a more advanced teacher'.[4] When he was ten, his family made sacrifices to send him to the Amsterdam Music Lyceum to study with Oskar Back who had been a pupil of both Ysaÿe and Thomson. In 1950, he was appointed co-leader of The Hague Philharmonic Orchestra with Theo Olof (b. 1924), who had remained a close friend since they were students. As well as being appointed leader of the Concertgebouw Orchestra and the Amsterdam Chamber Orchestra in 1962, Krebbers made solo appearances and was violinist in the Guarneri Trio; he also held teaching posts at the Sweelinck Conservatory in Amsterdam and the Robert Schumann Institute in Düsseldorf.

Then, in 1979, his life changed overnight. He was about to embark upon a solo tour of Australia when he was involved in a boating accident. Even the most experienced medical experts told him he would never play again. Committed as ever to his art, Krebbers decided he must turn this negative experience into a positive one. He revised his repertoire and discovered new ideas and new ways of approaching everything. Although he could not play his violin, he continued to teach his students. Because he could not play along with them, he acted as their eyes and ears. He sat on the juries of the Queen Elisabeth Concours, the Sibelius, the Carl Flesch and many other competitions; in 1995 he had the pleasure of sitting on the jury of the Herman Krebbers Competition in Maastricht. When Krebbers returned to playing six and a half years after his accident, many said he was playing better than ever. But long experience in his profession had taught him that it would be prudent not to return to an active stage career.

The name of Alberto Lysy is automatically associated with the International Menuhin Music Academy at Gstaad in Switzerland, of which he is director, and the celebrated Camerata Lysy which he founded in 1965. What is less well known is that Lysy played a Paganini concerto at the age of nine and could easily have followed a career as a soloist. Lysy was born in Buenos Aires in 1935, and had his first lessons from Ljerko Spiller, 'a remarkable teacher' to whom he owes his exacting standards in musicianship and his love of chamber music.

In 1955 Lysy won a prize in the Queen Elisabeth Concours. Menuhin was on the jury and afterwards told the young man that although he felt he had little to teach him personally, he could meet other musicians and broaden his horizons if he would join him at Gstaad. This was a watershed in Lysy's life. 'For the first time I met a great artist who said: "Try my way of playing but if you think your way is better don't just imitate me".'[5] Menuhin was anxious that Lysy should benefit from a wider influence, so he sent him to Budapest to study chamber music with Leo Weiner (1885–1960) and to Ede Zathureczki, successor to Hubay. Lysy also went to New York for a short period of study with Galamian.

Menuhin became more than a mentor to Lysy; a firm friendship developed and they travelled a great deal together: 'We would discuss technical problems of the Bach solo sonatas even in the railway carriage. It was not a case of just playing to him occasionally and then getting a few comments. He went into the minutest problems of technique and interpretation. I was living as a son in his family, playing and growing up with Menuhin's own children.'[6]

Menuhin's choice of Lysy as director was a wise one. A critic wrote in 1980: 'Alberto Lysy again proved at the Gstaad Festival concerts that he stands in the very front rank of the international élite of violinists, and year by year his musical personality becomes more and more exciting.'[7]

Lysy has strong ideas on teaching and is very much against teachers who have no set principles and only follow their instincts; he says: 'A young person is mixed up and needs guidance on definite lines. One must have a firm direction to follow and that should become one's personality as a violinist.'[8]

The Menuhin Music Academy and the Camerata Lysy are integrated: students of the Academy are also members of the Camerata. During the summer they give concerts throughout Saanenland, in village halls and churches in outlying villages, providing ample opportunities for the students to perform, often as soloists. The Camerata has become so popular that they are now invited to play in European festivals and throughout the world, but Lysy is wary of allowing the ensemble to become too commercial. 'We remain friends, play chamber music for the sheer joy of it and study together.'[9]

Katò Havas, born in Kezdivasarhely, Hungary, in 1920, has made a considerable impact as a violin teacher. But through her 'New Approach' she has reached out more widely by addressing the problems confronting all performing musicians. She has published many books and in one of her most popular, *Stage Fright*, she tackles the causes, effects and cure of the condition that has tormented the public performer from time immemorial. She maintains that the causes of stage fright are physical, mental and social. She teaches special exercises to overcome the main difficulties, maintaining that *anyone* can be cured provided they follow the training.

Katò Havas played the violin from early childhood and later studied with Imre Waldbaur (1892–1953), Antal Molnar and Zoltán Kodály at the Franz Liszt Academy in Budapest. She made her recital debut at Carnegie Hall in 1939, which was followed by concert tours throughout the USA. Her 'New Approach' grew out of her own battles with mental stress and physical tensions. From this time she devoted herself to teaching, founding and directing summer schools in Purbeck and Oxford, where she now lives. Menuhin endorsed her system wholeheartedly and, in 1974, wrote her a letter praising *Stage Fright*: 'It is the most realistic and practical approach imaginable. It stresses the real reasons and not the false ones, and gives in the most honest and lucid form the essential requirements of violin technique, violin playing and music-making. It is a book that should be worth its weight in gold to every student and many a performer.'[10]

## Notes

1. Flesch, *Memoirs*, p. 267.
2. Quoted from interview, M.C.
3. Quoted from interview, M.C.
4. *The Strad*, August 1995, p. 779.
5–9. *The Strad*, January 1980, p. 684.
10. Letter from Yehudi Menuhin to Katò Havas, 20 June 1974.

# 39  The Galamian Touch

Unquestionably, Ivan Galamian made a tremendous contribution to twentieth-century violin playing. Some found him a hard taskmaster while others worshipped him for his generosity. But his students all had one thing in common – they each developed their own musical personality – the hallmark of the great teacher.

Jaime Laredo was born in Bolivia in 1941 and, when his family moved to the USA in 1948, he became a pupil of Gingold at Cleveland. He entered the Curtis Institute at 14 to complete his studies with Galamian. Throughout his student years, Laredo gave occasional concerts and also made a successful tour of South America including his native Bolivia. In 1959, he gave a recital in Washington, DC, which alerted the critics to his exceptional talent; as a result he was recommended for entry to the Queen Elisabeth Concours in Brussels, carrying off the first prize at the age of 17, the youngest ever to win it.

However, his success in Brussels thrust him into the solo arena before he was ready. After his debut recital at Carnegie Hall that same year, the critics were equivocal: some praised his remarkable gifts while others felt he had much to learn. In discussing this particular concert, he said that he was more nervous after he won the competition than beforehand because everyone expected so much of him. Nonetheless, when he visited Bolivia he was given a hero's welcome and they even created a postage stamp in his honour, writing his name in *solfege* ('la re do').

In 1961, Laredo joined Serkin's group at Marlboro where he concentrated on chamber music and subsequently toured with Music from Marlboro, contributing virtuoso solo performances. In 1973, Laredo was engaged as leader of the Chamber Music Society of Lincoln Center and later established a trio with his cellist wife, Sharon Robinson, and the pianist Joseph Kalichstein. Boris Schwarz noted that, 'having tempered his virtuoso instincts, he had become a mature and beautifully balanced musician'.[1] These qualities are what Josef Gingold recognised when, in 1994, he appointed Laredo as his successor as honorary chairman and president of the Indianapolis International Violin Competition.

Another violinist from the same stable is Miriam Fried, who was born in Romania in 1946. Her family emigrated to Israel where she became a pupil of Alice Fenyves at the Rubin Academy in Tel Aviv, before going on to study with Gingold at Bloomington, Indiana. 'Gingold directed me in a way that I never thought about before. He made me so much aware of sounds. That is what the violin is all about.

I saw exactly how it differs from the piano [Fried's first instrument] and where its possibilities are. I am afraid I had neglected that before and he really opened up a new dimension for me.'[2]

Fried's next move was to New York to study with Galamian at Juilliard. Here again, she met progress. During her time there, Fried won her first major competition, the Paganini Contest in Genoa in 1968; the following year she made her solo debut at Carnegie Hall, with encouraging response from the critics. Then in 1971 she not only won the *grand prix* in the Queen Elisabeth Concours in Brussels, but became the first woman to win.

Fried has gone on to carve out an international career as soloist, recitalist, chamber musician and teacher. On the platform she is very relaxed and confesses never to be nervous, which may explain why she appears to be oblivious of her audience. Her playing is intense and very personal, and her tone warm and mellow, but never sugary. Fried has also made many recordings which include all the Bach solo sonatas and partitas. Her recording of the Sibelius concerto won a special award in Finland and sold over 25,000 copies. Teaching, for her, is also an important musical activity. She has been a professor of violin at Indiana University at Bloomington since 1986 and has taught at many summer schools including the Academia Chigiana in Siena.

Itzhak Perlman was born in Tel Aviv in 1945, the son of a Polish immigrant barber. Music was always present in the home and he cannot recall a time when he did not have the ambition to play the violin. At the age of four, Itzhak contracted polio which resulted in the paralysis of his lower limbs. However, the illness and a year's convalescence left his ambition unchanged. He took his first violin lessons at the Tel Aviv Music Academy and by the age of ten was a veteran performer.

Perlman insists he was not a child prodigy and that no pressure was ever exerted upon him either by parents or teacher. He loved the violin and enjoyed performing. It never occurred to him that there was anything unusual in a physically handicapped child seeking a career as a violinist.

When he was 13, Itzhak went to New York City to appear on the Ed Sullivan Show, leading to a three-month tour with the 'Ed Sullivan Caravan of Stars'. Shunted around the ballrooms of luxury hotels, a bunch of gifted children played their party pieces to a succession of weary audiences who had wined and dined too well. Their dressing room was the kitchen, where they sat until well after midnight, awaiting their call. Afterwards, Itzhak decided to stay on in New York, and he was awarded scholarships by the Juilliard School and the American–Israeli Foundation to study with Galamian and his assistant Dorothy DeLay.

On 5 March 1963, Perlman made his debut at Carnegie Hall, playing the Wieniawski Concerto in F sharp minor with the National Orchestral Association, under John Barnett. The concert took place during a newspaper printers' strike and, as a result, no reviews were published.

A year later, after winning the Leventritt Competition at Carnegie Hall, Perlman was engaged for a series of concerts with leading American orchestras, and his old mentor, Ed Sullivan, invited him back onto his show. Sol Hurok, his newly acquired agent, sent him on a coast-to-coast tour which took him to 50 major American cities. He was acclaimed, not only as an exciting new talent, but for his ebullient personality.

In January 1965, Perlman returned to his native Israel for a series of eight concerts. He had left as a talented youngster and now returned a fully fledged virtuoso. For him, the most emotional experience was when he went on stage at the Mann Auditorium in Tel Aviv, to play with the Israel Philharmonic Orchestra. The audience gave him a deafening welcome. 'Every kid in Israel dreams that one day he's going to play with the IPO . . . and then the dream comes true . . . .'3

In May of that same year, Perlman appeared at Philharmonic Hall, with the New York Philharmonic Orchestra under William Steinberg. He was recalled to the stage five times. By the age of 20, he had proved himself an artist of the front rank. When he appeared as soloist with the Detroit Symphony Orchestra under Sixten Ehrling, at the opening concert of the Carnegie Festival, playing the Sibelius concerto, Howard Klein wrote in the *New York Times*:

> Truly a sensation violinist. . . . The tone was voluminous-warm, throbbing and dead in tune. The octave playing was only surpassed by the way Mr Perlman whistled through the short section of the harmonics in the last movement . . . . Listening to him play produced joy on every level – technical, musical and above all the human. For the burly young man has that extra quality that raises music above technicalities and that is heart.'4

Perlman first visited Britain in March 1968 and made his London debut at the Royal Festival Hall playing the Tchaikovsky concerto with the London Symphony Orchestra. In 1968 he toured Britain with the Israel Philharmonic Orchestra and, in August, joined the cellist Jacqueline du Pré and Daniel Barenboim in a highly successful series of South Bank Summer Concerts. It was also at this time that he gave his first recital with Vladimir Ashkenazy – a partnership that has endured both personally and professionally over the years.

Perlman finds an audience stimulating and does not generally feel nervous. Curiously enough, the microphone makes him nervous, in spite of his regular recording schedule. He finds that playing without an audience is always a problem, and in recording sessions it is difficult for him not to fall into a trance.

He recalls the tour of 1975 when he and Pinchas Zukerman travelled all over Europe recording and filming their performances of violin duos. These two are not only colleagues but close friends and it was a pleasurable experience. 'The formality just goes out of the window . . . no keeping up appearances. Especially with Pinky, we know exactly what each one wants to do. We do it on the spur of the moment.'5 Here he is putting into practice one of his teacher's firm principles. 'The best performance always partakes of the nature of an improvisation in which the artist is moved by the music he plays, forgets about technique, and abandons himself with improvisatory freedom to the inspiration of the moment.'[6]

Perlman's impeccable left-hand technique and his bow hold, with fingers curved in a natural, relaxed way, ready to spring into action for every kind of bowing, are a source of amazement even to orchestral players who observe him at close proximity. This technique clearly has its effect. 'There is a joy and bounce to his playing that had oldtimers at Carnegie Hall reaching back in their memories to the days of the youthful Heifetz to find a parallel', wrote William Bender in 1964.[7] And this 'joy and bounce' are also the key elements to Perlman as a man. He has ignored his disability and reached the heights of his profession.

'He could be described as a violinist born; one of those rare musicians who play as if by light or nature, without effort. His violin seemed part of him',[8] wrote Joan Chissell in *The Times*, after the 21-year-old Zukerman's London debut recital at the Queen Elizabeth Hall in August 1969. He was accompanied by Daniel Barenboim in works by Mozart, Beethoven, Brahms and Schoenberg.

Pinchas Zukerman was born in a village outside Tel Aviv in 1948, the son of a fiddler-cum-clarinettist. Before he was six, he had mastered the recorder and clarinet well enough to accompany his father and the *ad hoc* ensembles who toured the hotels at weddings and other social events. At six he took up the violin and received his first lessons from his father. At eight he was admitted to both the Tel Aviv Academy of Music and the Israel Conservatory. He was assigned to Ilona Feher, who had herself been a pupil of Hubay in Budapest. He became her prize pupil and, in addition to his lessons at the Academy, spent many hours each day at her house playing duets and chamber music.

In 1961, Casals and Stern visited Israel and heard him play. They were greatly impressed and Stern recommended that he should go to New York for further training, and agreed to become his legal guardian. Although Stern was never his teacher, he kept a vigilant eye on his *protégé*. Stern arranged for Zukerman to live with the parents of the pianist Eugène Istomin. It was the Istomins who abbreviated 'Pinchas' to 'Pinky', the name by which he is now universally known.

His studies with Galamian at Juilliard were underwritten by the American–Israeli Cultural Foundation. He studied for five years with Galamian during a vintage period with Perlman and Kyung-Wha Chung sitting beside him on the front desks of the student orchestra. In 1967 Zukerman shared the Leventritt award with Kyung-Wha Chung. This led to a number of concerts and recitals in many of the leading cities of North America. Audiences responded warmly to this gifted young player who seemed more than able to tackle anything on the violin, and whose superb tone was being compared to all the great names in history. A year later, CBS signed Zukerman up on an exclusive recording contract. His first recording – of the Tchaikovsky concerto – was made in Britain, with the London Symphony Orchestra under Antal Dorati.

Zukerman's New York debut took place at the Philharmonic Hall in February 1969. He played the Mendelssohn concerto with the New York Philharmonic Orchestra under Bernstein. The *New York Times* tells us that the 20-year-old 'tossed off the event as it were a nursery rhyme' and praised his technique. 'His bowing and fingering are perfectly in hand and he negotiates the most difficult passages with ease. His tone is not huge but it is flexible and has a pleasing, poetic quality.'[9] That spring, Zukerman first appeared before the British public at the Brighton Festival. He and Daniel Barenboim gave a violin and piano recital at the Royal Pavilion, and later were joined by Jacqueline du Pré in a performance of the Brahms Double Concerto, with Barenboim conducting the New Philharmonia Orchestra.

Barenboim and Zukerman had first met in New York only a few months before. Barenboim had conducted when Zukerman was the soloist with the English Chamber Orchestra at a Carnegie Hall concert. They were so impressed with his playing of Mozart's Violin Concerto No. 4 in D major K218, that they invited him to repeat it at the Queen Elizabeth Hall in London. This association led to a close friendship which also includes Perlman. Together with Jacqueline du Pré they have made some memorable music – including the 1969 film of the Schubert 'Trout' Quintet, with Zukerman playing the viola, Zubin Mehta in a less familiar role on the double bass, and Daniel Barenboim as pianist.

Zukerman has the physique of an athlete and an inexhaustible supply of energy to match. His friend and colleague Christopher Nupen describes him as 'quite the most spiritually and materially generous person I know'.[10] His tremendous sense of fun sometimes gives the impression that he is happy-go-lucky: he may not take himself very seriously, but those close to him know that music is quite another matter.

Kyung-Wha Chung was born in Seoul, South Korea in 1948, the daughter of a lawyer. She is one of seven children, six of whom are trained musicians now pursuing careers in the West. Kyung took piano lessons when she was four but found no affinity with the instrument. She played all her exercises by ear and gave such good performances that nobody suspected that she had not learned to read the notes. She was then given a small violin on which she proceeded to teach herself. From the first sound of the bow on the string, 'I knew it would be my life'.[11]

At nine, Kyung played the Mendelssohn concerto with the Seoul Philharmonic Orchestra. She then passed through the hands of at least six teachers and, at 12, undertook a successful concert tour of Japan, sponsored by the Korean government. In 1961 her parents took her to the USA, where she had private lessons with Galamian and, subsequently, won a full scholarship to Juilliard.

Unashamedly a performer, Chung has no interest in teaching. She says: 'I have always loved audiences, and the more people there are the more exciting it is.'[12] In 1967, when she was 19, Chung shared the first prize in the Leventritt Competition with Zukerman. Shortly afterwards she made her debut with the New York Philharmonic Orchestra. Offers of engagements came thick and fast, but Chung did not feel that she was ready to embark upon an international career. Instead she decided to study for a further year.

In 1970, Chung came to Europe with one engagement in her diary. It was to play the Tchaikovsky concerto in a Charity Gala Concert with the London Symphony

Orchestra under André Previn at the Royal Festival Hall on 13 May. She walked onto the stage completely unknown; she left to a standing ovation.

Critics tend not to review such concerts for fear of causing embarrassment to artists who are providing their services free. Gillian Widdecombe, of the *Financial Times*, broke the unwritten law because it was 'an event of such musical excitement that it sincerely deserved more than the compliment of a full house and fulsome applause; more even than the compliment of the London Symphony Orchestra glued to their chairs in praise at the end'.

> I doubt whether Heifetz ever played the notes more accurately, and it's certainly a long time since Oistrakh or Stern played nearly as many. But what was so magnificent and moving about this performance was not its proud virtuosity, nor the vitality and intensity in the first movement, nor even the ruthless dominance Miss Chung exerted over every awkward corner of this unwieldy work. No, these points were marvellous features, but even more rare and rewarding was the expressive force of her performance: sweet, silken phrasing, soft and tender in the slow movement; beautiful playing, immeasurably mature.[13]

Within three days of her spectacular success at the Festival Hall, Chung was booked for 30 more concerts throughout Britain. There were also five BBC TV appearances and a concert tour of the Far East with Previn and the London Symphony Orchestra. Edward Greenfield, music critic of the *Guardian*, accompanied the tour. He tells a story that reveals the rapport that exists between the tiny virtuoso and an all-male orchestra. At a rehearsal of the Tchaikovsky, Chung was ready, tense and poised. The first violins began to play the introduction – not to the Tchaikovsky, but the Mendelssohn. Chung's lightning reflexes made her whip her violin under her chin, ready for the much earlier attack. Then she realised they were playing a trick on her. 'She stamped her foot in giggling anger, irritated to have been taken in but obviously delighted that she could inspire such joke-playing from the LSO.'[14]

Chung's repertory includes most of the standard works, many of which she learnt long before her American debut. But there are some eminent additions which show that she not only has the courage of her own choice, but can also meet a challenge with impunity. André Previn persuaded her to learn the Walton concerto. At first she was not happy with the idea; Chung, with characteristic humility, was not sure that she could do it justice. Now she finds it a 'rich and rewarding work'.[15] Chung's recording of this concerto, coupled with the Stravinsky confirms this opinion. Another work with which Chung has become closely identified is the Elgar concerto. Her recording of it, released in 1977, was exceptionally well received.

At first sight, Kyung-Wha Chung appears deceptively fragile. But after minutes in her company, one is aware of her great reserves of mental and physical strength. Highly disciplined, she aims at perfection in every aspect of her playing. She is a born performer and as soon as she appears, she has her audience in the palm of her hand.

She has a warmth of personality that is the hallmark of the communicator – Kreisler had it, and so did Menuhin.

Since the 1970s the sisters Ani and Ida Kavafian have brought considerable colour to the concert platform. Of Armenian parentage, they were born in Istanbul – Ani in 1948 and Ida in 1952 – and brought to the USA as children. They both had lessons from Mischa Mischakoff in Detroit and completed their studies at Juilliard – Ani with Galamian and Galimir, Ida with Galamian and Oscar Shumsky (1917–2000). Both sisters have had wide experience as soloists and chamber music players, and their duo recitals have gained them a wide following. They have a platform charisma which endears them to their audiences but, ultimately, it is their stylish playing and fine musicianship which makes their performances so compelling. Ida Kavafian was a member of the celebrated Beaux Arts Trio from 1992 until 1998.

Ruth Waterman was one of the few Galamian students who apparently derived little benefit from his method. Waterman was born in 1947 in Harrogate, Yorkshire, into a family of professional musicians over several generations. As a small child, she learnt both violin and piano, and at nine she attended the Royal Northern College of Music, first as a pupil of Endre Wolf and, later, György Pauk. She was 20 when she went to New York to study for two years with Galamian at the Juilliard. 'He was not what I would call a sophisticated musician. His main effect on me came as a result of the sheer immensity of his repertoire demands for each week's lesson. I was simply shocked into practising much harder than I ever had!'[16] Waterman is an experienced teacher herself, having held a professorship at the City University of New York and the Royal Academy of Music in London, and has given masterclasses in both the UK and the USA.

Waterman came to the public eye for the first time in 1966 when she was 19 and was invited by Yehudi Menuhin to step in, at 48 hours' notice, for an indisposed Milstein at the Bath Festival. She had already attracted national attention when she won third prize in the BBC Violin Competition the previous year, while at the same time having won a place at Cambridge University to read economics. When concert engagements began to emerge in a steady stream, she reluctantly decided to forgo Cambridge. However, she retained her lively curiosity in matters of the mind which led her to two main areas of concern: the process of interpretation, and the stylistic performance of Bach on the modern violin.

The experience of performing Bach's Brandenburg Concerto No. 5 with Rosalyn Tureck in New York's Central Park, in 1967, encouraged her to continue questioning the way violinists approach Bach. Having performed the preludes and fugues on the piano herself, she had long been puzzled by the discrepancy of stylistic awareness between keyboard and string players. Waterman feels she did not receive any help from Galamian in this area. She recalls that Galamian threatened to fail her if she played a gavotte 'anything like a gavotte', but decided it would never happen again.

Besides her solo engagements and teaching, Waterman has become known for her dynamic concert format, *Music Talks TM*, in which she combines performance with an exploration of the music – in effect, drawing listeners behind the notes. She has presented programmes in this fashion on the complete cycles of Bach, Beethoven, Schubert and Schumann sonatas, and the positive audience response is a clear indication that she has discovered an area that no one else inhabits at present.

> I am passionate about the performer's responsibility to the composer, as well as the audience, to bring the music to life by delving into stylistic performance practices in order to uncover the emotional character of each work, whether Mozart or Gershwin. My main joy lies in the search for the 'voice' of each piece and finally feeling absorbed into it. This process can be taught, and must be taught, if we are to emerge from the rather distressing current situation of fairly homogenised playing.[17]

The Korean Young-Uck Kim was born in Seoul in 1947, the son of a physician who was one of the first to practise 'Western' medicine. His mother entertained every Western musician who visited the city, one of whom was Rudolf Serkin, who suggested that the 12-year-old should go to the USA to study. Two years later, his teacher, Sascha Jacobson (b. 1897), at the Music Academy of the West in Santa Barbara, California, suggested he study with Galamian at the Curtis Institute. Kim studied with Galamian for eight years. 'I remember once having problems practising which I confided to him. He got me out of school and took me home with him, where I stayed three or four days. I lived in his house and practised in a little room at the back. He used to stop me from time to time to offer encouragement.'[18]

Kim made his concert debut at 15, while still a student of Galamian. Eugene Ormandy heard about him from members of the Philadelphia Orchestra and invited him to appear on a television programme with them, sharing the solo spotlight with André Watts, then a promising young pianist. The following year, he appeared with Leonard Bernstein in another programme, which was followed by offers to play in at least 100 concerts. At the time, Kim felt totally confused: 'I didn't know whether to say yes or no. . . . Frankly, I don't see how anyone in his teens is emotionally ready for the life of a touring musician. It's pushing a child into an unreal world and trying to convince that it's real. I kept playing but I felt that this had become my life without my having had anything to do with it.'[19]

By the mid-1970s Kim began to feel very unsure about his approach to performing. In retrospect, he thinks this was caused by the fact that he had been continually alone both emotionally and musically, lacking direct contact with any great artist who might have inspired him. By sheer perseverance he overcame this problem and made a successful debut recital in New York in 1976; his career has since gained momentum, both as a soloist and a chamber musician, with the trio formed in 1980 with pianist Emanuel Ax and cellist Yo-Yo Ma. He also gives sonata recitals with his close friend Peter Serkin, whom he first met at the Curtis Institute when they were both teenagers.

The Romanian Eugene Sarbu was born in 1950 in the small town of Pietrari at the foot of the Carpathian mountains. His father was a philosophy professor and good amateur violinist, who gave him his first lessons. Sarbu went on to study with Saul Nachmanovici (1899–1987), a pupil of Auer at St Petersburg and, at 13, won his first national competition; it was relayed on television which immediately made him into a household name. Two years later, he made his official debut with the Bucharest Radio and Television Orchestra, after which he was regarded as Romania's rising-star violinist.

Bucharest in the late 1960s was enjoying a cultural exposure far in excess of any other Soviet satellite state. The Enescu International Festivals attracted artists like Stern, Menuhin, Rubinstein and Karajan. Sarbu played for many of them; David Oistrakh, who had heard him when he was nine years old, had already offered to take him to Moscow as his pupil. At the time Sarbu's parents thought him too young, but in 1968, when Oistrakh renewed his offer – with a firm promise of a scholarship at the Central School of Music in Moscow – they accepted. However, at the eleventh hour, the Czech uprising intervened and Sarbu's plans were cancelled; instead, he entered the National Conservatory of Music (now the Bucharest Academy of Music) to study with Ionel Geanta (1913–80).

It was at this time that Menuhin came to Bucharest with the Bath Festival Orchestra and Sarbu was chosen to play with them. Acting upon Menuhin's recommendation, he won a scholarship to study with Galamian at the Curtis Institute. 'His [Galamian's] approach to violin technique was so logical – in other words, pure common sense. If there was not a valid reason for a particular fingering, he would not do it.'[20] In 1972 Galamian suggested that Sarbu should have a period of study with Milstein. Since childhood Sarbu had looked on Milstein as a god, so he was delighted. Sarbu remembers him with admiration. 'As a teacher he was very charismatic and had an almost magnetic power. I learned so much about freedom of phrasing and expression. He would say that Auer had always told his pupils: "You must be yourself." '[21] Sarbu went on to win prizes in almost every major competition in Europe and North America, and in 1978 he won the Carl Flesch Competition in London, where he also took the Audience prize. Two months later he won the Paganini Competition in Genoa.

Today, Sarbu is concerned with a project intended to benefit the younger generation of violinists in his country. Since Romania regained her freedom, Sarbu has been involved in a world campaign to help the country by giving benefit concerts for the Bucharest Academy of Music Scholarship Fund, established in 1995. For 20 years Sarbu was not allowed to perform in his own country, being a 'self-exiled person' under the dictatorial Ceausescu régime. When he returned to Romania in 1990, he was given a hero's welcome. The present scheme is a way of repaying his country for their loyalty and affection. In February 1996, the Bucharest Academy made Sarbu an honorary member of the Faculty.

The Korean Dong-Suk Kang was born in Seoul in 1954 and, at 14, was given a scholarship to study in New York with Galamian at Juilliard. He continued his lessons with him for many years after his scholarship had ended and remains grateful for the way in which this great master shaped his playing:

> He always had very good taste and was a very good person to be with. He was such an excellent guide that you never got lost on the way. When you are young the most important thing is how to play the instrument. Then you can use your equipment to express yourself. It takes time before you mature and have your own ideas, and Galamian was especially gifted in teaching how to play the violin itself. Although he could be very authoritative and demanding, I think one needs discipline.[22]

After Juilliard, Kang went on to Philadelphia, where he attended masterclasses and had lessons with Zino Francescatti at the Curtis Institute:

> In the masterclasses he was less critical than in private lessons which was good for me, because I wanted to learn something and not just be praised. The most impressive part was when I played the Beethoven concerto – he did not say anything but just picked up his fiddle and played the first ten bars or so of the first entry. He didn't *need* to say anything as he played without effort – not because it was so beautiful or technically perfect, but there was some quality which only people like Francescatti, who have been playing that concerto for 50 to 60 years, possess.[23]

Kang also had some lessons with Leonid Kogan (1924–82). Winning a prize in the Carl Flesch Competition in 1974 gave Kang a foothold in Europe. He consolidated his prospects by winning the 1976 Queen Elisabeth Concours. Menuhin, who was on the jury, said: 'He was the first to play and five days and 12 violinists later, his sound and his refinement were still in our ears and hearts. He has infinite subtlety in his playing, great precision and elegance.'[24]

### Notes

1. Schwarz, *Great Masters of the Violin*, p. 579.
2. Quoted from interview, M.C.
3. *Violin Society of USA Journal*, Spring 1977, iii, pp. 2 & 21.
4. *New York Times*, 30 October 1965.
5. Quoted from interview, M.C.
6. Galamian, *Principles of Violin Playing and Teaching*, p. 7.
7. *New York Herald Tribune*, 30 October 1964.
8. *The Times*, 25 August 1969.
9. *New York Times*, 6 February 1969.
10. Quoted from interview, M.C.
11–12. Quoted from interview, M.C.
13. Gillian Widdecombe, *Financial Times*, 14 May 1970.
14. Edward Greenfield, *Guardian*, 11 June 1971.

15. Quoted from interview, M.C.
16–17. Quoted from interview, M.C.
18–19. *The Strad*, April 1988, p. 310.
20–21. *The Strad*, April 1997, p. 372.
22. *The Strad*, February 1988, pp. 111–13.
23. *The Strad*, November 1997, p. 593.
24. Tennant publicity brochure.

# 40　The British Phenomenon

The Anglo-Saxon virtuoso violinist is a rare bird and only a handful of names have survived the centuries. We have already touched upon John Banister and Henry Holmes. John Dunn (1866–1940), who studied under Henry Shradieck at the Leipzig Conservatory, achieved considerable fame as a soloist and was a brilliant exponent of Paganini's works. Albert Sammons, born 20 years later, was the only English violinist until recently whose talents were considered to reach international standards.

One of Sammons' pupils, the New Zealander Alan Loveday, was a professor at the Royal College of Music in London. Born in Palmerston North, New Zealand in 1928, the son of a professional violinist, Loveday began to play when he was three on an eighth-size fiddle made especially for him. He received his first instruction from his father. At nine he played for the members of the Budapest String Quartet when they were touring New Zealand. So impressed were they by the child's talent that they gave a benefit concert at his home town to start a fund to finance his studies in Britain. Sammons heard the 11-year-old boy soon after his arrival in 1939, and predicted a bright future. Loveday became a private pupil of Sammons and later continued under his care at the RCM.

When in August 1946 Loveday gave a Prom performance of the Tchaikovsky concerto, *The Strad* critic commented on his effortlessly 'beautiful velvety tone' and his pure intonation. Loveday's playing has always been distinguished by his ability to maintain this purity, even at speed in the highest positions.

Another pupil of Albert Sammons who made a significant contribution to music making in the UK over several decades was Hugh Bean (1929–2003), born in Beckenham (Kent). His father, a marine engineer, was also an amateur violinist and as a child he was fascinated, not by the sound, but by the shape of the instrument. When his father found his small son trying to play his fiddle flat on his back, he decided it was time he gave him some lessons. Hugh made good progress and, at nine, won a prize in the Croydon Festival. The adjudicator suggested that he have some lessons with Albert Sammons, and their teacher–pupil relationship developed into a close friendship lasting until Sammons' death in 1957.

At 14, Bean won a scholarship to the Royal College of Music, where he studied violin and piano – continuing with Sammons – and later led both college orchestras, alternating with Alan Loveday and Tessa Robbins. He also carried off both the Principal Prize for Violin and the Queen's Prize. Sammons had given him a thorough grounding in the Elgar concerto; Bean's own score is very precious because it contains all Sammons' own markings for fingerings and bowings – doubly important because Sammons was Elgar's own personal favourite exponent.

Bean's first professional engagement in 1950 was with the Harvey Phillips String Orchestra, and, two years later, he won a Boise Foundation Travelling Award that enabled him to spend a year at the Brussels Conservatoire under André Gertler; he took home a double Premier Prix for solo and chamber music performance.

Bean had been playing for some time in the second violin section of the Philharmonia Orchestra when, in 1955, he was promoted to the position of co-leader to Manoug Parikian, before taking over as leader from 1957 to 1967. During his years with the orchestra, Bean enjoyed the experience of working with some of the world's greatest conductors and soloists. He admitted that he approached his first session with Karajan with some trepidation, but soon realised that the maestro was a good psychologist: 'After a brief "good morning", he totally ignored me for the rest of the session thus giving me time to play myself in.'[1] His first encounter with Klemperer was in sharp contrast; 'Although he was equally kind, I was summoned to his suite at the Hyde Park Hotel for what seemed a very long chat, after which I played him the solo fiddle part in the Mozart Serenata Notturno which we were to rehearse the following day. He said nothing, but apparently all was to his satisfaction because I subsequently led the orchestra under him for the next ten years.'[2]

From 1967 to 1969 Bean was co-leader of the BBC Symphony Orchestra, but resigned in order to devote more time to chamber music and solo work. He had already formed the Music Group of London in 1966 with the pianist David Parkhouse, cellist Eileen Croxford, horn-player Alan Civil and clarinettist Bernard Walton, and the Boise Trio with Croxford and Parkhouse.

In 1969, he was invited by Sir Adrian Boult to perform the Elgar concerto at the Three Choirs Festival in Worcester, which was broadcast by the BBC. The response from listeners was so enthusiastic that he repeated the performance several times with other leading British orchestras and conductors. His recording of the Elgar with the Liverpool Philharmonic conducted by Sir Charles Groves for EMI was reissued in the early 1990s on CD. Another classic reissue was Bean's recording of Vaughan Williams' The Lark Ascending, which has long been regarded as one of the finest performances of the work, demonstrating perfectly the lyrical feeling and warmth of expression by which his playing is distinguished.

In 1989 Bean returned as co-leader of the Philharmonia and, in 1995, he was made Leader Emeritus. He was appointed professor at the Royal College of Music in 1954, made a Fellow of the RCM and awarded the Cobbett Gold Medal in 1968, and retired some 40 years later.

The most phenomenal British violin talent of the mid-twentieth century must surely have been Ralph Holmes (1937–87), whose career was cut short by cancer. In 1966, he made his solo debut at Carnegie Hall, playing Vaughan Williams' The Lark Ascending and Ravel's Tzigane with the Houston Symphony Orchestra under Sir John Barbirolli.

Louis Biancolli, critic of the *World Telegram*, described him as 'that rare English phenomenon, a concert violinist to be reckoned with the upper echelon of the international string set'.[3] Holmes was born in Kent into a family where music was part of the furniture. His father, a schoolmaster, played both violin and piano, and his mother was a trained singer who relinquished her professional ambitions when she married.

In 1941, when his father was serving in the army, the four-year-old Ralph, hiding under the grand piano, tried out his father's violin. He said: 'I can remember the frustration of only being able to make scratchy noises and longed to make a beautiful sound.' Ralph's mother then bought him a small fiddle and took him to a local teacher, 'more in the interest of my father's violin than the idea that she might have a virtuoso on her hands. We hoped that by the time my father came home in a few months' time I might be able to play a scale'.[4]

When the war ended four years later, Ralph's progress was considerably in advance of the anticipated single scale. He had passed the final grade in the Associated Board examinations with the highest marks for violin playing, and had appeared in a number of local concerts.

Ralph was just eight when he began taking holiday lessons with the distinguished Canadian-born chamber musician David Martin. He was awarded a choral scholarship to the choir school of New College, Oxford, but it was not a welcome move. Although the standards of music were high and Ralph's musical education improved, he was unhappy. 'I was neither fish nor fowl and my violin practice suffered.'[5] In retrospect, Holmes felt that this incompatibility stemmed from the fact that during the war he had enjoyed an insulated existence with his mother, with regular lessons and most of his practice supervised. The sudden change to communal living was too abrupt. But matters improved when, at ten, he won a junior scholarship to the Royal Academy of Music. He was fortunate in being placed once again with David Martin. Three years later, Martin suggested that he should attend the Junior Orchestral Summer Course at Sherborne, directed by Ernest Read. Read was so taken with his playing that he invited him to perform the Mendelssohn Concerto with the Royal Philharmonic Orchestra at a children's concert in the Central Hall, Westminster. On these occasions it was customary for only one movement to be played, but Ralph was asked to play the entire concerto.

During the next two summers came the opportunity to study with Enescu in Paris. The experience proved a landmark in his musical life:

> He was a very real inspiration to me and had a profound influence upon my musical development. He helped me to understand the role of the violinist as interpreter and gave me vital help in grasping the essence of differing musical styles. Master of many languages, he would speak fluently in whatever the native tongue of his pupil and could accompany numerous concertos beautifully on the piano – naturally, from memory. And yet, with all his accomplishments, as violinist, composer, conductor, teacher, he also radiated a deep humility. A truly great man.[6]

Enescu was meticulous over fingering: 'It was particularly important in Bach, where each partita became a hobby. Enescu was insistent that in fingering the fugues one should maintain the integrity of each voice and not go careering over to other strings for odd notes. Conversely, however, he frowned upon shooting up to the top of the G string just for effect. His creed was honesty.' Holmes once recalled a lesson on Ravel's Tzigane: 'Enescu made so clear to me the comparison between the French Ravel writing in the *manner* of the gipsy idiom, and Sarasate's Zigeunerweisen where the composer was writing from the roots. Even today when I am playing any of the works that I did with Enescu, such as the Beethoven C minor sonata or the Bach unaccompanied partita, much of what he said comes winging over the years as if it had been said yesterday.'[7]

Every seat at the Wigmore Hall was sold before the doors opened for Holmes' debut recital on 29 October 1954. Gerald Moore was his 'most helpful'[8] partner at the piano. All the critics were enthusiastic. *The Times* critic judged that 'there is everything to suggest that he will end his career as one of the finest violinists this country has produced'.[9]

Inevitably, there were many forecasts as to the heights to which the young Holmes might aspire. On one occasion, Menuhin could not reach the studios in time for a rehearsal for the BBC TV programme 'Music For You'. The producer rang the Royal Academy of Music for a student to 'stand-in'. 'He needn't play much,' she said, 'just enough for the cameramen.'[10] They sent along the 18-year-old Ralph Holmes, who proceeded to play Menuhin's programme right through without batting an eyelid. Menuhin arrived during the rehearsal, but listened behind a curtain, delighted as always to discover young talent from an unexpected source. The conductor Eric Robinson's comment must have been the understatement of the year: 'Given ordinary luck, this young British violinist will become a successful concert artist.'[11]

On leaving the Academy, Holmes completed two years of national service in the Grenadier Guards. He found himself assigned to the string orchestra, playing at official functions. A special pass was issued to enable him to fulfil concert engagements, such as his first Prom with the National Youth Orchestra under Boult at which he performed Bruch's Violin Concerto No. 1. With national service behind him, and as many concert engagements as he could manage, all seemed to be set fair for the future. But in 1964 Holmes experienced a crisis. Although the critics were always kind, he himself began to have private doubts about his playing. He was particularly concerned about his bowing, but unable to address the causes. Then suddenly, in the middle of a performance of the Tchaikovsky concerto at the Albert Hall, he felt his bow arm tighten. When his vibrato also began giving him trouble, Holmes knew something was wrong. He decided to go to Galamian in New York.

The next four months were spent in an intensive period of study with Galamian who worked hard on Holmes's bowing. 'He greeted me with the news that he was going to make me my own doctor. And in the end he did.'[12] But Holmes was not readily able to change his bowgrip – understandably, when he had already been playing for 23 years. 'I realised that he was a wonderful teacher and naturally much of his general advice was invaluable, but the overall approach did not appear to be solving my particular problem.' On his return to Britain, Holmes was further discouraged to find that he was gradually returning to his old style. Then one day he tried out a beautiful Peccatte bow that belonged to friend and found he could not make it work properly:

> I knew then it was not the bow but me; I then went over everything that Galamian had taught me, analysing every detail. Suddenly I saw what he meant and in a few days I was able to put it into practice. Basically, as I saw it, was the necessity for me to make 'second nature' in the bow-hold the see-saw action of the fingers over the thumb as the bow travelled up and down the string, together with a much freer upper arm. And the vital concept of the arm as the lungs to a singer.[13]

Right up to his death, it was difficult to imagine that Holmes had ever experienced difficulty with bowing. The tone seemed to flow from an arm that could distil by instinct. His effortless technique was always subservient to the music. He made a melodic line sing like a bird, but his slashing bow-strokes as in the Ravel Tzigane or the Bartók Solo Sonata could bite with a vengeance. On the concert platform Holmes had that 'giving' quality that brought a warm response from his audience before he even played a note. He always looked as if he was enjoying himself. And yet each performance was born of a serious respect for the music itself. As one critic put it: 'At the heart of his playing was a great sense of integrity . . . no effects for the sake of effects, no extra trimmings. Always the style seemed to evolve from within the fabric.'[14]

Native British talent may be sparse, but the balance is redressed by a number of fine emigré violinists who have settled in the UK and taken out British citizenship. Three who have become known for many years as soloists and professors at the Royal Academy of Music in London, are the late Manoug Parikian, Erich Gruenberg and György Pauk.

Manoug Parikian (1920–87), was born in Mersin, Armenia (now western Turkey) but when he was a baby, his family moved to the more peaceful island of Cyprus. He had his first lessons on the violin when he was five and, at 16, was awarded a scholarship to Trinity College of Music in London to study with Louis Pecskai. His three years at college were difficult. He had come from an entirely different background, dominated by the Armenian church and Armenian culture, and London was a terrifying place to him. After he graduated another problem arose: his student visa expired and he was forced to return home to Cyprus. Then came what he described as 'four years in the wilderness' when everyone advised him to take up another job; all he wanted to do was to play the violin. After being refused many applications for a British passport, he was finally successful and, as it was then wartime, he joined ENSA and toured the Middle East giving concerts to the troops.

When the war was over, he returned to Britain for further study with Sammons. Concert-giving at that time depended upon rich patrons, so Parikian had problems breaking into the solo field. But finally, in 1947, after auditioning for almost every conductor in the country, he was engaged by Sir Malcolm Sargent to make his concerto debut with the Liverpool Philharmonic Orchestra; afterwards, he was offered the leadership of the orchestra, and stayed for a year. On his return to London he became the leader of the Philharmonia Orchestra, then enjoying what was the greatest period in its history. He played under all the great conductors and made recordings with Furtwängler, Guido Cantelli and Karajan; particularly memorable was Carlo Maria Giulini's recording of Vivaldi's Four Seasons, with Parikian as the soloist.

In 1957, he left the orchestra in order to concentrate on a solo career, and from this time enjoyed considerable success in Europe, the USSR, the Middle East and Canada. He was an exceptionally stylish violinist, producing a tone of great beauty based on an infallible technique. In the UK he also gave a number of first performances of works by contemporary composers including Alan Rawsthorne, Matyas Seiber, Gordon Crosse, Alexander Goehr and Hugh Wood, many of whom dedicated works to him.

Parikian taught at the Royal College of Music from 1954 to 1956 and at the Royal Academy from 1959. Considered to be a first-class teacher, he admitted that in his later years he enjoyed teaching more than in his younger days. His difficulty was that being a natural player, he found that he had to analyse what he was doing before he could help his students. For him, instinct was the 'guiding spirit' in every string player's performance, with a combination of instinct and analysis.[15]

A fine chamber music player, Parikian was fortunate in his duo partnerships in sonata recitals, playing regularly with Malcolm Binns, Lamar Crowson and Bernard Roberts; he and George Malcolm – on harpsichord – once gave the whole series of the Bach sonatas in the Queen Elizabeth Hall. He also performed the sonatas with Edwin Fischer on the piano, who in his opinion, 'played some of the most satisfying music'[16] he had ever heard. In 1977, he formed a piano trio with Roberts (later with pianist Hamish Milne) and the cellist Amaryllis Fleming, which thrived until Parikian's death ten years later.

Erich Gruenberg was born in Vienna in 1924, and received his first lessons on the violin when he was six. When Emil Hauser, leader of the original Budapest String Quartet, visited Europe on a talent-spotting trip, he awarded the 13-year-old a scholarship to study at the Jerusalem Conservatory. Gruenberg made his solo orchestral debut the following year, playing the Mozart D major Concerto. In 1946, Gruenberg arrived in London for the first time to study with Max Rostal. He won the Carl Flesch Medal the following year and, as a result, he was engaged to play the Brahms concerto with the London Philharmonic Orchestra. It is therefore not surprising that Gruenberg became a dedicated anglophile, made his home in the UK and took British nationality in 1951.

He was leader of the London String Quartet and a member of the Rubbra-Gruenberg-Pleeth Trio for many years, as well as the Boyd Neel Orchestra, the LSO and the RPO. Franz Reizenstein, Eric Harrison, William Glock and Fanny Waterman partnered him in memorable sonata recitals.

Today, Gruenberg devotes his energies to a solo career, touring internationally and premièring new music. He gave the first performance in the USSR of Benjamin Britten's Violin Concerto, with the Moscow Radio Orchestra under Gennadi Rozdestvensky. In addition, Gruenberg is professor of violin at the Royal Academy of Music in London. He gives masterclasses and sits on the juries of international competitions. Since 1997, he has chaired the jury and devised the programme for the Yehudi Menuhin International Competition for Young Violinists.

In 1993, BBC Radio 3's Saturday Review selected György Pauk's recording of the Mozart Violin Concerto in A major K219 from among 40 versions. Its defining qualities were a 'magical dimension' and 'an underlying serenity'.[17]

György Pauk was born in Budapest in 1936 into a musical family and began violin lessons at the age of five. His teacher was Madame Nogrady, who had a reputation for teaching young children, and she provided him with a sound technical foundation, for which he remains grateful to this day. At 13, he was the youngest student ever to be admitted to the Franz Lizst Academy, where he became a pupil of Zathureczki (a pupil of Hubay). He also studied chamber music with Leo Weiner and, in common with most Hungarian string players, has nothing but admiration for the great man: 'He was the father of chamber music in Hungary.'[18]

On graduating, Pauk quickly became established as a soloist in Eastern Europe. Then in 1956, on his first visit to the West, he won the Paganini Competition, and, equally significantly, became aware of the difference between the restrictions of Stalinist Hungary and the affluence of Italy. He was stunned in particular by the beautifully tailored clothes and spent most of his prize money on a new wardrobe. And, for the first time in his life, he saw the sea and found the opportunity to sit the whole day watching it.

After the unsuccessful uprising in Hungary that same year, Pauk decided to emigrate to the West; so, on his next foreign tour, he simply 'forgot' to return. He went first to Holland. Then in 1959, he won the Long-Thibaud Competition; Menuhin, who was on the jury, suggested he should come to England. When he arrived in 1961, he immediately felt at home and he has never changed his mind. At that time, London was a thriving centre of musical activity, with Ashkenazy, Barenboim and many other emigrés lending considerable colour to the scene. A meeting with Harry Blech brought about his orchestral debut at the Festival Hall, where he played the Beethoven concerto with the London Mozart Players. It was an unqualified success and led to his recording of the Tchaikovsky concerto with the LPO.

In 1962, Pauk gave his Wigmore Hall debut recital with Geoffrey Parsons. Not only praised by the critics, it also attracted the attention of a representative of the Australian Broadcasting Association who happened to be in the audience. He engaged Pauk and Parsons for an ambitious Australian tour, with 52 concerts in four months. Pauk was fortunate to play many times under Sir Georg Solti in London and in 1970, when Solti became musical director of the Chicago Symphony Orchestra, he was one of his first soloists. While on this US tour he acquired the instrument he now plays exclusively. A wealthy private collector, Howard Gottlieb, approached him after a concert and offered to lend him one of his Strads, the 'Massart', dated 1714. After five years Pauk began to feel uncomfortable holding on to it for so long and succeeded in purchasing it for what Pauk describes as a 'ridiculous price'.

Pauk taught for many years at the Guildhall School of Music and Drama and has been a professor at the Royal Academy of Music since 1987. Over the years, Pauk has become more and more involved in chamber music. He and the pianist Peter Frankl were fellow students at the Liszt Academy and have played together in sonata recitals and given many broadcasts for the BBC. Eleanor Warren, a producer at the BBC, suggested they form a trio with the cellist Ralph Kirshbaum. The rapport was immediate and, from the first minute they started playing together, they were a perfectly integrated ensemble.

## Notes

1–2. Quoted from interview, M.C.

3. *World Telegram*, 1 April 1966.

4–8. Quoted from interview, M.C.

9. *The Times*, 1 November 1954.

10. Quoted from interview, M.C.

11. *The Strad*, February 1956, p. 365.

12–13. Quoted from interview, M.C.

14. *World Telegram*, 1 April 1966.

15–16. *The Strad*, September 1983, p. 343.

17. *BBC Music Magazine*, 1993.

18. *The Strad*, April 1988, p. 291.

# 41   The Auer Inheritance

Although few of Auer's pupils are still alive today, his principles
continue to be passed on through second and third generations of
teachers worldwide.

For Pawel Kochanski (1887–1934), the influence was inherited through his first
teacher, Emil Mlynarski (1870–1935), but later studies with César Thomson made his
playing a classic blend of both the great Russian and Franco-Belgian Schools.

Born in Orel (Russia), he had his first lessons from his father and, at seven, entered
Mlynarski's class at the Odessa Conservatory. When Mlynarski was appointed
musical director of the Warsaw Opera, he took the 13-year-old Kochanski with him
and looked after both his general and musical education.

The following year Kochanski made his solo debut with the Warsaw Philharmonic
Orchestra and began giving regular concerts in the main Polish cities. Then, at 16, he
went to the Brussels Conservatoire to study with Thomson and, after only four
months, won a Premier Prix with the highest distinction. From this point onwards he
toured throughout Europe, attracting large audiences and receiving rave reviews.

He returned to Warsaw in 1907 where, in addition to what was now a busy concert
career, he was appointed professor at the Warsaw Conservatory. It was during this
time that he formed a professional partnership and close friendship with the pianist
Artur Rubinstein which lasted until Kochanski's untimely death from cancer at the
age of 46. In his memoirs, Rubinstein remarked on his 'tremendous core of vitality'
and, in particular, his eyes: 'coal black, formed like oblique almonds, with a velvety
deep expression which could be very moving, especially when he was playing'. 'Paul
loved above all, the company of musicians and a good game of bridge or poker.'[1]

In 1913, Kochanski succeeded Auer at the St Petersburg Conservatory, and since
he was unable to leave after the Russian Revolution, he also taught for some time at
the Kiev Conservatory.

Prior to the Revolution, Kochanski had married into a wealthy and influential
family; Rubinstein disapproved of the marriage, considering that the bride's father had
unduly influenced Kochanski with the gift of a beautiful Stradivarius known as the
'Spanish', and even refused to attend the wedding. However, the marriage turned out to
be a happy one. Kochanski returned to Poland in 1919 and two years later emigrated to
the USA, where he continued to delight audiences. Unlike so many virtuoso
performers, Kochanski was equally interested in teaching and those who studied with
him praised not only his expertise but his tireless dedication to his pupils. In 1924, he

was appointed violin professor at Juilliard and remained there until his death. Carl Flesch thought highly of Kochanski:

> Kochanski's tone captivated by its sweetness: he was moreover an inimitable interpreter, as well as an excellent arranger, of little Spanish violin pieces. . . . He was also a charming conversationalist; as a *raconteur* he was in the same class as Grünfeld, Rosenthal or Thibaud. Thus he would, at times, have his greatest successes *after* the concert when, having had their artistic fill, the music lovers had a wine with him and wanted to hear something about the human side of the artist. His death left a gap in American musical life that has not yet been filled.[2]

Kochanski was closely associated with Karol Szymanowski, whose Violin Concerto No. 1 (1916) was dedicated to him and became a regular part of his repertory. He also went to Warsaw in 1933 to give the première of Szymanowski's Concerto No. 2, although he was so ill at the time he had to play sitting down.

Writing in *The Strad* in September 1987, Henry Roth reflected that 'there can be no doubt that with the passing of Paul Kochanski, the world lost a violinist of redoubtable qualities; his recordings are an invaluable testament to an artist every violin enthusiast should know'.[3]

Over the years, Sascha Lasserson (1890–1978) has become a legend as one of the most distinguished and respected representatives of the Auer School. Lasserson was born in Vitebsk (Russia) and, at five, was given his first lessons by his father, a professional violinist. The following year, he entered the conservatory at St Petersburg under Nikolai Galkin and, at ten, he made his solo debut in Helsingfors playing the Spohr D minor Concerto. That same year he joined the class of Leopold Auer, won the Silver Medal and graduated with distinction in 1911.

From this time onward he was in constant demand as a soloist and played all over Europe, including Russia and Scandinavia. He made a successful tour of the UK in 1914. At the outbreak of the First World War, he was compelled to remain in the UK and, after the Russian Revolution, he decided not to return to his native country. He continued to appear with success as a soloist and, after the foundation of the BBC, made many broadcasts, which included a performance of all ten of the Beethoven sonatas. A critic once described his playing as possessing 'the requisite artistic power and consummate technique, coupled with a lack of all apparent effort'.[4]

However, Lasserson was also becoming known as a teacher and, as the word spread, he soon attracted students from all over the world. Eventually he abandoned the concert platform and concentrated on teaching. It has always puzzled his many admirers as to why this gifted virtuoso performer preferred teaching to a concert career, refusing many offers to go to the USA, where many other Auer pupils had made successful international careers. He was a modest self-effacing man, who taught because he loved teaching, and many famous violinists have Lasserson to thank for solving a problem nobody else could tackle. Despite his celebrity, he did not restrict his attention to the top players. He once took on a 60-year-old beginner and when asked why, he replied: 'That man a year ago could play nothing. Now you hear he makes a good attempt at a Tartini sonata and he gets pleasure out of having achieved something.'[5] The secret of his success as a teacher was his simplistic approach.

A contemporary of Lasserson, Kathleen Parlow (1890–1963) was born in Calgary and, as a child, had lessons from Henry Holmes in San Francisco. She visited London in 1905 and gave a debut recital at the Bechstein Hall that earned her praise from the critics and many orchestral engagements. However, she felt that there was still a need for further study and decided she would go to St Petersburg to join Auer's class; it was a choice she never regretted, for he solved all her problems and gave her the polish and encouragement she had been seeking. Auer regarded her very highly and called her 'Elman in a skirt'.[6] One of her first appearances after her final training period was to play the Glazunov concerto in the Musical Festival at Ostend, at the invitation of the composer.

She soon became one of the most sought-after women violinists of her day and undertook many international tours. Her playing was described as being very much in the Auer tradition: a big pure tone, suave legato and effortless technique. In 1926 she went to the USA, where she continued her solo career and taught privately at Mills College in Oakland, California. She finally settled in Canada in 1941 where she formed her own quartet, gave concerts, broadcast and taught at the Royal Conservatory of Music in Toronto. Needless to say, Auer's name was frequently evoked in her lessons.[7]

Franz von Vecsey (1893–1935), from Budapest, was a pupil of Hubay, Joachim and, finally, Auer. He had his first lessons from his father, a professional violinist, and went to Hubay when he was eight. Two years later, he undertook a concert tour as a child prodigy and made his Berlin debut; London heard the phenomenon in 1904 and his New York debut followed in 1905. In the meantime, he spent some time in Auer's class in St Petersburg. Elman was a fellow pupil and the rivalry between the two quickly became apparent in the class, although they would play duos together in private. Even when they were both established in their careers, the rivalry persisted. In 1908, Vecsey appeared in London with Hubay – who regarded him as his favourite pupil – in a performance of Hubay's Concerto No. 3, which was dedicated to Vecsey; later in the programme, master and pupil joined forces for the Bach Double Concerto which they 'played to perfection'.[8]

For some time, Vecsey enjoyed a solo career, playing all over Europe including Russia, although for some reason he was never as welcome in the USA. As the dedicatee, his name will always be associated with the Sibelius Violin Concerto (1903). The work was originally written for Willy Burmester, who withdrew before the first performance, which was then given by Karel Halíř under Richard Strauss in 1905. Critics were equivocal and the most celebrated violinists showed little interest: Joachim thought it 'abominable and boring' and Ysaÿe tried it but was disenchanted. So, Sibelius dedicated it to the 17-year-old Vecsey, who in 1910 played it successfully in Berlin and Vienna, and remained its most accomplished protagonist.

During the First World War, Vecsey served in the Austro-Hungarian armed forces and returned to the concert platform in the early 1920s. At the time, Boris Schwarz attended one of Vecsey's sold-out performances in Berlin when it was rumoured that he was still suffering from his war injuries, although it did not affect his playing. 'He performed with classical purity and inner detachment, letting the music speak for itself, as it were, without interjecting his own personality. His technique was absolutely perfect and effortless.'[9] Vecsey's concerts were always popular and attracted a full house, but his appearances grew more infrequent and he faded from the scene. He died at 42 following an operation.

Another Auer pupil who for many years enjoyed an international reputation was Cecilia Hansen (1897–1989), born in Stamiza Kamneska, a village near Rostov in Russia. At seven she attended the Rostov Conservatory for violin lessons, and two years later when her family moved to St Petersburg, she was accepted as a pupil of Auer at the conservatory. She graduated at 15 and was awarded a gold medal for her performance of the Beethoven concerto.

She would have been ready to travel abroad as a soloist, but the war years kept her in Russia, where her fame spread to every important city in the country. In 1921 she left Russia and settled in Finland with her pianist husband, Boris Zakharov, whom she had married in 1916. From this point her international career – as a soloist with orchestra and a recitalist with her husband – became a reality. In 1923, she played in the USA and made a great impression at her initial appearance with the Chicago Symphony Orchestra; this brought about further tours. In 1928, she was invited to play at the coronation ceremony of the Emperor Hirohito of Japan. Hansen settled in London in 1936 and, during the Second World War, she often played in Myra Hess' lunchtime concerts at the National Gallery.

Hansen was easily the most beautiful of Auer's students. She was tall and blonde and had a charismatic platform personality. She always dressed in white, and, after her death, Menuhin, who as a young boy had attended one of her concerts in San Francisco, wrote to her daughter: 'She looked like an angel, all dressed in white, and played like one.'[10] As to her playing, the opinions vary. Carl Flesch, hypercritical as always, said he would rather see her than hear her: 'She is one of the very few violinists whose posture and movements correspond to the laws of perfect physical harmony. Like Zimbalist, however, she does not belong to the inner circle of the Auer School. She has a charming personality without being in any way outstanding as a fiddler; her appearance helps the listener to forget her artistic flaws.'[11] Other reports say that her playing was 'scrupulously clean and stylistically correct' and also, '. . . as a player she excels as an interpreter of strenuous and romantic music'.[12] Her few recordings are proof that she was in fact a stylish and innately musical player.

When writing about the much neglected Toscha Seidel (1900–62), Flesch is uncharacteristically enthusiastic: '. . . the quality of his tone is one of the most beautiful I have ever heard in my career. Technically, too, he is excellently equipped, whence I regard it as an injustice of fate that he is not considered the third in a triumvirate with Heifetz and Elman.'[13] Seidel was born into an upper middle-class family in Odessa and started to play the violin when he was three; at seven, he was sent to study with Max Fiedelmann, an Auer pupil. The following year he performed a Bériot concerto so beautifully that it was decided that he should be sent to Berlin to study for the next two years with Adolf Brodsky at the Stern Conservatory.

His future was decided when he heard Heifetz play the Tchaikovsky concerto in Berlin. 'His bowings, his fingerings, his whole style and manner of playing so impressed me that I felt I must have his teacher, that I would never be content unless I studied with Professor Auer.'[14] The opportunity came to play for Auer at his summer residence in Loschwitz, near Dresden, and to his great joy, Seidel was accepted immediately.

Seidel studied with Auer both privately and at the St Petersburg Conservatory, and it is well known that Auer thought very highly of his playing and spoke of his two 'prodigies', Jascha Heifetz and Toscha Seidel. In fact, when they were attending Auer's summer classes in Loschwitz, they would perform the Bach Double Concerto. Seidel, in turn, worshipped his master.

In 1915, Seidel made his solo debut in Oslo, playing the Tchaikovsky concerto; critics and audience went wild. He repeated this success in St Petersburg the following year, having, in the interim, played in concerts all over Russia. In the USA in 1918, he made his Carnegie Hall debut, but while he received rave reviews, the city was already in a state of euphoria over the debut six months earlier of the young Heifetz. Needless to say, Seidel was not the only aspiring soloist to suffer as a consequence. However, while other violinists managed to carve out lesser solo careers for themselves, Seidel was not so fortunate. Why did he fail where so many others – often less talented – had succeeded? Henry Roth considered Seidel to be 'one of the most instinctive and exciting violin talents ever to draw a bow' but, despite his superb playing and sumptuous and voluptuous tone, he could not be considered a 'profound, perceptive, all-encompassing musician'.[15]

Seidel played for about ten years in his own string quartet, but it was in the film industry in Hollywood that he eventually found sustained employment. He was, for some time, leader of the Paramount Studio orchestra and as such had plenty of opportunity to play solos in the films; two which stand out in the memory are *Golden Earrings* (1947) and *A Place in the Sun* (1951). He also made many broadcasts and over 50 recordings of short pieces. Perhaps the most exciting example is the 1939 recording of the film score of *Intermezzo*, which endeared him to millions of listeners. In the late 1950s his contract was not renewed and Seidel was again facing a void; he was too naive to cope with the cut-throat operations of the freelance business and, in addition, his mental powers were degenerating. His once promising talent ended up being squandered in show orchestras in Las Vegas.

*The Times* critic, Hilary Finch wrote in 1985: 'Last night, as the veteran violinist played the time-honoured concerto, there was the feeling of being drawn once more into Shumsky's own world. And, for all its deceptive privacy and fragility, it is one which gives out warmth, space and at times even audacity in generous measure.'[16] Sixty years earlier, the eight-year-old Oscar Shumsky had just been accepted as Auer's youngest ever pupil.

Shumsky (1917–2000) was born in Philadelphia into a Russian immigrant family, in which everyone played an instrument. He began to play when he was three and, the following year, began lessons with the Russian-born Albert Mieff. He was playing in public by the time he was seven and, a year later, made his solo debut playing the Mozart Concerto K219 with the Philadelphia Orchestra under Stokowski. He was already studying in New York with Auer, who charged $60 per hour for lessons. Members of the Philadelphia Orchestra teased him, saying 'Hey, Oscar, are you an Auer pupil or a half-Auer pupil?' (Auer was eighty and Shumsky was eight.)

Shumsky remained with Auer until his death in 1930. By then he was already attending the Curtis Institute and was automatically accepted in Zimbalist's class. He graduated in 1936, but continued private studies with Zimbalist for three more years. However, throughout his student years, Shumsky continued to play in concerts with the Philadelphia Orchestra and undertook a tour of South Africa when he was only 15.

Nonetheless, Shumsky did not follow the usual pattern of the virtuoso. Highly intelligent, he tired of performing the same works over and over again and was outspoken in his criticism of unimaginative programming. For some time, he was employed as a staff musician with the National Broadcasting Company and, in 1939, he was invited to join the NBC Symphony Orchestra, which had been created for Toscanini. For the young musician, it was an exciting move and he made some lifelong friendships among his colleagues, two of whom were Josef Gingold and William Primrose. Shumsky sat on the outside second-stand chair, right under Toscanini's nose; what the maestro did not know was that his recently engaged first violinist had never played in an orchestra before. It seems that playing for Toscanini could be illuminating, but never relaxing.

> When players say they enjoyed playing for him, they are enjoying it *in retrospect*. One didn't enjoy it at the time because the old man's eye was everywhere. He had the ability to make the entire orchestra feel that every man was constantly under his gaze, which was uncomfortable. You never knew when he was going to fly off the handle. He got what he wanted through fear and a tremendous personal mystique.[17]

That same year, William Primrose formed the Primrose String Quartet, with Shumsky as leader, Gingold as the second violinist and Harvey Shapiro as cellist. Shumsky had played in quartets since he was 11 years old, so for him this was an immensely satisfying undertaking. Their success was phenomenal and their recordings remain a rich legacy. In 1942, Shumsky decided to leave the NBC Orchestra in order to concentrate on his solo playing. Although he had derived enormous benefit, Toscanini's influence was too powerful. In addition, he was offered a teaching post at the Peabody Institute and, since he had already done some private teaching and formed some important opinions on the subject, he accepted with enthusiasm.

For the next three years, during the Second World War, Shumsky served in the US Navy as a member of the Navy band along with other well-known musicians, including the cellists Bernard Greenhouse and David Soyer. Shumsky himself played some 17 concertos during the season, entertaining the Washington officials and their guests. On his return to civilian life, he went back into orchestral playing and teaching. He later taught at the Curtis Institute, Yale University and, in 1953, Juilliard. He quickly gained a reputation as a first-class teacher who understood how to handle his students. One said of him: 'The difference between him and every other musician I ever worked with was that he didn't just tell you things, he would help you to learn things. He made you think.'[18]

In the 1950s Shumsky turned to conducting, often directing from the violin. Despite his playing, teaching, conducting and recording, he never seemed to be caught in the limelight. That is until the 1980s when this prodigy of the 1920s was rediscovered. In 1981 he gave a London recital and British critics hailed him as an amazing new discovery. The *Daily Telegraph* glowed: 'It is not common practice here for audience members to leap to their feet in acknowledgement of outstanding playing, but it is a mark of Oscar Shumsky's achievement at the Queen Elizabeth Hall that so many did spontaneously just that.'[19]

At the age of 74 he gave a recital in Boston's Jordan Hall with the pianist Patricia Lander, and again the critics ran out of superlatives. The programme included Kreisler miniatures, Tartini 'Devil's Trill', and Beethoven Op. 30, No. 2 Sonatas. They received a standing ovation and responded with four encores. Shumsky finally turned to unaccompanied Bach and the critic declared: 'Most of us could have listened to that all night.'[20]

Steven Staryk, a second generation Auer pupil through his studies with Shumsky, was born in Toronto in 1932 into a family who came originally from Ukraine. He had early lessons with local teachers and later with Elie Spivak, then leader of the Toronto Symphony Orchestra and a former pupil of Adolf Brodsky. Staryk also studied briefly with Mischa Mischakoff and Alexander Schneider (1908–93) before going to Shumsky who had the strongest influence on his musical development.

Staryk was 18 when he joined the Toronto Symphony Orchestra and, after two years, was appointed leader of the CBS Symphony Orchestra. In 1956 he entered the Carl Flesch Competition in London and, although he did not win a prize, he impressed Manoug Parikian, who recommended him to Sir Thomas Beecham as a candidate for leader of the Royal Philharmonic Orchestra. Beecham engaged him at once; in 1960, Staryk became leader of the Concertgebouw Orchestra in Amsterdam. At the invitation of Georg Szell, he became leader of the Chicago Symphony Orchestra in 1963. Probably the most sought-after leader in the profession, he was also approached by Rudolf Kempe for the Berlin Philharmonic Orchestra and Eugene Ormandy for the Philadelphia Orchestra.

Staryk also held professorships at the Amsterdam Conservatory, Northwestern University in Evanston, Illinois and Oberlin College in Ohio, where he also formed a successful duo with the pianist John Perry.

In 1972, Staryk returned to Canada as a visiting professor. He was for many years on the music faculties of both Toronto University and the Royal Conservatory in Toronto. Then, in 1983, after many years' absence from the leader's chair, he accepted an invitation to lead the Toronto Symphony Orchestra. In 1987, he moved to Seattle,

Washington, where he is professor of violin and head of the string department at the University of Washington's School of Music. Drawing upon years of practical experience playing in orchestras, Staryk holds a weekly 'orchestral excerpts' class. Details of up-coming auditions are circulated and students with forthcoming auditions have the opportunity to give a mock performance in the classroom. With his vast experience of playing in some of the world's greatest orchestras he can solve most of the problems that arise in orchestral playing. When so many young players aspire only to be soloists, it is refreshing to find a teacher who has the skill and the incentive to train his students to excel in an alternative field.

Aaron Rosand is a second generation Auer pupil who was a student of Zimbalist at the Curtis Institute. Born in Hammond, Indiana in 1927, he first studied with Leon Sametini – a pupil of both Ševčík and Ysaÿe – before going to Zimbalist in 1944. He showed early talent for the violin, gave his first recital in Chicago when he was nine, and made his first orchestral appearance a year later playing the Mendelssohn concerto with the Chicago Symphony Orchestra, under Frederick Stock.

In addition to the Auer tradition, which Zimbalist represented, Rosand had had a grounding in the Franco-Belgian School from Sametini and, when he first went to study with Zimbalist, he had to take on an entirely different approach to bowing.

> While the Franco-Belgian School encourages a faster bow speed and triangular grip (i.e. the first and third fingers against the thumb), the Auer-Zimbalist approach calls for a denser sound resulting from more pressure on the index finger and flatter bow hair on the string. Having been trained in these two schools I try to adopt aspects of each in my own playing and teaching.[21]

While still a student, Rosand gave his New York recital debut at Town Hall in 1948. After he graduated, he appeared regularly as a soloist, receiving good reviews, but recognition did not come overnight. There was at this time a plethora of Russian violinists on the circuit and in general musicians had difficulty in getting engagements; many had to seek alternative ways of making money in order to live. Rosand made his European debut in Copenhagen in 1955 and has remained far more in demand there than in the USA.

He was finally recognised in his own country in 1970 when he gave a 'Romantic Recital' at Carnegie Hall which not only delighted his audience, but also prompted Harold Schonberg to extol his 'absolutely flawless playing' in the *New York Times*: 'Romanticism on the violin had a rebirth at Carnegie Hall.'[22] Rosand gives most of the credit for any of his performances to his 1741 Guarnerius del Gesù (ex-'Kochanski') violin, his 'faithful companion' to which he has been absolutely devoted for over 40 years. 'The passing of time and use have enriched its quality of sound. It is now even more brilliant and responsive, with extraordinary power and clarity. I feel blessed and privileged to be the owner of this legendary instrument.'[23]

Rosand teaches at the Peabody Institute, Mannes College and the Curtis Institute.

Elmar Oliveira (b. 1950) is an Auer pupil once removed – a student of Raphael Bronstein, who studied with Auer at St Petersburg, and his daughter, Ariana Bron. Oliveira was born in Waterbury, Connecticut, the son of an immigrant Portuguese carpenter who also made violins. When Oliveira was five, his father made him a tiny violin; he had his first instruction from his elder brother, John, who is now a member of the Houston Symphony Orchestra. At 11, he had made sufficient progress to be awarded a scholarship to study with Bron at Hartt College of Music, and, at 14, made his first solo appearance with the Hartford Symphony Orchestra.

At 18 he entered the Manhattan School of Music to complete his studies with Bronstein and made his recital debut in New York in 1973. Two years later, he won the Naumburg Prize, which brought him two New York recitals at Tully Hall. Encouraged by the positive response from the critics, he entered the 1978 Tchaikovsky Competition in Moscow and won a Gold Medal.

Today, Oliveira enjoys a busy international career and in 1983 he was awarded the coveted Avery Fisher Prize in New York for his services to music. More recently, he was given an honorary doctorate at the Manhattan School (now College) of Music, where for two years he occupied the Mischa Elman Chair.

## Notes

1. *The Strad*, September 1987, p. 689.
2. Flesch, *Memoirs*, p. 340.
3. *The Strad*, September 1987, p. 691.
4. *The Strad*, December 1990, p. 978.
5. *The Strad*, December 1990, p. 976.
6. Schwarz, *Great Masters of the Violin*, p. 448.
7. *The Strad*, October 1963, p. 213.
8–9. Schwarz, op. cit., p. 382–4.
10. *The Strad*, May 1991, p. 427.
11. Flesch, op. cit., p. 338.
12. *The Strad*, May 1991, p. 427.
13. Flesch, op. cit., p. 338.
14–15. *The Strad*, August 1989, pp. 639–40.
16. *The Times*, 27 April 1985.
17–18. *The Strad*, March 1987, pp. 213–16.
19. *Daily Telegraph*, 14 Setember 1981.
20. *Boston Globe*, 6 April 1991.
21. *The Strad*, November 1986, p. 470.
22. *New York Times*, 29 April 1970.
23. *The Strad*, October 1994, p. 999.

# 42 The Ševčík Legacy

As a teacher, Otakar Ševčík was either worshipped or questioned; in common with Auer and Flesch, a large proportion of his pupils – and their pupils – have occupied the top echelons of violin playing.

Jan Kubelík (1880–1940) was without doubt one of the most outstanding technicians of his time. As Ševčík's best-known pupil, it was through his example that his master's 'Method' was universally introduced to the musical world. His playing was firmly rooted in technique and although he included most of the classic concertos in his repertory, he was happiest when exhibiting the bravura gymnastics of the more virtuosic spellbinders.

Throughout his career the critics remained unmoved, if greatly impressed by his brilliance. In 1907, Richard Aldrich of the *New York Times* explained: 'There is something aloof in him as he plays . . . yet few have the power of so ravishing the senses with the sheer beauty of his tone, the charm of his cantilena, the elegance and ease with which he masters all the technical difficulties.'[1] On another occasion Aldrich admitted that in a performance of the Mozart Concerto in D major 'he showed a style of unaffected sincerity and strength', but in the Wieniawski Concerto in D minor, 'he was more at home'.[2]

Kubelík was born at Michle, a small town on the outskirts of Prague. His father was a market gardener and a good violinist who also conducted a local band. In his later years, when living in Beverly Hills, Hollywood, Kubelík reversed the process by becoming a keen amateur gardener. Having received his first instruction from his father, Kubelík had some lessons with Karel Ondříček (1863–1943), and then entered the Prague Conservatory under Ševčík at the age of twelve. He studied with him for six years and left the conservatory a proclaimed virtuoso after a performance of Paganini's D major concerto.

His Vienna debut in 1898 was equally successful and he continued to astound his audiences throughout Europe. In 1900 he appeared for the first time at a Richter concert at St James's Hall in London. The *Musical Times* critic wrote that 'fine orchestral playing and superb interpretations of the classics are very well in their way, but what can they avail with a London audience against a fiddler with a phenomenally developed technique, a dead-sure intonation, a beautiful tone, and an uncanny way of playing the most wonderful difficulties?' The critic went on to observe that Kubelík 'revels in surmounting seemingly impossible technical difficulties' and expressed the hope that 'as he grows older he may . . . revel equally in unravelling the beauties and depths that lie hidden in the aforesaid masters' [Beethoven, Mendelssohn, Bruch, Brahms] works'.[3]

Kubelík crossed the Atlantic in 1902 and here, as elsewhere, his audiences were bowled over by his facility, although, as we have seen, the critics described him as lacking depth of feeling. Nonetheless, by giving the public what they wanted, Kubelík amassed a fortune. His meteoric rise to fame as a prodigy meant that, before the age of 20, he became a very rich man. As early as 1904, he purchased an estate, complete with baronial castle, for $160,000 netted from his first American tour. He was also recording with the Victor Company and received substantial royalties. When Melba made her historic recording of Gounod's 'Ave Maria', it was Kubelík who supplied the violin obbligato.

In 1903 Kubelík married a Hungarian countess; the youngest of their seven children is the conductor Rafael Kubelík. In the USA there were many critics of the violinist's public image. The press constantly exploited stories of his castles, aristocratic connections and his 'highly valued fingers',[4] which appeared more important than good taste in musical performance. Certainly he managed to attract publicity that was not strictly concerned with his music-making. In 1902 he endured allegations that he was under the influence of a Svengali-like secretary, who directed him mechanically and pocketed the gain. Once, when travelling in an elevator in a Chicago hotel, he noticed a picture of Ignacy Jan Paderewski, the great pianist, on the wall. He tore down the poster, exclaiming: 'That's what you do for another artist, when I'm the man who made your hotel famous!'[5]

In the early 1930s Kubelík suffered a string of misfortunes. The depression drove him out of Europe, where his speculations had extended to five manorial estates in Bohemia and Hungary. At the time he also owned 16 valuable violins, including his famous 'Emperor' Stradivarius (dated 1715) and his Guarnerius del Gesù of 1735. In 1932 he was forced to sell many of his treasures, including the del Gesù (now owned by Kyung-Wha Chung), but he never parted with his 'Emperor'.

Although he returned to Europe and died in Prague in 1940, Kubelík settled for some time in California, where he retreated to a modest cottage high up in the Beverly Hills. Surrounded by orchards and high hedges of red poinsettia bushes, he devoted himself to composition, writing several concertos and small pieces for the violin. Kubelík did not play much in his later years because his hearing became so impaired that it affected his intonation. His place in the top echelon of violinists was finally taken by Jascha Heifetz.

One of the most brilliant of Ševčík's second generation pupils, Váša Příhoda (1900–60), had a short but distinguished career which flourished between the two wars. He was born in Vodňany in Bohemia, the son of a professional musician who ran a school. He received his first lessons from his father and, at ten, became a private pupil of Jan Marak (1870–1932), a professor at the Prague Conservatory, who had studied with Ševčík.

Váša began giving public concerts when he was 12 and appeared at the Prague

Mozarteum when he was 15; two years later he made his debut with the Czech Philharmonic Orchestra, and was warmly received by both public and press; the latter remarked upon the purity of his intonation and the powerful brilliancy of his playing. He was also extremely good looking, with a charismatic platform personality. Soon he was appearing successfully all over his own country as well as in Switzerland and Yugoslavia, but when he arrived in Italy, hoping to achieve a similar success, he was forced to earn his living by playing in a café orchestra in Milan. Toscanini heard him and was so sure he had found a second Paganini that he organised a subscription concert that brought enough money to launch him on an international career, with tours in Europe, South Africa and South America.

In 1921 Příhoda made his American debut, playing in several major American cities. His playing prompted some excellent reviews, but like so many other young violinists, he could not compete with the popularity of the established idols, Kreisler and Heifetz. On his return to Prague, he took on some private teaching and, in 1936, he took up an appointment at the Salzburg Mozarteum. During the Second World War, he chose to continue giving concerts in Germany, Austria and Bohemia and teaching at the Munich Academy of Music. In 1946 he returned to Czechoslovakia and was charged with being a Nazi collaborator. He left to settle in Italy at Rapallo and, in 1950, he took out Turkish citizenship before moving back to Austria where he was appointed a professor at the Vienna Academy of Music.

Příhoda finally made peace with his homeland in 1956 when he returned for some concerts in the Prague Spring Festival, but although he was still able to captivate an audience, he was past his prime. He died in Vienna of a heart attack a month before his 60th birthday. Those who heard Příhoda play at the height of his career remember his vibrantly expressive phrasing and passionate feeling which, to some extent, have been captured in his numerous recordings. He was also much loved by his colleagues and friends who described him as a sensitive human being whose greatest pleasure was to give pleasure to others. He sold his violin, a superb Stradivarius, the 'Camposelice', dated 1710, to the Czech state shortly before his death.

Louis Krasner (1903–95) was born in Cherkassky, Ukraine and brought to the USA when he was three. He had his first tuition on the violin when he was nine but, because his family were so poor, he had to pay for his own lessons from the age of 12 by playing in local theatres and at dances. At a 'smoker', he was noticed by an eminent physician, who introduced him to one of his wealthy patients, Mrs Arthur Livingston Kelly; she readily agreed to sponsor his studies with the Viennese Eugène Gruenberg at the New England Conservatory (Gruenberg had known Gustav Mahler and later introduced Krasner to Kreisler) and continued to meet all his expenses until his debut.

Krasner graduated at 20 with the highest honours and then went on to Europe where he had further periods of study with Flesch, Capet and Ševčík. He considered that it was the sheer variety of their methods which contributed to his musical development in a way that otherwise would not have happened. He was devoted to

Flesch and remained indebted to him for his analytical and logical approach. (Krasner tended to rely upon his instincts.) When Flesch left to take up his appointment at the Curtis Institute in Philadelphia, Krasner told him he intended to continue his studies with Lucien Capet in Paris; Flesch was vehemently opposed to the idea, but Krasner persisted with his plan and realised at once why Flesch had disapproved. 'It was so different from Flesch. Capet didn't try to interpret music in words. He would look at you and from that you got to know how something should go or not go according to the expression on his face. When he looked at you you felt the depth of his perceptions and concerns.'[6] Where Flesch suggested an up-bow, Capet played a down-bow; if Flesch used the third finger, Capet would use the fourth; Flesch's *piano* became Capet's point of departure for a *crescendo*.

Finally, for good measure, Krasner went from the analytical Flesch and the mystical Capet to the master technician, Ševčík, becaue he 'wanted to learn how to turn three somersaults on the high wire instead of two'. When he mentioned some virtuoso pieces that he wanted to learn, a world-weary Ševčík said: 'Why do all of you come and want to study technical things with me? Don't you think I have anything to offer in Mozart?' This impressed Krasner who wondered: 'How could this elderly man with such experience be so sensitive and all his master students be so *insensitive* to where the truth lies?'[7]

From this time onward Krasner lived mostly in Vienna, where he became acquainted with the composers Arnold Schoenberg, Alban Berg and Anton Webern, who first inspired his interest in contemporary music. Meanwhile, he travelled extensively throughout Europe as recitalist and soloist with the Vienna and Berlin Philharmonic and other leading orchestras. He also went to the USA where he met Alfredo Casella, then conductor of the Boston Pops, who invited him to give the premiere of his violin concerto.

On hearing Berg's opera, *Wozzeck* (1925), Krasner commissioned a violin concerto from the composer, hoping to break down the current prejudice against twelve-tone compositions. He gave the first performance in Barcelona in 1936 and subsequently played it all over Europe and the USA. He also premièred Schoenberg's Violin Concerto in Philadelphia under Stokowski in 1940. Since Europe was then in the throes of the Second World War, he was obliged to stay in the US and, in 1944, he became concert-master of the Minneapolis Symphony Orchestra, under Dimitri Mitropoulos.

Krasner was also an excellent teacher and in 1949 took up a post at Syracuse University, in upstate New York, where he stayed until 1972. While there, Krasner established the Syracuse Society for Chamber Music, followed by the founding of the Syracuse Symphony Orchestra, of which he was principal conductor. He also taught at the New England Conservatory of Music from 1969. He was greatly loved by his students for his endless patience and for his modesty and tireless efforts to help his fellow musicians.

Born in Vienna, Wolfgang Schneiderhahn (1915–2002) was taught by his mother when he was three, and first played in public two years later. At eight, he was taken on as a pupil by Ševčík at Písek, where in his first summer he had to learn from memory a programme that included the Tchaikovsky concerto, the Bach Chaconne and a great deal of Paganini. However – possibly because of his age – he was spared the famous exercises; instead, Ševčík wrote some studies especially for him. He stayed only a short time with Ševčík whom he remembered principally as a fanatic, who would have liked to make a Paganini out of every one of his students, but also as a great technician, who provided a firm basis on which his pupils could build.

Schneiderhahn completed his studies with Julius Winkler, one of the last representatives of the renowned Viennese school which could be traced back to Josef Böhm. It was Winkler who pointed Schneiderhahn in the right direction. 'With Winkler, I began to know what I *had* to do. He enabled me to go my own way and work on interpretation. Really, he taught me how to be a musician and how to read music.'[8]

Schneiderhahn's international career started when he was eleven playing the Mendelssohn concerto in Copenhagen; in 1933 he became the first leader of the Vienna Symphony Orchestra. After a brief spell with the State Opera Orchestra, he was appointed leader of the Vienna Philharmonic in 1937. 'I am very grateful for this experience. It teaches you to listen – how long the wind and brass leave to breathe. It is like playing in a string quartet, but the benefits are slightly different, and complementary.'[9] Chamber music always had an appeal for him and in 1937 he formed the Schneiderhahn String Quartet. However, in 1951 Schneiderhahn left the orchestra and disbanded the quartet in order to devote himself to a solo career, although he continued to play in a trio with Enrico Mainardi and Edwin Fischer.

Schneiderhahn had for many years been active as a teacher, first at the Salzburg Mozarteum and later at the Vienna Academy of Music. In 1949 he succeeded Flesch at the Lucerne Conservatory where in collaboration with Rudolf Baumgartner he formed the Lucerne Festival Strings in 1956. A fine exponent of contemporary music, Schneiderhahn gave a number of first performances, including works by Hans Werner Henze and Frank Martin, written specially for him. A stylish, elegant player, Schneiderhahn believed that by playing contemporary music, players are often able to solve problems associated with classical music. He once said: 'I always teach my pupils to balance their repertory with a good mix of modern music.'[10]

Josef Suk was born in Prague in 1929 into a family where music had been an integral part of their heritage for several generations. The composer, Antonin Dvořák was Suk's great-grandfather, and Josef Suk (1874–1935) the composer and violinist – who married Dvořák's daughter – his grandfather. Suk's own father was a fine amateur violinist who gave him his first lessons when he was six. Josef continued to study with Jaroslav Kocián (1883–1950), one of the most important of Ševčík's Czech pupils, and remained with him until his death in 1950. Suk then finished his studies with Alexander Plocek (*b*.1914) – another Ševčík pupil – at the Prague Conservatory.

From 1951 to 1952, while still a student, Suk was leader of the Prague Quartet; the three other members were veteran musicians at least ten years his senior. In 1952, he formed his own Suk Trio, with the cellist Miloš Sádlo and pianist Jan Panenka; later, Miloš Sádlo was replaced by Josef Chucro. When they played in London in 1990, Hilary Finch wrote in the *Times*: 'These are not performances taken out of the travelling case, pressed and polished for the occasion; rather the playing seems to grow out of a continuum of response and recreation constantly being regenerated in the players' lives.'[11]

In addition to his regular chamber music playing Suk was for two years leader of the orchestra for drama productions at the Prague National Theatre. In 1954 his solo debut recital attracted rave reviews. Five years later, he was invited to tour three continents as a soloist with the Czech Philharmonic Orchestra and in 1961 was named 'Soloist of the Czech Philharmonic'. When Suk made his British debut at the 1964 Proms, playing concertos by Mozart and Dvořák, he was highly praised for his silken tone, expressive fervour and technical skill.

Although Suk still appears as a soloist, his regular music-making is mainly with the Suk Trio. He has also made a number of recordings with the trio, and, with Jan Panenka has recorded the sonatas of Bach, Mozart, Beethoven, Brahms, Dvořák and Suk. With the exception of the music of Paganini, he has recorded most of the major works in the violin repertory.

Another of Suk's accomplishments is playing the viola – his second love. It came about many years ago at the suggestion of friends from the Smetana Quartet. His great-grandfather was a viola player and Suk – who has a hand of considerable size – realised that as he always had some difficulty with the high positions on the violin, he might try the viola. He not only mastered the instrument but became one of its great exponents, making several award-winning recordings.

A third-generation Ševčík pupil is the Polish Wanda Wilkomirska, who was born in Warsaw in 1929. She describes her family as 'an institution' in Polish musical life. Her father ran a music school and three of her siblings became members of the Wilkomirski Trio, who were already famous in Russia and Eastern Europe before she was born. She cannot remember when she learnt to read music, but her family assure her that she could sing before she could speak. As a child, she improvised on the piano; one day her father brought home a tiny violin and told her that the games were over and it was time she started to work. Although at first she resented being ordered to study, she finally admitted that she had benefited from her father's tuition, which consisted mostly of Ševčík exercises, and that he gave her a firm basic framework on which to build. She made her debut in Krakow when she was 14 and at the same time entered the Lodz Academy as a pupil of Irena Dubiska. But the greatest influence came when she went to study at the Budapest Academy with Ede Zathureczki – a pupil of Kocián. She describes Zathureczki as 'a pedagogical genius'.[12]

From the age of 15 Wilkomirska's concert career developed as a matter of course. Her family name opened every possible door and, in Poland, she could hardly walk in the street without being recognised. She made her highly acclaimed Wigmore Hall debut in 1951, and her American debut came in 1960 when she played the

Szymanowski Violin Concerto No. 1 with the Warsaw Philharmonic Orchestra on its first tour of the USA. The audience went wild and gave her an ovation that lasted for 20 minutes. Wilkomirska is philosophical. 'Maybe there was just a need for a violinist who did not play loud and fast like all the young people did. I came there and played very softly and sweetly because the piece [the Szymanowski] demanded it. . . . If I'd played maybe the Brahms Concerto, I'd have been "just another" brilliant young violinist.'[13] Vivacious, with a delightful sense of humour, Wilkomirska tells a story of how the late Sol Hurok failed in his attempt to make her stage personality more 'glamorous'. She refused to wear glittery dresses or flashy jewellery and told him: 'I don't like people looking at my earrings. I want them to listen to my music!'[14]

In 1982, Wilkomirska left Poland for Germany, and the following year took up a professorship at the Musikhochschule Heidelberg-Mannheim, where she is still very active; she is also a regular member of the juries for many international competitions. Many Polish composers have dedicated works to her.

**Notes**

1–2. *New York Times*, 11 November 1907.

3. *Musical Times*, 1 July 1900.

4. Richard Aldrich, *Concert Life in New York*, p. 118.

5. Lochner, *Fritz Kreisler*, p. 70.

6–7. *The Strad*, April 1986, p. 952.

8–10. *The Strad*, February 1985, pp. 749–50.

11. *The Times*, 1 February 1990.

12–14. *The Strad*, September 1986, p. 320.

# 43 Disciples of Oistrakh

D avid Oistrakh's students adored him and recognised the lasting influence he had on them; they also remember him as a warm and generous human being. 'I wonder if there has ever been another artist of his importance who devoted so much effort and time to his students. He had a way of getting involved with you, of getting to know you. You could trust him.'[1] This tribute was paid by Viktor Pikayzen. Born in Kiev in 1933, he was the son of a violinist who played in the Kiev Opera Orchestra. He received his first lessons from his father and made such progress that at nine he played the Wieniawski Second Violin Concerto for his successful audition at the Kiev Conservatory. When he was 13, he was invited to Moscow to play the Tchaikovsky concerto, attracting the attention of David Oistrakh, who was to be his teacher for the next 14 years at the Moscow Conservatory.

After leaving the Conservatory, Pikayzen embarked on a successful solo career and won several first prizes in various competitions, including the Paganini in Genoa in 1965. The following year he was appointed professor at the Moscow Conservatory, a post he held until 1986. In his teaching, Pikayzen tried to follow the principles established by Oistrakh.

> First, he demanded a constant effort to get at the artistic 'truth' and integrity of any piece. He was always ready to revise his analysis. Secondly, he insisted on technical perfection but he didn't go too far with that. You still had to make music out of everything. He worked out a kind of non-interrupted path, step by step, toward all the virtuoso goals. It was very logical.[2]

Pikayzen's playing is legendary: he is known for combining breathtaking brilliance of execution with an innate musicality. He has played all 24 Paganini Caprices in the same programme over 60 times and has the greatest respect for the Genoese master: 'You know, Oistrakh used to say that Paganini is the encyclopedia of the violin. But he also taught us to make music out of him.'[3]

Lydia Mordkovitch is yet another grateful Oistrakh student. She was born in 1944, in the railway station at Saratov near Kishinev; the relatives who were due to meet her mother never arrived. Later she learned they had been killed in the Nazi invasion. As a small child, Lydia wanted to learn the piano but her family could not afford to buy one, so she settled for the violin. At seven, she was admitted to the Special Music School at Kishinev, where she stayed for nine years. After briefly attending the

Stolyarsky School in Odessa, she completed her studies at the Odessa Conservatory and, in 1967, she was voted 'Young Musician of the Year' in Kiev. At that point, she was offered the opportunity to study in Moscow with David Oistrakh at the Tchaikovsky Conservatory, where she became his assistant. 'Oistrakh was a great inspiration. Everything he did was balanced, in the right proportion. He never exaggerated, and he was so sincere. . . . He would spend from two to four lessons on one piece, and this was enough because he gave everything in that time. It was then ready to perform on stage.'[4]

While studying with Oistrakh, she won a prize in the Long-Thibaud Competition in Paris that launched her solo career, with concerts all over the USSR and Eastern Europe. In 1974 her family decided to emigrate to Israel, and while waiting for her visa, she was not allowed to perform or teach.

Personally, Mordkovitch had not wanted to leave the USSR, and it was difficult to adjust to her first few years in the West, particularly as there were few opportunities to give concerts. She was more fortunate on the teaching side and was appointed professor at the Jerusalem Academy. Here she gradually began to establish a reputation and her concert appearances became more frequent. Soon she was performing successfully all over Israel and also toured South and Central America.

In 1979 Mordkovitch made her British debut in Manchester, playing the Tchaikovsky concerto with the Hallé Orchestra under Walter Susskind, and received glowing praise from the press. The following year she decided to move to the UK where she finally made her home and took out British citizenship.

Mordkovitch has continued her concert career and has made many award-winning recordings. She has taught at the Royal Northern College of Music since 1980 and the Royal Academy of Music since 1995.

The Bulgarian Stoika Milanova was born into a family of musicians at Plovdiv in 1945 and received her first violin lessons when she was four years old from her father, Trendaffil Milanov, director and professor at the local school of music. The family moved to Sofia in 1950, and at eight she gave her first recital; her orchestral debut with the Sofia Symphony Orchestra followed when she was 12. Two years later, she took First Prize in the Bulgarian National Competition. When she was 18, she played for Oistrakh, who invited her immediately to become his pupil at the Moscow Conservatory. For Milanova, these were the most exciting five years of her life. On one occasion she was playing the first part of the Brahms concerto for him and could not get it right. After refusing at first to play a passage, he took up his Strad; in a flash she saw all the beauty and depth she was looking for, and all obstacles were removed. Oistrakh would keep in touch with his students long after they had started on their performing careers and Milanova remembers what was to be their last meeting in London at the small pizzeria opposite the Royal Gardens Hotel. Just a short time afterwards while on tour in Germany she heard the news that he had died. She performed the Prokofiev Concerto No. 1 in his place, a very emotional experience, because she had lost not only a friend and teacher, but her 'spiritual father'.

During her time with Oistrakh, Milanova won the Special Prize at the 1962 Festival for Youth in Helsinki, second prize in the Queen Elisabeth Concours in Brussels in 1967, and both the First and the Audience prizes in the 1970 Carl Flesch Competition in London. Her career soon reached international proportions and she made many highly praised recordings. Her partner in duo recitals was the pianist Radu Lupu. She teaches at the Pantcho Vladigerov Bulgarian National Academy of Music in Sofia.

Liana Isakadze, an Oistrakh pupil who spent some seven years under his wing, was born in Tiflis in 1946. She showed early interest in the violin and began lessons when still a small child, first appearing in public in 1957 when she was 11 years old. In 1961, she won the second prize in the USSR National Competition; Oistrakh was on the jury. Impressed with her playing, he kept an eye on her until, in 1963, he took her into his class at the Moscow Conservatory. While his student, she won the first prize in the Long-Thibaud Competition in Paris and that same year made a highly successful tour of Eastern and Western Europe, Cuba and Finland. On her return she carried off several further prizes including the Tchaikovsky in Moscow and the Sibelius in Helsinki. Isakadze's repertory includes all the classical favourites, which she plays in period style, but she is also a champion of contemporary works.

Zakhar Bron inherits the Oistrakh influence through his studies with his son, Igor, at the Moscow Conservatory, and has emerged as one of the great teachers of his generation. He was born in Uralsk in 1946; his mother was a pianist and his father an engineer with a passion for the violin. Bron showed considerable talent and won prizes in several competitions including the Wieniawski and the Queen Elisabeth Concours, but he had no aspirations to be a soloist.

In 1974, Bron was appointed a member of the faculty at the recently established Special Music School in Novosibirsk. All lessons were private – in contrast to almost all the other schools where class-teaching was the norm – and Bron attracted many exceptionally gifted children, one of whom was Maxim Vengerov. Bron went on to teach at the Hochschule in Lübeck and is at present at the Hochschule in Cologne.

The death of Oleg Kagan in 1990 at the age of 44 deprived the musical world of one of the greatest violinists of his generation. He was born in 1946 in Sakhalin in the USSR, the son of a surgeon who loved the violin. Soon after the war the family moved to Latvia, and Oleg's first music studies were at the Riga Conservatory with Joachim Braun. At 13, he was heard by Boris Kusnetzov, who took him to Moscow to study with him at the Tchaikovsky Conservatory. The young boy lived with Kusnetzov, who supervised every detail of his training. Later Kagan said how grateful he had been for the strict discipline of this regime.

After the sudden death of Kusnetzov in 1964, Kagan was taken into Oistrakh's class and while still a student won many prizes in competitions: the Enescu in Bucharest in 1964, the Sibelius in Helsinki in 1965, the Tchaikovsky in Moscow in 1966 and the Bach in Leipzig in 1968. The experience of studying with Oistrakh was something he never forgot. 'Oistrakh exerted a tremendous influence on me. For his pupils he was like a father, a counsellor and a friend.'⁵ In Kagan's case, a firm friendship developed between master and pupil which lasted until Oistrakh's death. Oistrakh was particularly excited by Kagan's playing of Mozart, and conducted in Kagan's recording of all the Mozart concertos.

In the late 1960s, Kagan met Sviatoslav Richter, and again this engendered a close friendship and artistic collaboration that lasted for over 20 years. Richter was also a great admirer of Kagan's interpretation of Mozart and suggested they play all the Mozart violin sonatas, which also exist in a memorable recording. Over the years, the two artists made music in an infinite variety of venues from working men's clubs in Siberia, farms in White Russia and concert halls in the Caucasus to museums in Moscow. Although the classical composers held a firm place in their repertory, they were also attracted to twentieth-century music and gave many performances of compositions from the Second Viennese School; Berg's Kammerkonzert was a work with which they were closely identified. Alfred Schnittke and Kagan became close associates and the latter's performance of his Second Violin Sonata remained the composer's favourite. Schnittke wrote several works for Kagan, the first being the Third Violin Concerto in 1978.

Kagan was also a lover of chamber music and, over the years, played with most of the leading string players and pianists of the day, including his wife, the cellist Natalia Gutman. Another of his musical projects was the small festival he founded in the little medieval town of Zvenigorod in a lush green valley south of Moscow. Here he would invite his friends and they met every day to make music, even putting on operas together. As a man, Kagan was unaffected, modest and approachable. It is not difficult to visualise these qualities in the many recordings he made.

Gidon Kremer has been described as idiosyncratic, enigmatic and a maverick. He is not afraid to express opinions that are unorthodox, and it is therefore not difficult to imagine how he exasperated the authorities while living in the USSR. Of German extraction, Kremer was born in 1947 in Riga, into a family of professional musicians. He showed early musical talent and, at 18, was accepted as a pupil of Oistrakh at the Moscow Conservatory, remaining there for eight years. Only after Oistrakh died did the full significance of his teaching come home to him: 'He was a very generous artist and always sought to bring out the best in every student; he wasn't interested in producing so many little Oistrakhs. Although I admired him immensely and still do, I never tried to imitate his playing and I don't consider myself in any way his heir or anything of the sort. Thank God I never lacked the strength to be my own man.'⁶ Apparently Oistrakh was shocked when he first heard the 16-year-old Kremer play and declared him to be 'too anarchic and extrovert'. After Kremer had joined his class, Oistrakh realised that his student was not being intentionally awkward, but was trying to find his own way, and as such he accepted it. Kremer gives his reasons: 'I wasn't always happy with the received wisdom. This applies to the choice of repertory and cadenzas as well, not only the way of playing.'⁷

During the years with Oistrakh, Kremer carried off several first prizes: the Queen

Elisabeth Concours in Brussels in 1967, the Paganini and the Montreal in 1969, and the Tchaikovsky in Moscow the following year. Although this led to some 150 concerts in the USSR, he was at first refused a visa to travel abroad. In 1975, when he was finally given permission, he came to the UK and made his London debut; Karajan was in the audience and was so impressed that he invited Kremer to record the Brahms Concerto and to play with the Berlin Philharmonic at the opening concert of the next Salzburg Festival. From this time onwards, he travelled the world over, his career assured.

Although Kremer's repertory is vast and includes most of the classics, he has also made himself a reputation for performing contemporary music; he has performed works by John Adams, Philip Glass, Arthur Lourie, Arvo Pärt, Alan Ridout, Aribert Reimann and Alfred Schnittke, many of them written for him.

Václav Hudeček was born in 1952 in Rozmital – then Czechoslovakia – and received his first lessons from Bohumil Kotel, and later Václav Snftil, at the Academy of Music in Prague. He won numerous prizes, resulting in concert appearances, not only in his native country but also abroad; he made his British debut with the Royal Philharmonic Orchestra when he was only 15. While in London he played for Oistrakh, who invited him to study with him in Moscow. For four years he had private lessons with Oistrakh and was, in fact, his last pupil.

Hudeček considers that Oistrakh was the most important influence on his musical development, and when critics write about him, they often draw a comparison between him and his mentor. One critic wrote of Hudeček's recording of Bach's violin concertos: 'He plays with confident strokes and his strength of expression is perfectly controlled. His tone is wide and carrying, but never overdone.' In the double concerto he is joined by Dimitri Sitkovetsky – 'a partner of equal genius in this provokingly beautiful performance'.[8] Today, Václav Hudeček enjoys international status, and his recording of Vivaldi's Four Seasons was the most popular disc in the Czech Republic for many years.

## Notes

1–3. *The Strad*, September 1989, p. 760.
4. *The Strad*, August 1987, p. 599.
5. Notes from Maxim Panfilo to M.C.
6–7. *The Strad*, February 1997, pp. 125–9.
8. *Fonoforum*, March 1996.

# 44  Legends and Legacies

While the names of Flesch, Galamian and Ševčík dominate as teachers in the early twentieth century, there are other legendaries who will no doubt be remembered as having made their mark on the later decades of that century. Josef Gingold and Dorothy DeLay between them taught many of the young players at the top of their profession today. Franz Kneisel (1865–1926) was another highly respected teacher.

Louis Kaufman (1905–94) was born in Portland, Oregon, the son of Russian–Jewish immigrants – music-lovers who took him to concerts when he was a small child. He had his first violin lessons when he was seven and, at the age of ten, teamed up with a dancer and toured on the vaudeville circuit.

The following year Kaufman took some lessons with Henry Bettman, a pupil of Ysaÿe and, on the recommendation of Efrem Zimbalist, was accepted into the class of Franz Kneisel at the Institute of Musical Art in New York. Kaufman always contended that this was when his musical education really began; he remembered Kneisel as an excellent teacher, but also something of a tyrant, who insisted that his pupils practise for six hours a day. Since Kaufman was still at school, he could not comply, so he left Kneisel for a Jesuit priest, who proved an excellent teacher but a religious fanatic; after two weeks, his formal education came to an end.

In 1927 Kaufman won the Institute's Loeb Prize and the following year received the Naumberg Award, which brought about a solo recital at Town Hall in New York. In the meantime Kaufman had taught himself to play the viola and, when the word got around, he found himself playing chamber music with Kreisler, Elman, Zimbalist and Casals. This led to him joining the Musical Art Quartet, with whom he played until 1933. The previous year he had met and married a young pianist, Annette Liebole, and together they gave recitals all over the USA between his concerto appearances. Theirs was a harmonious domestic and musical partnership that lasted for over half a century.

In 1934, Kaufman was approached by MGM to play in Ernst Lubitsch's film *The Merry Widow*, and for the next 14 years he played solos in countless films, including *Gone With the Wind* and *For Whom the Bell Tolls*. In 1948 the Kaufmans decided to leave Hollywood for Europe, making Paris their base. This was the time when, with the advent of the LP, the recording industry was going through a period of change. Kaufman made over 100 major recordings with the world's finest conductors and orchestras, and although he was a fine exponent of the traditional repertory, he was also a strong advocate of contemporary music. He counted Milhaud, Poulenc and Copland among his friends and gave many first performances of works by Bohuslav Martinů, Dag Wirén, Leighton Lucas, Ralph Vaughan Williams and others.

The Kaufmans returned to the USA in 1956. He enchanted his audiences with his superb playing well into his 70s, but after an operation for a detached retina, he decided to retire. 'My credo has been simple. I never felt music owed me anything; whatever came my way I did to the best of my ability . . . and striven to give more than I received.'[1]

Shlomo Mintz was born in Moscow in 1957 and began playing the violin at three. His family later emigrated to Israel, where he had lessons with Ilona Feher when he was six. He made his solo debut at eleven when he replaced Perlman playing the Paganini Concerto No 1 with the Israel Philharmonic Orchestra under Zubin Mehta; as a result, Stern recommended him for a scholarship at the Juilliard School in New York, where he studied with DeLay.

Mintz made his Carnegie Hall debut at 16 and was acclaimed as a *Wunderkind*. But he has views on how that image affects the artist's later development: 'I think the *Wunder* itself has nothing to do with age. It takes different forms. Having observed other *Wunderkinder* as they develop, I note that if they grow very quickly they can often stop just as quickly. If a child shows an inclination to music at three years, he is simply beginning a process – one hopes a lifelong process.'[2]

According to the *Washington Post* critic, Robert McDuffie 'can make a violin do anything'.[3] McDuffie was born in Macon, Georgia in 1958, and his first musical memories are of his mother – a professional pianist – practising. At the age of three, he could pick out tunes on her piano, but soon showed a preference for the violin. He was fortunate in having lessons with Henrik Schwarzenberger, a Hungarian refugee who had settled in the USA. From him McDuffie gained a solid foundation, based on Rode, Dont, Kreutzer and Paganini, and developed over a ten-year period. Following studies with Margaret Pardee at Juilliard in New York, he was accepted by Dorothy DeLay. McDuffie remembers this time with gratitude. He maintains that she allowed her students to use their own imagination and grow on their own terms, so they are all different.

When McDuffie left Juilliard at 22 he had neither manager nor prospects. So for the next year he sat at the back of the violin section in the New York Chamber Orchestra – which he now regards as invaluable experience – after which he was taken on by one of the leading New York agents. But the real break came when he played for Menuhin and was invited to play chamber music with him at Carnegie Hall; this was followed by a US tour with the Warsaw Sinfonia, also under Menuhin. Today he is a fully fledged solo performer but continues to be actively involved with several chamber music groups.

Two British violinists, Nigel Kennedy and Simon Fischer, both born in 1956, with very different careers, were also pupils of DeLay at Juilliard. Nigel Kennedy was born in Brighton into a musical family. His mother, Celia Forbes, a piano teacher, recognised her son had an outstanding talent when he was able to play the piano at the age of two. He later had some lessons on the violin and, when he was eight, he won a scholarship to the Menuhin School, where he was a pupil of Robert Masters, whom he still remembers as one of his favourite teachers. He spent ten years at the school and in 1975 was awarded a scholarship to Juilliard.

On his return to the UK, Kennedy made his debut with the London Philharmonic Orchestra at the Royal Festival Hall. The critics raved and fame beckoned. In addition to concerts with all the leading British orchestras, in 1980 he performed with the Berlin Philharmonic and at the Proms the following year. He made numerous recordings and in 1985 won a Golden Disc for his recording of the Elgar concerto; he followed this with a phenomenally successful recording of Vivaldi's Four Seasons which made him a household name (and rather a lot of money).

Kennedy's well-publicised interest in jazz started when he was 15 and at the Menuhin School. When some of the teachers discovered that he was playing jazz in his practice time, they reported him to Menuhin. However, he thought it was a good thing and promptly introduced the rebel to Stephane Grappelli. Kennedy remains eternally grateful to Menuhin, not only for his support but also for introducing him to Grappelli, who gave him valuable new perspectives on the violin as an instrument of direct communication. He observed how Grappelli could get up and communicate with an audience's *mood* and enjoy every moment of it. From their first meeting, Kennedy was treated as Grappelli's protégé. From the great jazz violinist, he acquired the ability to play more with the feel of the music. Their respect was mutual.

In 1997 Kennedy decided to return to the concert platform and the traditional repertory and was welcomed back with open arms by audiences and critics alike. Many members of the general public had been introduced to classical music for the first time with his Four Seasons recording and the more established public recognised that, in spite of his 'punk' interlude, he was still a first-class violinist. In April, when his return to the fold coincided with the forthcoming General Election in the UK, politics seemed consigned to second place in the national press. *The Times* critic wrote: 'Only one British violinist in my lifetime has produced anything as bold and exhilarating … It is his playing, though, that most reveals Kennedy's new maturity. No other violinist on earth could manage the astonishing stylistic transition presented here.' He had been playing Bartók's Sonata for Solo Violin, which the critic described as 'one of the most fiendish challenges in the twentieth-century repertoire'. Kennedy – as he now wishes to be known – is still only in his forties; he tours the world ceaselessly, giving superb performances of the Elgar Violin Concerto and much of the traditional repertory, and his recordings sell in the millions. A great talent has found its true place.

Simon Fischer was born in Sydney, Australia into a musical family; his mother was a singer and amateur violinist and his father a professional pianist and teacher. The Fischers came to the UK in 1961 and shortly afterwards took out British Nationality. When he was nine, Simon won a scholarship to the Guildhall School of Music and

Drama Junior Department, and in 1974 went on to the main School, studying with Yfrah Neaman. He won further scholarships, enabling him to go to the USA where he had lessons with DeLay at Sarah Laurence College and Juilliard in New York. Fischer was greatly impressed by the standard of teaching in the States. 'Simple tone production exercises which I learnt from DeLay – and she from Galamian and he from Capet – transform the tone of the least well-equipped violinist in a matter of minutes. I came back excited by the idea of spreading these ideas around and I remain so today.'[4]

Back in the UK, after some time as a freelance orchestral and chamber music player, Fischer gained the opportunity to put his ideas into practice when he took up a post at Wells Cathedral School. From there he went on to the Purcell School and today teaches at the GSMD and the Royal Scottish Academy of Music and Drama. He joined the teaching staff of the Menuhin School in 1998.

Although he still plays concertos with a number of British orchestras, Fischer's main focus is on teaching. He has a special gift for explaining how to solve problems and is convinced that everything depends on a good basic training. In 1992, he contributed a series of almost 100 articles on string technique to *The Strad* magazine which he calls 'Basics'. The response was such that the collection was published as *Basics* in 1997.[5]

The Japanese Kyoko Takezawa is yet another of DeLay's pupil who has taken the West by storm. Born in Nagano in 1966, she began her training with a Suzuki teacher and switched to Kenji Kobayashi, another Suzuki student who had also studied with Galamian.

Kobayashi had often suggested that Kyoko should study with DeLay. In her second year at the Toho School in Tokyo, she attended masterclasses given by DeLay and knew he was right. She completed her studies at Juilliard, acquiring a final polish. In 1986, she was awarded the Gold Medal at the Second Quadrennial International Violin Competition in Indianapolis, which brought her a number of concert engagements and a recording contract.

Takezawa is now a well-travelled virtuoso, who is well received by critics everywhere. After her debut in Miami in 1992, in a performance of Bartók's Second Violin Concerto, one critic wrote that, for him, her playing was the high point of the concert – a supreme challenge, which she accepted 'with complete understanding of its rhapsodic, introspective and savage dream world'.[6]

Gil Shaham, born in Illinois in 1971, the son of two scientists, is one of the younger generation who seem to have inherited the old school style of playing, when virtuosity was combined with warmth and freedom of expression. The author was present at his Wigmore Hall debut in 1990 and the magical memory still lingers. Shaham had his first lessons with Samuel Bernstein at the Rubin Academy of Music in Jerusalem when he was seven; he is very grateful to this 'old Russian teacher from Vilnius' who was then in his eighties and imparted to his young student some of the traditions of the old school. 'There was a freedom musicians had back then – a feeling that you could really do anything on the violin. They each had their own voice. That's somehow lost today.'[7] Shaham made his solo debut when he was nine, playing Vivaldi's Four Seasons with Alexander Schneider and the Jerusalem Symphony Orchestra.

Shortly after this he went to the USA where he studied for a while with Jens Ellerman at Aspen before going to Juilliard as a student of DeLay. When he was only 18 he had one of those strokes of luck that every young musician dreams of: Perlman had been engaged for a series of six concerts with the LSO at the Royal Festival Hall in London, but a few days before the first concert, an ear infection prevented him flying. Shaham had one day to prepare programmes which included both the Bruch G minor and the Sibelius concertos. The concerts were highly successful, with warm response from the audiences and encouragement from the press. One year later, Shaham was awarded the Avery Fisher Career Grant and never looked back.

Midori, born in Osaka in 1971, had her first violin lessons with her mother, Setsu Goto, when she was three. A cassette made by a friend when she was eight found its way to Dorothy DeLay, who was so impressed she invited her to attend the Aspen Summer Festival in 1981. The ten-year-old gave a performance of Bartók's Second Violin Concerto that had Pinchas Zukerman in tears. She subsequently attended the Julliard School where she studied with DeLay, Ellermann and Yang-Ho Kim. She made her New York debut with the New York Philharmonic Orchestra at a Gala Concert in 1982. From this time, her career gained momentum and she began making highly successful appearances worldwide; at her London debut at a Prom concert in 1993 she played the Tchaikovsky concerto and brought the house down.

Today she has not only survived the dubious blessing of being a child prodigy, but has proved herself an adult performer of significance. She has a natural curiosity whereby she continually seeks new sources of inspiration and this imbues her playing with colour and imagination.

In the USA she established *Midori & Friends*. This is a foundation that presents a series of free solo and chamber music concerts at American schools throughout an area followed by a lively question and answer period; the response from both children and teachers has been encouraging. 'We hope that we have opened a door, however slightly, to a world children might explore more fully and which could enrich them all their lives.'[8]

Another DeLay student who has achieved international recognition is Cho-Liang 'Jimmy' Lin, born in Taiwan in 1960, the son of a physicist and frustrated musician. At the age of twelve he won the Taiwan National Youth Competition and was taken by his mother to Australia, where he spent three years at the Sydney Conservatory as a student of Robert Pikler, himself a pupil of both Bartók and Kodály. He is indebted to his old teacher for opening his eyes and ears to chamber music which he had not encountered in Taiwan. 'Pikler made me aware of the joy of playing quintets, and I began to see how it could enhance my solo playing through the discipline and camaraderie of working with other musicians.'[9]

It was hearing Perlman at a concert in Sydney that convinced him he must study with Perlman's teacher, DeLay, and this was confirmed by György Pauk who was playing in Sydney shortly afterwards. So, in 1975 Lin set out for New York and the Juilliard School. DeLay became not only Lin's teacher, but also a friend who helped him to adjust to the culture of his adopted country. 'Students in Taiwan were not encouraged to ask questions, let alone debate a point. Now that I'm teaching at Juilliard, I find it frustrating that my students won't talk back to me.'[10] DeLay recalled that at that time very few, if any violinists had come from Taiwan and she was surprised to find his playing so elegant and 'beautifully developed'.[11] Lin has made several visits to mainland China – the only Chinese violinist to have played both in China and Taiwan – and is greeted with an enthusiasm that leaves him exhausted. His hosts wanted to start around six in the morning with rehearsals, then masterclasses, then panel discussions and more rehearsals, and, of course, concerts at night. In 1997, Lin realised an ambition when he founded the Taipei Chamber Music Festival, a two-week event that attracts musicians from all over the world.

Another name to watch is that of Min-Jin Kym, born in South Korea in 1978. Her outstanding talent on the violin earned her a place at the Purcell School when she was only seven years old – the youngest pupil ever to have been accepted. At 11, she won the Martin Scholarship and the following year carried off the Mozart International Competition in Italy. She made her orchestral debut when she was only 13, playing the Lalo *Symphonie espagnole* with the Berlin Symphony Orchestra. Although she could have continued her career as a prodigy, she wisely decided to finish her schooling and complete her studies at the Royal College of Music where, at 15, she became the youngest student to be awarded a Foundation Scholarship. She was described by Ruggiero Ricci as: 'that rare species – a born violinist'.[12]

In November 1987, *The Strad* recommended its readers to note the name of a seven-year-old violinist as a great hope for the future; her name was Sarah Chang. She was born in Philadelphia in 1980, the daughter of Korean parents. She began picking out tunes on the piano when she was two and at four she begged to be taught the violin. Her first teacher was Julian Meyer, who considered she had the most phenomenal talent he had encountered in 19 years of teaching. Luis Biava, director of Temple University's Symphony Orchestra heard Sarah when the university created a 'Center for Gifted Young Musicians' and was equally astounded. He said that the intonation and accuracy she could achieve on her quarter-sized violin was nothing short of miraculous.

The rest of the story is legend. Chang was a pupil of DeLay by the time she was six and, like Midori, she has survived the prodigy years seemingly without problems; she now fulfils a busy concert schedule the world over, sending even the most waspish critics into raptures. In October 1994 she played Sarasate's *Carmen Fantasie* with the LSO in a gala 90th Birthday Concert conducted by Michael Tilson Thomas at the Barbican Centre in London; *The Times* wrote that 'the virtuoso violinist Sarah Chang, now all of 13, made a brief but stunning appearance' and that 'her assured technique and vibrant musicianship shone out like a beacon'.[13] When she performed Bartók's Second Violin Concerto in another celebratory concert – James Levine's 25th anniversary as conductor of the Metropolitan Opera – at Carnegie Hall, James R. Oestreich wrote that 'Ms. Chang delivered a beautifully coherent, superbly gauged reading that bespoke a musical understanding as prodigious as her technique'.[14]

The Greek Leonidas Kavakos was born in Athens in 1967 into a musical family and began his studies at the Greek Conservatory with Stelios Kafantaris. With the aid of an Onassis Foundation Scholarship, he attended masterclasses with Gingold at Indiana University at Bloomington. He made his concert debut at the Athens Festival when he was 17 and the following year won the Sibelius Competition in Helsinki, with the added distinction of being the youngest entrant. He went on to win both the Naumberg and Paganini competitions before he was 21.

From this time, he began fulfilling concert engagements in Europe, including Scandinavia and made his New York debut the following year when he also was awarded the silver medal in the Indianapolis International Violin Competition. London first heard Kavakos in the Proms in 1992 when he played the Stravinsky Violin Concerto with the BBC Scottish Symphony Orchestra. He gave his recital debut the following year at the Edinburgh Festival.

Kavakos has a natural talent and impeccable technique. After a sonata recital with the pianist Peter Nagy at the Lincoln Center in New York, Alex Ross of the *New York Times* called him a player of 'considerable fire and intelligence' and commented that he 'draws a grand golden tone from his violin, the sort of sound one is accustomed to hearing only through the acoustical haze of historical recordings'.[15]

The concerto with which Kavakos has been most closely identified is the Sibelius, which he has recorded in the original version. It is well known that Sibelius was a violin virtuoso manqué, but he also managed to compose one of the great concertos of our time. Its difficulties are well documented and it has been said that violinists needed six fingers on the left hand if they were to play all the notes. The original concerto was given its first disastrous performance in 1904 by Viktor Novaček, whose modest talents as a teacher and chamber music player were inadequate. The critics tore it to pieces and Sibelius withdrew the score and revised it drastically. It was performed in the version we know today in 1905. He felt so strongly about the original that he also forbade anyone to play it until the year 2007, but in 1990, Robert von Bahr, head of the Swedish recording company BIS persuaded the Sibelius family to allow a single recording to be included in the composer's complete works. When the recording was issued, Edward Greenfield wrote that 'Kavakos with pure tone and flawless intonation can convey total concentration. It says much that in the frequently-recorded revised version he bears comparison with the finest rivals; more thoughtful and inward than most.'[16]

Ulf Hoelscher has the distinction of having studied with three great teachers: Rostal, Gingold and Galamian. He was born in Kitzingen in 1942 and received his first lessons from his father, who was a music teacher. His progress was such that in his teens he went to study with Rostal in Cologne and, at 21, was awarded a scholarship to go to the USA where, over a period of three years, he studied with Gingold at Bloomington, Indiana and Galamian at the Curtis Institute.

Hoelscher's return to Germany was uneventful in that he had no great offers to appear as a soloist, although his ambitious father always had this in mind. His first string of professional appearances began with the 1967/8 season when Volker Schmidt-Gertenbach, music director of the Federal Society for Concerts for Young Musicians, engaged him for 30 concerts. His first international triumph came in 1971 with a concert in London. The critics were most enthusiastic, describing his playing as brilliant but also deeply musical. Hoelscher was soon snapped up by the recording scouts and he has a number of important discs to his credit and an array of awards. He plays concertos from Tchaikovsky, Berg, Schumann and Mendelssohn to Hummel and Spohr. He is also an advocate of contemporary works, many of which he has premiered.

One of the brightest stars of the younger generation is Joshua Bell, who through Gingold represents a direct line from both Auer and Ysaÿe. Joshua Bell was born in Bloomington in 1967, the son of two psychologists. When he was four he was given an eighth-size violin and took to it immediately. At eleven he was accepted into the summer camp at Meadowmount run by Galamian in upstate New York and found himself second youngest of 150 students, who included many of the top names in the profession. The following year he gave a recital in Bloomington and invited Gingold to attend. He begged for some lessons from Gingold, who was at first reluctant but finally agreed to take him on; there began what was to become a happy and compatible teacher–pupil relationship, lasting until Gingold's death in 1995.

At 14 Bell won a competition which led to a solo engagement with the Philadelphia Orchestra under Riccardo Muti, making him the youngest soloist ever to have appeared at a subscription concert with the orchestra. The following year he launched his full-time professional career and the rest is history; Bell has appeared in almost every country in the world and has made numerous recordings. Unlike so many of the 'Wunderkind' breed, Bell is rather shy and makes no effort to seduce his audience with extrovert charm; on the contrary, if anything he wears what one reviewer called 'a seraphic frown' and is completely lost in the music.

> Bell played the famous Prokofiev piece with a nice feeling for its lyrical line and sense of what might be called playfulness. This concerto is a wonderful blend of sweetness and devilishness . . . His tone was sweet and true, as that of a good singer must be.[17]

Bell also finds chamber music very satisfying, particularly because there is less pressure than in solo performances. He also enjoys playing with others so that they all feed off each other musically. In 1991 he formed a trio with the cellist Steven Isserlis and pianist Olli Mustonen.

Anne Akiko-Meyers was born in 1970 in San Diego, the daughter of a Japanese mother and American father, and made her first solo concert appearance when she was seven. She had some lessons with Alice Schoenfeld, then went on to Gingold at Bloomington, and at 14 entered the Juilliard School where she studied with DeLay, Masao Kawasaki and Felix Galimir.

She is convinced she has benefited from studying with several teachers of differing approaches. She loved Gingold's 'old-style' playing, and Akiko-Meyers' own playing is often praised for its sweetness of tone, which is almost certainly a legacy from her studies with Gingold. DeLay 'taught me to teach myself'.[18]

Her career has now reached international proportions and she has a long-term recording contract. She is also extraordinarily beautiful but critics, who have an uncanny insight into such matters, remark far more on her intelligent musicianship and melting sweetness of tone than her physical appearance.

When the 14-year-old Corey Cerovsek played the Mozart A major Violin Concerto with the Bournemouth Symphony Orchestra under Rudolf Barshai at the Royal Festival Hall, David Murray from the *Financial Times* not only gave him a glowing review but added that he was '…the nicest kind of prodigy, in short; not to be rushed after while he is still precociously clever, but to wait for while his astonishing talent matures'.[19]

Corey Cerovsek was born in Vancouver in 1972, the son of Czech-Austrian parents, and could read, write and play the piano by the age of four. The following year he took up the violin and, at nine, he won the Grand Prize in a Canadian Music Competition in which there were 3,000 entries. That same year he made his first public appearance with the Calgary Philharmonic Orchestra playing the Allegro from the Mozart G major Concerto. Bernard Levin described him as having 'the appearance of an angel and the talent of the devil himself' and added that 'the whole evening, as far as I'm concerned was black magic'.[20] When he played the slow movement of the Bruch Violin Concerto No. 1 with the Seattle Symphony Orchestra in 1984, there were gasps of disbelief from the audience and musicians alike. One critic wrote that 'he is a world-class virtuoso who happens to be 12 years old'.[21]

Cerovsek attended the Royal Conservatory in Toronto and graduated at the age of twelve. Of his several teachers, he learned most from the husband-and-wife team, Charmian Gadd and Richard Goldner. The Cerovsek family moved to Bloomington so that Corey could continue his studies at the University of Indiana with Gingold, who had taught Charmian Gadd. Two years later, Corey confounded the university's administrators by fulfilling all the requirements for a double degree in music and mathematics, and by 16 he had earned two master's degrees.

The pupil–teacher relationship between Gingold and Cerovsek soon developed into a friendship which – as with Bell – lasted until Gingold's death. Cerovsek is very conscious of the influence of Ysaÿe that he has inherited through his mentor. 'Mr Gingold showed me Ysaÿe's exercises for smooth string crossings, and taught me how to use fingering – which I had previously regarded as something mainly functional – in such a way as to explore all of the artistic resources of the violin.'[22] Gingold never emphasised technique *per se* because it was the fiddle's *spirit* he wanted to bring out.

There was also much discussion in every lesson on the fact that he wanted his students to understand what they were doing so that one day they could pass on the knowledge to others.

Cerovsek has played with most of the world's leading orchestras and conductors. He made his British debut recital at the Wigmore Hall in 1995 with his equally talented sister, Katja, two years his senior, and again had the critics gasping for superlatives. He still occasionally plays concertos on both violin and piano in the same concert. Cerovsek is not only a prodigy who has come of age, but is also a fully rounded musician, whose intellect and intuition are inseparable. When Gingold was asked about this phenomenon, he said: 'Corey will continue to grow because he is never self-satisfied. He has a great respect for his art. He always seeks to delve into the deepest aspects of every work he plays.'[23]

## Notes

1. M.C., *Independent*, 14 February 1994.
2. *The Strad*, December 1986, p. 578.
3. *Washington Post*, 23 November 1989.
4. Quoted from interview, M.C.
5. *Basics*, Peters Edition, 1997.
6. Hemsing publicity brochure.
7. *The Strad*, February 1996, p. 116.
8. *Signature*, Summer 1995.
9. *The Strad*, April 1987, p. 300.
10–11. *The Strad*, September 1995, p. 899.
12. Peacock publicity brochure.
13. *The Times*, 3 October 1994.
14. *New York Times*, 23 April 1996.
15. *New York Times*, 30 January 1993.
16. *Guardian*, 21 February 1991.
17. *The Plain Dealer*, 13 March 1992.
18. *The Strad*, May 1993, p. 461.
19. *Financial Times*, 26 January 1987.
20. *The Listener*, September 1981.
21. *Seattle Post*, April 1984.
22. *The Strad*, June 1992, p. 522.
23. *The Strad*, June 1992, p. 524.

# 45 The Soviet Torchbearers

T he October Revolution of 1917 changed the face of everything in Russia, including music. That summer, Leopold Auer – a monarchist through and through – spent his holidays in Norway as was his custom and simply failed to return to take up his post at the St Petersburg Conservatory.

The Russian Music Society, patron of music schools throughout the country, was dissolved and all their institutions were nationalised. The staff were not paid, the buildings were unheated, so lessons had to be given at the teachers' homes. Hunger was rife and public transport at a standstill during the winter months. Despite these arctic conditions theatres and concert halls remained open, and the musicians were obliged to perform wearing gloves. The composer Alexander Glazunov, director of the St Petersburg Conservatory, liaised with the Bolsheviks in order to keep the conservatories open. Inevitably there were radical changes; professors and students alike had to toe the party line and the curriculum was revised; as a result the quality of the teaching suffered.

Before examining further developments we should look at some pupil–teacher relationships that had considerable influence on the St Petersburg school. From Corelli to Somis, Pugnani, Viotti and Rode we have a direct line; Rode was the teacher of Josef Böhm, who in turn taught Joachim and Dont – two of Auer's teachers. As stated in an earlier chapter, it was Henryk Wieniawski – a pupil of Massart – who preceded Auer in 1860 when he became violinist to the Tsar and professor at the conservatory. He resigned in 1868 and Auer took his place. The foundations laid by Wieniawski provided the base from which Auer reached even greater heights.

Other violinists of significance in the St Petersburg school were Yuri Eidlin (1896–1958) an Auer pupil, Mikhail Vaiman (1926–77), who studied with Pyotr Stolyarsky and Eidlin, and Boris Gutnikov (1931–86), a pupil of Eidlin and Ioannes Nalbandyan (1871–1942). Following Auer's defection, a number of his former students achieved a modicum of continuity. Nalbandyan, Auer's assistant since 1895, remained a professor until 1942; Sergei Korguyev (1863–1938), a professor from 1900, was retained until 1925; Maria Gamovetskaya, a former assistant of Auer, held a class until 1931, and in 1928 Miron Poliakin (1895–1941), one of Auer's most talented pupils from the pre-Revolution period, returned to the conservatory in the city now called Leningrad.

In 1918, Moscow was declared the capital city of the USSR so that both politically and culturally it held pride of place. In the mid-1930s Moscow Conservatory gradually assumed the importance previously enjoyed by Leningrad; as a result, it attracted all the most talented teachers and students. In particular, the Moscow Conservatory built up a thriving violin faculty of mostly former students of Auer or those who had come under his influence: Lev Tseitlin (1891–52), Konstantin Mostras (1886–1965), Boris Sibor (1880–1961), Abram Yampol'sky (1890–1956), and later, Poliakin, were some of the best known. At the same time, another hotbed of violin playing was developing fast in the Odessa Conservatory, where Stolyarsky nurtured a number of budding talents. Over a period, graduates from his class went to Moscow for their postgraduate training, which engendered rivalry between the two schools, but obtained spectacular results. In 1937, the USSR had five among the first six prize-winners in the Ysaÿe Contest in Brussels: David Oistrakh – a pupil of Stolyarsky – took First Prize; of the other four, Yelizavita Gilels, Boris Goldstein (1921–87) and Mikhail Fikhtengolts (1920–85) were pupils of Stolyarsky and Yampol'sky, and Marina Kozolupova was a pupil of Mostras and Poliakin.

Ioannes Nalbandyan studied with Auer in St Petersburg and later became his most trusted assistant; he also had a period of study with Joachim at the Hochschule in Berlin. He enjoyed a successful solo career and favoured the classic repertory. He taught at the St Petersburg/Leningrad Conservatory from 1895 until his death in 1942, becoming a professor in 1908.

Piotr Stolyarsky (1871–1944) was born in a village near Kiev and received his early training at the Odessa Music School. As an adult he played from 1898 to 1919 in the Odessa Opera Orchestra, after which he devoted himself to teaching, working especially with young children: 'One of the fundamentals of his method was to instil confidence in the young pupil by assuring him that he had extraordinary talent.'[1] Stolyarsky gave his lessons in a room in his own apartment, where the under-fives played with toys while the over-fives had their lessons. Then, the smaller children would take their toy violins and imitate the older ones. Stolyarsky was just as expert at teaching his advanced students through the concerto and sonata repertory.

Abram Ilyich Yampol'sky was born in Ekaterinoslav (now Dnipropetrovsk) and graduated from Serguyev's class at St Petersburg Conservatory in 1913. He taught the violin at the local music college until 1920, appearing as a solo violinist and leading a string quartet. In 1920, he moved to Moscow, where he was a member of the Bolshoi Theatre Orchestra. Two years later, he was appointed director of the orchestral and violin classes at the Moscow Conservatory, becoming a professor and head of the violin department. Later he taught at the Gnessin Institute.

Yampol'sky was a key figure in the development of the modern Soviet Violin School who, by incorporating new ideas into the traditional school of Wieniawski and Auer, raised Soviet violin playing to a new artistic and technical level. 'His teaching method was based on a subtle combination of the performer's musical feeling with the all-round development of his mastery of the instrument.'[2] His students became known for their purity of intonation, refined tone, command of detail and depth of interpretation.

A pupil of Auer at the St Petersburg Conservatory, Boris Sibor also had some studies with Joachim in Berlin. As a soloist he appeared frequently at the Bolshoi Theatre and toured Russia with much success. He was greatly respected as a teacher and, in 1904, became senior tutor at the Moscow Philharmonic School, where one of his students was Konstantin Mostras, the teacher of Galamian. He taught at the Moscow Conservatory from 1921 to 1951 and was appointed professor in 1923.

Mostras was born in Ardzhenka in 1886, and clearly inherited the valuable influence of Auer through Sibor. He taught at the Moscow Philharmonic School from 1914 to 1922, and after that at the conservatory. Although an accomplished soloist he was also devoted to chamber music and became leader of the Lenin Quartet, founded in 1918, one of the first formed under the Soviet regime. During his years at the conservatory, where he became head of the violin department, he was known not only for his teaching skills, but also as one of the most important figures in the development of the Soviet School. He was intelligent, inventive and inquisitive, and his writings are still a significant contribution to the art of violin playing. Apart from publishing his own course on violin technique, in collaboration with David Oistrakh he edited the Tchaikovsky concerto, restoring it to something closer to the original version.

Mischa Mischakoff was a student of Korguyev at St Petersburg. He emigrated to the USA in 1921 where he accepted a succession of posts as concertmaster, a role for which he was well suited. Both Stokowski and Toscanini admired his playing, and the latter came to depend very much upon his assistance and experience when organising the string sections of the newly created NBC Symphony Orchestra.

Mischakoff's style of playing was 'ideally suited for his career as orchestra leader; his tone was strong but always beautiful, his rhythm robust, his technical command most reliable and unaffected by nerves'.[3] A stylish chamber music player, he formed his own eponymous quartet, which was active for many years. He also found time for teaching: among his pupils were the Kavafian sisters and Joseph Silverstein. He was also a connoisseur of fine instruments and once had in his collection two Stradivaris and a Guarnerius del Gesù.

Miron Poliakin was only 13 and already playing concertos with a musicality far beyond his years when he entered Auer's class at the conservatory. His temperament made him a difficult student, but after the 1910 examinations, Glazunov had only words of praise: 'Highly artistic interpretation. Marvellous technique. Enchanting tone. Sensitive phrasing. Temperament and atmosphere in his playing. A finished artist.'[4] Two years later, Poliakin performed at the 50th anniversary of the conservatory's foundation.

Poliakin stayed until he was 18, but did not graduate. He did have Auer's permission to give concerts in the provinces, and, after 1918, he toured Germany and Scandinavia. In 1922, he went to the USA where he made a successful New York debut, but at that time there were many talented violinists on the international circuit and the competition was such that, in 1927, he returned to the USSR, where he was welcomed with open arms; from this point, he achieved the success he deserved. Before leaving Soviet Russia he had favoured the virtuoso and popular works, but now he showed himself a master of the concerto and sonata repertory and the Russians took him to their hearts.

In 1936 Poliakin moved to Moscow where, in addition to his solo appearances, he taught at the conservatory, where 'he relied primarily on his own demonstrations, preferring to play rather than to discuss'.[5] Poliakin's class consisted of only two or three students. He could not bear to hear them play. After listening for a few seconds to a violin concerto played by a good young violinist, he interrupted him and criticised the performance in violent terms. Then he picked up the violin and, no matter how well the student had played, Poliakin always played better.[6]

Yuri Eidlin was born in 1896 in Ekaterinoslav (now Dnipropetrovsk) and studied at the St Petersburg Conservatory with Auer until the latter's departure in 1917, when he became a pupil of Korguyev. He taught at Baku from 1924 until 1926, after which he returned to Leningrad, where he taught at the newly opened School for Studies in Musical Technique. From 1927 he taught both solo and quartet playing at the Leningrad Conservatory and was made a professor in 1935. He was a good teacher who encouraged his students to play musically while thinking analytically about what they were doing. His own intellectual approach led to him publish his own system of violin playing, which had wide currency. Two of his best known pupils were Mikhail Vaiman and Boris Gutnikov.

Yury Isayevich Yankelevich (1909–73) was Yampol'sky's most celebrated pupil. He was born in Basle and studied with him at the Moscow Conservatory and later taught there. When Yampol'sky died in 1956, he took over his class and in 1969 he became head of the violin department. His students include Albert Markov, Vladimir Spivakov and Viktor Tret'yakov.

Mikhail Fichtengolz, a pupil of both Stolyarsky and Yampol'sky, was an outstanding violinist who completed postgraduate studies with Poliakin. He was a prize-winner in the Ysaÿe Contest in Brussels in 1937 and from this time achieved a reputation as a soloist. His career was interrupted by long years of illness, when he concentrated on teaching and music criticism. In 1992 he returned to the concert platform where he was greeted with great enthusiasm and recognised as an original interpreter of Bach's solo sonatas and partitas.

Boris Goldstein was born in Odessa in 1921 and had lessons with Stolyarsky from the age of five. When he was nine, he was taken to Moscow where he attended Yampol'sky's children's group and later completed his studies at the conservatory with Tseitlin. He appeared in his first concert at the age of 11 and immediately began playing all over Russia. At 16, he was a prize-winner in the 1937 Ysaÿe Contest in Brussels and, at 20, he was one of the youngest ever to be appointed as soloist of the Moscow Philharmonic Society.

Goldstein's large repertory included all the classic concertos and sonatas, but he also was a brilliant interpreter of contemporary Soviet music and gave many first performances. He was also a good teacher and taught at the Moscow Conservatory from 1948 until 1953, and at the Gnessin Institute until 1959, when he was able to leave the USSR and settle in Hanover, where he died in 1987.

One of the most important Soviet violinists in the mid-twentieth century was Mikhail Vaiman, a brilliant soloist and greatly respected teacher whom many said was the equal in many ways of David Oistrakh. He was born in Novy Bug in 1926 and had his first lessons from his father, Israel, a violinist and teacher at the Odessa School of Music. When he was eight years old, he entered Stolyarsky's class, where he made phenomenal progress.

Meanwhile, the USSR had become involved in the Second World War and Vaiman's father was killed in action. At the time, the family were living in Tashkent, where – fortunately for them – the Leningrad Conservatory had been evacuated. Vaiman was taken into the class of Yuri Eidlin, so inheriting the Auer influence. Recognising that he had an exceptionally gifted student on his hands, Eidlin sought to exploit every aspect of his talent and in 1943, when the Moscow authorities sent notification that they were reviewing young talent from music schools throughout the country, he entered his pupil with a strong recommendation. Yampol'sky, who was judging the entrants, was clearly impressed and, after Vaiman had played the Tchaikovsky concerto, he wrote that, in his opinion, the young man had one of the most outstanding talents he had encountered, adding that 'his execution was both technically perfect and innately musical.'[7]

After this, Vaiman won prizes in every competition available and appeared as a soloist not only in the USSR and Eastern Europe but also in the West and the Orient. Critics raved about his wonderful tone and impeccable technique, but they also praised him as being a thinking musician, who interpreted from both head and heart. He made numerous recordings, some of which are available today on CD.

Vaiman was a lifelong close friend of David Oistrakh, who also admired his playing, and when Vaiman made his New York debut, Oistrakh sent him a postcard from London:

2 June 1967

Dear Misha,

I am very glad that you were such a success in the US, but truthfully, I never doubted it. Greetings from Tamara and myself to you and Alla [Vaiman's wife].

Fondly,

David Fedorovitch

Vaiman was also a dedicated teacher. He taught at the Leningrad Conservatory from 1949, and in 1970 was appointed head of the violin department. His career was cut short by a fatal heart attack at the age of 52.

Boris Gutnikov was born in Vitebsk in 1931 and, from the age of five, had lessons from Nalbandyan and later, Lyubov Sigal. He had further studies with Eidlin at the

Leningrad Conservatory and, in 1953, won first prize in the World Festival of Youth in Bucharest. Gutnikov enchanted everyone with his beautiful tone and deep understanding of the music itself. Soon there was scarcely a town in the whole of Russia where he did not play. At the same time he continued to win first prizes in international competitions, including the Ondříček in Prague, the Long-Thibaud in Paris and the Tchaikovsky in Moscow. Efrem Zimbalist, a jurist of the Tchaikovsky Competition, said after the first round: 'At last I have heard from *that* young man, the St Petersburg tone!'[8] Gutnikov became a skilled teacher, whose students at the Leningrad Conservatory adored him because he was so patient and understanding, whatever the problem.

At his last concert, in the Tchaikovsky Hall in Moscow, when the programme included a Bach concerto and the Mozart Sinfonia Concertante, with V. Zhuk on viola, the public called him back again and again, almost as if they knew that it was his swan song. Gutnikov died in Leningrad in 1986 at the age of 55. Igor Oistrakh contributed an obituary in the *Soviet Music Magazine* in which he called him 'a knight of the violin', and described him as 'a charming man who combined modesty with nobility in every undertaking'. He recounted a story of the occasion when Gutnikov was playing on a bitterly cold evening in an open-air concert in Dzintari in Lapland; the acoustics were not good. Gutnikov made no complaints about the cold or the acoustics and filled the arena with beautiful sound, playing the Beethoven concerto as if nothing were amiss.[9]

Albert Markov was born in 1933 in Sverdlovsk, in the Ural mountains, and studied under Yankelevich at the Gnessin Institute. In 1959, he won the Gold Medal at the Queen Elisabeth Concours in Brussels, and, when Yankelevich died the following year, he took over his class and taught there for 15 years. He also followed a solo career and played all over the USSR and Eastern Europe and made many best-selling recordings. He belonged to that prestigious inner circle, the Moscow State Philharmonic Soloists, a distinction he shared with Kogan, Richter, Oistrakh and Rostropovich. He emigrated to the USA in 1975.

Markov's reasons for emigrating were the common ones; he had no freedom to make artistic decisions, no choice where to perform and his repertory had to be approved by the state. Markov did not defect; he left on a legal exit visa, but inevitably as soon as he made his application, he lost his job at the Gnessin Institute, and his wife, Marina – a violinist in the Bolshoi Orchestra – lost hers. When he finally arrived in New York, he learned from the impresario Sol Hurok of his unsuccessful efforts on his behalf to sponsor an American tour; not a word had been said to Markov.

Markov made his American debut in May 1976 when the Houston department store, Sakowitz, had offered in their Christmas catalogue 'the ultimate gift' of a chance to conduct the Houston Symphony Orchestra for one night at a cost of $14,500. A young New Yorker was given the gift by his family and he invited Markov to play the Paganini Concerto No. 2. The evening proved an unqualified success and the critics were astounded by this completely unknown virtuoso.

A debut recital in New York elicited similar praise and, a few days afterwards, Markov stepped in at the last moment for an indisposed Isaac Stern with the Baltimore Symphony Orchestra, again playing the Paganini No. 2 (Stern was to have given the première of the Rochberg concerto, 1974). Although Markov continues to perform, he devotes much time to teaching in New York at the Manhattan School of Music, Hunter College and the Hebrew Institute of Arts. He has also composed many works for violin, including a concerto, and written an invaluable tutor.

Albert's son, Alexander, born in Moscow in 1963, is one of the increasing number of the younger generation who are questioning today's intellectual approach to violin playing. The elder Markov gave his son his first lessons and, when they were living in the USA, enrolled him at Juilliard. At 14, Alexander was the youngest violinist to take part in the Juilliard Competition, taking First Prize, which involved a solo engagement with the Juilliard Symphony Orchestra. He later transferred to the Manhattan School of Music, where he finished his studies in his father's class. He possesses a flawless technique and his performances are charged with the emotional content we associate with the old school of virtuosos.

Alexander won the Gold Medal in the Paganini Competition in 1982 and has since achieved international recognition. He received rave reviews for his recital of all 24 Paganini Caprices at the Wigmore Hall in May 1997 and has made a CD and a film of all the Caprices, which has been televised throughout Europe. Both Markovs play violins made by the legendary Italian-born Sergio Peresson (1913–91); Alexander has often been approached by people asking if his is a Guarnerius del Gesù.

**Notes**

1. Schwarz, *Great Masters of the Violin*, p. 458.
2. *Grove*, 6th edn., 20, p. 569.
3. Schwarz, op. cit., p. 450.
4–6. Ibid., pp. 454–5.
7. *Moscow Report*, 28 December 1943.
8. Notes from Maxim Panfilo to M.C.
9. *Soviet Music Magazine*, 1986.

# 46  The Russian Heritage

With the Soviet school firmly established by Stolyarsky, Yampol'sky and Yankelevich, it was inevitable that a new generation of talented violinists would emerge.

Leonid Kogan (1924–82) was born in Ekaterinoslav (now Dnipropetrovsk), in the Ukraine, and at ten entered Yampol'sky's class for gifted children at the Moscow Conservatory (later the Central Music School). Yampol'sky was so impressed by his talent that he took the boy into his own home, so he could supervise his practising. Kogan made his official debut at 16, playing the Brahms concerto with the Moscow Philharmonic Orchestra in the Great Hall of the Moscow Conservatory.

Kogan attended the conservatory as an adult for eight years. In 1942, he married Yelizavita Gilels, also a superb violinist and sister of the pianist Emil. Their performances of Bach's Double Concerto and Ysaÿe's C major Duo Sonata – which they premiered – were highly acclaimed by the critics.

Another milestone came in 1947 when Kogan shared the first prize with Julian Sitkovetsky (1925–58) and Igor Bezrodnyi (1930–97) in the first Festival of Democratic Youth in Prague. He went on to win First Prize in the 1951 Queen Elisabeth Concours in Brussels. At Kogan's Paris debut in 1955 he played concertos by Mozart, Brahms and Paganini, and the audience at the Palais de Chaillot gave him a tremendous ovation which was echoed by the critics next day. In 1957, he made his American debut at Carnegie Hall, playing the Brahms concerto under Pierre Monteux and, although recognised as a superb artist, he was not as warmly received as Oistrakh. 'There was something remote and distant about Kogan's playing; it lacked the ultimate impact of a great musical personality, though it was beautifully chiselled and impeccably controlled.'[1]

Kogan went on to enjoy an international solo career and was particularly known for his interpretation of the Brahms and Beethoven concertos. But besides the great classical concertos, he also favoured contemporary Soviet music. He was the dedicatee of Khachaturian's Concerto-Rhapsody and also the first Soviet violinist to play and record the Berg concerto.

He was not a showy player – quite the reverse, he was 'reticent' on stage. 'His tone was lean, with a tight and sparse vibrato, his intonation infallibly pure, and his technical command superb.'[2] From 1952 Kogan taught at the Moscow Conservatory, where he was known for his inability to communicate. He was said to be 'stone-faced' when listening to the most talented pupils and made very little comment.

Nonetheless he was an excellent teacher and had a number of students who followed successful careers.

On the death of Oistrakh in 1974, Kogan was hailed as his successor, although in every way they were complete opposites. Kogan was lean and intense whereas Oistrakh was portly and easy-going; Oistrakh's playing was warm and mellow, Kogan's was clear and classical, yet both were stylish players who achieved perfection in their individual interpretations. According to Schwarz, 'there seemed to be a dark shadow over Kogan's personality; his colleagues spoke of him with guarded caution and without affection, though with respect for his violinistic achievements.'[3] However, Kogan also had another side. His son Pavel, also a violinist, tells us that he loved his work and his family, and that the seemingly remote image that he presented to the world was not a true one. His death at 58 came as a shock to the violin world.

Julian Sitkovetsky (1925–58) was a highly gifted violinist who, because of his untimely death from lung cancer, never achieved the international reputation he deserved. He was born in Kiev into a family where everyone played an instrument. He showed amazing talent at the age of four and, while still a child, was accepted by the Central School of Music. In 1933, Thibaud visited Kiev and was astounded at the nine-year-old's command of his instrument. He told him to learn languages, but the boy retorted: 'If people want to speak to me, they must do so in Russian!'

At the age of ten, Sitkovetsky played the Mendelssohn concerto at a music school concert and, when the school celebrated its 25th anniversary, he was chosen to play the Tchaikovsky concerto. Yampol'sky was so impressed that he offered to take him on as his student. The following year, Sitkovetsky began his studies at the Central Music School for Gifted Pupils in Moscow. During the Second World War, the school was evacuated to Penza, some 400 miles from Moscow. Life was difficult since the locals resented the Muscovites and with the Jewish pupils were openly hostile; even school football matches ended in knife fights. In 1943, Sitkovetsky graduated to the Moscow State Conservatory of Music in exile and, two years later, moved back to Moscow.

Sitkovetsky was soon performing all over the USSR and Eastern Europe and once played three concertos in one evening in East Berlin – the Sibelius, the Tchaikovsky and the Khachaturian, no less. He also took many prizes in international competitions, sharing the First Prize in the 1945 Prague Competition with Leonid Kogan and Igor Bezrodnyi and the Second Prize with Wanda Wilkomirska in the Wieniawski Competition of 1952 when David Oistrakh took the First Prize.

Sitkovetsky was known for his phenomenal aural and visual memory, which – allied to his impeccable technique and innate musicality – made his playing so appealing. Perhaps the best description is of his performance of the Tchaikovsky concerto, recorded on the final night of the Brussels Competition:

> Beyond the technical perfection, it contains an almost disarming pathos, panache and a total abandon which even the disciplined audience in the hall found difficult to ignore; applause between movements acknowledged their feelings while at the end of the third,

electrifying movement the audience simply lost all traces of reserve, bursting into tumultuous applause, stamping their feet and cheering. Perhaps the public knew best.[4]

Another Yampol'sky pupil, Igor Bezrodnyi (1930–97), was not only a fine violinist but an excellent teacher, who also added conducting to his accomplishments. When Rudolph Barshai left the USSR, he succeeded him as director of the Moscow Chamber Orchestra in 1976. Bezrodnyi was born in Tbilisi, Georgia, the son of two violinists, and began lessons with his father when he was six years old. Two years later, he was accepted into Yampol'sky's class at the Moscow Central Music School and, at 18, continued his studies at the Moscow Conservatory, also with Yampol'sky.

In 1947 he was invited to enter the Prague International Competition and shared the First Prize with Kogan and Sitkovetsky; while still a student, he played all over the USSR and Eastern Europe. Within five years he had taken two more first prizes, in the Jan Kubelík Competition in Prague and the Bach Competition in Leipzig. After graduation, Bezrodnyi quickly developed an international solo career. He was also a fine chamber musician and, from 1965 until 1972, he was the violinist of the distinguished Moscow Trio, with pianist Dmitri Bashkirov and cellist Mikhail Khomitser.

Bezrodnyi's teaching career began in 1953 during his period of postgraduate study, when he became Yampol'sky's assistant, and he soon realised that he enjoyed teaching as much as performing. In 1957 he joined the violin faculty at the Moscow Conservatory, eventually becoming the head. He later took up residence in Helsinki where he taught at the Sibelius Academy until his death. He was also in constant demand for masterclasses all over the world; he admitted that it was impossible to change anything fundamental in a few days but he enjoyed the contact with young players and was always very excited when he spotted a real talent.

Elvira Bekova, violinist of the Bekova Trio, studied with Bezrodnyi in Moscow for seven years and recalls that a lesson never went by without a mention of his mentor's name. Bezrodnyi considered Yampol'sky to be one of the great Russian teachers and wrongly overlooked by the younger generation of violinists. He made some sharp observations on the state of contemporary violin playing. On competitions, he would say that while he thought that they served a certain purpose, in general, they had got out of hand and had caused a deterioration in the artistic approach to performance. And on violin playing today:

> There are so few performers nowadays who honestly fulfil their artistic mission and use the violin as a singing, speaking instrument of the soul. There is so little indication of genuine life in the music, so little inspiration and imagination. Performers rarely offer new stylistic tendencies and new expressive means for the instruments. We should not forget that most of the masterpieces of violin literature were created by composers who were acting on contemporary styles of playing and on the artistic individuality of the outstanding masters of the time, exploiting their new conception of the violin and its capabilities. Lessons learned from the past are important to the future.[5]

When Felix Andrievsky emigrated from the USSR in 1972, the West gained one of the great teachers of the Soviet School. His first stop was Israel, where he held professorships at both the Jerusalem Academy of Music and the University of Tel Aviv. Today, he is a professor at the Royal College of Music in London and, over the years, has exerted considerable influence on the high standard of playing we know today. Andrievsky was born in Gitomar in the Ukraine in 1936. His father was a surgeon and his mother a music teacher; he decided from childhood that he would follow in her footsteps. He began lessons on the violin at eight with a 70-year-old Czech through whom he inherited a strong link with the nineteenth century. Within a few months, he won First Prize in a national competition and after some time at the Special Music School in Asherabad, he was accepted at the Central Music School in Moscow. From there he went on to the Gnessin Institute, in the class of Yampol'sky. When Yampol'sky died in 1956 his successor, Yuri Yankelevitch, accepted Andrievsky without an audition. In 1960, he joined the staff at the Gnessin and stayed for 12 years.

In 1963 he was invited by Yankelevitch to become his assistant at the Central Music School in Moscow. 'When this invitation came along I was prepared to give up everything else, including my ambitions for a solo career.'[6] Andrievsky is of the opinion that, at the time, Yankelevitch's class was by far the best. The students were outstanding and what Andrievsky appreciated most was their individuality. It is well to remember that this would have been unusual, and perhaps not always acceptable, since teaching at that time was geared to preparation for entering competitions and winning at all costs was the maxim. Andrievsky always had reservations on the exaggerated technical preparation which, in his opinion – shared with Bezrodnyi – could damage musical creativity.

From the time they first met in Moscow many years ago, Andrievsky and Menuhin were closely associated. Menuhin invited him to come and teach at his school, which was then newly opened, and, in 1972, this was finally possible. Subsequently Andrievsky also taught at Menuhin's International Music Academy at Gstaad and in 1984 became professor at the Royal College of Music in London. Menuhin thought him 'a wonderfully flexible and responsive teacher, always ready to listen to the ideas of his students – but at the same time demanding very good reasons for them!'[7]

Vladimir Spivakov was born in 1944 in Ufa, in the Ural mountains, and cannot recall a time when music was not present in his life. His mother was a pianist who gave him lessons when he was four. Two years later, he switched to the violin and made such progress that he auditioned for the Central Music School, but was not accepted (for political rather than musical reasons). Instead, he attended the local Regional Music School, where he was unhappy at having to go back to open strings. By chance, he heard one of the older pupils playing Tchaikovsky's Meditation and surprised his teacher by playing it by ear, correctly and perfectly in tune.

After a year, Vladimir was invited to study with Lyubov Sigal at the Central Music School. He made excellent progress, especially with his vibrato as Madame Sigal – an Auer pupil – was an expert on this point. At the Leningrad Conservatory, he had another period of study with Veniamin Sher, a man of considerable culture, who inspired his young pupil to take an interest in literature and art. It was during his studies with Sher that he entered the competition of the White Night's Festival and won First Prize, despite the fact that he was three years below the age for entry (16).

From this success, the teenage Spivakov went to Moscow Conservatory to study with Yankelevich for eight years, a period that he regards as being his greatest inspiration, musically and technically. Spivakov subsequently won a number of prizes in international competitions and followed a successful solo career. His first appearance in the West was as soloist-director with the Chicago Symphony Orchestra, when he played the Mendelssohn concerto and conducted a Mozart symphony. As a result, he was offered an extensive tour with the orchestra, but because of the Cold War the tour had to be called off. It was then that Spivakov formed his own orchestra, the Moscow Virtuosi. His London concert debut took place in 1977 at the Royal Festival Hall, playing the Tchaikovsky concerto with the LPO under Maxim Shostakovich. Joan Chissell wrote in *The Times* that 'with honeyed tone Mr Spivakov could sing (and trill) like a bird as well as make child's-play of the bravura'.[8]

Mayumi Fujikawa was born in Asahigawa City, Japan in 1946 and had her first lessons from her father, followed by further training at the Toho School of Music; after being awarded a scholarship by the Alex de Fries Foundation, she continued her studies at the Antwerp Conservatory. In 1968 she became a pupil of Kogan.

The turning point came when she shared the Second Prize with Spivakov in the 1970 Tchaikovsky Competition. Oistrakh's comments at the time gave some idea of what the future could hold for her: 'In her are united an astounding violinist and a marvellous musician. To hear her play is pure pleasure. She was the great revelation of the Tchaikovsky Competition.'[9] That same year she also won First Prize in the Grand Prix Henri Vieuxtemps Competition in Belgium and from this time her international career took off with a vengeance. Critics everywhere seemed genuinely affected by her performances.

Viktor Tret'yakov was born in 1946 in Krasnoyarsk, in Siberia, and at seven began his violin studies at the Irkutsk Music School. At 13 he became a pupil of Yankelevich at the Central Music School in Moscow and continued as his student at the conservatory. He was only 20 when he won First Prize in the Tchaikovsky Competition and Oistrakh, who was chairman of the jury, said that he was a clear leader from the first round and he 'fascinated everyone with the universatility of his style and the virtuosity of his performance'. He also commented on the ease with which he tackled both a Paganini concerto and the Tchaikovsky.[10]

From this point, Tret'yakov's future was assured. He made his British debut in 1967 and his American debut, with the Philadelphia Orchestra under Ormandy, followed by a recital at Carnegie Hall – all this while still a student at the conservatory, from which he graduated in 1970. The New York critics called him the Soviet 'violin ambassador' and whenever one of the leading Soviet orchestras visited the USA, he was the soloist. Tret'yakov is an engaging personality on stage and the audiences love him.

Although he has since played with most of the world's leading orchestras, Tret'yakov devotes much time to chamber music and performs with Svyatoslav Richter, Rostropovich, Yuri Bashmet, Natalia Gutman and, until his death in 1990, Oleg Kagan.

Boris Belkin – now a Belgian subject – was born in Sverdlovsk in 1948. He had lessons on both piano and violin and attended the Central Music School in Moscow when he was six. He admits that at the time he developed a kind of hatred for both instruments since, for him, soccer and ice hockey seemed much more attractive options. Belkin's keyboard facility led him to play more piano than violin, but at 16, when he entered the Moscow Conservatory and began his studies with Yankelevich, he decided to concentrate on the violin. This was the beginning of a long and close relationship. 'Yankelevitch was wonderful. He was *very* intelligent and this was especially important, because he guided me in areas that went far beyond the four strings of the violin. And when it comes to technique and method, he was extraordinary.'[11]

Belkin followed the path of the successful virtuoso in the USSR, playing all over Eastern Europe, and won First Prize in the Soviet National Violin Competition in 1972. But two years later, thoroughly disenchanted with the regime, he emigrated to Israel. Belkin is truly an individualist and it is not difficult to see how he would have resented the inflexibility of the Soviet system. For example, he had prepared all the repertory necessary to enter the 1971 Paganini Competition in Genoa, but at the last moment – without any explanation – he was forbidden to leave. And, even after winning the Soviet contest in 1972, when he applied for a visa in order to enter the 1973 Paganini Competition, his application was again refused.

Looking back on his musical education in general he has many reservations. He felt that the training at the conservatory was too intensive and the spirit of competition overwhelming. 'I felt that winning contests was the entire purpose of our existence. Musicality was often sacrificed just to sharpen our contest-orientated skills.'[12]

Belkin is still very much the individualist. In complete contrast to his reluctance to practise as a child, he now practises four to six hours a day. 'I never take a vacation from my violin . . . When I am not playing a concert, I am practising, and when I am not practising, I am playing a concert!'[13] However, his attitude towards competitions has not changed; he has refused many requests to judge competitions and even declined an invitation to sit on the jury of the Queen Elisabeth Concours in Brussels: 'I would be almost afraid to play such a role. I find it disturbing.'[14]

Belkin is known not only for his violin's beautiful singing tone, but for his passionate approach to the *musical* requirements. Of his performance of the Tchaikovsky Violin Concerto, Hilary Finch of *The Times* wrote: 'Boris Belkin performed with the mind and sensibility of a grand Russian choreographer . . .'[15]

When Julian Sitkovetsky died in 1958, it was his ambition that his three-year-old son should one day become a violinist. Today, Dimitri Sitkovetsky, born in Baku in 1954, has fulfilled his father's hopes and enjoys the international reputation that the latter himself never lived to achieve. His mother, Bella Davidovitch was a distinguished pianist, so he was exposed to music from birth. He showed early talent and learnt to play both piano and violin when still a small child. He was sufficiently talented to be accepted, at the age of seven, by the Central Music School in Moscow into the class of Yankelevich and continued with him when he went on to the Moscow Conservatory in 1972. After Yankelevich's death he completed his studies with Igor Bezrodnyi.

As a child, Dimitri's main problem was being from a famous family where so much was expected of him. He thinks that had his father lived, he might never have become a violinist since he would always walk in his shadow. As it was, he was encouraged by his mother and also had the opportunity of mixing with the musical elite of Moscow. When he was ready for the concert platform, the agency Goskonsort gave him permission to play outside Russia, so that when he emigrated in 1977, he did not leave because of restrictions, but rather to explore wider horizons in the West. When he arrived in New York he auditioned for the Juilliard School and was awarded a full scholarship as a graduate student in Galamian's class. He looks back on those two years as the most crucial in his life, because he had finally arrived at a place where nobody knew either him or his parents, and where he could set his own goals. 'It was wonderful to be in an environment where a real love of music exists, not just careers and how well you do, but a wonderful place to make friends and exchange ideas.'[16]

In 1979, Sitkovetsky won the first Kreisler Competition in Vienna. He made debuts with the Berlin Philharmonic Orchestra in 1980 and the Chicago Symphony Orchestra in 1983; his UK debut in August 1986 was at a Prom at the Royal Albert Hall, with the BBC Philharmonic Orchestra under Edward Downes. He played Shostakovich's First Violin Concerto, stepping in at the last moment for the indisposed Russian bass Paata Burchuladze, and received rave reviews from the press.

In 1988 Sitkovetsky and his mother returned to Russia on a concert tour that included a Gala concert with the Moscow Philharmonic Orchestra under Dimitri Kitaenko, in which together they performed three concertos. The concert was a sellout and for Sitkovetsky it was one of the most important concerts he had ever played. Sitkovetsky is constantly adding to his extensive repertory, and at the Proms in 1995, he scored a triumph with the premiere of John Casken's Violin Concerto.

Viktoria Mullova successfully defected from the USSR in 1983 and has since established herself on the international circuit. She was born in Moscow in 1959, her father an engineer and her mother a school teacher; she began playing the violin when she was four. At nine she was accepted at the Central Music School in Moscow as a pupil of Volodar Bronin, Kogan's assistant and a former student of Oistrakh. She stayed there for ten years, then entered the conservatory as a pupil of Kogan, who had been her childhood idol.

Mullova won First Prize in the 1980 Sibelius Competition and in 1982 – the year of Kogan's death – she was awarded the Gold Medal in the Tchaikovsky Competition. She was soon fulfilling many engagements as a soloist and received rave reviews everywhere. But Mullova has a highly individual personality and felt stifled by the restrictions of the Soviet regime on her artistic development. So, in 1983, when on a tour of Finland – leaving her government-owned violin in her hotel – she and the conductor, Vahktang Jordania, took a taxi to Stockholm, where they were granted political asylum in the USA.

Mullova has since played with most of the world's great orchestras and under the leading conductors. The *Chicago Sunday Times* critic once wrote (in *The Strad*):

> Trained by Leonid Kogan, the greatest of the Soviet violinists, she is certain to be one of the dominant musical figures of the last two decades of this century. What sets her apart is her phenomenally accurate intonation. Her playing contains expressive nuances far beyond the ordinary fiddler. Her purity of tone is matched by the purity of line she sets forth.[17]

Conversely, she has also been accused of being 'poker-faced' like Kogan, since she hardly moves at all while playing. She is delighted at such criticism and maintains that Kogan and Heifetz both played like that and she has no intention of developing a more mobile manner just to please the audience. Mullova has also made numerous recordings which have elicited warm praise from the critics.

### Notes

1–3. Schwarz, *Great Masters of the Violin*, p. 471.

4. *The Strad*, December 1990, pp. 983–5.

5. Letter to M.C. from Elvira Bekova.

6. *The Strad*, January 1985, p. 680.

7. Letter from Menuhin to M.C.

8. *The Times*, 3 October 1977.

9. Publicity brochure.

10. Schwarz, op. cit., p. 473.

11–14. *The Strad*, December 1989, pp. 1047–8.

15. *The Times*, 17 April 1987.

16. *The Strad*, May 1986, p. 24.

17. *The Strad*, February 1990, p. 133.

# 47 Italian Renaissance

In the latter part of the eighteenth century and early nineteenth century, Italy produced two of the greatest violinists in the history of the instrument: Viotti and Paganini. Yet although the Italians almost live and breathe music – mainly through their singing traditions – since the passing of these two legends, great Italian violinists have been thin on the ground. Two who belong in their pantheon are Franco Gulli and Salvatore Accardo, born almost 20 years apart.

Franco Gulli (1926–2001), a much-loved professor at the Music School of the University of Indiana at Bloomington, enjoyed a distinguished career as a soloist before leaving Europe to settle in the USA in 1971. Born in Trieste into a family of professional musicians who ran a large private music school, Gulli received his first lessons from his father, who had studied with Ševčík and Marak in Prague, and later with Arrigo Serato and at the Accademia Chigiana at Siena.

Gulli was taken to concerts as a small child and he recalled, at the age of eight, hearing Milstein play the Bruch concerto with a *subito piano* in the last movement that he would never forget. He was also greatly influenced by the recordings of Szigeti. When Szigeti moved from the USA to Switzerland, they became acquainted and Gulli would seek advice from the master.

Gulli's solo career began as a prodigy, but the war intervened; when it ended he joined I Poeriggi Musicali in Milan as a third violin, and became their leader within a year. The young Gulli performed under Leonard Bernstein, Sergiu Celibidache, Lorin Maazel, Carlo Maria Giulini and many others, thus gaining quite different approaches to the repertory. He recalled performing the Schumann concerto with Rafael Kubelík and it soon became clear that for him it was a very emotional experience; it was the last work in which he had played the piano accompaniment for his father, the great Jan Kubelík.

After some seven years with the orchestra Gulli resigned in order to concentrate on his expanding solo career. In 1967, Gulli made his La Scala solo debut, playing the Paganini D major Concerto under Celibidache. In Milan, he met the pianist Enrica Cavallo – later to become his wife – and they gave many recitals together.

One of the very important events in the season of 1960/61 was the discovery of the Paganini Concerto No. 5. Gulli was invited to give the premiere in Siena. His recording of the work was, for many years, the only one available. As violinists everywhere wanted to perform it, it became very popular; the impresario Arthur Judson of New York offered Gulli a string of engagements in the USA and, over the years, he played with most of the major American orchestras. Gulli's performance of the Paganini No. 5 also led to his first teaching post at the Accademia Chigiana in Siena, one of the oldest and most prestigious institutions in the world (among the violin teachers of the past there had been Serato, Enescu and guest professors, Milstein, Kogan and Szeryng). Josef Gingold heard part of Gulli's recording on his car radio and liked the performance, although he had no idea who was playing. He and Gulli later met at the Paganini Competition in Genoa and, in 1971, Gingold invited him to take over the summer course at Bloomington. It was so successful that he was subsequently offered a permanent post.

Salvatore Accardo, from Turin, was also the son of a violinist. Born in 1941, he took naturally to the violin and, at six, was accepted into the Conservatorio S. Pietro a Majella in Naples. His teacher was Luigi d'Ambrosio, a pupil of Wilhelmj, bringing him in a direct line to Ferdinand David. D'Ambrosio was a stickler for good basic technique and Accardo was reared on a diet of scales and Ševčík exercises.

Accardo made his professional debut in Naples when he was only 13 in a programme which included Paganini Caprices. His teacher had suggested earlier that on completing his studies at the Conservatorio he should study with Enescu, but the master's death in 1955 made that impossible. So, instead, he took some postgraduate studies the following year with Yvonne Astruc, Enescu's former assistant at Siena; at the time, they had Casals, Segovia, Celibidache, Cortot and Michelangeli on the faculty and, for Accardo it was a milestone in his career. 'I began to learn the importance of meeting great musicians. One needs to talk to them and play with them in order to grow up musically.'[1]

In 1958, Accardo was the first winner in the newly formed Paganini Competition in Genoa and was engaged for concerts all over Europe and North and South America. There was one disadvantage: he was labelled as a Paganini specialist, with the implication that if you play only Paganini you are a wizard, not a musician. In Accardo's case, the assumption is far from the truth since his repertory includes works from Bach to Penderecki. He also considers that this verdict on Paganini is grossly unfair: 'He wrote great music in the Italian operatic tradition of Rossini, Donizetti and Bellini. Even his concertos are operatic, with an overture, love duets, tenor and soprano arias and recitative; Schubert, Schumann and Liszt were crazy about him and recognised him as a great composer. Schubert once said of him: "I have heard an angel play."'[2] Ysaÿe is another composer for whom Accardo has great respect: 'The solo sonatas are a very important part of our repertoire. Ysaÿe's writing is very polyphonic – in a way it is a kind of "modern" Bach. He was such a great violinist himself so he knew what it was capable of – both technically and harmonically.'[3]

For eight years, Accardo taught at the Accademia Musicale Chigiana in Siena, but found himself constantly questioning the lack of attention to chamber music, which he considers to be the foundation of all violin playing. Today Accardo teaches at the Scuola di Perfezionamento in Cremona, founded in 1986 by the Swiss benefactor, Walter Stauffer. Tuition is both free and private and although Italian students have preference over foreigners, choices are on a highly selective basis. The teachers all play chamber music with the students and tuition may continue as long as teachers and pupils require it.

## Notes

1–3. Quoted from interview, M.C.

# 48   New Sounds in Old Music

By the late twentieth century, the performance of early music on period instruments, played with the baroque bow, had become well established worldwide. However, despite the number of distinguished musicians who have been quoted as being responsible for the early music revival, the real pioneer was Arnold Dolmetsch (1858–1940), who was giving performances of seventeenth- and eighteenth-century music in the 1880s. Originally a violinist, he was a private pupil of Vieuxtemps in Brussels and also studied at the Brussels Conservatoire; in 1883, he came to London and was one of the first intake of students at the newly opened Royal College of Music.

As violin master at Dulwich College, he revolutionised standards of playing and also gave concerts of early music at his home, first in Dulwich and later in Bloomsbury and Haslemere, Surrey, where he founded the Haslemere Festival in 1925. From the 1890s onwards, he used only original instruments and bows. Dolmetsch's *The Interpretation of the Music of the XVII and XVIII Centuries*, published in 1915, is still regarded as an important work on the subject.

The cellist Nikolaus Harnoncourt (*b.*1929) started his career in 1952 as a member of the Vienna Symphony Orchestra, but had always been interested in early music. With his wife, the violinist Alice Harnoncourt, he founded the Vienna Concentus Musicus in 1953, one of the first professional orchestras to use original instruments. They have made numerous recordings and toured widely.

From a predominantly scholarly viewpoint, the American composer, Sol Babitz (b. 1911) was one of the first in the twentieth century to make extensive researches into how the violin was played in the Baroque period. In 1948 he founded the Early Music Laboratory in Los Angeles and he has written a great deal on the subject which is of value to the student of early performance practice.

Another early exponent of historical violin playing is Marie Leonhardt, born in Lausanne in 1928. She attended the Geneva Conservatoire where in 1952 she won the Prix de Virtuosité. She undertook further studies at the Schola Cantorum Basiliensis and with Max Rostal at the Guildhall School of Music and Drama in London. She led the Musica Antiqua Amsterdam with Ton Koopman and the Leonhardt Consort under the direction of her husband, the harpsichordist Gustav Leonhardt, with whom she has made over 70 recordings, mainly of seventeenth-century music.

Since 1968, she has been director of the Baroque violin class at the Rotterdam Conservatory as well as giving masterclasses throughout the world. Since 1980, she has directed the Summer Academy of the Casa de Mateus in Portugal. Leonhardt avoids the word 'authentic': 'We now have the right instrument, the right bow, the right strings, original scores and treatises on technique; but unless we replace the music in its cultural context, unless we uncover the old concept of rhetoric, "affects" and emotions, we will never touch and convince our audience, nor convey the intentions of the composer.'[1] Today, facsimiles of the original scores are available and there is no longer any need to rely on highly personal editions, dominated by editorial fingerings and bowings.

In the USA, Stanley Ritchie is an early music pioneer, who combines solo and chamber music playing with teaching at the School of Music at the University of Indiana in Bloomington. He was born in Yenda, New South Wales, in 1935 and, at 15, entered the Sydney Conservatorium to study with Florent Hoogstoel; he graduated four years later with diplomas in performing and teaching. He continued his studies with Ernest Llewellyn and during this time won a national competition that brought him solo engagements with all the principal Australian symphony orchestras.

In 1958 he was awarded a Ginette Neveu scholarship and a French government grant to study with Jean Fournier in Paris, and from there went to the USA for further study with Joseph Fuchs and Oscar Shumsky. He later settled there and held a number of orchestral posts as concertmaster, including New York City Opera, the Metropolitan Opera and the New York Chamber Soloists.

Ritchie's interest in Baroque performance dates back to 1970, when he met the harpsichordist, Albert Fuller. They founded Aston Magna in 1973 and, for some 20 years, gave workshops, academies and festivals throughout the USA. With his wife, the harpsichordist, Elisabeth Wright, he formed Duo Geminiani, while also making frequent solo appearances with John Eliot Gardiner, Roger Norrington, Anner Bylsma and many others in the early music field. He now specialises in teaching Baroque violin and finds it 'a fascinating challenge, not only from the point of view of technique, which differs significantly from that of the modern violin, but also of the interpretation of music of that period, whose principles diverge so radically from modern concepts'.[2]

Simon Standage (b. 1941) is a violinist who divides his time between playing both the Baroque and modern violin. He studied with David Martin (1911–82) and after four years as a member of the Netherlands Chamber Orchestra with Szymon Goldberg, he was awarded a Harkness Fellowship to study with Galamian in New York. 'His teaching was very sound, sorting out problems of both technique and musicianship. Where he helped me most was in the right arm and hand – how to draw a straight bow, a necessary attribute of the Baroque performer.'[3]

On his return to the UK, Standage played for some time in London in various orchestras and, in 1973, became co-founder with Trevor Pinnock of the English Concert, serving as both leader and soloist. Since this time, he has founded a number of important ensembles and, from 1991 to 1995, was Associate Director of the Academy of Ancient Music with Christopher Hogwood. Standage teaches at the

Dresdener Akademie für Alte Musik and is professor of Baroque music at the Royal Academy of Music in London, where at first students took this subject only as a second study. One of the department's achievements is the formation of an orchestra for playing early music on modern instruments.

Marilyn McDonald has an international reputation as a teacher and performer, both as a soloist and as a chamber music player. She was born in Milwaukee, Wisconsin, in 1943 and began playing the violin when she was a small child. Her main teachers were Angel Keyes and Josef Gingold. She began playing the Baroque violin in the early 1970s and was mainly self-taught, but was later greatly influenced by Jaap Schröder while playing in the Smithson Quartet. She has been on the faculty of Oberlin Conservatory for many years and is a member of several Baroque ensembles; she has also made many recordings with the Castle Trio.

The name of Kuijken is well known in the Baroque field. Sigiswald Kuijken was born in Dilbeek, Belgium in 1944, and from the age of seven came into contact with Renaissance music and instruments through his elder brother, Wieland who played the viola da gamba. Sigiswald taught himself to play the gamba while learning the Modern violin, studying in Bruges and Brussels. In the meantime, he had also taught himself to play the Baroque violin. By 1969, he was an accomplished exponent, who played with neither chin rest nor shoulder rest, holding the violin on his collar bone as did all violinists before Paganini.

Kuijken was a member of the Alarius Ensemble for eight years, during which time he explored seventeenth- and eighteenth-century repertory and its performing practices. He also led various groups with his brothers Wieland and Barthold and with the harpsichordists Robert Kohnen and Gustav Leonhardt. In 1972, he formed his own orchestra, La Petite Bande, to record Lully's *Le Bourgeois Gentilhomme*. Although at first concentrating on French music, they went on to play and record music by Bach, Handel, Haydn, Gluck and Mozart. Kuijken also appears as guest conductor/director of a number of other Baroque orchestras including the Orchestra of the Age of Enlightenment, whose debut concert he directed in 1986.

John Holloway must surely be one of the most ubiquitous violinists in the field of historically informed performance at the present time. Born in Neath, Glamorgan in 1948, he studied first with Yfrah Neaman, with whom he continued at the Guildhall School of Music and Drama when he was 17. Holloway went on to win a number of competitions and began a freelance career in London, but in the early 1970s he became interested in early music. This led to leaderships with the Academy of Ancient Music, the Taverner Players, the London Classical Players and others and, in 1976, he gave what was probably the first recital on Baroque violin in London. Holloway continues to perform, record, teach and give masterclasses the world over. His recordings, in particular, have won considerable acclaim.

Holloway is certainly outspoken on performance issues and holds imaginative but practical views on teaching: 'I try to develop in all students the pleasure to be had in finding and nurturing their own musical instincts, and educating those instincts by getting interested in all aspects of the music they want to play.'⁴

Monica Huggett's recording of the twelve Corelli sonatas with the Trio Sonnerie inspired a reviewer to say that she 'brings a sweetness of tone and a perfection of technical control that cannot but inspire admiration on their own account, but in combination with such unerring musical insight as is to be found here makes these into quite masterly interpretations'.⁵ She was born in London in 1953, into a large musical family, and was reared with a background of almost every type of music. She chose the violin, began lessons at the age of six and completed her studies with Manoug Parikian at the Royal Academy of Music. She was introduced to the Baroque violin while in her teens, felt an immediate sympathy with the instrument and undertook studies in performance practice with Sigiswald Kuijken, Gustav Leonhardt and Ton Koopman. She has since become one of the most distinguished exponents of the Baroque violin and remains one of its most fervent champions.

With Koopman, Huggett founded the Amsterdam Baroque Orchestra and she led the ensemble for seven years. In 1982, she formed the Trio Sonnerie with Sarah Cunningham (viola da gamba) and Mitzi Meyerson (harpsichord). Huggett has toured the world as soloist, director and chamber musician; she is artistic director of the Portland Baroque Orchestra in the USA and teaches at the Koninklijk Conservatorium at The Hague.

Catherine Mackintosh, born in London in 1948, also successfully combines performing and teaching. She was given her first lessons on the violin when she was seven and from the age of eight played in the school orchestra. Her first introduction to early music came from a seemingly unlikely source – the composer Harrison Birtwistle, who was music master at her school in Wiltshire. He conducted a choir in which she sang music from Machaut to Bach.

Mackintosh went through the conventional violinist's training at the Royal College of Music, where she also taught herself to play the Baroque violin. After leaving the college, she played in a number of chamber music groups and, in 1969, made her first recording, with Anthony Rooley and the Consort of Musicke, of which she was a founder member. In 1973, she became leader of the Academy of Ancient Music under Christopher Hogwood and later founded the Purcell Quartet with Elizabeth Wallfisch (violin), Richard Boothby (viola da gamba) and Robert Woolley (harpsichord); they have sustained a busy concert programme and made many recordings. Mackintosh is equally fluent on the Classical violin, viola and viola d'amore, and plays regularly with the Orchestra of the Age of Enlightenment. She also teaches at the Royal Scottish Academy of Music and Drama in Glasgow and has been professor of Baroque and Classical violin at the Royal College of Music in London since 1977.

A contemporary of Mackintosh, the Australian Elizabeth Wallfisch, today enjoys a busy career as a soloist, chamber musician and teacher of both Baroque and Classical performance using period instruments. She was born in 1948 in Sydney, into a family of professional musicians going back three generations, but it was through her father, an amateur clarinettist, that she was initiated into the world of early music.

At 18, she left Australia to study at the Royal Academy of Music in London and was taught the Carl Flesch method. But when she left the Academy, she developed problems in her arms through over-practising and was obliged to stop playing for a year. After her recovery, she joined L'Estro Armonico, an ensemble who played eighteenth-century music on modern instruments. When they began using period instruments, the director, the violinist Derek Solomons recognised that she had a natural talent and lent her a Baroque violin and bow.

> I picked it up and never looked back. That was a huge turning point for me. I re-learned how to play. If you have the right instruments, you can take them to the limits in every direction – the limits of virtuosity, of colour, of shape and articulation. On a Baroque violin you can contrast a beautiful, sweet tone with one that sounds like a drum if you want. I find so much freedom.[6]

Although Wallfisch still appears as a soloist, it is the very breadth of her experience that she most enjoys. She performs regularly with a number of orchestras and ensembles, including the Raglan Baroque Players and Convivium (formerly the Locatelli Trio), with cellist and viol player, Richard Tunnicliff and harpsichordist Paul Nicholson. She has made a number of award-winning recordings and holds professorships at the Koninklijk Conservatorium in The Hague and the Royal Academy of Music in London.

One of the most controversial figures in the world of early music is Reinhard Goebel, founder and director of Musica Antiqua Köln, who holds strong views about performance practice. He was born in 1952 in Siegen, Westphalia, and began lessons on the violin at 12. His fascination with Baroque music came about early, inspired by an old recording of Bach's Second Brandenburg Concerto. He spent five years in conventional training at the Musikhochschule in Cologne, where they scoffed at the very idea of early music performance, and then went on to several other teachers who also proved unsympathetic. It was only when he undertook a further period of study with Marie Leonhardt that light dawned and he realised that his instinct had been the right one.

In 1973 Goebel founded Musica Antiqua Köln and, to his surprise, it attracted attention from the onset; by 1978 they had a contract with Deutsche Grammophon. He is known as a perfectionist and his musicians hold him in awe because he is capable of fiery outbursts of temperament, for which he makes no excuses. His passion is embodied in the music itself, which is confirmed by one of the members of the group: 'I think he is truly moved by the music; there is a force that drives him that has only to do with the musical language he's learned.'[7]

Perhaps the most significant example of his sheer indomitability came in 1991, when Goebel, who was then 40, had signs of paralysis in one of the fingers of his left hand and was diagnosed as suffering from focal dystonia. He felt sure that his career as a violinist was at an end when a friend suggested he try to play with the other hand. Goebel practised for two years on an instrument specially made for him by Roger Hargrave and by 1993 was touring again – as a left-handed violinist. 'It actually makes no difference musically. It is more difficult to suddenly have to listen to the instrument with the right ear.'[8]

Ingrid Seifert is best known for her performances with London Baroque and her many recordings of seventeenth- and eighteenth-century violin music. She was born near Salzburg, Austria, in 1952 and studied the violin at first with Jaroslav Suchy and later in Vienna with Joseph Sivo. After graduating, she attended Nikolaus Harnoncourt's performance practice classes at the Mozarteum. The Mozarteum awarded her a scholarship to study with Sigiswald Kuijken at The Hague. For a time she played with Harnoncourt's Concentus Musicus Wien and other groups, but in 1976, she went to live in London, where she founded London Baroque with her husband, the cellist and viol player Charles Medlam. Since then, she has dedicated her professional life almost wholly to the ensemble; she also teaches at summer courses in Europe, including Scandinavia.

> Rather than a vain attempt at reproducing the style of seventeenth- and eighteenth-century playing, I have aimed at a way of playing which puts the music into its own terms of reference. This of course involved the study of art, architecture and literature contemporary to the music. Playing this music on the Baroque violin has given me the opportunity to enjoy new sounds in old music.[9]

The Italian Enrico Gatti is now a name to be reckoned with, not only as a performer but as a teacher who encourages the younger generation of period instrument specialists. He was born in Perugia in 1955, studied with Chiara Banchini at the conservatory in Geneva and completed his studies with Sigiswald Kuijken at the Koninklijk Conservatorium at The Hague. From the onset of his performing career, Gatti dedicated himself to seventeenth- and eighteenth-century repertory, leading a number of specialist ensembles, including La Petite Bande and Les Arts Florissants. In 1986 he founded the Ensemble Aurora, with whom he has toured extensively and made a number of excellent recordings. He now teaches at the Conservatoire in Toulouse and the Research Centre for Early Music at the Civica Scuola di Musica in Milan.

It is not long ago that Andrew Manze was 'discovering the Baroque violin as a postgraduate student at London's Royal Academy of Music'.[10] Today he is much in demand as a soloist and director of period orchestras across Europe. Born in Beckenham, Kent in 1965, Manze was a music scholar at Bedford School, where the music was of a high standard; he led the orchestra from the age of 14 and even played concertos. After playing for some time in the National Youth and the European Communuity Youth Orchestras, he read Classics at Cambridge. During this time he had a few lessons on Baroque violin with Simon Standage and Marie Leonhardt, and in 1986 he attended Marie Leonhardt's Summer School in Portugal. When he first arrived in Cambridge he was not over-impressed with the Baroque violin and was far more interested in contemporary music, mainly because performance could benefit from the composer being alive and available for discussion; but this all changed when he began to understand more about Baroque music. He realised that either you imagine that the composer is close at hand and you are making decisions with him, 'or else, in the case of seventeenth-century music, you just have to imagine that you *are* the composer, because almost all of the composers were players'.[11]

On leaving university, he spent a postgraduate year with Simon Standage at the Royal Academy of Music followed by another at the Koninklijk Conservatorium at The Hague, which led to his meeting with Marie Leonhardt:

> She tried to teach me freedom of everything – freedom of mind, physical freedom and freedom from preconceptions. She was one of the first people to strip off the layers of nineteenth- and twentieth-century things that had been applied. It was very inspiring to see someone who'd probably played things like the Purcell Chacony hundreds of times still get so excited and make it sound so thrilling. There aren't many people like that around.[12]

Manze has since played with or led most of the best-known Baroque orchestras and in 1988 formed his own trio, Romanesca, with lutenist Nigel North and keyboard player John Toll, with the express aim of presenting music from the seventeenth and eighteenth centuries in a way that is lively, expressive, and accessible to contemporary audiences. Their recordings of sonatas by Vivaldi and Biber have received awards. One Dutch critic wrote perceptively:

> Freedom plays a central part in Manze's own approach to music-making; you can hear it in every note of his playing, which has the priceless gift of being able to make you gasp with surprise at some audacious stroke, smile with pleasure at a humorous twist or bask in its sheer expressive warmth. It is not surprising, then, that he would like to introduce a greater element of improvisation in the performance of Baroque music.[13]

Another violinist who has contributed significantly to the Baroque revival as a soloist, quartet player, chamber musician and teacher is Jaap Schröder, born in Amsterdam in 1925. He started to play the violin when he was eight and later entered the Sweelinck Conservatory. After the war, he was awarded a scholarship to study for a further year in Paris at the Ecole Jacques Thibaud, where he took the Premier Prix and also undertook studies in musicology at the Sorbonne.

On his return to Holland in 1949, Schröder was appointed leader of the Radio Chamber Orchestra in Hilversum and was later associated with a number of prominent orchestras, which he either led or conducted, including the Netherlands Chamber Orchestra. Upon reflection he realises that he enjoyed playing Dvořák and

Brahms, but when it came to works by Haydn and Mozart he was not so happy and felt the need to search for a different approach. In the early 1960s, he met Gustav and Marie Leonhardt, the cellist Anner Bylsma and flautist Frans Bruggen, which opened up a whole new world to him. He founded and directed a string group, Concerto Amsterdam, for recording purposes. He also investigated the Classical period and its instruments, and together with Christopher Hogwood and the Academy of Ancient Music in London, he directed the first complete recording of the Mozart symphonies on Classical instruments.

Schröder succeeded his old teacher, de Clerck at the Sweelinck Conservatory in 1963, retiring in 1991; over the years, he has held professorships and given master-classes throughout the world. Lucy van Dael, a pupil of Sigiswald Kuijken, in turn succeeded Schröder at the Sweelinck Conservatory, and also teaches at the conservatory in Krakow. She is a creative and versatile player, who for some 16 years led the Orchestra of the Eighteenth Century and, since 1991, has been a member of the Archibudella Quartet. Today, she is mentor to the third generation of Baroque violinists in Amsterdam.

**Notes**
1. Quoted from interview, M.C.
2. Quoted from interview, M.C.
3. *The Strad*, March 1985, pp. 841–2.
4. Letter from John Holloway to M.C.
5. *Gramophone*, September 1990.
6. *Strings*, January/February 1996, p. 38.
7. ABC Radio 24 Hours, October 1995, p. 30.
8. *The Strad*, September 1993, p. 800.
9. Quoted from interview, M.C.
10–11. *Tijdschrift Voor Oude Muziek*, January 1997, pp. 5–7.
12. Quoted from interview, M.C.
13. *Tijdschrift Voor Oude Muziek*, January 1997, pp. 5–7.

# 49 The Younger Generation

In the last 20 years the talent that has emerged throughout the world surpasses anything in previous generations. Olivier Charlier was born in 1961 in Albert, near Amiens, into a family of amateur musicians and had his first lessons on the violin from his father when he was five years old; that same year he attended the Amiens Conservatoire in the class of Robert Postel. When he was still only ten, he was admitted to the Paris Conservatoire as a pupil of Jean Fournier. During this time he met Nadia Boulanger, who was most encouraging, and he also worked with both Yehudi Menuhin and Henryk Szeryng, who in 1976 offered him a personal scholarship to study with him.

Charlier won a number of prizes in international competitions, which gave rise to a number of highly successful international tours. Charlier now enjoys a busy solo career and has many recordings to his credit. When he played the Khatchaturian Violin Concerto with the Ulster Orchestra in 1991, one critic wrote that on this occasion there were no problems in tackling the virtuoso requirements: 'Indeed, this was as well informed and technically brilliant an account of this demanding work as one could hope to hear, with a lot more character to the rather long-winded cadenza that one sometimes gets. The slow movement was beautifully shaped and the dancing rhythms of the finale captured brilliantly.'[1]

Charlier has been a professor of violin at the Paris Conservatoire since he was 20. He finds he has a special affinity with his young students and they in turn find it satisfying to work with a professor who inhabits their world.

Thomas Zehetmair was born in Salzburg in 1961 and played chamber music with members of his family from early childhood. He had his first lessons from his father, Helmut Zehetmair, a professor at the Salzburg Mozarteum, and continued with him until his graduation. He later attended the masterclasses of Franz Samokyl, Max Rostal and Nathan Milstein. At 16 he made his debut at the Salzburg Festival and, in 1978, won first prize at the International Mozart Competition. His first recording – of Mozart concertos – was released in 1980, and that same year he made his debut in Vienna at the Musikverein. Zehetmair has since enjoyed a successful international career as a soloist and chamber music player. His repertory contains most of the traditional works, but he is also interested in contemporary music and has given a number of first performances.

Zehetmair's platform manner has a natural authority and control that makes him at one with his instrument. In the 1995 Edinburgh Festival, he gave three late-night recitals of Bach that had the critics spellbound. Conrad Wilson wrote: 'Being the most meticulous of performers, he ensured that not a single detail of Bach's writing went for nothing. Yet there was no hint of pedantry in his precision, because it was invariably placed at the service of a profound yet instinctive musical understanding.'[2]

Mayumi Seiler was born in Japan in 1963, the daughter of a Japanese mother and German father, and played the violin from the age of three. The family moved to Salzburg and when Mayumi was six, she studied violin at the Mozarteum with Sándor Végh. Mayumi and her three sisters formed the Seiler String Quartet and toured Europe and Japan with considerable success until they each went their own way in the music profession.

After further studies in Aachen, Mayumi spent ten years in London as a member of the Schubert Ensemble, with whom she made many recordings. She moved to Canada in 1996, following her marriage to the Toronto Symphony Orchestra timpanist, David Kent. As a soloist and chamber musician she has travelled the world, and is also highly respected as a teacher; when she was in the UK she taught at the Guildhall School of Music and Drama (GSMD), the Dartington International Festival and Chetham's Music School; she is now at the University of Toronto.

Xue Wei was born in Beijing, China in 1963, when Mao Tse-Tung's cultural revolution was in full swing. Under his régime, most young children were sent to live on communes to carry out farm labour, but because Xue's father played the violin and had taught his son to play, he was able to play in the government orchestra. Western music was forbidden and only works like the Yellow River Concerto and Eastern Red were allowed. To learn Western repertory, Xue Wei studied in secret with the leader of the Peking Opera Orchestra. He first heard a recording of the Mendelssohn concerto when he was 14. The cultural revolution ended that same year, enabling him to attend Shanghai and Beijing Conservatories, where the teachers were all Russian graduates.

In 1982, Xeu Wei arrived in London for the Carl Flesch Competition in one of the first groups to represent China after the revolution, so no one knew what to expect. To everyone's surprise, he took the Outstanding Merit Prize and, the following year, won Third Prize in Japan's International Violin Competition. He caught the attention of Yfrah Neaman, who had been impressed with his playing at the Carl Flesch Competition the previous year; Neaman offered to teach him at the GSMD and he organised his financial support through two of the UK's leading bankers. The Lord Mayor himself intervened in order to obtain his Chinese exit permit.

Meanwhile, Xeu Wei had become a hero in his own country and a name to be reckoned with in the West. Today, he enjoys a busy solo career and the critics praise his sensitive and musical approach to every undertaking. When looking back on the main influences, he singles out Neaman, who was both friend and teacher when he first came to London. 'He was very supportive in the transition from student to professional and gave me an understanding of the culture of Western history. . . . He was a musical father figure.'[3]

Tasmin Little must surely be the most outstanding British talent since the late Ralph Holmes. She was born in London in 1965, the daughter of the actor George Little. She had her first violin lessons when she was seven and it was soon discovered she had perfect pitch. She became a pupil at the Yehudi Menuhin School, where her teacher was Jacqueline Gazelle. The grounding she received has stood her in good stead ever since. She went on to the GSMD, where she was a pupil of Pauline Scott and carried off the prestigious Gold Medal (awarded to only one student per year). Awarded an ESU scholarship, she attended masterclasses with Lorand Fenyves at Banff and was so bowled over by his teaching and charismatic personality that she stayed on in Canada for a further six months to study with him at Toronto.

Little achieved international status in 1986 by giving the Leipzig premiere of the Delius Violin Concerto with the Gewandhaus Orchestra under Kurt Masur. In London, she made her recital debut in 1988 at the Purcell Room on the South Bank with the pianist Piers Lane; her Prom debut followed in 1990 with the London premiere of the Janáček Violin Concerto with the Welsh National Opera Orchestra under Sir Charles Mackerras.

Tasmin Little enchants audiences everywhere, not only with her brilliant and innately musical performances, but also with her enthusiasm and ebullient platform personality. She walks on stage as if she loves every member of her audience and is privileged to entertain them; this is another quality she shares with Holmes.

Frank Peter Zimmerman, born in Duisburg, Germany in 1965, started playing the violin at five, studied at the Folkwang-Musikhochschule in Essen with Valery Grodov and later with Saschko Gawriloff at the Staatliche Hochschule in Berlin. He first attracted public attention by winning the 1976 Jugend Musiziert competition at the age of 11, and was only 15 when he went to Amsterdam to complete his studies with Herman Krebbers. Zimmerman made his Salzburg Festival debut at 17 and his US debut in 1984, with the Pittsburgh Symphony Orchestra. Today he enjoys an international reputation.

Zimmerman is one of the increasing number of younger players who admire the 'old school', romantic style of playing exemplified by David Oistrakh. He bemoans the fact that today precision takes precedence over personality and the kind of individual playing that made Kreisler or Busch immediately recognisable is almost non-existent. Despite his fears, Zimmerman's own playing does have its own personality. When he played the Ligeti Violin Concerto (1990) at the Queen Elizabeth Hall in 1997 with the Philharmonia Orchestra under Esa-Pekka Salonen, Andrew Clark wrote that it was 'little short of a revelation' and that 'it is good to find a violinist of Zimmerman's stature taking the concerto into his repertoire'.[4]

The Dutch Isabelle van Keulen is a rarity among violinists in that she is not only a talented performer and teacher but plays down the virtuoso aspect of her career:

> A soloist is not just someone who closes her eyes and plays her part. A soloist is just one person and can fit so easily with an orchestra when she listens carefully. It is nearly

always the fault of the soloist when the ensemble is not together – the reaction with an orchestra should be like playing quartets. I don't want to be a soloist – I am just a musician.[5]

Van Keulen was born in 1966 in the village of De Hoef, near Amsterdam. She decided at the age of three that she wanted to be a violinist and had her first lessons when she was six from a local teacher. She began part-time study at the Sweelinck Conservatory in Amsterdam under Davina van Wely and, during the next few years, proceeded to win a number of competitions; she also attended masterclasses by Gutnikov, Spivakov and Rostal. Then in 1984 she won the Eurovision Young Musician of the Year Competition in Geneva, which led to invitations from orchestras all over Europe and the USA, including the Berlin Philharmonic and the Concertgebouw. In 1986, van Keulen attended masterclasses by Sandor Végh at the International Musicians Seminar at Prussia Cove and was so impressed with his individual approach that she went to Salzburg for further studies with him. Végh taught her independence: he told her that she had so many ideas of her own she should try to figure them out for herself.

Van Keulen has since appeared with a number of celebrated quartets and in 1995 founded her own, Isos. In 1989 she took up the viola 'just for fun' and now performs regularly on both instruments. When she performed the early D minor Mendelssohn Concerto one critic from the *Scotsman* wrote: 'Van Keulen, noted as a viola virtuoso as well as a violinist, produced here what seemed a fusion of both instruments. The soprano, fresh and clear swoops to rich contralto; into a work which seems to have poured from the composer's pen with scarcely a blot in the ink, she brought intellectual flow and powerful persuasive melodic force.'[6]

Since 1989, Van Keulen has taught at the Koninklijk Conservatorium in The Hague. For relaxation, this remarkable young musician occasionally sings with a pianist friend, Reinild Mees, in an Amsterdam bar where they have a group made up of a saxophone, double bass, timps, piano and two singers.

Christian Tetzlaff was born in Hamburg in 1966 into a musical family. He began studies on both violin and piano at the age of six. He claims never to have worked very hard at his playing and that his parents never insisted upon practice. When he was 14 he attended the Lübeck Conservatory to study with Uwe-Martin Haiberg, who 'put his finger on the dark spots' in his playing.[7] Tetzlaff remained at school until he was 18, finishing his general education, and never once entered a competition. He was 21 when he made his debut and from that point his career blossomed, taking him all over Europe and the USA. He devoted a further year to study with Walter Levine, of the La Salle Quartet, at the University of Cincinnati, and spent two summers at Marlboro.

Pamela Frank was born in New York City in 1966, the daughter of two concert pianists, so she cannot recall a time when she did not hear music. When she was five, she began lessons with Shirley Givens, who made the violin 'fun'. She went on to Szymon Goldberg, first at the Juilliard Pre-College department and then at the Curtis Institute. Goldberg was known for being ruthlessly demanding: 'You had to justify everything you did, to explain every note you played. He was always the sceptic you had to convince.'[8] Goldberg was from the Flesch school, whereas Givens came from the Galamian, and so Frank feels that despite the gruelling time she had with Goldberg, she has benefited from the influence of both schools, especially where her bowing was concerned. Then in her last year at Curtis she had some useful coaching from Jaime Laredo.

In her early teens, Frank became a member of the New York String Orchestra, which holds seminars for the young musicians who are coached by Alexander Schneider, Felix Galimir, the Guarneri Quartet and other distinguished musicians. She played for two years with them; at 19, she made her solo debut with the orchestra at Carnegie Hall, performing a Vivaldi concerto.

Pamela Frank now receives rave reviews wherever she goes. She is certainly an all-round musician in that she gives sonata recitals with her pianist father and plays duos with the cellist Yo Yo Ma. Her repertory ranges from Mozart and Beethoven to Stravinsky, Barber and Takemitsu; after a performance of the Barber Violin Concerto in Seattle, a critic from the *Seattle Times* wrote:

> Here is a young violinist who seems to grow in strength with every performance; a player of intelligence, fire, taste, technique, and a big luscious tone. Whether she is tearing into the wicked perpetual-motion finale or pouring out the soulful lines of the lyrical slow movement, Frank compels you to listen to one of the brightest talents of her generation. She's still enough of a music lover to slip into the orchestra and play along in the Franck D minor Symphony, as she did following her concerto.[9]

Pip Clarke was born in 1968 in Warrington, Cheshire and began lessons on the violin at seven. She went on to study at Chetham's, the Royal Northern College of Music and Guildhall School of Music and Drama, and made her chamber music debut at the Purcell Room when she was 16; her solo debut there followed three years later. After further lessons with Christopher Ling, the teacher whom she considers has exerted the greatest influence on her playing, she emigrated to the USA and now enjoys a busy international solo career.

Maxim Vengerov is by far the most exciting talent to have emerged in recent years. Not only does he have a faultless technique, but from a very early age he has possessed an uncanny insight into the music itself, which enabled him to express almost any emotion or colour at will. He was born in 1974 in Novosibirsk, in Western Siberia, and before he could walk, he would be found listening intently while his parents, an oboist and a choir director, rehearsed. Hearing a recording by David Oistrakh inspired him to learn the violin, and at seven he began lessons with Galina Turtschaninova. Three years later, he went to study with Zakhar Bron who recognised that he had a phenomenal talent on his hands. Bron encouraged him to play in public and within a year, Maxim won first prize in the Junior Wieniawski Competition in Warsaw.

Vengerov made his Moscow debut at 11 playing the Schubert Rondo Brilliant and, the following year, performed on the opening night of the Tchaikovsky Competition in Moscow, although he was too young to compete. He subsequently appeared in all the major cities in the USSR and made his German debut in the 1987 Schleswig-Holstein Music Festival. In 1989, when Bron moved to Lübeck, Vengerov followed. He went on to win prize after prize at festivals and competitions; his Wigmore Hall recital debut had the London critics searching for superlatives. The following year he won the Carl Flesch Competition, also winning a prize for interpretation and the Audience Prize.

Shortly afterwards, Vengerov and his family emigrated to Israel and, following performances with the Israel Philharmonic Orchestra, he made his US debut with the New York Philharmonic Orchestra in 1991. He returned to the UK for Prom appearances in 1992 and 1993 and, in every case, the critics were hard put to find words to do him justice. He has already become a legend, having appeared with the world's leading orchestras and conductors, and made numerous award-winning recordings.

Vengerov's playing was aptly described by Robert Henderson in the *Daily Telegraph* after his recital at the Barbican in March 1994: 'The mystifying thing is how he has managed to acquire at so young an age, and so perfectly, so many facets to his expressive personality, from his quicksilver poise and rococo elegance in a little Mozart sonata to his lyrically contained depth of feeling and emotion in Brahms's G major Sonata Op. 78.'[10]

Vengerov has been compared to Heifetz on many occasions: Dr Herbert Axelrod, friend and biographer of Heifetz, presented Vengerov with Heifetz's bow after hearing his New York recital debut, saying: 'I know I have found a worthy successor to Heifetz.' The bow, named the 'Henryk Kaston' is a sister bow to the one that the master used every day and donated to the San Francisco Museum of Fine Arts along with his Guarnerius del Gesù violin. Vengerov knew from the first moment he held the bow that it was wonderful: 'When I played, I felt the ghost of Heifetz .... Violinists often blame their bows for any problems they are having with their playing. If I have problems now, I know it's my fault.'[11]

**Notes**

1. Transart publicity brochure.
2. *Glasgow Herald*, 24 August 1995.
3. *The Strad*, August 1989, p. 625.
4. *Financial Times*, February 1997.
5. *The Strad*, July 1991, p. 612.
6. *Scotsman*, 30 January 1995.
7. *The Strad*, March 1995, p. 263.
8. *The Strad*, March 1996, p. 220.
9. *Seattle Times*, 7 March 1995.
10. *Daily Telegraph*, 5 March 1994.
11. *The Strad*, April 1994, p. 320.

# 50  The Way Ahead

In four centuries of development, standards of violin playing have never been higher than they are today. It is not surprising that, in striving to reach perfection, young virtuosos have influenced general standards of performance, although sometimes their facility has outstripped their artistic mastery. It is possible for an artist to circle the earth by jet plane and appear in New York on one night and Berlin the next – a formidable contrast to the leisurely travels of Spohr in his carriage or even the boat and train journeys of the early part of the last century. The dilemma we face at the present time is that whereas the playing of yesterday's performers matured more slowly, virtuosos today are often forced into bloom and placed on show very young. It is much to their credit that so many players appear to survive the pressures of TV, recording and ceaseless globe-trotting.

In an age when technical mastery is taken for granted and musicianship is often sacrificed to the inordinate demands of recording, how can a young player make a personal statement that distinguishes him or her from the uniformity of professional excellence? Only by ignoring fashionable trends and standing rock-firm on the impression the music makes upon the individual performer, can this be achieved, and the full meaning of the music reach the audience. Sándor Végh believed that spontaneity and inspiration must match a player's technical ability. He firmly believed in European traditions and was convinced that we must preserve what we have had in the past or we will lose ourselves. The individuality of violinists like Ysaÿe, Kreisler, Thibaud and Heifetz can immediately be identified from recordings, however old and scratched. Of the modern violinists, only a handful have that personal dimension; they include Isaac Stern and Salvatore Accardo.

The twentieth century could well be called 'the Century of the Competition'. Most aspiring virtuosos enter at least one of these contests – regarded by many to be of dubious worth. On the one hand, a prize can bring a violinist out of obscurity into the limelight, and, provided he or she can face the heat, it may well be the start of an international career. But it is also a further example of how a budding artist can be exposed to the elements too soon. Many prize-winners become competition casualties and never fully recover.

The first International Tchaikovsky Competition was held in Moscow in 1972. Although its technical demands are formidable, the challenge appears to attract an ever-increasing number of applicants. There are three rounds in which the contestant must play from memory music that ranges from a Bach sonata to the Tchaikovsky concerto. In the first round, the competitors play Bach and Mozart. In rounds two and three, the pieces are all drawn from the Romantic or contemporary repertory, a practice that has emphasised technical facility over musical ability. Until recently, the Leventritt, in New York, was considered one of the most prestigious of the American competitions. The winner was awarded a cash prize and a series of engagements with leading American orchestras. Now it operates as a foundation, offering a bursary to the winner to enable him or her to continue studies, after which a concert series is undertaken.

The Paganini Competition has been held in Genoa for the last quarter of a century. The first prize-winner receives a cash prize and is allowed to play Paganini's violin at a concert to celebrate the close of the event and at another during the season following the competition. Many Japanese have taken prizes in this competition, and a number of French and Italians; Salvatore Accardo won at the age of 15.

The Carl Flesch International Competition was, for many years, Britain's most important contribution. Held every two years, it was inaugurated at the Guildhall School of Music and Drama in 1945 to commemorate the life and work of Carl Flesch. It gradually expanded from modest beginnings into one of the world's major international competitions; it was last held in 1992.

The original Ysaÿe Concours, created from an idea of the great Belgian violinist Ysaÿe, was first held in 1937 and won by David Oistrakh; but after the outbreak of war in 1939, the competition was suspended. In the late 1940s Queen Elisabeth of the Belgians – who had been a close friend of Ysaÿe – agreed to give her name as patron to a new competition based on the same rules as the Ysaÿe. The first Queen Elisabeth International Music Competition was held in 1951 with Leonid Kogan as the first prize winner. This competition for violinists is held every four years. The year 2001 celebrated the 50th anniversary of this event.

The Yehudi Menuhin Violin Competition, which includes a senior and junior section, was first held in 1983 with Leland Chen (senior) and Wang Xiao-dong (junior) as the first winners. The competition is held every two years.

Over the last few centuries, certain nationalities appear to have produced an abundance of great players, whereas others have yielded only an occasional virtuoso. From early in the nineteenth century up to the present time, the Jewish race seems to have produced a wealth of great soloists, with their origins mainly in Hungary, Poland, Russia and Ukraine. The large number of Jewish violinists born in and around Odessa makes nonsense of coincidence. The exodus of so many who have achieved international status in the USA, caused Stern to remark: 'They send us their Jews from Odessa, and we send them our Jews from Odessa.'[1]

A significant feature of the 1970s was the astonishing upsurge of talent from the Far East: the technique, dedication and musicality manifest in the oriental virtuosos – despite not having been reared in a Western culture – is not only surprising but seemingly inexplicable.

The high standards of performance engendered by this multi-racial excellence presages well for the future. The superlative quality of contemporary recorded sound will provide definitive examples by which unprecedented comparisons may be made by succeeding generations. However, whether we learn about technique and style from eighteenth-century tutors or the latest digital recording, one quality is shared by them all. The great violinists are the supreme romantics, and it is through their gift of direct communication that we have experienced and will continue to experience the impact of music as a living, transcending force.

**Notes**
1. *Stagebill*, ii, 1978, p. 1.

# Bibliography

ABRAHAM, GERALD, *A Hundred Years of Music*, Duckworth (London 1966).

ALDRICH, RICHARD, *Concert Life in New York*, Putnam (New York 1941).

APPLEBAUM, SAMUEL AND SADA, *With the Artists*, Markert (New York 1955).

AUER, LEOPOLD, *Violin Playing as I Teach It*, Duckworth (London 1960).

AXELROD, DR HERBERT R., ed., *Heifetz*, Paganiniana Publications (New Jersey 1976).

BACHARACH, A. L., ed, *The Musical Companion*, Victor Gollancz Ltd (London 1934).

BACHMANN, ALBERTO, *An Encyclopedia of the Violin*, Da Capo (London 1976).

BEECHAM, SIR THOMAS, *A Mingled Chime*, White Lion (London 1973).

BERLIOZ, HECTOR, *The Memoirs of Berlioz*, ed. D. Cairns, Panther (London 1970).

BLUNT, WILFRID, *On Wings of Song*, Hamish Hamilton (London 1974).

BOULT, SIR ADRIAN, *My Own Trumpet*, Hamish Hamilton (London 1973).

BOYDEN, DAVID D., *The History of Violin Playing from its Origins to 1761*, Oxford University Press (Oxford 1965).

BROOK, DONALD, *Violinists of Today*, Rockliff (London 1948).

BURNEY, CHARLES, *A General History of Music*, ed. F. Mercer, Foulis (London 1935).

BUSBY, THOMAS, *Concert Room and Orchestra Anecdotes*, printed for Clementi & Co. (London 1825).

DE COURCEY, G. I. G., *Paganini the Genoese*, 2 vols., Oklahoma Press (Oklahoma 1957).

DOLMETSCH, ARNOLD *The Interpretation of the Music of the Seventeenth and Eighteenth Centuries*, University of Washington Press (Seattle 1969).

ELKIN, ROBERT, *Queen's Hall (1893–1941)*, Rider (London 1944).

ELKIN, ROBERT, *Royal Philharmonic (1893–1941)*, Rider (London 1946).

ELKIN, ROBERT, *The Old Concert Rooms of London*, Arnold (London 1955).

EMERY, FREDERIC B., *The Violin Concerto*, 2 vols., Da Capo (New York 1969).

EVANS, EDWIN, *Brahms Chamber and Orchestral Music*, W. Reeves Ltd (London, undated).

FARGA, FRANZ, *Violins and Violinists*, Rockliff (London 1950).

FERRIS, GEORGE T., *Great Pianists and Great Violinists*, 3rd edn., W. Reeves Ltd (London, undated).

FLESCH, CARL, *The Art of Violin Playing*, Carl Fischer (New York 1939).

FLESCH, CARL, *The Memoirs of Carl Flesch*, trans. Hans Keller, Bois de Boulogne: W. Reeves Ltd/Rockliff (London 1973).

FOX, CHARLES, GAMMOND, PETER AND MORGAN, ALUN, *Jazz on Record: A Critical Guide*, Arrow (London 1960).

FULLER-MAITLAND, J. A., *Brahms*, Methuen (London 1911).

GAISBERG, FRED W., *Music on Record*, Robert Hale (London 1946).

GALAMIAN, IVAN, *Principles of Violin Playing and Teaching*, Faber & Faber (London 1962).

GIBSON, J. C., *A Musician's Life*, Frederick Books (London 1956).

GREENFIELD, EDWARD, LAYTON, ROBERT AND MARCH, IVAN, eds., *Penguin Stereo Record Guide*, 2nd edn., Penguin (London 1977).

GREER, DAVID, *Hamilton Harty, His Life and Music*, Blackstaff Press (Belfast 1979).

*Grove's Dictionary of Music and Musicians*, 5th edn., Macmillan (London 1954).

*The New Grove Dictionary of Music and Musicians*, 6th edn., Macmillan (London 1980).

*The New Grove Dictionary of Women Composers*, ed. Julie Anne Sadie and Rhian Samuel, Macmillan (London 1994).

HAENDEL, IDA, *Woman with Violin*, Victor Gollancz Ltd (London 1970).

HANSLICK, EDUARD, *Music Criticisms 1846–99*, trans./ed. Henry Pleasants, Penguin (London 1950; Baltimore 1964).

HARLEY, JOHN, *Music in Purcell's London*, Dobson (London 1968).

HAWEIS, R. H., *My Musical Life*, W. H. Allen (London 1884).

HILL, RALPH, *Brahms: A Study in Musical Biography*, Dennis Archer (London 1933).

HILL, W. HENRY, ARTHUR F. AND ALFRED E., *Antonio Stradivari: His Life and Work (1644–1737)*, Dover (London 1963).

HORTON, JOHN, *Brahms Orchestral Music*, BBC Music Guides (London 1968).

JAFFA, MAX, *A Life on the Fiddle*, Hodder & Stoughton (London 1981).

KOLNEDER, WALTER, *Antonio Vivaldi: His Life and Work*, Faber & Faber (London 1970).

KRAUSE, ERNST, *David Oistrakh: Ein Arbeitsporträt*, Henschelverlag Kunst & Gesellschaft (Berlin 1973).

LAHEE, HENRY C., *Famous Violinists of Today and Yesterday*, Page (Boston 1899).

LAURIE, DAVID, *Reminiscences of a Fiddle Dealer*, Virtuoso Publications (Cape Coral 1977).

LOCHNER, LOUIS P., *Fritz Kreisler*, Rockliff (London 1951).

MACLEOD, JOSEPH, *The Sisters d'Aranyi*, George Allen & Unwin (London 1969).

MENUHIN, YEHUDI, *Unfinished Journey*, Macdonald & Jane's (London 1977).

MENUHIN, YEHUDI, *Violin and Viola*, Macdonald & Jane's (London 1976).

MOSER, ANDREAS, *Joseph Joachim*, trans. Lilla Durham, Philip Welby (London 1901).

MOSER, ANDREAS AND JOSEPH JOACHIM, *Briefe an Brahms und Joachim*, ed. Moser, Verlag der Deutschen Brahms Gesellschaft (Berlin, Vol. I 1908, Vol. II 1912).

MOZART, LEOPOLD, *A Treatise on the Fundamental Principles of Violin Playing*, trans. Editha Knocker, Oxford University Press (London 1948).

NEUMANN, WERNER, *Bach and His World*, Thames & Hudson (London 1961).

PINCHERLE, MARC, *Vivaldi, Genius of the Baroque*, Norton (New York 1957).

PLEASANTS, HENRY, *The Musical Journeys of Louis Spohr*, Oklahoma Press (Oklahoma 1961).

PUGH, PETER AND HEATH, DOUGLAS, *The Tom Jenkins Story*, Cambridge Business Publishing (Cambridge 1995).

PULVER, JEFFREY, *Paganini the Romantic Virtuoso*, Herbert Joseph (London 1936); repr. Da Capo (New York 1970).

RONZE-NEVEU, M. J., *Ginette Neveu*, Rockliff (London 1957).

SALTER, LIONEL, *The Gramophone Guide to Classical Composers and Recordings*, Book Club Associates (London 1978).

SCHOLES, PERCY A., *The Mirror of Music 1844–1944*, 2 vols., Novello and OUP; Arno (London 1947).

SCHONBERG, HAROLD, *The Great Pianists*, Victor Gollancz Ltd (London 1974).

SCHULLER, GUNTHER, *Early Jazz: Its Roots and Musical Development*, Oxford University Press (New York 1968).

SCHWARZ, BORIS, *Great Masters of the Violin*, Robert Hale (London 1984).

SONNECK, O. G., *Beethoven: Impressions by his Contemporaries*, Dover (New York 1968); Constable (London 1968).

SPOHR, LOUIS, *Louis Spohr's Autobiography*, Da Capo (New York 1969).

*The Strad*, Novello (London 1898–1986); Orpheus Publications Ltd (London 1987–2001).

SZIGETI, JOSEPH, *With Strings Attached*, Alfred A. Knopf (New York 1967).

SZIGETI, JOSEPH, *On the Violin*, Cassell (London 1969).

TARTINI, G., *Letter to Maddalena Lombardini*, trans. Charles Burney (London 1779).

THOMPSON, A., ed., *International Cyclopedia of Music and Musicians*, 10th edn., Dent (London 1975).

VAN DER STRAETEN, A. E., *The History of the Violin*, 2 vols., Da Capo (New York 1968).

VAN DER STRAETEN, A. E., *History of the Violoncello, the Viola da Gamba, Their Precursors and Collateral Instruments*, W. Reeves Ltd (London 1914).

VAN DER STRAETEN, A. E., *The Romance of the Fiddle, The Origin of the Modern Virtuoso and the Adventures of His Ancestors*, Rebman (London 1911).

WILSON, JOHN, ed., *Roger North on Music*, Novello (London 1959).

YSAŸE, ANTOINE, *Eugène Ysaÿe*, Editions Ysaÿe (Brussels 1974).

# Index